RED FLAG

ALSO BY MICHAEL ASHCROFT

Blue Ambition: The Unauthorised Biography of Kemi Badenoch (2024)

Red Queen? The Unauthorised Biography of Angela Rayner (2024)

All to Play For: The Advance of Rishi Sunak (2023)

In the Shadows: The Extraordinary Men and Women of the Intelligence Corps (2022)

First Lady: Intrigue at the Court of Carrie and Boris Johnson (2022)

Life Support: The State of the NHS in an Age of Pandemics (2022)

Falklands War Heroes: Extraordinary True Stories of Bravery in the South Atlantic (2021)

Red Knight: The Unauthorised Biography of Sir Keir Starmer (2021)

Unfair Game: An Exposé of South Africa's Captive-Bred Lion Industry (2020)

Jacob's Ladder: The Unauthorised Biography of Jacob Rees-Mogg (2019)

White Flag? An Examination of the UK's Defence Capability (2018)

Victoria Cross Heroes: Volume II (2016)

Call Me Dave: The Unauthorised Biography of David Cameron (2015)

Special Ops Heroes (2014)

Heroes of the Skies (2012)

George Cross Heroes (2010)

Special Forces Heroes (2008)

Victoria Cross Heroes (2006)

Dirty Politics, Dirty Times (2005)

For full list, visit www.LordAshcroft.com

www.LordAshcroftPolls.com

www.LordAshcroftMedals.com

www.LordAshcroftWildlife.com

www.LordAshcroftOnBravery.com

@LordAshcroft

MICHAEL ASHCROFT

RED FLAG

THE UNEASY ADVANCE OF SIR KEIR STARMER

This revised edition published in Great Britain in 2025 by
Biteback Publishing Ltd, London

ISBN 978-1-78590-981-8

10 9 8 7 6 5 4 3 2 1

A CIP catalogue record for this book is available from the British Library.

Set in Minion Pro and Futura

Printed and bound in Great Britain by
CPI Group (UK) Ltd, Croydon CR0 4YY

CONTENTS

AUTHOR'S ROYALTIES

Lord Ashcroft is donating all author's royalties from *Red Flag* to charity.

ACKNOWLEDGEMENTS

Among the scores of people who kindly agreed to be interviewed for this book, some asked not to be named publicly. For this reason, it is not possible to identify here everybody who deserves thanks; suffice it to say their background briefings were extremely useful.

The following people were notably generous with their time and help by assisting or advising in different and important ways: Prof. Bill Bowring, Sean Davey, Peter Burgess, David Jones, David Johnson, Mark Dixon, David Wharton, Margaret Crick, David Griffith, James Hanning, Safia Bugel and the staff of Haringey Archive and Local History Centre.

Thanks must also go to the formidable Angela Entwistle and her team, to Kevin Culwick and to those at Biteback Publishing who were involved in the production of this book. And special thanks to my chief researcher, Miles Goslett.

INTRODUCTION

When this book was first published as *Red Knight* in the late summer of 2021, Sir Keir Starmer's political prospects looked distinctly shaky. His principal problem was that after barely eighteen months as Labour leader, nobody could be sure what he stood for. In his defence, he had been busy. First, there was the job of trying to patch up a Labour Party that was still badly damaged by its poor showing at the 2019 general election. On top of that, he had to oppose a Conservative government led by Boris Johnson that basked in the glory of an eighty-seat majority – a task that was hugely complicated by the disruption of the Covid-19 pandemic. To compound matters, he had just suffered a string of disastrous local election results and the humiliation of losing the solid parliamentary seat of Hartlepool to the Tories in a by-election. Furthermore, his dysfunctional relationship with his deputy, Angela Rayner, had left him open to mockery.

His critics, chief among them Tony Blair, did not hold back. What was his overall plan, they demanded? What were his economic policies? And was he as dull and plodding as he seemed? This disparagement prompted doubts in some quarters about whether Labour would even survive under his leadership. What nobody knew at the time was that he had already had a crisis of confidence and come close to resigning. Only the soothing words of his wife, Victoria, and the advice of his loyal political aide Morgan McSweeney stopped him throwing in the towel. Then his fortunes changed. In November 2021, the Conservative government embarked on the long journey of self-destruction that ended, ultimately, in the ruling party's worst ever general election defeat in July 2024. Starmer was installed as the first Labour tenant of 10 Downing Street for fourteen years.

Making the transition from shadow Cabinet minister to Leader of the Opposition to Prime Minister in the space of a single parliamentary term was no mean feat. With the help of a small group of trusted lieutenants, he achieved it by jettisoning MPs and party members whose hard-left political opinions he feared might stand in the way of regaining power, and by giving the public the impression that Labour had returned to the centre ground. All this happened with miraculously little damage being sustained to Labour's image. Starmer's ruthlessness surprised many – not least one of his former colleagues in Doughty Street Chambers who told me he'd always assumed he was a 'political wet'. Yet certain thoughts nagged. To what degree was the 2024 general election result a positive vote for the Labour Party as opposed to being just an anti-Tory vote? The turnout was not quite 60 per cent and Labour's share of the vote was a mere 33.7 per cent – the lowest of any majority party on record. Put another way, 80 per cent of registered electors did not back Labour at the ballot box. What's more, were Starmer and his top team ready for government? The answers to these questions soon showed themselves.

On paper, Labour's haul of 412 MPs against the Conservatives' rump of 121 MPs should have marked the beginning of a period of supremacy for the new Prime Minister. Yet his political honeymoon was cut drastically short and his – and Labour's – poll ratings plummeted during his first 100 days in office. In part, this was thanks to a series of self-inflicted blunders including manifesto breaches and sleaze scandals. These missteps raised doubts about Starmer's integrity and his political nous. Confidence in him suffered. More widely, he is also felt to have failed to carve out a reputation as an interesting and original thinker. Most crucially, on the economy his government stands accused of returning to the default setting of previous Labour administrations, via Chancellor Rachel Reeves dishing out public sector pay rises while imposing higher taxes and more bureaucracy on business and enterprise. In doing so, Starmer's own claim of wanting to put economic growth at the heart of his government's programme has proved hollow. Additionally, in defiance of the millions who voted for Brexit in 2016, he has forged closer ties with the EU. And his insistence on trying to make Britain net zero by 2050 is set to cost taxpayers multiple billions of pounds. After nearly a year in power, it is not difficult to see why his government is scrambling for consistently better poll ratings, even taking into account the role he began to play in world affairs at the time of going to press. For very different reasons, his position is weak again, just as it was in the late summer of 2021.

Little was then known about Starmer other than that most of his adult life had been spent outside elected politics, as a barrister from 1987 until 2008 and as the Director of Public Prosecutions from 2008 to 2013. He became a Labour parliamentary candidate in December 2014 and entered the Commons in May 2015 at the relatively late age of fifty-two. Five years afterwards, he was elected Labour leader. In *Red Knight* I sought to find out more about him, but it became clear in the early stages of the project that he did not want the book to be written. Indeed, he actively obstructed it, telling friends – who then told me – that he would rather they did not co-operate. I wrote in 2021 that while I am the first to accept that everybody is entitled to a private life, I also believe that any politician who wishes to present themself to the country as the Prime Minister in waiting should have a skin thick enough to be untroubled by a study of their character. He seemed to think it would be acceptable for him to stand for the highest office in the land without some probing questions about him being asked in a truly unrestrained way. This reaction confirmed that he is by nature cautious and defensive. He is also uncomfortable with the rough and tumble of politics.

As it turned out, many people who have known Starmer at various stages of his life were happy to help. Some did so publicly; others preferred to do so anonymously. Their recollections contributed to the book's accuracy. This can be stated with certainty because in 2023 Starmer agreed to give a series of interviews to the journalist Tom Baldwin. Their conversations formed the basis of what became Baldwin's sanctioned biography of Starmer. Much of the independently researched detail found in the pages of *Red Knight* also features in Baldwin's book.

Starmer is hard to fathom at the best of times but is easily portrayed as a man of contradictions. Having attended a fee-paying school and the University of Leeds, gone on to study for a year at the University of Oxford, become a successful barrister, been appointed Director of Public Prosecutions, accepted a knighthood, entered the Commons and now become Prime Minister, he is undeniably a member of the establishment. And yet despite having succeeded in life thanks to his own hard work, he seems always to be at pains to distance himself from the establishment by speaking so often of his 'working-class' roots and his socialism. It is as though he is worried that the public will think less of him for having done well off his own bat.

This perception of him facing in two directions at once dominated his first years in Parliament. Having become a knight of the realm in 2014, he made it clear that he would rather not be addressed as 'Sir Keir'. When he took up the post of shadow Secretary of State for Exiting the European Union from 2016, he promised to honour the Brexit referendum result, only to demand a second vote later on. He remained in the shadow Cabinet when Labour was plagued by allegations of antisemitism but did not speak up publicly in any meaningful way for the Jewish community – despite his wife's Jewish background. He campaigned for Jeremy Corbyn to become Prime Minister twice, at the 2017 and 2019 general elections, and then denounced him, saying he had never considered him a friend and was always 'certain that we would lose the 2019 election'. As Leader of the Opposition, he was at pains to portray himself as being of the left but, under him, Labour was rebuilt by those on the party's right. This has naturally made some wonder whether he was interested in gaining power for the sake of it, or whether he is driven by something more principled.

Starmer calls himself a socialist and yet, although well-off in his own right, he and his wife were happy to accept thousands of pounds' worth of clothes paid for by the Labour donor Lord Alli, a multi-millionaire proponent of capitalism. His key election promise was to grow the economy, but his government's policies appear to have hindered that aspiration. As for his popular appeal, all the signs are that despite his image as a football-mad man of the people, he struggles to connect with the electorate – and they have difficulty identifying with him. Most polls conducted since July 2024 have served as a reminder that he has never been as liked or as respected as Britain's most successful leaders have been. His lack of captivating communication skills has not helped him, though, in a way, it does make his victory in 2024 more remarkable.

Having looked at Starmer's life before he entered No. 10, it seemed only right that I should chart his first months as premier. As well as tracking his progress from 5 July 2024, the day he formed his government, I have revised and updated sections of the original text. It struck me as appropriate to retitle the book *Red Flag* in recognition of the Labour Party's traditional anthem and, at the time of writing, to acknowledge the concerns of so many voters, pollsters and commentators about what Starmer's rule could mean for the future of Britain.

Sir Keir Starmer reached the political summit as quickly as he could have done. The points arising are: how did he achieve this; what has he done with the power he has gained; and what is the outlook for Britain under his stewardship? This book sets out to answer these, and other, questions.

Michael Ashcroft
April 2025

CHAPTER 1

'THE POSHER THE VOICE, THE MORE VULGAR THEY ARE'

Any mention of the county of Surrey tends to inspire in some people's minds the hackneyed idea that everybody who lives there owns a large house, works in the City of London and belongs to at least one members-only club. This stereotypical view, given credence by the label that the area is quintessential Stockbroker Belt territory, certainly has a ring of truth to it. Yet it is also undoubtedly simplistic. The upbringing of the self-declared socialist Sir Keir Starmer, who was raised and went to school in Surrey, serves as adequate proof that it has also always been home to people of more ordinary means, no matter how aspirational they are. The question becomes whether Starmer's background can be considered truly working class, as he has often been at pains to suggest when making his pitch to the electorate, or whether he is really a 'posh Trotskyist', as some newspapers have claimed.

Tracing his paternal line back to the early nineteenth century, it is clear that four of the five generations of Starmers that came before his were solidly working class. His great-great-great-grandfather, George Starmer, was born in Lincolnshire in 1819 and was a labourer there until his death in 1870. His son, also called George, began life as a farm labourer in the same county before marrying a servant, Matilda Buswell, and moving to Yorkshire in 1890, where he was employed as a gamekeeper and then became a farmer. Their son, the colourfully named Gustavus Adolphus Starmer, who was Keir's great-grandfather, was born in 1882, also in Lincolnshire. He, too, was a gamekeeper though by 1907, he and his wife, Katherine, had moved south to Surrey, where he was employed at Marden Park, an estate owned by Sir Walpole Greenwell, one of the wealthiest stockbrokers in the country. Gustavus and his family were allowed to live in Marden Castle, a nineteenth-century gothic turreted folly that was built as a hunting lodge and sometimes used by Greenwell's guests on shoot days. Gustavus began the Starmers' connection with the region, which lasted for more than a century via Keir Starmer's younger sister, also called Katherine. She remained in the area, close to where she and her siblings were brought up, until 2021.

During the First World War, Gustavus was a driver in the Army Service Corps. In 1917, he was found to be unfit for service because of heart disease. He was granted a gratuity of £35 and awarded the Silver War Badge, which was given to those who were honourably discharged due to wounds or illness. He died in April 1974, when Keir was eleven years old, and was still a resident of Surrey at that time. Gustavus's son – and therefore Keir's grandfather – was Herbert Starmer, known as Bert, who was born in 1905. Although he was born in Liverpool, he lived and worked in Surrey almost all his life. According to the 1939 Register, the national census compiled by the British government on the outbreak of the Second World War, he was an agricultural wheelwright based in the village of Woldingham. Later, in the 1960s, he worked there as a mechanic at a garage. His wife, Doris, who was Keir's grandmother, was born in Surrey in 1907. The couple had four children – three boys and a girl. Their third son, Rodney, was Keir's father. He was born in 1934 and grew up in Woldingham. Rodney was certainly born into a situation most people would accept as being 'working class'. It is debatable, though, whether he can be described as having stayed in that social bracket throughout his life or whether, for reasons which will be shown, he managed to open a door through which his children could potentially make their way in order to live what would surely be thought of as a more middle-class existence.

Being overly critical of private individuals whom one has never met is never wise, particularly if, like Rodney Starmer, they are no longer alive to explain themselves. With that said, when researching this book it has been noticeable that he was not considered by every interviewee who encountered him to be an easy man to know. On a visit in late 2020 to the street on the outskirts of Oxted in which he lived from 1963 until his death in 2018, for example, those neighbours who felt qualified to discuss his personality agreed to do so on an 'off the record' basis only. The reason for their polite reticence was soon clear. Speaking of an often scruffily dressed man, who wore a pair of shorts and a T-shirt on most days of the year and who sported an almost Victorian-era beard for much of his adult life, they variously described him as 'eccentric' and 'a bit of a strange character'. One neighbour said, 'The Starmers were staunchly Labour, and many others round here were Conservative. At election times their house would be plastered with Labour posters.' When asked if a clash of political views might have influenced their attitude to Rodney Starmer, they insisted this was not the case. With some reluctance, one of them added, 'He was just not very nice.'

An acquaintance of Rodney's also mentioned that he could remember receiving a round robin Christmas letter from him in December 2014 which contained at least one barbed comment – something he thought rather incongruous given the context. In the letter, a copy of which this person was willing to share, Rodney did indeed refer bluntly at one point to 'some of the residents in Oxted', of whom he clearly disapproved. In what sounds rather like a battle cry from a class warfare activist, he wrote of these residents: 'The posher the voice, the more vulgar they are.' As sweeping generalisations go, this one does seem to be somewhat gratuitous and may be said to shed some light on his personality and opinions, which those who knew him have made clear were unmistakably left-wing. To what extent such views shaped the outlook of his children is an open question, but it has to be considered at the very least possible that his judgement might have rubbed off on an impressionable young mind. Andrew Cooper, a childhood friend of Starmer, says his recollection is that whenever Keir spoke of his father, 'He was always described as quite strict.' Another friend, Paul Vickers, has said:

> Keir's dad was a very powerful, almost slightly intimidating, figure, a very big man and was always very principled. He was probably what you might call somebody from the traditional Labour left. I'm pretty sure that's where Keir picked up his first political insights: from his dad. His father … would always ask you, and ask Keir, questions which revolved around politics. He expected us to be interested in politics.

Tony Alston, a friend of Rodney's who knew him through their shared interest in competitive cycling, also suggested that his was a slightly unusual personality. '[Rodney] was what one might call a character,' Alston says. 'He was one of those bluff but really kind-hearted people. He would turn up to a funeral wearing green plus twos and a baggy top. He was perfectly respectable; he was just unconventional.' Alston knew him mainly through the long-established Southern Counties Cycling Union, of which Rodney, a cycling enthusiast throughout his life, was president for several years. He suggested that some people who were involved in organising and running cycling events avoided getting on the wrong side of Rodney.

> I never argued with [Rodney] because I don't argue with people, but, if he had a view, he wanted it his way. Certainly, he would fight his corner, but not in an unpleasant way as far as I remember. He was certainly popular in his own club, but he could be a trifle awkward if he thought he was right and you were wrong.

In view of the mixed feelings which Rodney Starmer seems to have generated among some of his friends and acquaintances, perhaps it is fairest to rely for a character reference on the man who spent more time with him than all those quoted: his eldest son. When he was interviewed on BBC Radio 4's *Desert Island Discs* in November 2020, Keir Starmer said: 'I don't often talk about my dad. He was a difficult man, a complicated man. He kept himself to himself. He didn't particularly like to socialise so wouldn't really go out very much, but he was incredibly hard-working.' He added: 'I understood who he was and what he was, but we weren't close.'

By contrast, his mother, Josephine, seems to have been far more popular. Those same neighbours who were so reluctant to talk openly about Rodney Starmer described his wife in glowing terms as a kind and friendly woman who was always cheerful. They were quick to add that they believed all four of her children had inherited her good nature. She was born in Woldingham in July 1939, four months after her parents' marriage and six weeks before the outbreak of war. Her father, Ronald Baker, who was also born in Surrey, was an electrical engineer. The 1939 Register records his profession as a driver and fitter for road passenger transport. The origins of her mother, Marjorie, are less clear, though it appears she died in Croydon, Surrey, in 1959. Looking back to the beginning of the nineteenth century, Josephine's forebears were employed in a wide range of jobs every bit as humble as those done by the Starmers. Records show that among her ancestors was an attendant in a Surrey County Council lunatic asylum, a printer, a miller, a general labourer, a servant and a laundress.

Josephine's path through life was far from straightforward. By the time she was ten years old, a recurring pain in her joints caused her parents to seek medical advice. Eventually, she was sent to Guy's Hospital in London for tests. There, aged eleven, she was diagnosed with juvenile idiopathic arthritis, also known as Still's disease; so called because the condition was first described by the English paediatrician George Still in 1896. This rare illness, the cause of which remains unknown, is characterised by fever and rashes as well as joint pain, and it can have a profoundly destabilising effect on those who live with it. The symptoms and frequency of episodes vary between individuals and are hard to predict. Sadly, Josephine was not spared the worst of what the disease is capable of inflicting.

According to the eulogy given at her funeral in 2015, she was quickly taken under the wing of the consultant who was in charge of her, Dr Kenneth Maclean. As Josephine was facing the prospect of being confined to a wheelchair for the rest of her life, Maclean was granted permission by her parents to, in effect, experiment on her with the new steroid cortisone. It had never been administered to children before the 1950s, but it had been shown to reduce swelling in the joints of adults suffering with rheumatism. In Josephine's case, it proved something of a wonder drug, enabling her to live a fuller life for much longer than might otherwise have been the case, albeit with consequences for her physical health as she entered middle age and beyond.

Josephine had to spend a considerable amount of time in hospital during her childhood, but that fact did not prevent her from passing the entrance exam to Whyteleafe County Grammar School for Girls in Surrey. It was while she was a pupil there, aged sixteen, that she first met Rodney Starmer, at a local dinner and dance being held by the cycling club of which he was a member. They struck up a close friendship immediately, despite a five-year age gap. By then, he had left Purley County Grammar School, had completed two years' national service with the Royal Electrical and Mechanical Engineers and was apprenticed to a local toolmaking firm. After Josephine left school, she became a student nurse at Guy's Hospital, allowing her to maintain her contact with Dr Maclean, whose pioneering treatment improved her quality of life so markedly and guaranteed that she remained able to walk. Her friendship with this highly respected doctor had one further, significant benefit. When she and Rodney married in the late summer of 1960, he was a guest at their wedding. According to Rodney, who delivered the aforementioned eulogy, he took the couple aside at their reception and told them quietly that if they intended to start a family, the unknown side effects on Josephine of the cortisone treatment meant they should not wait. He also promised Josephine that if she ever had any children, he would arrange personally for her to give birth to them at Guy's.

In a demonstration of how robust Josephine remained as a young woman, she and Rodney took their honeymoon in the Lake District. There, Rodney wanted to share with his new bride his passion for climbing hills and mountains – an activity he had first enjoyed a few years previously when visiting the Dolomites in northern Italy. They stayed at the Dower House guesthouse in the grounds of Wray Castle on the western side of Lake Windermere and, not yet owning a car, made their way around the area by bus. Halfway through the holiday, and having already climbed eight mountains, they got into difficulties on Loughrigg Fell, a situation that was exacerbated by Josephine's lack of stamina compared to her husband. By chance, they soon came across a pipe-smoking middle-aged man who was sitting on a rock with a sketching pad. Showing some concern, he asked if they were all right and, noting Josephine's obvious exhaustion, advised them on the best way to descend the great hill.

The following day, they explained to Barbara Smith, the landlady of their guesthouse, the circumstances of this brief meeting. She told them that the man who had helped them was almost certainly her friend Alfred Wainwright. He was already reasonably well known by then in Britain as a fellwalker, author and illustrator, but he would go on to become a television personality who sold millions of books, many of which are still in print today. The best known of these is *A Pictorial Guide to the Lakeland Fells*, a seven-volume series detailing the hills and peaks of the Lake District, which is still regarded by many walkers as the definitive guide to the Lakeland mountains. Mrs Smith arranged for the Starmers to see Wainwright again the following year when they returned to the area. They got on well, and this resulted in a friendship which lasted for the next thirty years, until Wainwright's death in 1991. The Starmers also remained on good terms with Wainwright's second wife, Betty, until she died in 2008.

Rodney Starmer believed that Wainwright – who, not unlike himself, had a reputation as a rather gruff man of few words – acted as a crucial beacon of hope to Josephine over those three decades. He was always kind to her and concerned about her condition, and he would write to her when her illness flared up and left her bedbound or, as was often the case, in hospital. He is also said to have inspired her to continue climbing as many of the Lake District's fells as she could by ending his letters to her with the words 'Get well, the hills are waiting for you.' Such was the respect the Starmers accorded Wainwright that Rodney confessed in *Encounters with Wainwright*, a book of tributes which was published by the Wainwright Society in 2016, that he and Josephine 'shed a tear' when they read his obituary in *The Guardian*. He also declared that both of them 'loved him like a father'.

It is clear that Cumbria itself became equally important in the lives of Rodney and Josephine Starmer, for they visited there at least once a year throughout their marriage until 2014, the year before Josephine's death. Despite her increasing incapacity, the couple managed to 'claim', or scale, 212 of the 214 Wainwright fells – an achievement which gave them much joy. This impressive statistic also features in *Encounters with Wainwright*, which, furthermore, includes a list of the health problems that dogged Josephine as the years passed by. They included her twice needing new knee and hip joints; her contraction of the MRSA superbug in hospital in 2000; and, finally, a fall in 2008 which broke a femur and resulted in her having a leg amputated just above the knee. In fact, this fall occurred while they were in the Lake District and required them to be driven by ambulance from there to London, where the operation was performed. Remarkably, thanks to Rodney's engineering ingenuity, even after the partial loss of a limb and when Josephine was confined to a titanium wheelchair, they continued to climb to heights of more than 2,000ft. The modifications Rodney made to the chair meant it could cope with the terrain. He also designed a walking frame for his wife.

Rodney and Josephine took seriously the advice offered to them in 1960 by Dr Maclean about having children as early as possible. Having married, Rodney took a job as a works manager at a large toolmaking firm at Ashford in Kent. In a sure sign that they were keen to upend their own working-class roots, the young couple secured a mortgage which allowed them to buy a bungalow on the edge of Romney Marsh. In June 1961, Josephine gave birth to their eldest child, Anna. On 2 September 1962, Keir was born. It has become standard practice in media reports to state as fact that he was named after Keir Hardie, a founder of the Labour Party and its first parliamentary leader, yet Starmer admitted in one interview in 2015 that he had no evidence for this because he had never discussed it with his parents. Still, this idea has stuck, and he has never disabused anybody of it. Anna and Keir were followed in March 1964 by twins Nicholas and, thirty-two minutes later, Katherine. Thanks to Dr Maclean, all the siblings were born at Guy's Hospital, despite the fact the family lived nowhere near the London Borough of Southwark, where it is situated. For any young woman in good health, the relentless nature of having to look after four young children who were born within three years of each other would be a challenge. That Josephine Starmer managed this task seems nothing short of extraordinary, particularly because her own mother was not alive to help her.

Shortly after Keir's birth, the family settled at 23 Tanhouse Road, a three-bedroom semi-detached house close to the commuter town of Oxted, which sits at the foot of the North Downs. The house was built alongside a few dozen identical properties between 1928 and 1930. With barely more than 1,100sq. ft of floorspace and only one small bathroom, it would have been cramped for a family of six, particularly as the children grew older. A two-plate Aga in the kitchen was perhaps the only outward sign of what might be thought of as anything approaching domestic luxury. The house had a driveway at the front, on which was eventually parked the family's Ford Cortina, and a back garden overlooking several acres of undeveloped land, meaning it was in an open and bright position. Today, Tanhouse Road is a reasonably busy thoroughfare, but its semi-rural location means it remains pleasant. Horses graze in the surrounding fields and a brook flows yards from what would have been the Starmers' front door. In the 1960s and 1970s, when there were fewer cars on Britain's roads, it must have been a relatively peaceful place in which to live. As a young boy, Keir had other children to play with locally, too.

Diana Watson, who was the same age as Starmer, says she can remember visiting him at home as a little girl more than fifty years ago. 'I went to Keir's house for a birthday party or something,' she says.

> Their house was very modest. Even though Surrey is traditionally quite affluent, they came from a very modest background. Surrey is thought of as being very much part of the Stockbroker Belt, but east Surrey is really quite rural. It's near the Kent border. The Starmers were unpretentious. They were normal people.

She adds:

> I remember his mother had curly brown hair and brown eyes, and I'm sure I remember noticing her hands were mis-shapen and asking my mother what was wrong with them, and she told me Mrs Starmer had arthritis. She had very kind eyes. I think they were quite like Keir's in a way.

Paul Vickers recalled visiting the house when Starmer was in his teens and found it to be slightly chaotic but friendly: 'I used to love going there. It was always like a building site and there were holes in the wall, there was bits of masonry missing. It was always as though they were trying to finish the house but never actually got quite around to completing the job.'

Having moved to Tanhouse Road in 1963, Rodney Starmer continued to work in the toolmaking trade, but, due to his eldest son's ambiguous explanations, there has always been a certain amount of confusion as to his employment status. This uncertainty justifies examining the complicated question of whether he could objectively be thought of as working class or whether he was in fact a member of the middle classes. In March 2018, Starmer gave an interview to BBC presenter Nick Robinson, in which he discussed his father's career. He said he 'was a toolmaker working in a factory and working every hour, basically'. He added:

> My dad was a toolmaker, he was a very good toolmaker, but he had to live through the policies of Margaret Thatcher, and that decimated manufacturing. I remember distinctly, he went out to work at eight o'clock in the morning, came back at six o'clock for his tea, and went back to work till ten o'clock at night.

The following year, he again talked about his father's occupation, telling the BBC Radio 4 *Today* programme that he 'worked in a factory' as a toolmaker. And during a subsequent interview on *Desert Island Discs*, he returned to the pattern of his father's working day, this time changing the hour that his father returned home after his first shift, saying:

> He worked as a toolmaker on a factory floor all of his life, and my enduring memory as a child was him, as he did, go[ing] to work at eight o'clock in the morning. He came home at five o'clock for his tea, went back at six o'clock and worked through till ten o'clock at night, and that was five days a week.

The inference that listeners to any of these broadcasts might have drawn is that Rodney Starmer was employed by somebody else, perhaps even in a lowly capacity, and may have been one of many toolmakers who toiled at a works. Yet this was not the case. For reasons best known to himself, Starmer did not use any of these opportunities to explain that his father in fact ran his own business, the Oxted Tool Company. Initially, he operated from a unit on a farm in the Hurst Green area, close to where he lived. When this premises was no longer available, he moved to a light industrial estate at Gaywood Farm in the village of Edenbridge, just over the nearby county border in Kent. Nicky Kerman, who still runs the site, says he can recall Rodney Starmer well because he was a 'cheerful chap with a big beard', who was one of the first people to rent a workshop there.

> He was in Unit A, which is probably about 1,500sq. ft in all, and he almost always worked alone, to the best of my knowledge. He gave it up to look after his wife in the 1990s, as far as I'm aware. I think he specialised in making tools for other people. I remember he had a lot of machines and was clearly very good at his job.

No records of the Oxted Tool Company exist in the historical files of Companies House. This makes it difficult to assess how successful Rodney Starmer's business became and indicates that he may have remained a sole trader – as opposed to running a limited company – throughout his working life. Keir Starmer did specify that money was tight when he was growing up, saying in 2019 that 'there were many times when the electricity and the telephone bill didn't get paid'. This suggests that the business may have struggled at times. It is thought that if he did ever employ other people, he did so only on a small scale or on an ad hoc basis. He was certainly more than an ordinary labourer, however. Indeed, his friend Tony Alston says Rodney Starmer told him he had once secured a piece of work from a government department. 'Rodney was a precision engineer,' says Alston.

> At one time he was very left-wing. His company won a job working for the Ministry of Defence. I don't know if it's true, but he always used to say, 'I rang them up and pointed out I was left-wing,' and they said, 'We know exactly what you're like, Mr Starmer, and we've offered you the contract,' so he took the contract.

Alston adds: 'He used to do jobs that people couldn't get done elsewhere. It was machine work, high-quality stuff. I'm under the impression that he employed other engineers from time to time.'

While it is fair to say that a person's own sense of who they are and of the class they feel they belong to certainly matters, it is hard to accept that Rodney Starmer was a straight-up-and-down member of the working class, as his son has often suggested. This poses the important question of how Starmer regards himself. When, in December 2019, he hinted publicly that he was considering standing to succeed Jeremy Corbyn as Labour leader, he tackled this topic by telling the BBC Radio 4 *Today* programme:

> And as for the sort of middle-class thrust, as you know, my dad worked in a factory, he was a toolmaker, and my mum was a nurse, and she contracted a very rare disease very early in her life that meant she was constantly in need of NHS care, so actually my background isn't what [people] think it is.

Technically, everything he said on that occasion in relation to his father is true, of course. Yet as a skilled manual worker who was self-employed and who owned a house (with a mortgage), it is certainly arguable that Rodney Starmer would be thought of by some social scientists as being a cut above other toolmakers who *did* work in factories for other people. None of this would matter in any way, of course, but for the fact that Keir Starmer has not been totally explicit about it when asked, presumably for self-protective reasons.

Aside from their cycling and walking hobbies, Rodney Starmer and his wife enjoyed opera and classical music, and they would regularly attend plays and concerts all over Surrey, especially at the Barn Theatre in Oxted, which is known for amateur dramatics. Its chairman, Bruce Reed, describes them as 'a lovely couple' who would often attend the same musical two or three times because they enjoyed it so much. He says, 'Rod would do anything for anyone. They were both salt of the earth.' He also remembers that, in 2005, they posed happily for a photograph at the theatre with the Duke of Kent, the Queen's first cousin, to mark the occasion when he opened a £300,000 extension containing a new wheelchair lift. In view of Rodney's previously mentioned comments about a 'posh voice' being indicative of a 'vulgar' person, it is amusing to reflect on Reed's account of the reverence Rodney showed the visiting royal. Reed adds: 'Rod usually insisted on wearing shorts, apart from the one day that the Duke of Kent visited. He told me he'd been out and bought a pair of trousers especially for the occasion. He was a shorts and sandals and socks man throughout the year otherwise.'

Family holidays were always spent in the Lake District, though, perhaps oddly, the Starmers never took their children to meet Alfred Wainwright during these visits, fearing they would intrude on his privacy. Another of Josephine's enthusiasms was keeping donkeys, and from the 1970s, they usually had at least two of these beasts living in their back garden. Rodney even became a director of the Donkey Breed Society, a national charity. They also offered a home to dogs that had been abandoned or needed to be rescued. All this was fitted in around Josephine's thirst for knowledge and education. In the mid-1970s, she enrolled with the Open University and received a degree after three years of study. Religion is not thought to have played an especially prominent role in the lives of the Starmers, though Josephine is understood to have attended a local church into her eighties. Starmer has been open about being an atheist, telling one interviewer in April 2021 when asked if he believes in God: 'This is going to sound odd, but I do believe in faith. I've a lot of time and respect for faith. I am not of faith; I don't believe in God, but I can see the power of faith and the way it brings people together.'

As a result of Josephine's illness and Rodney's unsociable working hours, there were few adult visitors to the house during their son's childhood. The family lived under the appalling shadow of Josephine suddenly having to be admitted to a high-dependency unit. Such was Rodney's devotion to his wife that he stopped drinking alcohol so he would be able to accompany her to hospital at any hour of the day or night if need be. There, he would remain with her for as long as necessary, sleeping in a chair if it came to it. He became so well versed in her illness that he knew exactly what symptoms to watch out for and what combination of drugs she was to take depending on her state. Starmer has even recalled a time when he was aged thirteen or fourteen and his father rang him from a hospital to warn: 'I don't think your mum's going to make it. Will you tell the others?' Such unwanted and painful responsibility, placed on his shoulders at a young age, certainly forced him to grow up quickly and perhaps to take life more seriously than most of his peers. Inevitably, as shall become clear, it left its mark on his personality as well.

The four Starmer siblings were all sent to a primary school

in the village of Merle Common, approximately four miles from Tanhouse Road. It was a small, Victorian building with only about fifty pupils and is described by Diana Watson, who lived next door to it and was an exact contemporary of Keir Starmer, as ‘rather sweet and idyllic’. It has long since closed. She says: ‘It was an old, purpose-built village school with an outside toilet block and a little village hall over the road where we would go for dancing and other activities.’ She says one abiding memory she has of this time is that Keir was ‘very protective’ of his younger brother, Nicholas, who was apparently prone to ‘making mischief’. Starmer has also discussed his brother in passing, once saying:

> My brother struggled at school, whereas I did all right, and I remember my parents instilling in me that we were both as successful as each other and that you always measured what people were dealing with in front of them, and so they never singled me out as a golden boy. They were proud; they wanted me to do what I did; but they always brought it back to, ‘And your brother’s doing just as well in what he’s doing,’ so now I never use the word that someone is ‘thick’ or ‘stupid’ or not able to do things. I hate that language. Or that people are ‘bright’. I see it completely differently: that people are very good in different fields at what they do, and we measure them in that way.

Nicholas lived in the north of England and for some years worked as a mechanic. He died aged sixty in December 2024. Of his other siblings, Katherine is a careworker and Anna is believed to have worked in the NHS.

When they were aged eight, Starmer and his classmates moved to the newly built Holland Middle School nearby. Diana Watson joined him there and, like him, sat the 11-plus examination in order to determine whether, from September 1974, they would attend the local comprehensive school, Oxted County School, or one of Surrey's grammar schools. Diana says that she has no memory of the school forcing them to work particularly hard in order to prepare for this rigorous test, perhaps because there was less competition for it at the time. In any case, she says, Starmer's work ethic and attention to detail was already on show by then, in contrast to the vast majority of his classmates, suggesting that he did not need to be pushed. She says:

> Holland Middle School was in a bigger catchment area, so there were kids from Hurst Green who went there as well. It was the feeder for Oxted County School, a comprehensive which at that time was less desirable than it is now. Keir was quite hardworking and serious. In our year, probably four or five pupils got into a grammar school. Keir was one of them; I was another.

There is no question that his passing the 11-plus was a source of great pride to his family, not least because his elder sister, Anna, did not go to a grammar school. Of the four Starmer siblings, Keir would be the only one to take this academic route through his senior school career. His parents decided that he would go to Reigate Grammar School, some twelve miles from their house – a distance long enough to require him to catch a bus every day. It is striking that it was on these bus journeys that he would forge some of his thoughts about politics, religion, justice and equality, therefore marking not just the beginning of the next phase of his life but also the birth of his belief system.

Having considered Keir Starmer's background, perhaps it would be most accurate to say that it was neither 'working class' in the strictest sense nor 'posh', as some journalists have attempted to prove. Instead, it was closer to what marketing employees in the 1980s would have called C2 – a member of the skilled worker social class that was instrumental in returning Margaret Thatcher to Downing Street three times – and what some sociologists and academics in the more distant past would have termed petit bourgeois. This French term, akin to lower-middle-class, is one that would undoubtedly be well understood by Starmer, whose deep interest in Marxist theory was to fill hundreds of hours of his time as a young man.

CHAPTER 2

SCHOOLBOY SOCIALIST

When Keir Starmer entered Reigate Grammar School in September 1974, it was on the cusp of great change. Having been founded in 1675, it was one of the oldest and most traditional educational establishments in the country. Set in grounds close to the centre of the market town of Reigate, it was not a particularly grand place, but it did bear many of the characteristics of a public school. It was academically selective; it was open to boys only; it operated a house system; masters wore gowns; rugby took precedence over football; there was a thriving Combined Cadet Force; corporal punishment was standard practice; and a steady stream of alumni went to Oxbridge. Such outward projections of exclusivity might have appealed to a certain type of parent in Surrey, but, for a host of reasons, one would not have thought automatically that Rodney and Josephine Starmer would be among them. Not only did they support Labour, a party whose ideological opposition to such institutions was well known, but the school was in fact fee-paying for most of the time that their son was a pupil there – something many people in left-wing circles considered to be beyond the pale, even if they could afford to educate their child privately. In the past, Starmer has been accused of deliberately concealing his attendance at Reigate Grammar, so, given the level of public comment his apparent defensiveness over his secondary education has attracted, it is worth examining how this toolmaker's son ended up at an independent school before considering the impact of this experience on his life and career.

One of the biggest political battles being fought during Starmer's schooldays related to the very path on which his parents set him: the fairness of selective education in England and Wales. This vexed question had dominated British politics for decades. Rodney Starmer's assumed political hero, Keir Hardie, had even spoken about the issue during the previous century. It was reported in the *Westminster Gazette* on 1 August 1896 that Hardie had attended an international conference of socialists, and he was quoted afterwards as saying that he believed everybody should receive a full education which was 'free at all stages, open to everyone without any tests of prior attainment at any age – in effect, a comprehensive "broad highway" that all could travel'. Attitudes towards the 11-plus examination specifically and grammar schools in general had only intensified since the 1950s, and many radicals and progressives considered the entire system to be nothing short of immoral. A central charge was that grammar schools created a publicly funded elite whose members were destined for university, while those children who did not attend them had to make do with lesser expectations. All this was said by detractors to reinforce social divisions.

This was the backdrop to the decision in 1965 by Harold Wilson's Labour government to instruct all 163 local authorities in England and Wales to close the 1,200 or so grammar schools which existed and replace them with non-selective comprehensive schools. Although this comprehensivisation process picked up speed during its first five years, its rhythm was interrupted in June 1970, after the Conservative Party won the general election. The new Prime Minister, Ted Heath, appointed Margaret Thatcher as his Secretary of State for Education and Science.

As the product of a grammar school herself, Thatcher believed in academic selection as the best way for bright children from poorer backgrounds to advance through life. Although she accepted the idea of non-selective education (she approved 3,286 comprehensives during the forty-four months she held the Education brief), she also wanted to protect good schools. In this vein, her first act as Education Secretary was to overturn Labour's policy and issue what was known in her department as Circular 10/70. This directive meant that no education authority should be forced any longer to subscribe to the blanket policy of comprehensivisation. Education therefore became a matter of choice at a local level, potentially allowing some grammar schools to determine their own fate rather than having change thrust upon them. The importance of a common education for everybody may have been dear to many within the Labour Party, but Rodney Starmer was on Thatcher's side of the argument when it came to the schooling of a member of his own family. He believed in having options rather than adhering to diktats.

The headmaster of Reigate Grammar School throughout Starmer's seven years there was Howard Ballance. He had been in post since 1968 and was of a conservative frame of mind. He is widely remembered as a man who was devoted to his job. He was of the generation of schoolmasters which had served in the army during the Second World War, but that didn't mean he was an authoritarian figure. For example, he made a point of memorising the Christian names of all 700 pupils in his care at a time when most teachers referred to boys by their surnames only. He was also aware that as the head of a county grammar school, he was responsible for boys from every social background, some of whom were less privileged than others. He would even liaise with the local police if a boy got into a scrape which might have led to him being charged with an offence, persuading officers to allow him to deal with the problem. He cared deeply about the ethos of his grammar school and the success of those in it. During his fourteen-year stewardship, the school prospered, with improved exam results, greater sporting success and more emphasis on drama, music and the Duke of Edinburgh's Award. Most crucially of all, however, Ballance is credited with saving Reigate Grammar School from being incorporated into the comprehensive system and with setting it on a new course, of which Starmer was a direct beneficiary.

Reigate Grammar School was set up in the seventeenth century by Henry Smith, an alderman of London, when he bequeathed £150 towards the purchase of land for a 'free school'. Later, it was linked to the local parish church of St Mary's, until the mid-nineteenth century when it was reformed as an independent establishment. After this, it developed and expanded, leading to a Victorian building programme, the results of which still stand today. In the early twentieth century, the county began paying for able boys to attend the school as well, but by the time of Starmer's arrival, it stood at a crossroads. Three decades earlier it had opted to be taken over by Surrey County Council under the terms of the 1944 Education Act. This meant it became a voluntary-controlled school. The school's foundation owned most of its land and buildings and appointed some of the school governors, and the local authority funded the school and employed the staff.

Although Surrey County Council was dominated by the Conservatives, there was great enthusiasm among its reform-minded members for scrapping Reigate Grammar and creating a new comprehensive school and a new sixth form college in Reigate. When Ballance learned of this in March 1971, he took legal advice from a London law firm, Blyth Dutton, about how to break free of local authority control and, through Mrs Thatcher's adjustment, revert to independent status. Two months later, on 23 May, the chairman of the school's governors, Albert Channing Owens, wrote to Thatcher explaining that, following a vote, the governors wished to apply to discontinue as a voluntary-controlled school and become fee-paying. This request was made under Section 14 of the 1944 Education Act. The letter stated that the school had made financial arrangements with the Crusader Insurance Company Ltd, of Reigate, to buy from the local education authority any property and equipment not already owned by its foundation. Noting that it was bound to give two years' notice to disentangle itself from the tentacles of Surrey's education authority, it was also made clear that Reigate Grammar hoped to reopen as a fee-paying school in September 1973.

This move by a voluntary-controlled school was considered worthy of national attention. *The Times* picked up the story a few days later, quoting the chairman of the governors as saying:

> We feel there is a great need in our part of Surrey for the sort of education we offer. There are 700 boys in the school, which is about the right number. The governors have agreed to the plan and now have been told that the teachers are 100 per cent behind it. Indeed there is absolutely no doubt that many would go elsewhere if we went comprehensive.

It seems highly unlikely that anybody in Surrey who took an interest in education would have been unaware that the future of Reigate Grammar was being fought over, and that, one way or another, it was on course to become a very different kind of school. Interested parties would almost certainly have included Rodney and Josephine Starmer, because their eldest son's 11-plus exam was beginning to show on the horizon.

Surprisingly, more than two years passed before any meaningful response from Thatcher was forthcoming. Then, on 21 June 1973, a representative of hers in the Department for Education wrote to Owens to explain that the Secretary of State could not accept the application. The school was advised that a second application could be made but 'only in association with proposals submitted by the local education authority under Section 13 relating to other maintained schools which would, if approved by [Thatcher], have the effect of leaving no place for the school in its present form'. The plans of Ballance and the governors were frustrated, forcing them back into talks with Surrey County Council.

Just over six months later, in February 1974, a snap general election was called by Ted Heath, which resulted in a hung parliament. Labour, still led by Harold Wilson, returned to government and Thatcher was replaced as the Secretary of State for Education by the Labour MP Reginald Prentice. By this point, Starmer had passed his 11-plus. Then, in June 1974, three months before he started at Reigate Grammar, the *Surrey Mirror* reported it was 'almost certain' that the school would become fee-paying after the council's overtures had been met with 'total rejection' by the governors. By the time of Starmer's first day in the school, Ballance was working six and a half days a week to secure the necessary funds to make it viable as a private institution.

David Jones taught languages at Reigate from September 1975 until July 2011. One of his first pupils was Starmer, to whom he gave French lessons. Jones says that Starmer's first few terms would have been overshadowed by its unclear future but that many parents stepped in to help Ballance. 'A very active, very accomplished parents' committee was formed to promote and attain the independence of the school,' Jones remembers. Their collective efforts paid off.

As Ballance negotiated a hefty loan with the local branch of Barclays Bank, teaching staff were promised a 5 per cent pay increase if they agreed to stay on at what he hoped would be the new fee-paying school. At the same time, provisions were made to take extra pupils – including girls in the sixth form – to increase revenue. Donations from wealthier parents were sought as well. Ballance's second application to become independent, in line with Thatcher's advice, was finally approved by Prentice in May 1975, at the end of Starmer's first year. It was decided that the changeover would take place on 1 September 1976, the beginning of Starmer's third academic year. Ballance became the first headmaster of a voluntary-controlled school in England to achieve the status of independence. Not only that but Surrey County Council eventually agreed to cover the cost of every pupil who had entered the school via the 11-plus for the duration of their stay – a figure which ran to more than £300,000 (about £2 million in 2024). Only the parents of new pupils arriving from September 1976 would have to pay.

This was the convoluted process by which Starmer came to spend five years at a fee-paying school, albeit free of charge. Ultimately, his good fortune was made possible by Margaret Thatcher's decision to issue Circular 10/70, giving grammar schools some say in their destiny. As David Jones says, 'Mrs Thatcher had approved the loophole through which the school squeezed to become independent in September 1976.' Jones says he remembers the period with a certain amount of affection:

> It was quite an exciting time, in a way. The school had to build its resources and establishment pretty much from scratch. Howard Ballance was a tremendous force for good through all of that. I suppose that forged some of the spirit of the time, because at that point all the boys were 11-plus pupils and there was tremendous gratitude for the substantial undertakings that were given and there was enormous parental commitment as regards extracurricular help and, indeed, fundraising.

There is no argument that Rodney and Josephine Starmer knew

before their son joined the school that fundamental change in its status was on the cards, but they obviously believed that the prospects it offered him trumped the beliefs of progressive-minded politicians. Not only is it normal for every parent to want the best for their child, but it is equally true that no child can be responsible for decisions taken by their parents about their schooling. With this in mind, it is noteworthy that when the *Daily Mail* discovered in September 2009 that Starmer had omitted to mention Reigate Grammar School in his *Who's Who* entry, it concluded that this was a piece of chicanery which reflected badly on his character. By then, he was the DPP, and the *Mail* was deeply unimpressed. 'Despite the fact that the school almost certainly made him the man he is, it didn't fit with his image as a man of the people,' it thundered in a leading article. 'Those who utter small lies invariably tell big ones as well. Don't such small acts of deception tell us something significant about these public figures?'

As with the questions raised in the previous chapter about what Starmer has had to say regarding his father's profession, the fact that he attended a grammar school which became a private school should not matter to anybody. A more interesting point is why he should feel any sensitivity about it. Certainly his parents did not. They kept a careful record of his progress, with school reports and photographs filed away with pride. Conceivably, he may have regarded it as somehow compromising that, in a way, he owes his schooling – and everything that sprang from it, starting with his attendance at a good university – to Margaret Thatcher, a politician he has repeatedly condemned in public. Alternatively, it could be that he feels some misplaced sense of guilt at being the only one of four siblings who was given a grammar-school-style education. Whatever the true explanation, it is striking that after the *Mail* took him to task in 2009, he updated his *Who's Who* entry by confirming in its pages the name of his alma mater in Surrey. It would have been strange if he had not done so, because it is quite obvious that he flourished there.

• • •

Travelling from Tanhouse Road to the town of Reigate every morning involved Starmer having to leave home early to catch a bus. The twelve-mile journey took more than half an hour each way. He was not the only boy in his year to use public transport to get to school; several of his exact contemporaries did as well, including Andrew Sullivan. Although it would soon become clear that their politics were very different, Sullivan says he and Starmer always had a friendly rivalry. Sullivan also sat directly behind Starmer during their first three years at school, until they were aged fourteen, giving him a ringside seat on Starmer's early years. In retrospect, he likens them to two characters from Alan Bennett's play *The History Boys*, which is set in a fictional northern grammar school in the early 1980s. 'The thing that made us different was that we lived quite a long way from the school,' Sullivan says.

> He and I were both on the other side of the county. Generally speaking, over the years we just got into this fight. We would constantly argue. It was the 1970s, so everything was quite political. These were the years of Wilson, Callaghan and Thatcher. She was elected Tory leader in 1975 and that, I think, is when the arguments really started. On most days we would have some kind of knock-down argument on the bus, and it would often continue through the day at school. We would pick up other people along the way. It became a bit of a performance after a while. Someone told me recently they had vivid

memories of these arguments, including me at some point debating Keir about Thatcher.

Another exact contemporary on those journeys was Andrew Cooper. 'He got on at Oxted; I got on at Godstone,' remembers Cooper.

> He was very popular and likeable and widely liked. He was very into sport, certainly in the early years. He was bright but was not the very brightest. Nor was I. He was in the upper echelons. He was a very funny guy; a jokester. His personality is much more relaxed and light-hearted than comes across. If there was a group of teenage boys on a bus larking about, Keir would always be at the heart of that. He was charismatic. He stood out as having a personality and would initiate jokes and conversations. There was a lot of Top Trumps played to begin with and then, as we got older, political discussions. Andrew Sullivan was often on the same bus. We were untypically interested in politics from a young age.

Sullivan, now a political commentator who has lived in America since the 1980s, attributes his and Starmer's 'precocious' interest in politics to both of their families having had strong political opinions. 'His parents were very socialist and committed to the left, and it was clear that he was already committed there,' he says. But he remembers that their discussions were not restricted to politics:

> It was also a fight about religion. I was a pretty devout Catholic and happy to argue about transubstantiation and abortion with anyone at the age of twelve; he was an atheist. At school there were some very bright kids, and these sorts of conversations

> were going on. We would have fights about it. He remembered last time we got together, actually, that he would even go into the Christian Union, where I would go after class, to pick a fight with me there, just to keep the argument going. We got it into our heads that we were at war.

During Starmer's first year, the boys were split into three forms, each consisting of about thirty pupils. As he moved up the school, a new system developed in which forms were reorganised according to which house a pupil was in. There were eight houses, each named after a local geographical feature or area. The house system was not pastoral and existed primarily for the purposes of competition on and off the sports field. Each house had two assemblies a week, which were held in two small classrooms. Starmer was put in a house called Linkfield. In the sixth form, pupils were again divided into sets depending on the A-Level subjects they were studying. As would be expected for a selective school, academic matters were paramount, with Howard Ballance pushing everybody to do their best at all times.

In addition to termly reports, monthly reports were issued in a process overseen by Ballance personally. Andrew Cooper remembers that these assessments were posted on a classroom wall, meaning there was no hiding place for anybody who had performed badly. 'You'd be graded one to five for effort as opposed to achievement, with a one being excellent and a five being poor,' he recalls. 'If you got a four or five you had to go to the headmaster. From a schoolboy point of view, those monthly reports were how we judged one another's ability. You had to get your parents to sign them.' He says that, certainly during their first three years in the school, 'I would guess Keir was in the one to three range.'

Peter Wheatley, a physics teacher at the school from 1975 who taught Starmer at A-Level, says that the academic ability of most boys of Starmer's vintage was never in question anyway, whether they were being put under pressure or not. 'When the school was a proper state grammar school, the ability level of the pupils was amazingly high,' he says.

> In forty-three years of teaching, I never taught classes as bright as those proper grammar school classes at Reigate. They were outstandingly good. It was because the school covered such a big catchment area. The boys were so intelligent. The brightest boy I ever taught was one year older than Keir. He was ridiculous. His dad was a jobbing builder, and he went to read maths at Cambridge. When we went independent, for the first few years it was more about who had the biggest purse. There was a hell of a change of standard. That wouldn't have affected Keir. He got in as a proper grammar school entrant, so he was in one of the seriously bright years.

Starmer had several close friends as he moved up the school, including Mark Adams, Paul Vickers, Steve Wheddon and Geoffrey Scopes. He was not able to spend all his spare time gadding about with them, though. From the age of fourteen, he was encouraged by his parents to get a holiday job working on a farm, so he could earn his own money. Another friend in his year was Quentin Cook, subsequently known as Norman and by his DJ name Fatboy Slim. They took violin lessons together, though Cook left Reigate Grammar aged sixteen, and they appear to have lost touch thereafter. Music remained a very important part of Starmer's life as a schoolboy, however. He also played the flute, the piano and the recorder. Mark Dixon began his teaching career at Reigate Grammar in 1978 and rated Starmer's musicianship highly. 'He was a very good flute player and played in the school orchestra,' he says.

> I ran an early music group [at Reigate]. We were a group of recorder players and crumhorn players. He got quite keen on this. He used to come along at lunchtimes. We performed at various concerts and competitions. I remember we once played our recorders in a competition in Redhill and won. His parents were also very keen. They were kind enough to invite the group to tea at their place in Oxted. They were very supportive of the school and his musical interest.

In fact, Starmer was good enough at the flute to be an exhibitioner at the Junior Guildhall School of Music, which was linked to the main Guildhall School of Music, one of Europe's premier conservatoires. Every Saturday morning, at the insistence of his parents, he would travel to London to attend lessons given by staff who played in professional orchestras. The expectation was that most of the students would go on to study music at undergraduate level before turning professional themselves. The Guildhall has destroyed the records of many former students, and Starmer's file would appear to be among them, making it difficult to assess just how good a musician he was. He did volunteer in a 2015 interview that he realised at the age of seventeen that while other students at the Guildhall were 'hugely talented' he 'just practised hard', suggesting he never harboured ambitions of making a career out of playing music. Yet he put his talent to use. His flute teacher, Deirdre Hicks, died in 2020, but the archives of Reigate Grammar record that during his sixth form he set up and ran a wind ensemble which featured on a float during the 1980 Lord Mayor of London's procession. He played lead flute during school productions of *Joseph and the Amazing Technicolor Dreamcoat* and *Oliver!*, and he would perform in local concerts in Surrey with Ms Hicks. As a teenager, he also toured Malta with the Croydon Youth Symphony Orchestra, one of south London's leading amateur orchestras, which performed concerts several times a year.

Reigate Grammar had a reputation for being a strong sporting school in the 1970s, and Starmer was a keen partaker. During the autumn and spring terms, rugby was the main game, though hockey and cross-country running were also on offer. Sixth formers could play football if they preferred. In the summer term, it was a choice between cricket, tennis and athletics. Alan Reid was in charge of the cross-country and athletics teams and remembers Starmer as a decent middle-distance runner. 'From my point of view, he was quite a quiet lad,' he says. 'I've dealt with a lot of extroverts, but he was a quieter boy. My recollection is that he was in the school athletics team until he was about fifteen.' The school magazine, *The Pilgrim*, also notes that in his lower sixth, between 1979 and 1980, he was part of the 1st XI football team. He played in the midfield position and was rated as a 'talented ball player' who 'increased in stature as the season progressed', doing well enough to win his colours. In his final year, he won his colours again and was awarded the Paul Lynch Cup for being the player of the year. Graham Best, who was in charge of the team, is nothing but complimentary about his ability, even if he was not blessed with great height, at 5ft 8in. 'Keir was a very skilful and keen footballer at school and always played with great energy and commitment,' he says. 'Although the team was not hugely successful, Keir captained the side in his last year and proved a good leader both on and off the field.'

In another non-academic department he was just as determined to succeed, completing his Duke of Edinburgh's Gold

Award aged seventeen. In order to achieve this goal, he had to undertake a series of five self-improvement exercises over a period of at least a year, including volunteering in the community. The award culminated in planning and completing an adventurous journey in Britain. For that final stage, he was among a group of fourteen pupils who went on a five-day hiking expedition during the summer holidays in 1980. Dartmoor was the chosen location. Mark Dixon was one of the masters who supervised the trip. 'They would have covered fifty miles in four days carrying all their equipment, including tents and food, with them, so it was pretty arduous,' he says.

In a report Starmer wrote about the trip for *The Pilgrim*, he noted that there were 'minor disagreements about map-reading' between himself and his friend Steve Wheddon, adding, 'But I was always right!' It seems his desire to lead was already on show – a suggestion which chimes with Dixon.

During Starmer's top year in the school, he was made a prefect and was considered the ideal candidate to describe – again for *The Pilgrim* – a summary of the results of his house in the various inter-house competitions. Once more, his serious and sensible side was apparent, as was a politician's skill for making mediocre achievements sound positive. 'This year saw Linkfield do very well in most House competitions,' he wrote, 'and there is a genuine feeling of being part of a team when we assemble for House prayers. Although we did not actually top the list in many competitions, we were nearly always in the top three, and congratulations must be given to everyone who took part.' He was pleased to announce that Linkfield had come second in the speaking competition – something he called 'a really good result' considering it was 'a House with no outstanding orators'. He was also proud of the results of the quiz and chess teams and the cross-country and hockey teams. Rugby and basketball were less successful, he admitted, 'but the spirit was there for both and that's what counts'. He went on: 'To sum up, I think we can now look at Linkfield as a House of dedicated young people who can be relied upon to put a fine effort into anything they are called upon to do.'

The culture of Reigate Grammar started to change after it became an independent school. Not only was this because the number of children who had to sit the 11-plus had diminished; it was also because of the arrival of girls in the sixth form. 'By the time we got to the sixth form [in September 1979] there were perhaps twenty girls,' says Andrew Cooper. 'He was very popular among the girls because he was funny and charismatic. I don't think he had a girlfriend from among those girls; he did have girlfriends, but I don't remember a steady girlfriend from that period.' Groups of friends including Starmer would meet at weekends and during school holidays. 'It would usually be at someone's house or more probably in a pub,' says Cooper.

> We would often meet either in the Reigate area or sometimes at points roughly halfway between Reigate and Oxted, like Nutfield. There was a village hall there, which was sometimes used as a venue for parties. I'm sure we were all guilty of drinking beer under the age of eighteen but nothing more dangerous than that.

Andrew Sullivan says that, inevitably, Starmer's personality changed as he grew older. Whereas he remembers himself being 'uptight and ordered' and someone who 'wore his school cap at all times and said thank you to the bus driver', Starmer became 'much more one of the lads'. He goes on:

> People liked him. He was quite popular. But he always seemed

> a little angry about the world. There was a rough edge to him. He was physically more rough and ready, and he was not totally conformist. You got the impression he did not like the school very much. He certainly wasn't going to go down the Oxbridge route. That was a big difference [between us]. At some point, he didn't seem to be doing the conventional thing, but he was obviously very clever.

This non-conformist dimension to Starmer's character was certainly in evidence outside school. He became active in left-wing politics, joining the East Surrey Young Socialists – the youth wing of the Labour Party – when he was sixteen years old. Andrew Cooper, who was a Conservative member of the House of Lords and now sits as a crossbencher, was at the forefront of this organisation before Starmer joined it. He says there was little formal debating at school, and, if there had been, it wouldn't have been very dynamic anyway.

> East Surrey was obviously a very Conservative area, and our school was, by 1976, a private school. Most of the students probably reflected the politics of their parents, so there weren't very many Labour-supporting people there. I grew up in a Labour-supporting house and got involved when I was not quite fourteen, in 1977. The Labour Party Young Socialists group was already well established by then. It was chaired by Guy Morris, who became quite a good friend of mine and who lived not far from Oxted. The secretary was Jane Robinson.

Nobody seems to know definitively why Starmer became involved in the group, beyond acknowledging the obvious reason: his parents voted Labour. Cooper says he can recollect one early conversation about politics on the bus to school before Starmer joined. 'I remember him being very supportive of the fire brigade pay strike [between November 1977 and January 1978]. I remember having a discussion with him about it upstairs on the bus. I was less sure about it; Keir was very strongly supportive of it.'

Despite his parents' devotion to Labour, it is interesting to note that he has said that his father was too busy to get involved in the party locally. 'He wasn't active because he was a toolmaker working in a factory and working every hour, basically, so he didn't have time for activism, but he was a strong Labour supporter,' he told the BBC in 2018. Neither was the schoolboy Starmer force-fed left-wing doctrine by his parents. In the same interview, he was asked if politics was talked about at home, or whether he was ever taken out by his parents to campaign. He answered, 'No, no... [my dad] wasn't there during the week for those [political] conversations.' Even when pressed on *Desert Island Discs* to state what exactly sparked his interest in politics as a teenager, he did not answer the question directly.

It seems likeliest that, having inherited some political beliefs, he had the intellectual curiosity to explore them. He was not usually forthright in expressing his opinions as a teenager, according to Cooper, though he did discuss his father sometimes. 'He did talk about his dad quite a lot but not his mum. Rodney was always described as quite strict. He never shared the fact that he had those challenges [relating to his mother's illness] in his home life. I don't recall him often expressing strong personal views on everything,' Cooper says. 'But I don't remember a time when I didn't know Keir was a Labour person through and through.'

Nationally, the Young Socialists was considered to be in the grip of the Trotskyites in the late 1970s, but the picture in east Surrey was different. Cooper goes on:

> For reasons I was never able to make sense of, the Labour Party

in east Surrey – which was obviously in a Conservative-supporting area – was on the other fringe of the Labour Party altogether and was affiliated with a group called the Campaign for a Labour Victory (CLV), which was the forerunner of what became the Social Democratic Party.

One of the first Labour Young Socialists meetings I went to had a speaker from the CLV. I remember it vividly because Labour HQ, who ran the Young Socialists nationally, were so perturbed that this group wasn't aligned, they sent a speaker down to talk to us and try to whip us into line.

Cooper became chairman of the East Surrey Young Socialists in 1978, and it is from this point that he can clearly remember Starmer's active participation in the group. Meetings would usually be held in the top-floor room of an outbuilding at the back of Cooper's parents' house, which was on the village green in Godstone.

> I certainly remember Keir coming to those meetings. I think it's true that I was in the Labour Party before he was, and I remained in it until I went to university in 1981. I sometimes joke that perhaps it was me who brought Keir into the Labour Party, though probably that's not true.

The group met every four to six weeks, but it was a very social kind of socialism, and they would invariably seek out refreshments when the serious business of politicking was over.

> We didn't just meet to pass motions. Mostly we would sit around and natter about politics for a bit and then go to the pub. Keir definitely had a passionate, positive belief in equality. I don't think I had at the time a great sense of to what extent he was an

> out-and-out socialist, as opposed to a moderate, but if we argued with people about the Conservatives, the arguments were good natured. There was no animus. If you'd looked around the room at that time and said, 'One of you will one day be Labour leader,' you wouldn't have thought it would obviously be Keir, but certainly he would have been on the shortlist.

The Young Socialists also helped the local Labour Party when it came to canvassing and campaigning. A small number of Labour councillors sat on the district council, elected by wards in Caterham and Oxted. Cooper says Rodney Starmer's connections may have been influential in fostering his son's political activities, as there were two centres of left-wing activity around Oxted, each dominated by a personality faction.

> Keir knew from his father, I think, the leading Labour figures from the Oxted camp. One was Robin Harling, who was the chairman of East Surrey Labour Party for most of the time that I was in it. He had a brother called Jim. They both lived in Oxted, near Keir. And there was also a legendary figure called George Cornish, who was a very popular Labour councillor. Keir knew the Harlings, who were a big Labour force. Keir then became involved with a few people from school [in the Young Socialists]. I think there were ten or twelve of us in the Young Socialists. Not that many. I think we were quite highly valued because we were willing to go out canvassing.

The constituency Labour Party was supportive of Tony Benn at the time.

> They found us quite puzzling because they expected us to be more left-wing than them, and we were less so. I remember

> somebody from the regional Labour Party came to see us. They were checking up on the Young Socialist groups because they were worried about extremism, and he wrote me a letter afterwards saying we were like a ray of light because we were so mainstream.

Cooper left the Labour Party to join the SDP when it was founded in March 1981 by the so-called 'Gang of Four' Labour politicians, comprising Shirley Williams, Roy Jenkins, David Owen and Bill Rodgers, but Starmer stayed on.

Jon Pike, who lived in Caterham, a short distance from Oxted, was a few years Starmer's junior. Through his interest in left-wing politics, and because his mother knew Starmer's mother, he got to know Starmer and also joined the Young Socialists. According to him, nobody was off-limits to the group – not even the local Conservative MP for East Surrey, Sir Geoffrey Howe, who was at the time Margaret Thatcher's Chancellor of the Exchequer. 'We ran jumble sales and held public meetings and poked fun at the Tories,' Pike has recalled.

> We weren't always politically or socially astute. One time, we found out that Geoffrey Howe was starting a fun run in Oxted. We all signed up so as to go to the start and heckle him. Heckling done, it then dawned on us that we had to actually run the course. A certain amount of walking and smoking of fags may have occurred.

One wonders what the teenaged Starmer would have said if he had been told that in the future he, just like Howe, would go on to be called to the Bar by Middle Temple, would become a QC, would be elected as an MP and would also accept a knighthood for his abilities as a lawyer.

Despite having a fairly packed extracurricular life, those who taught Starmer remember that he did not ignore his studies. The consensus is that he was academically solid, if not brilliant. He chose maths, music and physics as his A-Level subjects. Mark Dixon taught physics and occasionally came across him in lessons. 'Keir was a very well-meaning lad with a good sense of humour, with an occasional hint of mischief,' he says. 'He was always very organised at school, very lively, versatile and wide-ranging. Academically he was pretty sound. He was not absolutely at the top of the pile, but he was in the top set. He was pretty sharp.' His parents took a close interest in the progress of his studies as well. Dixon adds:

> I remember at parents' evenings, they always came and always wanted to have a chat and were fully supportive and thankful for what one had done for their son. They very much appreciated everything that was being done for him and talked about how he was having a great time at school and getting the most out of it. It doesn't surprise me he's got to where he has.

Peter Wheatley, who also taught Starmer physics at A-Level, concurs. 'They were all very bright,' he says.

> He's not one of those names that leaps out as having been absolutely outstanding, but he was in a very outstanding year. The proper grammar school pupils were sharp and highly motivated. They were good fun to teach. Typical of them would be if I set them a selection of questions at the end of the chapter in a textbook for homework, several members of the class wouldn't just do the eight or ten questions I'd asked them to do, they'd do all twenty or thirty questions. It was hard work for me, but it was quite interesting to come across kids so highly motivated.

> As I say, the catchment area was so big that the school was able to be very selective.

In his final term at school, in the summer of 1981, Starmer scored two Bs and C in his exams – enough to win a place at the University of Leeds. Before he left, he was, with three other pupils, a recipient of the CE Deacon Prize for Service to the School, illustrating the esteem in which he was held. Even if, by then, some of his contemporaries were 'suspicious of his political views!', as his form master Mr Bullen noted in one of his final reports, it is beyond question that his secondary schooling was successful on all fronts – socially, academically, in terms of handling responsibility and also in getting the most out of the extracurricular activities that were on offer. All these achievements were a tribute to him but also to his parents, especially his mother. Making them proud mattered to him very much. Going to Reigate Grammar also afforded Starmer his first independent taste of left-wing politics, thanks to his friendship with Andrew Cooper. And yet despite all this, a fundamental contradiction remains.

Starmer has stayed close to Reigate Grammar since leaving it. Not only are some of his best friends today also his former schoolmates but it seems he has always been happy to lend his support to the school when required. Former member of staff David Jones recalls that he has regularly put in an appearance at events when asked. 'Certainly during his time as DPP, he was always outstanding when it came to attending functions at the school to which he'd been invited. He not only attended the functions but he would always come and have a pint with us afterwards,' he says. In February 2014, Starmer also delivered the Henry Smith Lecture to pupils at the school. That year, a new organisation, the Henry Smith Club, was established. It is aligned with a Reigate Grammar bursary campaign which pays the fees for five children whose parents cannot afford to fund a private education. Starmer has willingly backed this charitable initiative and, moreover, has played an active role in it. At least once, in 2017, he was the guest of honour at its fundraising dinner, held at the East India Club in London. On that occasion, he 'spoke of his fond memories of his time at school, and of the first-class education he received, which laid the platform for his successful career'.

Notwithstanding all that he has achieved courtesy of a selective grammar school education, however, he has also made it plain that, ultimately, he rejects the system through which he came. 'I don't agree with separating children at eleven, because I think children develop at different ages,' he said during an event at the Labour Party conference in 2019. 'I also profoundly disagree that you're either, as it were, a talented child, or a not-talented child. Everybody is good at different things.' Instead, he has said he would advocate a comprehensive system in which pupils are put into streams according to their ability. This would, he believes, create a state education system that is so strong that private schools would become 'irrelevant'. To what degree this motivated him to make adding VAT to independent school fees one of his party's flagship policies during the 2024 general election campaign is an open question. What is more definite is the charge of hypocrisy he faces for imposing a tax on the type of private education that he enjoyed. Of course, his fees were covered using taxpayers' money in order to avoid disrupting his schooling. Had that public money not been available, he would have had to leave Reigate Grammar School, a point he has never addressed publicly.

As proof of his commitment to the state sector, his own children have not been educated privately, and he is adamant that they never will be. 'Going to a grammar school allowed me to have that focus, but I still don't think it's the right thing to have done,' he said. 'I didn't have a lot of choice about it at the time.' All of which prompts the question: why bother to help raise money for less-well-off pupils to attend the fee-paying school of which you were a beneficiary if you do not believe such institutions should exist in the first place? Perhaps enquiries of this nature, which demand a proper explanation, throw some light on the reason why Reigate Grammar School was omitted from Starmer's *Who's Who* entry until the *Daily Mail* picked up on it.

CHAPTER 3

KING OF MIDDLE-CLASS RADICALS

The idea of taking a year off between school and university was less commonplace in 1981 than it is today, but one early adopter was Keir Starmer. Many young people who did decide to have a gap between receiving their A-Level results and becoming an undergraduate often chose to go in search of adventure by backpacking around Asia or South America, or perhaps doing voluntary work in Africa. Others wanted to sample the world of commerce by working in an office somewhere in Britain. In a move which says much about his character as a young man, Starmer trod an altogether more altruistic path by spending several months in Cornwall looking after disabled people and then going to work in his father's toolmaking business.

The place to which Starmer went first was Churchtown Farm Field Studies Centre. It had been established in 1975 by the Spastics Society, which is now known as the charity Scope. It was located in idyllic countryside in the village of Lanlivery, close to Bodmin Moor, and was primarily intended to encourage nature studies and outdoor pursuits. In the late 1970s and early 1980s, there were very few establishments in Britain, or indeed in Europe, like it which were devoted solely to those with physical, sensory or learning disabilities. It catered for all ages, from young children to middle-aged adults all the way up to those who were in their nineties. Clients came from both the UK and other countries, including France, Germany and America.

Churchtown's overriding philosophy was that learning should be fun. It was quite normal for a child in a wheelchair, for example, to be immersed – in their chair – in a large pond in the centre's grounds, so they could get as close as an able-bodied person to insects and plants, which they would then be taught about. Some visitors to the centre lived for most of the year in residential hospitals, meaning that a trip to Churchtown was for them a holiday. Others were at school or college studying for O-Level or A-Level exams in biology or geography, and the type of fieldwork on offer at Churchtown was considered essential to their progress. Clients were also taught about farm animals and were able to learn practical tasks, such as how to milk a goat or groom a horse. Outdoor activities including rock-climbing, orienteering, hiking, swimming, fishing and birdwatching were on offer, too, as was sailing on the river at the nearby town of Fowey or day trips to the seaside.

David Griffith was the bursar and administrator at Churchtown in 1981 and says that it was in many ways a revolutionary place. 'At that time, we were in the forefront of taking disabled people out of doors on field trips and outdoor pursuits. Now it is the norm, but then it wasn't,' he says.

In 1981, the village of Lanlivery consisted of a church, a pub, a school and a few houses. Churchtown was based in disused farm buildings which had been converted for use by those in wheelchairs. It employed its own professional care staff, but it always needed non-professional voluntary assistants. Its status meant there was no shortage of offers of help throughout its busiest months, from May to November, and it was not even necessary for it to advertise. Most volunteers were selected because of what their CV suggested they would be able to contribute. It is thought that some voluntary work with the disabled, which Starmer had done as part of his Duke of Edinburgh's Gold Award, probably recommended him for this unpaid role. A maximum of eight Churchtown assistants could be accommodated at any one time, most of whom had quarters in a manor house that was just over the road from the central site. 'The minimum age for volunteers was eighteen,' says Griffith. 'We didn't encourage people to stay longer than six months because part of the ethos of the centre was that the enthusiasm that young volunteers brought was important.'

In spite of the beauty of Cornwall's countryside, decamping to such a remote area to care for strangers with a range of complicated conditions would not be the first wish of every teenager straight after leaving school. Demonstrating admirable strength of personality, however, Starmer stuck with it. The number of clients visiting at any one time varied according to their disability. A maximum of seventy mentally disabled but ambulant clients and visiting staff could stay there at once, though if a group comprised individuals who were primarily physically disabled and required a wheelchair, that number shrank to about thirty. Courses lasted for one week. 'Voluntary assistants didn't get involved in personal care, but their core function was to support our clients at mealtimes and, most importantly, to be additional pairs of hands while out in the field in various activities,' says Griffith. 'They would have had an interest in either environmental studies or in outdoor pursuits so that they could get stuck in with abseiling or rock-climbing or sailing.'

Although hundreds of volunteers worked at Churchtown during the years Griffith spent there, he says that he and another member of staff can recall Starmer. According to them, he volunteered with two other young men from the London area and looked after disabled girls and boys from mid-summer 1981 until the end of the year. Griffith says Starmer was well suited to the work, and his time there was considered a success. 'I remember three of them came down,' he recalls.

> There are certain people who stand out in a crowd. I think it's probably that there were three of them together that triggered memories. They had a stronger presence than an individual coming to stay with us; they had that bigger impact. I remember they were very good with the clients. I remember in the evenings we always had social activities, and very often we would encourage the volunteer assistants to lead in entertainment if they could, whether it was a quiz or whatever. We had a piano. This group of three were quite good at entertaining our clients in the evening. [Starmer] had a classical musical interest and would have been fully involved in the life and work of the centre.

Starmer returned home in time for Christmas and had a further nine months of freedom at his disposal before he began studying for his degree at the University of Leeds. Surprisingly, he did not stray far from Surrey for long during this period, spending six months working alongside his father learning how to operate a production machine in his workshop. He was paid a small sum for his time but got little else from the experience.

The fact that he did not escape his parents' clutches as soon as possible suggests that he was either a very dutiful son or felt pressurised into remaining in Oxted, conceivably for financial reasons. Who is to say that his father did not expect him to pull his weight if he was about to become a full-time university student requiring some level of support? Whatever the explanation, Rodney Starmer did later acknowledge that the period they spent together might not have been regarded by his son as the most fruitful or interesting use of his time; he admitted that he knew Keir had found it 'dead boring'.

Little did either of them know then, however, that there would be one upside to Starmer's stint in the toolmaking business. Thirty-seven years on, in 2019, he was able to tell members of the Labour Party who he hoped would elect him as their leader that he was not the middle-class man some might assume but in fact had working-class roots. He cited as evidence the experience of this dull manual work. 'I actually had never been in any workplace other than a factory until I left home for university,' he said in 2019. 'I had never been in an office. The idea that somehow I personally don't know what it's like for people across the country and in all sorts of different circumstances is just not borne out.' He had been able to make exactly the same point during an interview at the Labour Party conference three months previously.

In September 1982, not long after his twentieth birthday, Starmer finally travelled north to start the next phase of his life. Leeds is one of the original redbrick universities, founded in the early twentieth century, and it has long been regarded as one of Britain's better seats of learning. It is a campus university which is based in the heart of the city, guaranteeing its popularity with students who feel they can enjoy the best of both worlds. In the early 1980s, Leeds was still associated in many people's minds with the murders carried out there by serial killer Peter Sutcliffe, dubbed the Yorkshire Ripper. Indeed, Sutcliffe's last known murder victim, Jacqueline Hill, was a Leeds University student who was killed in November 1980, and the month before that another young woman, Maureen Lea, had been attacked by Sutcliffe in the grounds of the university. The case had only been resolved in May 1981, when Sutcliffe was jailed, and the shadow cast by his crimes was long.

Yet as a metropolis and as a university, Leeds was always

considered fun and lively. It had a thriving social and sporting scene and the era's best-known bands, such as The Undertones, The Cure and The Smiths, visited regularly to play gigs. With a population approaching 1 million, this West Yorkshire urban centre was a world away from the small Surrey town where Starmer had grown up, and he is known to have had a happy time there.

He was the first person in his family to attend university, and his parents were adamant that he should not waste the opportunity. They certainly exercised a certain amount of control over his university career. Originally, Starmer had expressed an interest in reading politics. Given his devotion to the Young Socialists, this was unsurprising. Furthermore, the politics department at Leeds was held in high esteem by many at that time. For example, Ralph Miliband, the prominent left-wing intellectual and father of Starmer's two future friends, the politicians David and Ed Miliband, had been professor of politics there until 1978. Yet in a sure sign that Rodney and Josephine Starmer expected their son to gain a degree in a subject that would equip him to enter a profession after he graduated, they insisted that he should read law instead. Starmer acquiesced, even though this subject is notoriously time-consuming even at undergraduate level, and despite his legal knowledge being minimal when he began the course. As he has admitted, when he arrived at Leeds, he had never met a lawyer before and he didn't know the difference between a solicitor and a barrister. He has also claimed that he didn't know what lawyers did, though it should be noted that in his sixth form his form master, Mr Bullen, referred to him in a school report as 'an aspiring lawyer', suggesting that he must have done at least some research into how the law worked before embarking on his degree. Nevertheless, over the ensuing nine terms, spread over barely thirty-six months, he had to grasp an enormous amount of information.

In the early 1980s, Leeds was considered a good institution at which to read law. One former tutor of the era says that it was 'not generally thought by those in academic circles to be in the first rank, but it was proudly in the second rank'. Most of those studying alongside Starmer would have been undergraduates for whom Leeds was their second choice after Oxbridge, UCL, Bristol or perhaps Manchester or Birmingham. The tutor recalls that the course then involved getting to grips with the standard subjects used by every respectable law faculty in the country, except at the universities of Oxford and Keele.

In the first year, four compulsory subjects were taught: contract, tort, English legal system and constitutional law. In the second year, there were two compulsory subjects: land law and crime. In the third year, trusts and jurisprudence were obligatory. During years two and three, students had to choose three further subjects to achieve the requirement of five subjects. The list of options available to them was Roman law, legal history, European law, international law (peace), international law (war), family law, employment law, revenue law, social security law and conveyancing. The course was arranged to ensure that graduates had a Qualifying Law Degree for the purposes of entry to the profession. With very few exceptions, subjects were taught by a combination of two lectures per week – making a total of forty for the year per subject – and one tutorial group consisting of a lecturer plus four students, which met once a fortnight, making a total of ten tutorials per year per subject. By the standards of many undergraduate degree courses, this was a rigorous regime which made fairly sizeable demands on a student's time.

During his first year, Starmer lived in a room in Charles Morris Hall on the university campus. Luckily for him, at least one friend from Reigate Grammar School, Geoffrey Scopes, was also at Leeds, giving Starmer an immediate advantage over other new students who had arrived knowing nobody else. Starmer has said that he was prone to drinking pints of snakebite, an intoxicating lager–cider mix, in the union bar. He was apparently a regular attender of the university's Thursday night disco and an enthusiastic football player. He also made an attempt to remain engaged politically. One of his first acts on arriving at Leeds was to become a member of the university Labour Club, which was chaired by a third-year student called John Erskine. 'I do remember signing [Starmer] up to the Labour Club at the freshers' fair,' Erskine says. 'The name does stay with you. I signed him up. I took the money. It cost £1. We were quite busy, so he moved on, but I ran into him at subsequent Labour Club meetings.'

Leeds Labour Club was one of the biggest university Labour clubs in the country, with several hundred members. Erskine had secured the chairmanship in June 1982 by beating the Militant tendency, the Trotskyist faction which dominated Labour politics at the time. 'The alliance with which I took the Labour Club [from Militant] was made up of radical lesbian feminists, Jewish students and Labour moderates,' he says. The battle with Militant continued throughout Starmer's first year and beyond, as the club sought to cement itself into a position that was firmly on the democratic left rather than anything more radical.

Yet despite the intriguing challenge that this fight represented to some, including Erskine, there is no suggestion that Starmer had much appetite for it. Frankly, there is little evidence that he had any inclination towards becoming too heavily involved in any aspect of student politics. Certainly, he did not hold any official position within the club. 'We did try and make contact with [Starmer] about internal Labour Club elections, and he was a bit circumspect about taking on Militant in the way that I would have,' Erskine says. 'Even then, he was quite legal about things. In those days I was not above cutting corners in terms of dealing with Trotskyites. I was also always committed to taking people on, whereas I think he was more measured.'

It was not only Militant's presence that made politics so diverting during Starmer's first twelve months at Leeds. With Margaret Thatcher's Britain beginning to take shape; curbs on the trade unions becoming a fact of life; the 1983 general election proving disastrous for the Labour Party; and Michael Foot's resignation triggering a leadership election, there was no shortage of engrossing matters to occupy the Labour Club. 'It was a time of great energy,' says Adam LeBor, who was also a member during Starmer's first year.

> It galvanised everyone. I was also active in the Union of Jewish Students (UJS) as well. Both UJS and the Labour Students spent a lot of time fighting the Trots and the Socialist Workers Party, politically speaking. It was a time of massive political awakening. I had always been a Labour Party supporter, and there was such a range of people in the Labour Club, some from working-class backgrounds, some quite posh people, some from everyday middle-class backgrounds. It was great. I learned so much about politics. It fizzed with energy.

Despite this atmosphere, neither Erskine nor LeBor has any memory of Starmer being notably active or showing any zeal for political debate. The club met in a lecture theatre for an hour every Wednesday at lunchtime, and meetings would be overseen by Erskine. Guest speakers would be invited, or student discussions would be held. The South African social campaigner Denis Goldberg was one well-known figure who addressed the club, and the human rights campaigner Peter Tatchell was another, as was the veteran Leeds MP Denis Healey. Erskine says he strived to get a variety of speakers from different backgrounds, as long as they were of the non-Trotskyist left. 'Keir wasn't that regular an attender of the meetings,' says Erskine.

> I'd say he'd come to every two or three. I don't remember him being particularly regular [in his first year]. Looking back on it, he was someone who was obviously very thoughtful and intelligent and concerned about behaving in a legal kind of way. The one speech I remember him making was quite measured and concerned with what was happening in the party.

LeBor adds that he 'can't remember Starmer at all', although he is at pains to stress that almost nobody's powers of recall are perfect four decades later. Still, it is as if Starmer saw things in black-and-white terms, simply believing there were no enemies on the left. Matt Tee, who ran the Labour Club between 1983 and 1984, when Starmer was in his second year, also says he has no memory of meeting him at that time.

The student union is another arena in which many national Labour politicians who have attended university often forge their debating skills and mould their principles. Again, though, there is no hint that Starmer showed any serious intent in this context. From June 1983 until June 1985 – the year Starmer graduated – Erskine became a convenor for the National Union of Students in Leeds, placing him at the heart of the union. He says he does not remember Starmer putting forward motions or participating in any set-piece debates at union meetings and events. It seems that even though Starmer's student days covered what is now regarded as a seismic period in Britain's political history – including the 1984–85 miners' strike, which began in Yorkshire, and the struggle to rebuild the Labour Party under its new leader, Neil Kinnock – whiling away endless hours in coffee bars and pubs talking politics was not for him.

As well as being active politically, Adam LeBor edited the student newspaper, the *Leeds Student*, between 1983 and 1984, when Starmer was in his second year. LeBor says he has no recollection of Starmer showing any interest in journalism during his editorship and does not believe he was well-known enough within the university to be written about in the paper either. The *Leeds Student* was an independent newspaper that represented those who attended Leeds Polytechnic, as well as those who were at the University of Leeds, though its principal focus was the university. It was printed weekly each term, meaning that it published approximately twenty-four editions every academic year. Each one was sixteen pages long, with sections covering news, comment, arts, music and sport at both institutions. Approximately 4,000 copies were printed in each run. Having examined all seventy-two editions that were produced during Starmer's time at Leeds, it is clear that student politics received a wealth of coverage, from reports on rent strikes to the manifestos of Union Council and NUS candidates. The activities of the Labour Club also featured fairly regularly, either because of its ongoing row with Militant, or through its involvement with campaigns such as 'anti-fascist week' (October 1982), or for its call for a mandatory £20 weekly grant for students (February 1983). Starmer, however, was not mentioned or pictured in relation to any of the reports on the Labour Club between 1982 and 1985. Moreover, he never wrote for the paper and was not named or quoted in any other articles.

In order to locate his name in the *Leeds Student* for the purposes of this book, it was necessary to scour every single corner of the publication. It did crop up – just once. The paper ran a 'Personals' section, where students could leave birthday greetings or, sometimes, more obscure messages and wisecracks for each other. In the edition published on 27 January 1984, somebody left an anonymous note for Starmer, which was cryptic but, in its way, rather telling. It read: 'Keir Starmer, King of Middle-Class Radicals.' This was almost certainly an in-joke between friends, but, if nothing else, it proves that since he was twenty-one years old, this former Surrey private school boy has been fending off accusations of being more bourgeois than he would care to admit.

When it came to his involvement in student politics at Leeds, Starmer could be described as the man who wasn't there. He did not seek the spotlight but was instead cautious, modest and restrained. Why should this have been so? John Erskine believes he knows the answer to that question: 'At the time it might have annoyed me that someone with a bit of talent [like him] was like that,' he says.

> I wished he'd get stuck in. I wished he didn't have the scruples he did. But I can see it as being of a piece. He was someone who was serious about getting a good law degree and not letting down his parents. The law department at that stage was very good. People like Brian Hogan taught there. They cracked on and expected people to deliver academically, so I'm not surprised [to find] that he concentrated most of his efforts on his studies.

At the start of his second year, Starmer and Scopes were among six students who rented a terraced house together at 22 Chestnut Avenue in the Hyde Park area of the city. The others were fellow law student John Murray, Simon Head, Alison Jenkins and Deborah Bacon. It was from this point that Starmer began to show a deeper interest in his degree. The law faculty was based in buildings in Lyddon Terrace, away from the main campus, and was in a sense self-contained, in that it had its own common room and study area. There was also an active university Law Society. As there were only about 100 law students per year, many of them knew each other quite well and didn't necessarily mix much with students who were reading other subjects.

Leeds had a strong criminal law element and some well-regarded professors, including Charles Drake, Brian Hogan and Horton Rogers. Among its senior lecturers was Peter Seago, who was also a Justice of the Peace. This environment may have fostered in Starmer, some of whose future career was spent working as a criminal barrister, an interest in criminal law. Yet he has often said that his attraction to working in an international human rights context was developed as an undergraduate, when he made up his mind to become a barrister and eventually to specialise in this branch of the law. 'I became absolutely fascinated with the idea that at the end of the Second World War and the atrocities of the Second World War, the countries around the world came together and made commitments to each other to honour human rights,' he has said. 'I became fascinated and really taken with the idea behind human rights, really. It's not so much the individual rights, but it's the human dignity that sits behind human rights, how we treat individuals, how we treat them fairly, equally.' Having taken up this cause, he began to study harder than ever – and not only in order to keep his parents happy.

One of his principal tutors at Leeds was Clive Walker, who became a lecturer there at the start of Starmer's second year and is now professor of criminal justice studies. He has always thought Starmer was one of the most capable students he has ever taught, and, according to another of Walker's former students, he was always convinced that Starmer would succeed in the law. As he is not significantly older than Starmer (Walker graduated from the University of Leeds with a law degree in 1975), their relationship was perhaps less formal than many other student–tutor associations are, and they remain in close contact. In light of this, it was surprising that Walker refused point-blank to talk about Starmer for the purposes of this book. 'My role demands *uberrima fides*,' Walker said by way of explanation. Assuming that I know no Latin, he then kindly added: 'Which is lawyer-speak for "my lips are sealed".' It remains unclear why Prof. Walker should consider his role in Starmer's life to be strictly off-limits. He and Starmer even worked together on two law books in the 1990s. The first of these, *Justice in Error*, was published in 1993, and Walker and Starmer are credited as co-editors. It comprises a series of essays by academics and campaigners concerning aspects of the criminal justice system which have resulted in the conviction of innocent people. The second, *Miscarriages of Justice*, follows a similar theme and was published six years later.

Starmer clearly worked extremely hard at university. By his own admission, his studies were at the centre of his life, and he spent much of his time with his head in his books because he is naturally driven and industrious. Nobody was surprised when, in the summer of 1985, he took a first-class degree in law. It is worth saying that in the mid-1980s, achieving this result from a decent redbrick university was still considered unusual enough to be fairly impressive. One former member of staff says Starmer was among only three or four people in his year to have reached this height. He has certainly always been thankful for the platform which his tertiary education provided for him. And as is the case with Reigate Grammar School, he has been careful to maintain strong links with the University of Leeds, opening its new law faculty building in 2011 and serving as a member of its advisory board.

Having enjoyed academic success as an undergraduate, Starmer was not entirely sure which direction to take, though it was quickly apparent that he was in no mood to rest on his laurels. One source familiar with the set-up at the University of Leeds at the time says they believe that Prof. Horton Rogers may have advised him to have a word with another academic, Adrian Briggs, in order to help him reach a decision about next steps. Briggs had worked in the law faculty at Leeds between 1979 and 1980, and by 1985 was based at St Edmund Hall, Oxford. Rogers and Briggs had stayed in close touch, meaning talented students who were leaving Leeds were well-positioned to be given a steer on what the University of Oxford might have to offer them, specifically in relation to a graduate course called the Bachelor of Civil Law (BCL), Oxford's postgraduate law degree. No sooner had he finished his business at Leeds than Starmer was accepted onto this course, joining St Edmund Hall (known affectionately as 'Teddy Hall') for the academic year 1985–86 as a mature student on a scholarship.

According to the lawyer Ken Macdonald, himself an alumnus of St Edmund Hall who went on to become the Director of Public Prosecutions in 2003, only the most able students are accepted onto the BCL course. 'The BCL is probably the best graduate law degree in the common law world,' he says. 'It's very competitive to get on. The brightest graduates in law from around the UK and the Commonwealth tend to compete to get on that degree, and [Starmer] got on it.'

A senior member of St Edmund Hall staff during Starmer's year there agrees, explaining:

> The BCL is a graduate degree, but it's not an ordinary graduate degree. It's not a doctorate. It insists on a fair coverage so that when you leave you haven't been sitting in the law library by yourself hunting out one particular subject. You're expected to be prepared on a range of subjects. It's a tough course.

Starmer's time in Oxford was academically unrelenting and really quite brief. He studied there for just twenty-four weeks, spread over three eight-week terms. He barely had time to appreciate his surroundings before he had left, let alone to make much of an impression on other students there. St Edmund Hall is located on Queen's Lane, just off the High Street, and occupies a small site based around a quadrangle. In the 1980s, it had a strong sporting reputation and, having begun admitting female students only a few years earlier, was known as a college with a fairly masculine atmosphere.

During Starmer's period of study, the University of Oxford was awash with future front-rank politicians. David Cameron, Michael Gove and Jeremy Hunt were all students there at the time. And in early 1986, Boris Johnson, then in his penultimate year at Balliol College, was elected president of the Oxford Union, the influential debating society. (There is no known evidence that the two ever met at this point.) Some future Labour Party MPs were also undergraduates while Starmer toiled away on his postgraduate course, including Ed Balls, David Miliband and Stephen Twigg. It was natural that Starmer should have wanted to join them in signing up to be a member of the Oxford Union Labour Club (OULC), and it is certainly known that he and Miliband became friendly at this time. Perplexingly, no official OULC records from the period survive, but one person who is familiar with the history of the club says it is 'highly unlikely' that Starmer would have held any sort of executive role, partly because the OULC has always been much more of an undergraduate phenomenon.

As Starmer had done at Leeds, he kept a low profile. With that said, he did become friendly with one left-wing undergraduate, Benjamin Schoendorff, who was the chairman of the OULC in the year before Starmer arrived. As shall become clear in the next chapter, their friendship would endure beyond Starmer's Oxford career.

In contrast to its right-wing equivalent, the Oxford University Conservative Association, the OULC rarely made the student or national press in 1985 or 1986, perhaps in part because it chose to boycott the Oxford Union. Instead, anti-Apartheid activism was the principal means by which it captured the attention of the student press, especially in relation to the activities of Barclays Bank in South Africa. For example, on one occasion in November 1985, some OULC members – including Stephen Twigg – were at the forefront of a sit-in at the entrance to the Randolph Hotel in Oxford, in protest at a Barclays 'milkround' recruitment event being held in the city. A few months later, David Miliband, then the president of the Corpus Christi Junior Common Room, stopped the college from banking with Barclays. These were the issues which appear to have taken precedence at the time, and Starmer seems to have had little opportunity to join in with them. He worked hard enough to gain what has been described by his friend Geoffrey Robertson, a leading barrister, as a 'goodish' BCL in the summer of 1986.

Starmer, who is now an honorary fellow of St Edmund Hall, has spoken of his memories of this period of his life in refreshingly frank terms. 'When I arrived at St Edmund Hall, I had a first-class degree from Leeds University behind me, but I was still not clear what path I should take next,' he has said. 'My time at St Edmund Hall – an intense year studying for the BCL – confirmed me in my choice of pursuing a career as a human rights advocate, both here in the UK and abroad. From then on, I did not look back!' Having originally thought of becoming a solicitor – a job which some in legal circles believe would have suited him just as well because it does not usually require any public speaking skills – Starmer has claimed that he became convinced at Oxford that he wanted to present arguments in court instead and, therefore, to be instructed as a barrister by a solicitor. For a young man who had hitherto shown little, if any, interest in debating in any formal context, this was surprising. One lawyer who would work with Starmer years later casts doubt on his suitability for his chosen route. 'The BCL is quite competitive to get on to, but if you do your homework, you can get on it,' they say.

> Keir can read what the law says and apply it, but that's not what being a human rights lawyer is all about. Anyone can do that. Human rights law – or any legal practice that's pushing the boundaries – is not about accepting the status quo and trying to take the path of least resistance, but about trying to battle new frontiers, and that is so not Keir Starmer.

Could Starmer open up new horizons in a legal sense? His first challenge was to gain a place at Bar School in London. With two solid academic qualifications to speak of, this presented no problems at all and, having done so, he chose to spend two weeks of the summer of 1986 at what has been described as a 'work camp' in the Czech village of Lidice, just outside Prague. By day, he and sixteen European students helped to restore a memorial to victims of a 1942 Nazi war crime in which more than 300 civilians were murdered in retaliation for the Czech resistance assassinating SS chief Reinhard Heydrich. At night, he washed in primitive facilities and slept in a military tent. As the Cold War was at its height when Starmer embarked on this austere adventure, Czechoslovakia was not easy to enter, requiring a special visa and, for a Briton, guaranteeing the interest of the secret police. Starmer's details were recorded in Communist spy files, as would be expected, and are still accessible in the state archive today. When asked about the trip in 2024, he refused to comment.

CHAPTER 4

ALTERNATIVES

An idea has taken hold that when Keir Starmer first moved to London in the autumn of 1986, he lived above a brothel. This is not quite true. To be strictly accurate, it would appear that he rented a room in a flat above a sauna. The flat in question was on the top two floors of 285 Archway Road, part of a parade of shops located directly opposite Highgate Underground station. The brothel story is not without basis, however. In August 1985, the year before Starmer's arrival, Victor Mehra, the owner of a business called the Highgate Sauna Centre, which was indeed based at 285 Archway Road, was found guilty at the Old Bailey of living off the earnings of prostitution. *The Times* reported that Mehra received a sentence of nine months in prison. A sauna supposedly continued to operate from the same shop in 1986, though it is not clear who ran it. The premises had apparently ceased to be a house of ill repute by the time Starmer moved in. According to some accounts, though, it remained a fairly insalubrious place.

Starmer came to be living in these surroundings thanks to his old school tie. His exact contemporary at Reigate Grammar School, Andrew Cooper, had lived in the flat until late 1984 while attending the London School of Economics. Another school friend, Paul Vickers, had taken on the digs from Cooper. 'Waves of people then started to live there, including Keir,' says Cooper.

It was an unbelievably grubby place. We used to joke about

> the fact that we lived above a brothel. It was a massage parlour, very sordid, with a reception area on the ground floor and stairs down to the basement where there were just rooms with dirty mattresses on the floor. We joked about it until the landlord went to prison, at which point we realised it really was a brothel.

The hole in the kitchen floor and the broken windows which Cooper remembers must have been repaired at some stage, and some other improvements made, because, according to the electoral roll, Starmer remained at that address for at least four years, until 1990, and some of his later flatmates were young women. It seems unlikely that they would have been happy to live above a den of vice.

Initially, Starmer shared the flat with Vickers – who later worked for the BBC and *Private Eye* magazine – and another old Reigatian, Mark Adams. Stephen Bunyan made up the quartet. Of this period, Vickers, who died in 2017, once observed: 'Keir was one of the more important figures in the social whirl. He was a great party animal. He was very keen on Desmond Dekker, and I think his favourite record was *The Israelites*, which we would have to listen to dozens of times a week.' He added: 'Keir's politics were hard left and with that hard leftness came responsibility, so any decision that was made had to be made collectively, but of course Keir, as the strongest personality in that collective, usually got his own way.'

By day, Starmer, who had turned twenty-four in September 1986, attended the Inns of Court School of Law at Gray's Inn Place in Holborn. There, he took what was then known as the Bar Vocational Course, the obligatory nine-month professional training course for would-be barristers in England and Wales before they began their pupillage. All aspiring barristers must belong to one of the four Inns of Court, the ancient professional associations whose appearance and characteristics are much like some Oxbridge colleges. Starmer was fortunate in that his Bar School fees were partially covered by the Inn he had joined, the Honourable Society of the Middle Temple. Having been interviewed by some of Middle Temple's senior members, he had been awarded a Queen Mother Scholarship, which is considered one of the most prestigious bursaries on offer and is usually given in recognition of academic excellence. According to the recipient of a similar award at about the same time, it might have been worth approximately £1,500.

In order to be called to the Bar so that he could eventually begin practising as a barrister, Starmer also had to attend twenty-four dinners in Middle Temple's fabulous Elizabethan dining hall. These formal dining sessions were mandatory and were considered an important part of a barrister's education, though many in legal circles regarded this tradition as something of an anachronism. Starmer was lucky in one way, though. While studying for the BCL at St Edmund Hall, he had got to know Anthony Metzer, who was in his final year at Wadham College, reading law. They had struck up a friendship. Metzer then attended Bar School with Starmer and had also joined Middle Temple, guaranteeing that at least one friendly face would be in the Inn's dining hall.

In tandem with his legal studies, Starmer continued to put his energy into a very different sort of endeavour, with which he had been preoccupied since leaving Oxford: namely a magazine called *Socialist Alternatives*. Between July 1986 and August 1987, five editions of this Marxist journal were produced on what could be described as a professional-amateur basis. In other words, the title gamely took a dive into the choppy financial waters of the commercial publishing business, but the end product appeared to be hastily cobbled together and was often as error-strewn as a local parish newsletter. Given the relative youth of those behind it, its inexpert appearance was probably unsurprising. Starmer was a member of its seven-strong 'editorial collective', which was led by Benjamin Schoendorff, who was at the time in his final year of a PPE course at Oxford. As explained in the previous chapter, Schoendorff, who was born and raised in France, had been chairman of the Oxford University Labour Club between 1984 and 1985, and Starmer had first fallen in with him while he was a mature student at St Edmund Hall. The periodical listed as its address 22 Charles Street in Oxford, a house which, by coincidence, had been owned until 1984 by the future publisher and Labour MP Derek Wyatt and was rented to students thereafter. Most members of the editorial collective studied at Oxford during the magazine's brief existence.

In 1984, while waiting to begin his studies at Oxford, Schoendorff had approached the Paris office of the International Revolutionary Marxist Tendency (IRMT) seeking its financial backing to start a magazine in Britain. The IRMT agreed to help and as part of his preparation for the venture he was introduced to some prominent British left-wingers, including the politicians Ken Livingstone and Tony Benn. Having arrived at Oxford, the young Frenchman recruited about a dozen Oxford students who shared his brand of socialism. Among them was John Foot, son of the journalist Paul Foot and great-nephew of Michael Foot, the former Labour leader. Another recruit was Starmer, who, it seems, had in the short time he had been at Oxford already immersed himself in far-left politics. 'Keir Starmer was fresh from Leeds … I remember also [he was] selling *The Militant* outside the Oxford University Labour Club meetings, believe it or not, and had invited Derek Hatton to Oxford,' said Schoendorff.

The Militant was the house newspaper of the Militant tendency, the Trotskyite group in the Labour Party, and Hatton was one of the most prominent Trotskyites in the country. He had been the deputy leader of the Militant-controlled Liverpool City Council in the early 1980s when it went to war with the Thatcher government's proposed cuts to its budget. He was expelled from the Labour Party in 1986 for his membership of Militant.

Socialist Alternatives was inspired partly by the thinking of a Greek revolutionary commonly known by the moniker 'Pablo'. His real name was Michalis Raptis, or Michel Raptis, and during his life he was a leading member of the Fourth International, a Trotskyist organisation whose aims are to overthrow capitalism and establish world socialism. Raptis, who was born in 1911, is said to have met and got on well with Fidel Castro, Che Guevara and Ayatollah Khamenei, and after the Second World War he established himself as one of Europe's more prominent left-wing radicals. A common misconception is that *Socialist Alternatives* was a Trotskyist magazine, but according to Richard Barbrook, one of its unpaid contributors, this is wide of the mark. 'I met Jane Alexander, who was on the editorial board of *Socialist Alternatives*, at a party,' says Barbrook.

> I think I was the only person at this party who had heard of the Pabloites. Jane invited me to some of their meetings and got me to write this article. People say Keir was a Trotskyist, but he wasn't a Trotskyist. That's the mistake they make. They assume that merely because Michel Raptis, who was the leader of this little faction, had been a Trotskyist, but he stopped in the 1960s. He then got really into self-management and red–green politics. It would be completely accurate to say that Keir was a member of a group that had been founded by an ex-Trotskyist.

Having ditched Trotskyism in the 1960s, Raptis led a breakaway group, the International Revolutionary Marxist Tendency, and turned his attention to women's liberation, among other things. He developed a cult following, especially in Paris, and the left-wing clique that pored over his essays and discussed his philosophy became known collectively as the Pabloites. *Socialist Alternatives* was, in effect, the London franchise of the Pabloite movement. Barbrook says he can recall attending some of their meetings at a flat in Hampstead 'near where George Orwell had worked in a bookshop in South End Green', and at which it is possible that drugs may have been smoked on occasion. 'We used to sit around; we used to talk,' he says.

> I'm pretty sure we smoked dope but [Keir] was a lawyer, so I know lawyers at the time used to avoid doing that. He was a very committed lawyer. That's what I knew him as. We probably broke the Misuse of Drugs Act, but I wouldn't think he did. It's so long ago I can't remember. I don't even know if he was in the room when that happened. Keir struck me as straight shooter who mixed with a bohemian crowd that he didn't really suit.

Its first issue, vol. 1, no. 1, published in July 1986, had a cover price of 90p – roughly the price of a pint of beer at the time – and introduced itself as 'a journal with a difference'. The opening editorial declared: 'Thatcherism is rapidly loosing [*sic*] its hold over British politics and yet the Left finds itself in such a mess that it appears unable to present a coherent socialist alternative.' It went on to outline its vision of socialism as 'the generalised self-management of society as a whole' and claimed it was 'concretely working towards a radical extension of popular control over wealth and power' by 'building a new kind of alliance from the bottom up integrating both the traditional wing of the labour movement and the new social movements'. It spoke of 'sexual', 'racial' and 'economic' oppression and exploitation and also blasted the Labour Party's right wing for its 'unholy alliance' with the 'realigned left' over the expulsion of Militant tendency members from the Labour Party.

For reasons best known to himself, Schoendorff, despite being the magazine's de facto editor and the driving force behind it, sometimes wrote under the pseudonyms 'Harry Curtis' and 'John Walter'. In middle age, Schoendorff has claimed that the views he held when he was involved with *Socialist Alternatives* remain important to him, commenting in 2019: 'I remember Keir very well … we were radical anti-imperialist ecosocialists. My personal stance hasn't changed much since.' In an attempt to explain what it was all about, Starmer once told the BBC:

> [*Socialist Alternatives*] was an organisation looking at how you grow politics from the bottom up rather than the top down, and there was a lot of interest at the time in self-management and how you change the economy through that, so that was the next [political] phase that I went through when I went to college.

On that occasion he did not, however, manage to explain what self-management is. For the avoidance of doubt, others have defined it as a social and economic model instituted by the Communist Party of Yugoslavia from 1950 until 1990, which was advocated by President Tito, among others.

The first edition of *Socialist Alternatives*, which was thirty-six pages long, featured an article on Marxism by Raptis himself. Another contributor was the Labour MP Tony Benn, whose recent speech to the Brussels Conference was reproduced. Starmer's principal piece in the magazine's opening offering argued for the expansion of trade unions in light of the ongoing Wapping dispute – the printworkers' strike held between January 1986 and February 1987 that was sparked by Rupert Murdoch's decision to relocate his British newspaper operation from Fleet Street to east London. Starmer then endorsed the idea of handing greater control over the economy to trade unions, opining:

> These are important examples of how trade unions can begin building horizontally within and beyond the union, thus extending the challenge from simple workplace control to control over industry and community … the challenge of control can only be met if unions are radically enlarged to encompass the political elements of control throughout society.

A second piece by Starmer took the form of a critique of a campaign launched by Neil Kinnock, called Freedom and Fairness. In the article, Starmer took issue with what he regarded as its pro-capitalism approach, writing, 'Freedom and Fairness, like its industrial counterpart [Jobs and Industry], presumably safeguards the freedom of capital in Britain whilst showing little regard for the freedom of the workforce and community to extend their political control.' He went on:

> The 1979 defeat can be seen as a rejection of corporatism and statism by the electorate. It is unfortunate however, that Freedom and Fairness should interpret this as a reaffirmation of market values coupled with an extension of home ownership … Unfortunately, by turning back to the market economy, it misses a third alternative, that of participatory socialism based on democratic planning.

The next edition, published in October 1986, anticipated the 1987 general election and stated that '*Socialist Alternatives* will continue to argue for a radical extension of popular control over wealth and power'. In it, Starmer co-wrote an article with his close friend Alex Harvey, another member of the editorial collective, assessing the recent TUC conference. By the third edition, the magazine's editorial page covered what it saw as a world 'ecological crisis' and spoke of how 'capitalism feeds on all forms of oppression'. A few paragraphs later, it was reduced to begging its readers for 'material' and also for 'financial' help, presumably to stay afloat.

Starmer's contribution to this issue again saw him back on the trade union beat, this time devoting three pages to what he called 'a new type of industrial pluralism' to combat the 'authoritarian onslaught of Thatcherism'. The degree of Starmer's brain power this type of article used up was discussed many years later by his flatmate Paul Vickers, who recounted that on one occasion two burglars walked into their flat in Archway Road while Starmer was working at his desk and stole their television and video recorder. The thieves arrived and left without Starmer realising, bumped into Vickers on the stairs, dumped the electrical items and ran off. Starmer, apparently lost in thought, was oblivious to the crime. 'He was so obsessed with the books, he was so buried in his texts, that he didn't notice these two burglars walking round … helping themselves to our stuff,' said Vickers.

Perhaps Starmer's proudest *Socialist Alternatives* moment came in April 1987, when he interviewed Tony Benn at his Holland Park Avenue townhouse for the fourth issue of the magazine. While firing questions at Benn in his kitchen, he was invited to sit on one of Benn's prized possessions: a wooden chair that had been owned by Keir Hardie. The subject on which they reflected concerned whether the Labour Party needed to be 'refounded' if it was to survive. At one juncture, Starmer asked Benn: 'Would you say then that overall the Labour Party should become the united party of the oppressed, rather than the party of any one section of the oppressed, for example the working class?' Although Benn's answer was characteristically fluent, the very fact that Starmer asked him this captured the eye of the political journalist Nick Robinson more than thirty years later. When he challenged Starmer about it during a BBC interview in 2018, Starmer sounded defensive. 'Well, that's very much how it felt to me and in the era of Thatcher and as I say this searing sense for me that manufacturing was being destroyed, that the economic model was wrong and that there needed to be radical change,' he said. He added: 'Well, that was obviously me thinking I had cracked all the answers at an early age; language which doesn't make much sense, actually.' At the time of their meeting Tony Benn may well have agreed with Starmer's subsequent critique of his own position, for their encounter failed to merit a mention in Benn's assiduously kept diary for 1987.

The fifth edition of the magazine, produced in August 1987, was in large part devoted to an examination of the recent general election, in which Thatcher had claimed a third successive victory. (Incidentally, in this election Starmer's own MP in north London, Sir Hugh Rossi, a Conservative, had also held his seat.) Starmer's byline appeared on four articles, indicating that he was spending an increasing amount of time on the magazine despite having to revise for his Bar exams. Richard Barbrook is not surprised at the level of his devotion to the cause. 'He was the guy who got the magazine done,' Barbrook recalls.

> The thing I remember is that he got all the articles in, he got it laid out, he got it to the printers and he got it back from the printers and distributed it at the bookshops, and that's what I remember he was like. The rest of them probably sat around and talked about it and had interesting ideas. [Starmer] wasn't

> the leader, this other guy, Benji Schoendorff, was the leader. [Starmer] was the number two, the organiser basically. The other guy knew Raptis.

Despite Raptis apparently ditching his Trotskyist leanings, *Socialist Alternatives* continued to plough a furrow that made it unashamedly hard left. It condemned the Labour Party under Neil Kinnock, lambasting the 'Labour right's hopeless neo-Keynesian economic programme'; it called for a 'radical extension of common ownership over wealth and power'; it argued in favour of prisoners' rights; and it pushed for the working week to be cut to thirty-two hours. Starmer also queried police activity in the context of the dispute between printworkers at Wapping, whom he supported and where he had attended the picket lines as a legal observer. He wrote of 'paramilitary policing methods' and said: 'This leads to the question of the role the police should play, if any, in civil society. Who are they protecting and from what?'

Yet Barbrook believes that, for all its presentational faults, the magazine, which he describes as 'avant-garde', was in fact visionary. 'I think it was ahead of its time,' he says.

> They were really ahead of their time on green issues. The trouble is, it was too green for the reds and too red for the greens. If Keir dusted off all his old issues of *Socialist Alternatives* and studied them, he would be a much better leader of the Labour Party.

Another reader of the magazine who got to know him at this point was Peter Tatchell, the human rights activist. '*Socialist Alternatives* was radical left but democratic and modernising enough to embrace human rights, ecology, feminism and LGBT+ equality,' Tatchell says. 'It was very anti-Stalinist, libertarian and anti-statist. I'd describe Keir as being on the radical, thoughtful, questioning left. He was always very open to explore new ideas and perspectives. Unlike some people on the left, he was not at all dogmatic or sectarian.'

It is certainly true that one of its major preoccupations, environmental matters, enjoys mainstream press coverage now. At the time, though, it must have felt to Starmer that he was fighting an uphill battle. Each issue of *Socialist Alternatives* is thought to have had a print run of between 500 and 1,000 copies. It was sold mainly in left-wing bookshops, including Collet's on Charing Cross Road and the Camden-based shop Compendium, and had a limited readership. Paul Vickers even said dismissively that because the magazine consisted of nothing more than 'dense political theory' it was 'totally unreadable'. He added: 'As a result, we used to sit [in the flat] surrounded by boxes of thousands and thousands of unsold copies of *Socialist Alternatives*.'

To what extent Vickers exaggerated its poor sales for effect is not clear. What is more certain is that, almost forty years later, Schoendorff has said that although he likes Starmer personally, he still regards him as something of a puzzle.

> One thing that is strange is I don't really remember having to argue very long or very deep with [Starmer] for him to join us, even though in terms of Trot groups [we] could hardly be more distant from the Militant tendency than we were at the time ... There is something strange about Keir in general. It's a mystery to me how he went from being [a supporter of] Militant to being a Pabloite in weeks. Normally when you recruit someone from another tendency it takes a while, you need to go through lots of stuff.

Reflecting on Starmer's politics a few days before the 2024 general election was called, Schoendorff was withering.

> I really don't get a sense of intellectual evolution, for lack of a better word, which to me means the guy is actually an empty suit. I don't think he is a master, I think he's just a puppet, saying whatever he's been told to say, and it's going to be the worst you've ever seen ... Every day it seems he is able to insult our intelligence and morals in a new way which is beyond comprehension.

Back in the 1980s, however, Starmer could not be faulted for trying to maximise the magazine's chances of success. Not content with distributing it via bookshops, he made sure it was also available to those who attended meetings held by the Socialist Society, a radical movement of activist intellectuals formed in 1982 that was independent of the Labour Party and committed to making 'socialism the common sense of the age', in the words of its founding statement. Among its members were the left-wing academic Ralph Miliband, the future Labour leader Jeremy Corbyn and Caroline Benn, an author and campaigner on education who was married to Tony Benn. Another principal figure was Hilary Wainwright, who made a couple of contributions to *Socialist Alternatives* herself, including giving Starmer an interview for the April 1987 edition.

Wainwright recalls that some members of the magazine's editorial collective managed to get themselves voted onto the Socialist Society's steering committee. The significance of this is that the Socialist Society was instrumental in helping to co-organise with the Campaign Group of MPs an annual Chesterfield conference. The inaugural Socialist conference was in October 1987, a meeting of 2,000 radical left activists in Tony Benn's Derbyshire constituency. These conferences were sometimes attended by the leader of the National Union of Mineworkers, Arthur Scargill and, among others, the Labour MPs Ken Livingstone, Bernie

Grant, Audrey Wise and Eric Heffer, another occasional *Socialist Alternatives* contributor. Its purpose was to build a broadly based movement against Thatcherism in the wake of the defeat of the miners and the abolition of the Greater London Council. This confirms that key players within *Socialist Alternatives* were tangentially linked to national politics.

'There was a group of boys in the Socialist Society from *Socialist Alternatives*,' Wainwright says.

> I think they were still students. I think they'd all come from Oxford. I remember one was called Alex Harvey. They must have turned up at a Socialist Society AGM and got themselves elected to its steering committee. We were quite a significant organisation, but not a huge one. We had quite a big paper membership – maybe 500 or so. We were mainly a group of politically active intellectuals, politically active inside and outside the Labour Party. That inside–outside theme was important. We rejected the notion the big division on the left was about whether to be inside or outside of the Labour Party. There was a significant group inside the party who shared a lot of ideas with people outside the party; through the Socialist Society we created a space where the most important point wasn't whether you were in or out of the Labour Party but rather whether you were committed to working in a non-sectarian way on developing new ideas and promoted political education. We produced three or four Penguin books like *What Is to Be Done About Health?* and *What Is to Be Done About Education?* and we would have educational conferences. Our members were mainly teachers at schools and universities and polytechnics and higher education colleges, as they were then, and also journalists. So it was a body of socialist intellectuals of a committed and practical kind.

Starmer's ties to the Socialist Society continued for several years. For example, in 1989, he and another barrister, Robin Oppenheim, participated in drawing up the socialist policy review document for the third socialist conference, as an alternative to the Labour Party policy review of the same year. The event was sponsored by Tony Benn and the Campaign Group of MPs, and the policy review was published in the Socialist Society's journal, *Interlink*. Oppenheim and Starmer's contribution, titled 'The Judiciary and the Legal System', featured ideas on a new democratic constitution and on human rights. Andrew Coates, a Marxist writer who met Starmer in the 1980s, says:

> Socialist Society meetings were monthly at one point. Meetings were held all over London in various university buildings. [Starmer] was a very committed, serious person, quite amiable. Some of his comrades were quite annoying, but he wasn't. Benjamin Schoendorff was what we call a faction leader, and he was just a bit annoying. They were formally on the steering committee, but they weren't very intensely involved in it and they were just a group who were trying to press this thing about 'the alternative' and it was the forerunner of green–red politics. [Starmer wrote] pretty serious stuff on legal reform and human rights. He was pretty respected in that sphere already. He was active for quite a long period of time.

The Socialist Society has been defunct for almost thirty years, having held its last meeting in 1993. This long passage of time perhaps helps to explain why Hilary Wainwright has no vivid memory of Starmer. As with Barbrook and Coates, however, one of Starmer's colleagues – Schoendorff – did lodge in her mind, leading to the impression that Starmer was more of a background personality. 'I remember the guy who led *Socialist Alternatives*,

Ben Schoendorff, was quite a dynamic character,' Wainwright says.

> He rather dominated their contributions. When Keir became DPP [in 2008], people said, 'Do you remember he was in the Socialist Society?', and then I became aware that he had been, but I can't say I remember him sitting across the table from me. I haven't had anything to do with him since. He didn't strike me as a distinctive political figure at the time.

As for the magazine, Wainwright says,

> I probably would have read *Socialist Alternatives*. I can't say that I can remember any good ideas [in it]. I would have taken it seriously, as I would have any publication coming up with interesting new ideas. Through Schoendorff it had quite a strong French connection which could have been quite interesting. It wouldn't be a reference point, but occasionally I would read it.

• • •

By the summer of 1987, Starmer had completed his Bar Vocational Course. His final stage of preparation to be a barrister required him to secure a pupillage. In effect, this is a twelve-month training contract in a set of barristers' chambers. As the profession is so oversubscribed, and each set takes on only a few pupils every year, clearing this hurdle is difficult. In the 1980s, the legal world remained pretty traditional, and it was still tilted in favour of those who were white, male, had been to a private school and had attended Oxbridge. Starmer, of course, ticked all these boxes, whether he would care to admit it or not. His academic qualifications, and his acquaintance with a string of well-placed academics from the universities of Leeds and Oxford who could vouch for him, meant that he was at least as well equipped to succeed as most of his rivals. In light of the set of chambers he eventually ended up in, however, his background probably served him less well than did his political beliefs.

Aspiring pupils could apply to as many sets of chambers as they wished. The process required them to write a personal letter to a chosen set explaining why they wanted to be in pupillage there. If they were lucky enough to be asked for an interview, they would be seen by two senior members of chambers, usually on a Saturday. They might then be invited to return for a second and possibly a third grilling before a final decision was taken. It seems appropriate at this point to quote the late barrister and author John Mortimer, creator of *Rumpole of the Bailey*, who once wrote of 'the splendid miseries' of being a pupil in a barrister's chambers. Mortimer was by no means the only legal figure to have regarded this early stage of a young lawyer's career in such agonising terms, but he would have been better placed than most to monitor Starmer's progress. For at the age of twenty-five, Starmer was accepted as a pupil at 1 Dr Johnson's Buildings, a mixed common law set in the legal district known as the Inner Temple. Mortimer was still an associate tenant of these chambers, despite his various literary triumphs. Situated in a handsome Grade II-listed nineteenth-century property close to the Royal Courts of Justice, it was well-regarded and, crucially for a young man with Starmer's politics, less stuffy and more liberal than other sets. Several young left-wing barristers were already in situ there, and, as we shall see in the next chapter, Starmer had already got to know them.

One of those who conducted Starmer's pupillage interview was Gavin Millar, whose sister, Fiona, is the partner of Alastair Campbell, Tony Blair's former press secretary. Another was

Stephen Irwin, a medical negligence specialist who became a High Court judge in 2006 and who was appointed a Lord Justice of Appeal in 2016, a role he relinquished in 2020. The third was Peter Thornton, who would go on to become the Chief Coroner of England and Wales. The interview did not go as smoothly as Starmer might have hoped. During it he quoted the maxim 'property is theft' – which is attributed to the nineteenth-century French socialist Pierre-Joseph Proudhon – while explaining why he thought non-violent burglars should not necessarily have to go to prison. This remark caused some consternation among some of the senior barristers at 1 Dr Johnson's Buildings. Allegedly, it was Stephen Irwin who came to Starmer's defence, saying he was clearly 'absolutely brilliant' and should be taken on.

The head of 1 Dr Johnson's Buildings in the autumn of 1987 was Lord Hooson, a Welshman who was among the last of a dying breed that had been active in both the law and politics simultaneously. He had been a barrister since the late 1940s and was also, from 1962, a Liberal MP. He remained in the House of Commons for seventeen years until losing his Montgomeryshire seat at the 1979 general election, whereupon he was elevated to the House of Lords. His legal career was no less high-profile. He was perhaps best known for having defended Ian Brady, the Moors Murderer, at his trial at Chester Assizes in 1966. Other notable personalities in the set were Louis Blom-Cooper, a fierce opponent of the death penalty; Alex (now Lord) Carlile, one of the youngest QCs in the country, having taken silk a few years earlier aged thirty-six; and Geoffrey Robertson, an Australian who had acted for the defence in a string of newsworthy cases such as the *Oz* magazine trial and who was dating the future television cook Nigella Lawson. Starmer must have counted himself lucky to be rubbing shoulders with such colourful figures as he negotiated the foothills of his chosen occupation, for others of his vintage would have found themselves working in comparatively drier and dustier environments. Some of the younger members of the set at 1 Dr Johnson's Buildings may not have been as glamorous as their elders, but, as alluded to already, they certainly shared the same trenchant left-wing opinions as Starmer, and he was well known to them.

Pupillage is usually split into two terms, each lasting six months, which are known as 'sixes'. Pupils work under a pupil master or pupil mistress. First, they operate in a non-practising capacity and must watch and learn by shadowing their superior in court and helping them in chambers, for example by assisting with research or by drafting skeleton arguments. During their second six months, they are allowed to begin handling their own cases and clients at a low level. Over the course of their year-long traineeship, they are assessed by the seniors in their set. They are then invited to apply for a permanent position, known as a tenancy, which enables them to base themselves in chambers as a self-employed barrister. If their face fits after a year in pupillage, they are likely to become a tenant, but this is by no means guaranteed. Generally, tenancy is awarded only after a vote of all members of chambers, including the clerks, who distribute most of the work.

Colin Wells was a pupil alongside Starmer between 1987 and 1988. Another pupil was the aforementioned Anthony Metzer, Starmer's friend from his spell at Oxford. All of them, according to Wells, were 'centre-left', which defused the situation immediately. 'In those days there was a lot of competition to get [a pupillage], but the three of us got on very well,' says Wells.

> Hundreds of people applied to that set. They had a very good reputation. If you were accepted for an interview, you might be in competition with 100 or so other people. I had a good

> reference. I suppose being politically active in the Labour movement helped. The chances of me getting anywhere were quite remote because I went to a polytechnic, I was working class and I have a strong accent.

Despite the fact that he and Starmer were both ultimately gunning for a tenancy, Wells says that Starmer was always friendly towards him. 'He could look at things from left field,' he recalls.

> He was always someone I could discuss cases with. He's a very bright guy, very intelligent but humble as well. He would help out. When you're pupils, you're thrown together for quite an intensive twelve months or so and tend to live in each other's pockets, but you have to get on with the work.

As is the case with many young barristers, Starmer's legal career began in earnest with minor criminal briefs. The hours were long, and the work was often hard. 'You have to remember, when you're doing a pupillage, you're probably putting in twelve- to fifteen-hour days and commuting all over the country doing court appearances,' says Wells. Occasionally, he recalls, they might have a quick drink of an evening, but there was not a great deal of time for socialising. In any case, Starmer had a laser-like focus on his work, and his public-spirited approach to the job was apparent from the word go. 'He was someone who was very well prepared to get his hands dirty, roll his sleeves up and get involved,' remembers Wells.

> It wasn't just for his career. It was a true commitment to representing those who'd been wronged. That's the impression I still have of him to this day. I was delighted when he became leader of the Labour Party because everyone asked me what he was

> like and I was able to say he's a true socialist. He's a political animal in that sense, not just a careerist. He actually genuinely believes in it. You can't say that for a lot of politicians. You can't say that about a lot of barristers, either.

During the summer of 1988, Starmer, Metzer and Wells all applied for tenancy at 1 Dr Johnson's Buildings. Of the three, Wells was not accepted, but he was allowed to 'squat' there temporarily and apply again later. Metzer and Starmer were taken on, but just as had been the case the year before when vying for pupillage, Starmer's interview did not exactly go swimmingly. His senior colleague, Geoffrey Robertson, who considers himself to have been Starmer's mentor, once said that he 'looked about fourteen, was nervous and awkward in the interview and (worst of all, for my colleagues on the panel) was poorly dressed'. The item of clothing they found particularly disagreeable was, apparently, his cardigan. In retrospect, the idea that Starmer thought it sensible to attend such a formal meeting wearing something which in the 1980s was most closely associated with the breakfast television presenter Frank Bough did show a complete lack of *savoir faire* on his part. Robertson added, 'It needed all my powers of persuasion to get [Lord Hooson] to accept him.' A glowing reference from one of his better-known tutors from his days at Leeds University was apparently crucial to his success.

Having become a tenant, Starmer could start to earn his first self-generated income by running his own cases and by acting as junior counsel to some of his older colleagues who were able to take on bigger briefs. Six years after becoming a law student at Leeds, he was finally on the move. By this time, his personal life was looking up as well, insofar as his girlfriend, Angela O'Brien, whom he had first met at Leeds, had moved into his flat at Archway Road. She was one of three young women living there with

Starmer and the aforementioned Mark Adams and Paul Vickers. She would go on to become a clinical psychologist, and they were obviously serious about each other. Starmer had even published a piece written by O'Brien in the final edition of his beloved *Socialist Alternatives.*

CHAPTER 5

SOCIALIST LAWYER

Socialist Alternatives was not the only left-wing publication to preoccupy Keir Starmer during 1987. Although he devoted a considerable amount of energy to pushing the message of the Pabloites that year while he was working long hours as a law student and later in pupillage, he also found time to become a member of the editorial committee of another new magazine, called *Socialist Lawyer*. It is the official journal of the Haldane Society of Socialist Lawyers, which was founded in 1930 and describes itself as 'an organisation which provides a forum for the discussion and analysis of law and the legal system from a socialist perspective'. Independent of any political party, its membership consists of lawyers, law teachers, law students, legal workers and trade unionists. Starmer's link to the Haldane Society has rarely been mentioned outside of legal circles, and he has never advertised his involvement in it – for example, it is not listed in his *Who's Who* entry. For professional and personal reasons, however, it was an important part of his life, and this phase of his career warrants examination.

Starmer's contemporary at 1 Dr Johnson's Buildings, Colin Wells, who was also a Haldane member in the 1980s, says that the group was considered a key platform for barristers and solicitors on the left at the time. 'If there were strikes and industrial disputes, we would help out in a legal sense,' he says. 'There would be picket lines that we would act as legal observers on; there would be advice that we would give.' Indeed, it was through the Haldane Society that Starmer volunteered to be a legal observer at Wapping during the 54-week printworkers' dispute. As noted in the previous chapter, the strike came about as a result of Rupert Murdoch's decision to scrap the hot metal printing presses of Fleet Street and embrace the electronic revolution by building a modern printing plant in east London. From there, the four British newspaper titles which he owned at the time – *The Times*, the *Sunday Times*, *The Sun* and the *News of the World* – would be produced.

As this move placed thousands of printing jobs in jeopardy, the dispute became increasingly bitter and led to violent clashes between protesters and the police, in which hundreds of arrests were made. The night of 24 January 1987 marked the first anniversary of the strike and was a particularly tense occasion, with bricks, bottles and iron bars being hurled at officers, 162 of whom were injured. Mounted units then charged at parts of the crowd. After a confrontation lasting for several hours, Wapping High Street was covered in debris, and it looked as though a battle had indeed been fought there. Starmer has claimed he was present that night, though in what capacity remains unclear. An independent group called the Wapping Legal Observers was formed with Haldane Society backing, after the print unions asked for help in monitoring and reporting on police activity and arrests. In a report it produced subsequently, however, which was written by the future KC Ben Emmerson, there was no mention of Starmer's name, so perhaps he was there under his own steam.

Whatever the case, this was dangerous work which certainly showed Starmer's commitment to the cause, even if there was a certain paradox in his risking his safety in the name of people who were employed by newspapers which he probably did not read, whose editorial line he almost certainly opposed, and whose proprietor had a famously strong relationship with his bête noire, Margaret Thatcher. The ultimate defeat of the print unions in February 1987, two years after the miners were overcome, dealt a hammer blow to union power in Britain, but at least Starmer would in future be able to talk about Wapping with the authenticity of personal experience.

It is noteworthy that another lawyer who belonged to the Haldane Society at that time, Bill Bowring, claims that until the 1980s it was dominated by Communist Party lawyers. He adds: 'The initial leaders of the Haldane in the 1930s were Stalinists. They probably adopted the name Haldane – after Viscount Haldane, the first Labour Party Lord Chancellor – as camouflage.' According to Bowring, who was chair of Haldane while Starmer was secretary, several of the communist lawyers have gone on to join the ranks of today's legal establishment, leaving their political past quietly behind them.

Starmer's name first cropped up in the *Socialist Lawyer* in its second-ever issue, published in the spring of 1987, when he was halfway through Bar School and more than six months before he joined 1 Dr Johnson's Buildings as a pupil. It had been launched the previous year as a quarterly magazine and was edited by Nick Paul and Andrew Buchan, two youngish barristers who were themselves members of 1 Dr Johnson's Buildings. Starmer was listed alongside them as one of six members of its editorial committee. The others were Heather Williams, Alastair Smail and Beverley Lang. Other than Starmer, Smail was the only one who did not at that point have a seat in 1 Dr Johnson's Buildings. In fact, that set of chambers appears to have been the effective office of *Socialist Lawyer*. Anybody who wished to write for the magazine was asked to submit their ideas to its address and Lang, who is now a High Court judge, doubled up as its secretary and would take telephone calls concerning society business there.

Another member of 1 Dr Johnson's Buildings, Helena Kennedy, who was one of the first Labour peers appointed by Tony Blair in 1997, was listed as a vice-president of the Haldane Society at the time Starmer became involved. It will come as no surprise to anybody that networking has always been an essential ingredient of success for aspiring barristers. Whether or not Starmer had his eye on a pupillage at 1 Dr Johnson's Buildings in early 1987 – and whether he thought he might achieve that aim via the Haldane Society – is an open question. What is not in doubt is that he was mixing with a group of people who were already established there and who would be useful to him in the future.

He served in various roles on the magazine for more than five years, during which time it published articles by a range of lawyers, politicians and activists, including the barrister Marina Wheeler, who later married Boris Johnson; Tony Benn; and Peter Tatchell, the human rights campaigner. Starmer's first ever contributions to the magazine hardly ranked as earth-shattering. One was a discussion with two solicitors about the rights of tenants versus landlords; the other was a short piece on his pet subject: the need for trade union reform after two successive Thatcher administrations. His radical spirit was evident elsewhere, though. In the fourth issue, published in the winter of 1987, he reviewed a book titled *Immigration Law and Practice*, written by Ian Macdonald, in which he appeared to support the claim that immigration law is imbued by a 'racist undercurrent'. He wrote:

> Ian Macdonald does not let the establishment off the hook by accepting the argument that any immigration law is bound to distinguish between 'us' and 'them', instead he points to the

> preferential treatment of EEC visitors and settlers in this country to show the racist undercurrent which permeates all immigration law, whether implemented by the Tories or Labour. It's not a question of numbers, it's a question of racism.

Then, in the winter of 1987, Starmer and Robin Oppenheim tried to overturn more than fifty years of history by suggesting that the Haldane Society should change its name, ditching 'Haldane' and instead calling itself either the National Association of Socialist Lawyers or the National Society of Socialist Lawyers. The justification for this idea was that the name Haldane apparently sounded like a 'London-orientated barristers' club'. In their manifesto, published in the *Socialist Lawyer*, the pair wrote that they considered broadening the society's membership to be vital because 'the context of the present hostile political climate, the inevitable attacks on civil liberties, jury trial, legal aid and the legal rights of trade unions will require us to turn ourselves outward and to build an effective national campaigning organisation'. This proposal was contested vigorously by many of Haldane's most senior figures, including John Platts-Mills, its president. As a former Labour MP with communist sympathies, Platts-Mills, by then in his eighties, can hardly be accused of having held small 'c' conservative opinions. Yet he and others wrote of their 'deep concern' at the Starmer–Oppenheim suggestion, on the basis that the name Haldane was 'an important part of our history' which 'is known throughout the British trade union movement and throughout the world as the name of Britain's organisation of socialist lawyers'.

In March 1988, a meeting was held at 1 Dr Johnson's Buildings to settle the question. Bill Bowring, who was there, remembers the occasion was 'really stormy with a lot of shouting'. He adds: 'Keir was the kind of Young Turk of the time, with quite a few supporters.' But not enough, it seems. His plan was voted down, and the name Haldane survives to this day. Bowring, though, says the episode is one indication, together with Starmer's proposals for Haldane's reform ('Haldane Forth') and his project for the 'modern prosecutor' while he was DPP, that Starmer is at heart 'a moderniser'.

By the fifth edition of *Socialist Lawyer*, in the spring of 1988, Starmer interviewed two other lawyers: his colleague Gavin Millar, and another barrister, Nick Blake. The premise of their discussion was the apparently inherent injustice of the judicial system. Starmer described the judiciary as 'notoriously white male and educated at Oxford or Cambridge', stating it is 'class-based and cannot be said to reflect the aspirations and anxieties of ordinary people in any way'. His opening question to Millar and Blake was: 'There is little dispute amongst socialists that the present judicial system needs changing. However, it seems that the left is not able to put forward a united and coherent alternative. What do you think are the most promising alternatives on offer?' Later, he asked them if they thought it was time for judges to be elected. If he wished to let Millar and Blake know that he was just as forward-thinking in his attitude as the next socialist lawyer, he went the right way about it. But of course, the 'radical' conversation that this trio enjoyed now appears somewhat hollow. All of them are white men who attended Oxbridge, though none of them thought fit to acknowledge this at the time. Furthermore, Starmer went on to become a silk, then DPP and to accept a knighthood; Blake is now Sir Nicholas Blake, a retired High Court judge; and Millar is a KC.

It was in early 1988 that Starmer also joined the Haldane Society's executive committee. Bill Bowring was appointed at the same time. 'Keir's first activity in Haldane was as a member of the editorial team for *Socialist Lawyer*,' he says.

> He joined Haldane shortly after I did, though for different reasons. I joined because [while a Labour Party councillor in Lambeth] I had deliberately broken the law and was being prosecuted by Margaret Thatcher for wilful misconduct. I was willingly taking the consequences. I wanted solidarity. Keir is someone who would never knowingly break the law under any circumstances.

This observation, Bowring believes, says much about his character. 'Keir's certainly not a Marxist,' he says.

> He has probably read some [Marxist] material. It's alleged that because he wrote for *Socialist Alternatives*, which was one of the fifty-seven varieties of Trotskyism called Pabloism, people say he was a Pabloite in his younger days, but I never heard him utter the words Pablo, Marx or Trotsky. I would put Keir down as a middle-of-the-road social democrat. I don't think Keir is in favour of an armed insurrection or anything like that. He would very strongly oppose it, because he's a law-and-order chap. Crucial to understanding Keir is that I think if there's a really bad law, one should break it, and of course one will then be punished. But he would have a really strong opposition to breaking a law under any circumstances.

By the autumn of 1988, Starmer had been appointed as the joint secretary of the society's executive committee along with Pam Brighton. Bowring was made its vice-chairman. Starmer had also taken on responsibility for the administration of another publication, *The Employment Law Bulletin*, which was described as 'a highly successful quarterly journal published by the Employment Law Committee of the Haldane Society' and which had a wide circulation among trade unions and labour lawyers. From the spring of 1989, he was the Haldane Society's sole secretary, shouldering ever more responsibility and, alongside his *Socialist Lawyer* duties, having to focus on the minutiae of the society's running. For example, if anybody wanted to bring a non-Haldane member to a committee meeting, they had to inform Starmer first. And he had to be notified of all proposals for the AGM. All this occupied much of his spare time, when he was not engaged as a barrister.

To have a cheerleader or mentor in the workplace is essential for almost any young, thrusting professional, and Starmer was no exception. That is why it was extremely useful to him that, by 1988, he had been taken under the wing of his senior colleague at 1 Dr Johnson's Buildings, Geoffrey Robertson. Robertson had recently been appointed a QC, and his own ambitions knew few bounds. Robertson is understood to have rated Starmer as a barrister in large part because he had solid qualifications, he was good at paperwork and he was happy to put in long hours at his desk. Starmer's reward for showing such devotion to his career was to be asked in late 1988 to accompany Robertson on a trip to the European Court of Human Rights at Strasbourg. This was to be Starmer's introduction to human rights law.

Things got off to an embarrassing start for the novice, however. A story circulated afterwards that when they landed at Strasbourg Airport, Robertson made it through customs successfully but Starmer did not. It transpired that he had lost his passport en route. With Starmer being threatened by the local gendarmerie with being locked up and returned to Gatwick Airport the next morning, Robertson had to telephone the British consul, who was persuaded to go to the airport and vouch for the hapless Starmer so that he could remain in the city for twenty-four hours. Miraculously, this ploy worked, and Starmer was able to witness Robertson acting for his client Mogens Hauschildt, a silver bullion dealer from Denmark who had been arrested for an alleged fraud but denied bail by the Danish authorities. Ultimately, Denmark lost the case – and Robertson therefore won it – and the country had to change its criminal justice procedures, as did some other European countries. Incidentally, *Hauschildt v Denmark* remains a leading authority when it comes to judicial bias, meaning that Starmer witnessed a little bit of legal history on that occasion.

Despite Starmer's work rate, he did allow himself some time off occasionally – as long as it allowed him to explore new left-wing ideas with like-minded people. Peter Tatchell recalls a trip they took together with others to a green–left summer camp in France in 1989. 'I first met Keir around 1987,' Tatchell says.

> He was a fellow left-wing activist. He struck me as very intelligent, passionate and committed to a radical vision of what Britain could be. He was well to the left of Neil Kinnock, the then Labour leader, but what struck me was that he combined radicalism with pragmatism. His ideas were achievable and not far-fetched like some other people on the left. He was very much in the orbit of the emerging confluence between greens and socialists. He was quite in advance of Labour thinking at the time.

Tatchell remembers that whenever they met, they discussed a range of ideas which were not considered mainstream in Labour Party circles in the 1980s and early 1990s.

> Both he and I were already thinking about the potential of Europe-wide collaboration between socialist parties, trade unions and civil society groups to advance a progressive agenda. This went against the grain of traditional left-wing hostility towards what was then the EC. Keir was very strong

> on human rights. He also embraced new ideas on feminism, ecology and LGBT+ rights when some in the Labour Party – even on the left – were still quite hesitant.

Their joint interest in working with those who were involved in European politics was what took them on their Gallic exploit, yet there was little glamour about the trip on which they embarked. While some of Starmer's colleagues from chambers were jetting off to Greece or Italy for a few weeks in the sun, he and Tatchell were among a group who travelled by coach to the Massif Central in order to attend a green socialist summer camp, which had been organised by the European Alternatives Youth Network. Starmer's girlfriend of the time, Angela O'Brien, did not go with them.

The journey began with the forty-strong delegation leaving Britain to visit Paris for the 200th anniversary of the Storming of the Bastille. They departed from Victoria station on the morning of 14 July and arrived in the French capital that evening for the celebrations. The next day, the group reboarded their coach and headed south, ending their journey when they reached the countryside close to the ancient village of La Couvertoirade, about an hour's drive north of Montpellier. The camp was held on farmland which belonged to a French left-wing activist. According to Tatchell, a couple of hundred activists from across Europe gathered there for seven days of radical lectures, debates and music.

'It was on the Larzac Plateau, a centre of Maquis resistance during the Second World War,' recalls Tatchell.

> We all camped out in tents in the fields and mucked in to cook meals and clean. Most of the people involved [from Britain] were from the *Socialist Alternatives* milieu, people like Ben Schoendorff and his then girlfriend, Flo Bertorelli. There were

> various people there, including the German Green MEP, Frank Schwalba-Hoth, plus some British Green activists, Dutch socialists and French radical leftists, all of us committed to left–green collaboration, Europe-wide co-ordination and a new kind of progressive politics.

So-called red–green parties were very much on the rise at the time, with several having sprung up in time to stand candidates in the 1989 European elections which had taken place the month before. They included the Dutch party GreenLeft, a political alliance comprising the Communist Party of the Netherlands, the Pacifist Socialist Party and two left-wing Christian parties, the Evangelical People's Party and the Political Party of Radicals. Unity List was the name of a similar socialist pick 'n' mix operation which had formed in Denmark.

Tatchell says he delivered several lectures during the conference:

> My talks at the summer camp were on building a Europe-wide red–green alliance and urging pan-European collaboration to push the EC in a more progressive direction on social justice, environmental and human rights issues. The overall focus was green socialist. Everybody there came from the green socialist milieu. There were daily talks, debates and musical performances. I can't remember if Keir played any music. He probably did, but I can't recall.

Nor does Tatchell have any memory of Starmer, who by this time was six weeks shy of his twenty-seventh birthday, taking to any of the platforms to make a speech. It seems that he preferred, somewhat characteristically, to stay under the radar, and adopted a more relaxed approach at this political festival. 'As well as the formal discussions, there were also lots of informal chats,' Tatchell says, throwing up the possibility that Starmer enjoyed talking one-to-one instead of addressing large crowds. English was the *lingua franca* at the event, allowing all those present to exchange ideas and information as they sought to advance their green and socialist agenda into all corners of Europe. 'People from France, Britain, Germany and other countries would link up and talk together over coffee or a beer,' Tatchell remembers. 'All the meals were communal. We prepared them together on a rota system, we ate them together and we washed up afterwards. It was a fantastic event. I was a bit sceptical when I was invited, but I was really glad I went.'

Tatchell adds that he and Starmer left the camp separately. He thinks Starmer caught the bus home, while he joined Schoendorff and Bertorelli to drive back to London by car. 'On the way back, we stopped off and met Pierre Juquin, a former member of the French Communist Party who had [by that point] broken with them.'

• • •

As well as his work as a barrister and his duties for the Haldane Society, Starmer also found time between 1987 and 1990 to take up a post as a legal officer for the National Council for Civil Liberties (NCCL), a civil liberties watchdog now known as Liberty. At the time he joined it, the NCCL was an organisation with a sordid recent past. Under the banner of promoting freedom, it had campaigned in the 1970s to liberalise the law on paedophilia and reduce the age of sexual consent to fourteen. In 1976, for example, the NCCL argued that 'childhood sexual experiences, willingly engaged in with an adult, result in no identifiable damage.' And in 1978, a group called the Paedophile Information Exchange (PIE) affiliated itself to the NCCL. As has been well documented, members of the PIE essentially tried to make paedophilia respectable by campaigning to lower the age of consent and resist controls on child pornography. Astonishingly, it was only in 1983 that the NCCL cut its ties with the PIE and its evil agenda. In holding a formal position within the NCCL, Starmer was following in the footsteps of other prominent Labour figures, including the future Cabinet ministers Patricia Hewitt and Harriet Harman, both of whom worked there in the 1970s, and in Harman's case in the early 1980s, too. Another future Labour MP, Diane Abbott, was also linked to the NCCL shortly before Starmer joined its ranks.

In the 1980s, the NCCL campaigned vigorously against various rights violations through the channels of the United Nations and the European Court of Human Rights in Strasbourg. By 1989, it viewed Margaret Thatcher as having decreed what its general secretary, Sarah Spencer, said was 'a peacetime state of emergency' through media censorship and extensive police powers. Spencer refused to co-operate with this book, saying, 'If you attempt to imply that I have suggested [Starmer] either did, or did not, contribute [to the NCCL] then you will be misrepresenting what I have said.'

Be that as it may, Starmer has been happy to state himself that he was linked to the group between 1987 and 1990. Records show that under Spencer's direction the NCCL also advocated introducing a Bill of Rights for Britain focused on civil rights. Harold Pinter, the playwright, was one of the NCCL's most prominent supporters. In February 1989, it changed its name to Liberty and embarked on a modernisation programme, shedding its intellectual image and adopting a more populist approach. Despite being apolitical, it was generally regarded as being on the libertarian left, lobbying to scrap the poll tax and proposals to introduce football ID cards.

Starmer's most public work for the NCCL and Liberty seems to have come at the very end of the 1980s. In June 1989, for example, he was linked to a battle against a clause in the Local Government and Housing Bill which sought to prevent officers who dealt with the public, earned more than £13,500 or worked in restricted areas from being politically active. And in August 1989, he gave press interviews on behalf of Liberty in which he picked to pieces proposals to introduce video identification parades. That month, he also used his position as Liberty's legal officer to reprimand the police for their attempt to crack down on an open-air acid house party in an area just outside Lambourn in Berkshire. After officers from Thames Valley Police set up roadblocks and confiscated electronic equipment to prevent the party from going ahead, Liberty chose to back the organisers in a court action. Starmer was quoted as saying that the police operation was 'outrageous and unlawful' and 'an incredible abuse of police powers'. He is not thought to have been a regular attender of acid house parties, where taking proscribed drugs such as MDMA and LSD was not unusual, though one friend who prefers to remain anonymous says he was certainly not averse to 'smoking weed' at social occasions when he was a younger man.

• • •

By this point, Geoffrey Robertson was putting the finishing touches to his long-held ambition to shake up the legal establishment by abandoning 1 Dr Johnson's Buildings so he could set up a new 'post-modern' set of chambers. Since joining the Bar in the 1970s, Robertson had been uncomfortable with what he regarded as its outmoded quirks and had been ruminating on how to operate in a more contemporary environment. He wished to dispense with traditions such as having clerks who earned their money on commission and to appoint a practice manager on a salary instead. He also wanted to run a chambers that welcomed a wider variety of people – women, ethnic minorities and those who did not come from middle-class backgrounds. Being physically situated away from the legal district was a priority for him. Robertson chose as the location of his new set some buildings in Doughty Street in Bloomsbury, far enough outside the confines of the Inns of Court but within walking distance of the High Court. The barristers bought the buildings collectively. All this was considered to be revolutionary at the time.

Starmer was one of twenty colleagues from 1 Dr Johnson's Buildings who decided to accompany Robertson on this adventure in July 1990. This breakaway move was said to be entirely amicable, with no hard feelings from those who remained at Dr Johnson's. Although Starmer was the youngest barrister on board this enterprise, he is remembered as having played a contributory role in its planning and negotiations and was said to be very excited by it. Among other figures to decamp to Bloomsbury were Helena Kennedy, Louis Blom-Cooper, Gavin Millar and Starmer's Oxford friend Anthony Metzer. During the first year of its existence, a further eight barristers from other chambers joined them. The new practice was founded upon what Robertson has called an 'imperishable commitment to the legal aid system', with barristers split equally between civil and criminal practitioners. Robertson insisted that all barristers observe the so-called cab-rank rule, whereby they must accept any client whose case comes within their field of practice as long as they are available to do so. The only exception to this rule related to any case in which the death penalty would be upheld.

Colin Wells was one of the group that left 1 Dr Johnson's Buildings to join Doughty Street Chambers from its inception. 'We wanted to consolidate into a new, quite exciting radical set,' he recalls.

> *The Guardian* at the time called us the Young Turks, which was quite funny really, because we weren't that young. We were at the bottom, but the QCs were older. There was a group of us with a common interest in pursuing the human rights of individuals. We were all ages, from the bottom up.

Everybody contributed to the purchase of the building in Doughty Street, and the reputations of those involved apparently ensured the chambers would be a success. 'It was very secure from the outset,' says Wells.

> Although we were a new set, there was strength in depth, so we knew that financially we were secure and we had good quality people. So, for me as a junior of two or three years' call, it wasn't a risk at all; it was quite an exciting project. We didn't change the work we did; we carried on with the work we were doing, but it was a consolidation of ideas into one set.

Another Doughty Street figure says:

> Doughty Street is a very good set because one of the problems about being a barrister is that an awful lot of barristers are pompous twerps. People like that were remarkably thin on the ground at Doughty Street, and Keir reflects that. He's just a thoroughly nice guy. He's a much more genial character than his persona in 2021 portrays. Usefully for him, there were always people at Doughty Street who were very closely involved in the Labour Party. They lived in north London and spent a lot of time discussing Labour politics. Everybody knew that. Some were Labour councillors. Their involvement varied. It is almost a question of who wasn't involved! I'm thinking of

Robert Latham, Nick Toms, Helena Kennedy, Phillippa Kaufmann and Martin Westgate, to name a few.

The sense of modernisation at Liberty and also at his chambers seems to have rubbed off on Starmer. At the same time as Doughty Street Chambers was being set up, he and the executive committee of the Haldane Society were mulling over a series of proposals aimed at preparing the organisation for the new decade. In a trenchant piece for the *Socialist Lawyer* published in the autumn of 1990, Starmer wrote a rather bossy manifesto, stating that the society needed to raise its profile in the national left-wing press, citing titles including *The Guardian*. He also castigated other members in this document by stating, 'The Society is weak on policies. The Annual General Meeting is a farce. Largely irrelevant and wordy resolutions are passed and then forgotten.' He called for more money to be pumped into *Socialist Lawyer* and suggested that a designated office worker be hired to handle all administrative matters. He also advocated a recruitment drive so that it would achieve a membership of at least 2,000 people. All this was rounded off with a warning that the society's finances were 'in an appalling state, perhaps worse now than ever before'. He then shared his idea to set up a charitable trust called the Haldane Educational Trust, which would finance all the society's educational research and publication work.

According to Bill Bowring, some of this worked – but not for long. 'He set out his plans to turn Haldane into something like [the pressure group] Liberty, with premises and a worker and an educational charitable trust, running professional development courses for money,' Bowring observes. 'We had premises in Took's Court and in Red Lion Square over Conway Hall. But it did not last more than a few years.'

As a footnote, it is worth adding that in February 2021 the Haldane Society seemingly attempted to humiliate Starmer by passing a motion at its AGM which stated, 'Sir Keir Starmer QC MP does not qualify for membership of the Haldane Society … because he is demonstrably not a socialist.' In a sense this was a futile gesture, on the basis that Starmer had ceased to play an active role in the organisation since 2008, when he resigned from its executive committee, and has had nothing formally to do with it since then. Not being able to expel him, the next best thing that those behind the motion could do was to state that he would 'not be permitted to rejoin the society unless and until his re-admittance is agreed by a future general meeting'. This would, of course, have required him to try to rejoin in the first place. However empty these words may seem, though, it must have stung Starmer to some degree to be subjected publicly to such treatment by a group to which he had devoted a considerable amount of his time over the years. The irony of a self-declared socialist being disowned for demonstrating insufficient socialism by a socialist group whose name he had tried to change thirty years earlier because it did not sound socialist enough cannot have been lost on him either.

CHAPTER 6

UPHOLDING THE RULE OF LAW

Two significant things happened to Keir Starmer towards the end of 1991 which confirmed that, on the cusp of turning thirty, he was making progress both personally and professionally. First, he and his girlfriend, Angela O'Brien, bought a flat in north London, thereby cementing their commitment to each other. The maisonette at 60 Ellington Street, a smart Victorian terrace close to Highbury & Islington Underground station, certainly represented a step up the ladder for them. Compared with their shared rental accommodation in Archway Road, and another flat at 32 North Road in Highgate where they had stayed briefly, 60 Ellington Street was in a more fashionable part of town. Having arranged a mortgage, they joined Britain's property-owning classes for the first time.

The second development that autumn concerned Starmer's decision to travel to Northern Ireland. His interest in the province can be traced back to two years earlier, in December 1989, when Kader Asmal, a senior lecturer in human rights law at Trinity College, Dublin, and president of the Irish Council for Civil Liberties, had delivered the D. N. Pritt Memorial Lecture for the Haldane Society. During his speech, Asmal put down British lawyers for failing to hold the British state to account over what he regarded as its poor record in Northern Ireland. He said:

> The list of abuses and catalogue of malpractices arising out of the current emergency which has now lasted twenty years may be well known, but whether they have made an impact on the consciousness of professional legal bodies – on your Bar council, your Law Society, your law schools or your voluntary associations – is doubtful.

These words are said to have made a strong impression on Starmer. A few months later, in April 1990, he attended the Appeal Court hearing in London of the so-called Winchester Three, sitting in as a legal observer for the pressure group Liberty and also on behalf of the Haldane Society. This case concerned three young Irish people, John McCann, Finbar Cullen and Martina Shanahan. In 1988, they had each been found guilty at Winchester Crown Court of involvement in a plot the year before to murder the then Northern Ireland Secretary, Tom King. The trio, who had exercised their right to remain silent, were sentenced to twenty-five years in prison. Their convictions were overturned after serving just two years, however, because during the course of their original trial, the British government had announced its intention to abolish this legal principle in terrorist cases in Northern Ireland. King had spoken publicly in support of this move and made comments about terrorist suspects abusing the right to refuse to answer questions.

The Appeal Court ruled that King's words could have prejudiced the original trial of those suspected of planning to kill him. This was a highly controversial decision, and the group's release from prison was heavily criticised by some, including by the former Master of the Rolls Lord Denning. Starmer, however, was delighted. In the next edition of the *Socialist Lawyer*, published in the summer of 1990, he wrote triumphantly under the headline 'King Size Blunder':

> Much work was done by the Haldane Society on the case of the Winchester Three. *The Guardian* printed our letter shortly before the appeal and I observed the hearing of the appeal on behalf of the Society. The Court of Appeal found that statements made by Tom King during the trial in which he equated silence with guilt created a serious risk of prejudice to the fairness of the trial. The case is a glaring example of the miscarriages of justice that would result if the government's proposals to limit the right to silence were carried into force and vindicates the campaign to retain the right to silence of which the Society has been a long supporter.

Although he obviously felt it right that this principled position had won the day, it could be argued that he overplayed his hand. It is sobering to recall that on 30 July 1990 – around the time his words were published – another Conservative MP, Ian Gow, was murdered by an IRA bomb that was planted underneath his car outside his house in Sussex. Nobody has ever been convicted of Mr Gow's murder.

Over the course of the next eighteen months or so, Starmer assembled a delegation of lawyers and arranged for them to visit Belfast on a four-day fact-finding mission to investigate criminal justice in the province under the Emergency Powers, which were still in place. Under the umbrella of the Haldane Society, he and thirteen colleagues left London on 26 September 1991. It is no exaggeration to say that in making this trip, they ventured into a potentially deadly environment. Only the week before their arrival, a prominent Protestant businessman had been murdered by the IRA in Belfast. By a bizarre coincidence, he was called John Haldane. He was a father of four who had been dictating a letter to his secretary at his timber firm in the docks area when two men walked into his office and shot him three times at close range. Mr Haldane had been the sixty-first person to die violently that year in Northern Ireland. The IRA said he was killed because his company supplied materials to the security forces. Then, during Starmer's visit, a Catholic newsagent, Laurence Murchan, was murdered in the Falls Road area. The Loyalist Retaliation and Defence Group, a previously unknown organisation, claimed that Mr Murchan had stocked the IRA paper *Republican News* in his shop and said his killing was in retaliation for John Haldane's murder by the IRA. At the time, Mr Murchan was reported as being the 2,000th civilian to be killed in the conflict in Northern Ireland since 1969.

While there, Starmer's team observed the so-called Diplock Courts, in which criminal trials were held without a jury; they explored the effect of the removal of an arrestee's right to silence (a right which remained in place elsewhere in the United Kingdom); they scrutinised allegations of ill-treatment among those who had been detained by the Royal Ulster Constabulary; and they studied the Casement Park trials, which took place as a result of the deaths of British Army Corporals David Howes and Derek Wood in March 1988. Their deaths, also known as the Corporals Killings, were among the most dramatic and grisly of the Troubles.

Starmer and his team certainly used every hour available to them during their mission. In the context of their work, they met High Court and Appeal Court judges; they interviewed prisoners; they spoke to the Independent Police Complaints Commission and the Standing Advisory Commission on Human Rights; and they spent time gathering material from solicitors and academic researchers. Among those who accompanied Starmer were Phillippa Kaufmann, who is now a KC; Stephen Cragg, also now a KC; Nadine Finch, who went on to be an immigration judge; Stephanie Harrison, who is now a KC; and barrister and academic Bill Bowring.

In mid-1992, a report detailing their observations was published under the title 'Upholding the Rule of Law?' It concluded that the Diplock Courts were 'failing to secure reliable convictions based on properly tested evidence' and should be abandoned. It also claimed that Catholic detainees were being subjected to interrogation techniques which amounted to physical and psychological torture. It further called for the right to silence to be reinstated. And, in a section devoted to the Casement Park trials, it alleged that the sentences of those found guilty of the murders of Corporal David Howes and Corporal Derek Wood were unsafe. 'It is plainly shown that these convictions cannot be sustained either on the basis of the evidence that came before the courts or the law which was applied,' the report stated. According to Bowring, who was then chair of Haldane and who wrote the introduction, the report was 'a collective effort', and it remains a project with which he is proud to be associated. 'It was a great team which went [to Northern Ireland],' he recollects.

In light of work for the Police Service of Northern Ireland which Starmer would take on later in his career, it is worth noting that the report's own authors acknowledged that their findings could be criticised on two levels. First, the group said it had no means of testing the testimonies it received, nor could it 'carry out empirical research over any period of time to determine whether the abuses reported to us were indeed taking place'. Second, and of more interest in relation to Starmer specifically, the Haldane Society had a clear policy at that time of supporting a united Ireland. 'We call for British withdrawal,' the report declared. 'We did not hide the fact we had such [a] policy.' This, therefore, cannot be classified as an impartial piece of work. Bill Bowring is cited as the person who wrote these words, which appeared in the introduction, but it seems highly unlikely that Starmer – the serious-minded convenor of the trip, which was co-funded by the Haldane Educational Trust, a body he was instrumental in setting up – did not know about them prior to the report's publication. This fuels questions about how neutral Starmer was, then and subsequently, on the Northern Irish question and gives pause for thought when it comes to assessing to what extent his own feelings about Northern Ireland have ever been examined or understood. What is not in doubt, according to Bowring, was the effect that this delegation would have on his career. 'This experience was Keir's initiative,' remembers Bowring. 'He did all the spadework and had already done important work on terrorism and human rights. The mission gave him the contacts and experience which helped him to get so deeply involved in the peace process some years later.'

By the spring of 1992, Starmer the barrister was tackling the kinds of difficult and traumatic cases through which he would make his name as a representative for the hard-pressed and those who felt they had been hard done by. This sort of work may not have made him wealthy, but it certainly identified him as a lawyer who was driven by a desire to use his position to help others. For example, he was a junior to his head of chambers, Geoffrey Robertson, in a case which was highly inconvenient to the British and American governments. Robertson and Starmer represented the relatives of six privates from the 9th Royal Fusiliers Regiment who were among nine British soldiers killed by so-called 'friendly fire' during the Gulf War. The soldiers died, and eleven other men were injured, when an American A-10 aircraft fired on two British armoured personnel carriers on 26 February 1991. Robertson and Starmer were instructed by a young litigation solicitor called Mark Stephens, who is now a longstanding friend of Starmer. Unusually, the soldiers' families applied for a jury inquest into their deaths to make sure that public confidence in the case was not undermined. This request was granted by Nicholas Gardiner, the Oxford coroner, and the subsequent inquest determined that all nine soldiers had been killed unlawfully. One lawyer who remembers this case says it left a mark as far as Starmer is concerned. 'It had a powerful effect on Keir, who was very sympathetic to the bereaved parents,' says the lawyer. 'It also made him sceptical, both of the class system in the British Army and of the military alliance with the US.'

And in October 1992, he was a junior member of a team that tried to defend two murderers at the High Court who had been released on parole and then sent back to prison for leading an unsettled lifestyle. The men, Anthony Creamer and James Scholey, applied for a judicial review of decisions of the parole board not to recommend their release on licence, but this was denied by Lord Justice Rose. The judge appeared, however, to believe that Creamer and Scholey, who brought their action in an attempt to force the Home Office to disclose the unpublished reports on which its decisions were based, had a point. The refusal to show the pair the reports, Rose said in judgment, was 'a breach of natural justice'. He added: 'A prisoner's right to make representations is valueless unless he knows the case against him. Secret, unchallengeable reports, which may contain damaging inaccuracies and which result in continuing loss of liberty, are or should be anathema in a civilised, democratic society.' Rose concluded that he was bound by legal precedent, meaning there was nothing he could do about his judgment.

This was exactly the sort of project in which Starmer appears to have relished being involved. With that said, it does throw up a rather more challenging question about certain beliefs he has held regarding imprisonment in general. One highly respected lawyer recalls with incredulity an occasion around this time when Starmer shared his views on this subject. According to this person, he certainly seemed keen to convert the idea of civil liberties for all into a practical reality. 'I remember sitting in the pub with him listening to him seriously say he doesn't believe in imprisonment for anything, ever,' reports the lawyer. 'We all say stupid things when we're young, but he wasn't that young. He was a practising barrister; he wasn't a teenager.'

Soon after Lord Justice Rose's decision, in December 1992, Starmer acted for another controversial client, the National Union of Mineworkers, whose president was Arthur Scargill. The case, which was heard at the High Court, challenged decisions made two months previously by British Coal and the then president of the Board of Trade, Michael Heseltine, to close thirty-one coal pits. The industrial relations specialist John Hendy QC, who now sits in the House of Lords as a Labour peer, led Starmer and another barrister, Jennifer Eady, who is now herself a judge. Mark Stephens was again the instructing solicitor. 'When you're a junior barrister, it's the icing on the cake to get brought into a case with a leader, particularly a big case that's in the newspapers and is going to set a legal precedent for the future,' says Hendy.

> It was a massive case at the time. It was a very urgent case, and we worked on it over a period of weeks. [Starmer] would have been drafting the legal documents for the case, the pleadings, the skeleton argument and so on and working on the strategy of how we were going to argue the case, what legal arguments we were going to put together. He was a very bright, hard-working young barrister. He was very talented. Both of the juniors were. We had a great team.

The judicial review was successful for Hendy, Starmer and Eady. The closure of the pits was halted, essentially on the grounds that the British Coal Corporation had failed to consult with the unions. Indeed, the outcome has been of use to Hendy subsequently. 'I've used the judgment in the pit closures case many times since because it became one of the leading cases on what constitutes proper consultation. [Starmer] was innovative and committed. Both the juniors were very good. It was a pleasure to have a team like that.' He adds: 'The outcome of these difficult cases is completely unpredictable, so of course it's satisfying to win a case rather than lose one, but you put the same intensity in no matter what the outcome is. You don't know what the outcome's going to be when you start, of course.'

Unsurprisingly, not every brief Starmer took on as a relatively young barrister of just over five years' standing was as high-profile or as successful. In April 1993, he represented Elizabeth Marsh, who had produced a booklet claiming that a wonder drug could cure cancer and AIDS. She was being prosecuted by the Department of Health under the Medicines Act 1968, which makes it an offence to sell or produce any product that has not been through clinical trials. Marsh's booklet was sent with a covering letter to a gay pub in Camden, north London, asking for volunteers for clinical trials for the drug, which would be distributed free, although there would be an initial consultation charge of £95. Starmer argued that this did not amount to a commercial interest in the medicine, which the prosecution needed to show to prove Marsh's guilt. He said that even though Marsh had contracted for 300 copies of the booklet to be printed in November 1990, the Crown had produced no evidence to support the idea that she was responsible for its distribution. Furthermore, said Starmer, the booklet stated from the outset that it was merely a discussion document looking at possible cures for cancer. As an explanation, it didn't stand up to scrutiny, and Marsh was jailed for six months.

It would be another case that crossed Starmer's desk soon after this one, also involving contentious literature, which would help to make his name, however. The action in question was a High Court libel trial involving two campaigners of modest financial means, Helen Steel and Dave Morris, and the hamburger chain McDonald's. Steel and Morris were environmental activists linked to a small protest group called London Greenpeace, which in the 1980s had begun producing leaflets titled 'What's wrong with McDonald's? Everything they don't want you to know'. The leaflets questioned the fast-food firm's practices in relation to animal cruelty and rainforest destruction, the nutritional value of its products, the exploitation of children in its advertising and employees' working conditions, among other things. In 1990, Steel, Morris and three London Greenpeace colleagues were served with a writ by McDonald's. A letter to them made clear that a court case would ensue unless they apologised. Of the five, Steel and Morris were the only ones who refused to comply with this order. They were entitled to two hours of legal aid, after which they were on their own and would have to defend themselves as so-called litigants-in-person.

This marked the beginning of what has become known colloquially as the 'McLibel' case. A total of twenty-eight pre-trial hearings were held before proceedings began in earnest in June 1994. As legal aid was not available for defamation actions, Steel and Morris had to represent themselves in court against some of the country's top libel lawyers led by Richard Rampton QC, who reputedly charged McDonald's £2,000 per day for his services. A solicitor friend of Steel's advised her to contact Starmer, believing that he might offer her and Morris some free advice. In fact, Starmer agreed to write their defence and to help draft the relevant documents without charge. Over the course of the trial, others helped Steel and Morris as well, including the aforementioned solicitor, Mark Stephens; representatives from the campaign group Liberty; and lawyers from the firm Richards Butler. Steel and Morris did not dispute handing out the leaflets, and McDonald's accepted that they did not write the material contained within them, but the company was determined to sue. Things got off to a dire start for the defendants when the High Court ruled that the case should be heard by a judge alone, as McDonald's wanted, and not, as is usual in libel, by a jury. Given that the burden fell on Steel and Morris to prove their case, the odds were well and truly stacked against them.

The McLibel trial was scheduled to last for twelve weeks. In fact, it was heard over 314 days, making it the longest-running libel trial in English legal history. A total of 170 witnesses gave evidence. Steel and Morris argued that the case was in essence about censorship, as McDonald's had previously used England's libel laws to quieten its critics. The pair cited at least fifty groups, including newspaper and television companies, which had been forced to apologise to the hamburger chain over the previous few years. Undoubtedly, it was a captivating contest, and Steel and Morris emerged from it as two brave individuals who were willing to take on a fight that others with substantial resources had ducked. When the judgment was handed down in June 1997, the judge, Mr Justice Bell, found largely in favour of McDonald's, though he also concluded that several of the points raised in the London Greenpeace leaflet were accurate, meaning the hamburger chain won only a partial victory.

Ultimately, McDonald's was awarded damages of £76,000, a sum of money which neither Steel nor Morris had and which they were open in saying they would not pay. It was a pyrrhic victory for McDonald's, however. Not only is the case thought to have cost the firm in the region of £10 million in legal fees but it gained worldwide attention and enough negative press coverage for McDonald's to ensure that its executives shied away from ever chasing Steel and Morris for the money they owed. The case is still universally regarded as an infamous corporate public relations failure. Shortly after the judgment, Jeremy Corbyn, then a backbench MP, even used the result as the basis of a parliamentary Early Day Motion in which he condemned England's libel laws.

Most profiles of Starmer that have been written since then have made a point of mentioning the McLibel case as a highlight of his legal career. It is certainly true that he played a significant role in it by helping the defendants on a pro bono basis. Some Doughty Street colleagues further recall that he extended to the pair not only the benefit of his professional wisdom but also the use of his chambers so that they could photocopy documents and access legal textbooks if need be. Yet one legal figure who knows Starmer believes that his role may have been misinterpreted by some members of the public, not to mention some journalists, insofar as Starmer did not actually defend Steel and Morris in court in the way that might be assumed by those who are unfamiliar with the law but have perhaps watched too many courtroom dramas on television. Neither was he the only lawyer involved. As Steel and Morris became known as 'DIY lawyers' during the trial, because they were doing a job normally undertaken by professional solicitors and barristers, it does not seem unreasonable to pursue this argument. 'The [McLibel] case isn't what it's purported to be,' says the person concerned.

> Keir didn't represent Helen Steel and Dave Morris. They used to go into his chambers and use the research facilities. Keir would occasionally draft documents for them because they

> were representing themselves. That's the whole point about that case – those two people represented themselves in a libel action that went on for about eighteen months. It was the longest libel action in English legal history. Keir did do the case in that he was like a litigation friend, but he didn't do any advocacy as far as I know.

This analysis is entirely accurate. Starmer did not appear at the High Court to cross-examine witnesses, nor did he appear as an advocate for Steel and Morris. In fact, he himself said in August 1996 that Steel and Morris had been legal novices when he first met them, but over the course of the trial they had learned enough about the law to be able to 'draft stuff on their own'. Such was their ability, he said that he thought they would make good lawyers themselves, and he even encouraged them to follow him into the profession. Moreover, it wasn't as though he wasn't busy with other matters at this stage of his career. In March 1996, under the umbrella of the Haldane Society, he organised a 45-strong delegation to fly to South Africa to attend a conference arranged by the International Association of Democratic Lawyers at which Nelson Mandela gave an address. It attracted about 260 participants from thirty-three countries, though the British contingent was the largest. Among those on the trip with Starmer was Phillippa Kaufmann, his Doughty Street colleague who was, like him, a member of the Haldane Society's executive committee.

During the course of the McLibel hearings, Starmer also found the time to co-write, with Francesca Klug and Stuart Weir, a book called *The Three Pillars of Liberty*, which is described as an audit of British compliance with international human rights standards. In September 1996, he even drew attention to its publication by writing a letter to *The Times*. In it, he backed a call by Norma Major, wife of the then Prime Minister John Major, for the introduction of tougher privacy laws, which would bring the UK into line with other European nations. And he took on other work. In 1995–96, his clients included a Druid called King Arthur Pendragon, who was accused of trespassing while observing the summer solstice at Stonehenge. Defending him, Starmer was alarmed to discover that he would only swear an oath on his sword, Excalibur, forcing Starmer to research the law on oaths and then persuade Salisbury Magistrates' Court that this would be acceptable. It worked.

He also represented two people involved in what came to be regarded as a test case about the freedom to protest. Dr Margaret Jones, a university lecturer from Bristol, and a student in his mid-twenties called Richard Lloyd had taken part in a peaceful roadside demonstration, also at Stonehenge, in June 1995. They were the first two people to be charged with the new criminal offence of 'trespassory assembly' of twenty people or more, which had been brought in under the 1994 Criminal Justice and Public Order Act. Having been found guilty by Salisbury magistrates, Starmer believed that this meant the police were legally entitled to use the new public order powers to ban peaceful demonstrations. He recognised it as a case which touched upon issues concerning fundamental public freedoms, which were perhaps under threat from wider law and order reforms introduced by the then Home Secretary, Michael Howard, who had signalled his intention to crack down on squatters, trespassers and protesters. When Jones and Lloyd appealed at Salisbury Crown Court in January 1996, Starmer represented them, arguing that the convictions could stand only if it were proved that his clients and others had exceeded their rights to be on the highway. He said there was a 'clear trend towards recognising peaceful, non-obstructive assembly as a reasonable and usual use of the highway', and said the evidence showed the appellants had been peaceful and non-obstructive. Michael Butt, for the Crown, claimed this submission was a 'thinly disguised' attack on the Criminal Justice Act and accused Starmer of wasting the court's time. Butt added that if Starmer was successful, a whole section of the Act banning assemblies within prohibited areas would be nullified. Starmer was successful – initially. The convictions were overturned that day, inducing the Crown Prosecution Service (CPS) to appeal to the High Court. There, in December 1996, Starmer tried to argue that if the CPS appeal was successful, it would mean that any group of twenty or more people gathered together on the highway could run the risk of breaking the law. It did not hold. The following month, it was ruled that there was no right in law for members of the public to hold a peaceful, non-obstructive assembly on the public highway. Despite this failure, Starmer had chalked up some more runs as a lawyer in whom a radical spirit burned. He was making a name for himself.

The High Court's finding in the McLibel case in June 1997 was not the end of that matter. Seven years later, in September 2004, Steel and Morris went to the European Court of Human Rights in Strasbourg. On that occasion, Mark Stephens was their solicitor and Starmer represented them in person. He argued on their behalf that the British government had failed to meet the requirements under the Human Rights Convention to guarantee them a fair trial and to safeguard their right to freedom of speech. At the centre of the affair was the fact that no legal aid was available to Steel and Morris and that they were forced to represent themselves in court despite having no legal experience and no money to pay for so much as evidence transcripts. Starmer told the Strasbourg court that the 'inequality of arms' between a multi-national corporation and two largely unemployed and unrepresented campaigners could not have been greater. 'The result was that, without legal assistance, the case was under-prepared, unready for trial and was advanced by two inexperienced, untrained and exhausted individuals who were pushed to their physical and mental limits,' he said.

The seven judges hearing the case agreed that Steel and Morris had been denied their rights to free speech and to a fair hearing. In February 2005, the British government was ordered to pay them compensation of £24,000 plus £32,500 towards their legal costs. Afterwards, Starmer called the ruling a 'milestone for free speech'. He said, 'Until now, only the rich and famous have been able to defend themselves against libel writs. Now ordinary people can participate much more effectively in public debate without the fear of being bankrupted.' Some of his fees were awarded by the British government.

The entire saga, which had begun fifteen years previously, was made into a documentary, called *McLibel*, which was directed by Franny Armstrong with input from the left-wing filmmaker Ken Loach. An impeccably coiffed Starmer can be seen at various points of this film discussing developments in the case. The DVD of *McLibel* also features seven minutes of extra interviews given by Starmer which did not make the final cut. In one such scene, recorded in 2005, he talked about his recent appointment as a Queen's Counsel, commenting that his accepting this award was 'odd, since I often used to propose the abolition of the monarchy'. Years later, in February 2021, he came to regret his candour when the footage was rediscovered by some sections of the media and used against him at the very time the Labour Party was trying to be more patriotic in its attempt to win back voters.

There is another, rather more fascinating, aspect of the McLibel trial which in a sense haunts Starmer to this day, however. During proceedings at the High Court between 1994 and 1996, it came to light that McDonald's had placed some members of London Greenpeace under surveillance, using private investigators to monitor their activities and their personal lives. The sense of violation that this inspired in Helen Steel led her to question the true nature of a romantic relationship she had formed in the early 1990s with a man who called himself John Barker. They were involved with each other for a couple of years and had even lived together at one point, but by the time the McLibel trial began he had vanished, having written her a letter in which he claimed to have had a mental breakdown and moved to South Africa.

Understandably, Steel was devastated, and she began trying to find out more about this man, spurred on by a nagging feeling that he was not who he said he was. Her instincts were right. During the McLibel trial, her own detective work eventually confirmed that the name 'John Barker' was an alias. Just like the protagonist in Frederick Forsyth's book *The Day of the Jackal*, 'Barker' had assumed the identity of a dead child. He had lied to Steel about many aspects of his life. Steel eventually established that his real name was John Dines, and in 2010 she discovered that he was an undercover police officer who had been working for the Metropolitan Police's Special Demonstration Squad, which spied on political activists, including those linked to London Greenpeace.

In 2015, Steel, who was one of seven women who had been tricked into relationships of this nature, was awarded compensation by the Metropolitan Police. That year, the Undercover Policing inquiry was set up by then Home Secretary Theresa May. Its purpose was to examine the activities of the Special Demonstration Squad and the National Public Order Intelligence Unit since 1968. More than 100 of these so-called 'spy cops' are said to have targeted individuals and groups linked to political and social justice campaigns. The inquiry was slated to last for three years but at the time of writing it remains active and looks likely to last for comfortably more than a decade. While giving evidence to the inquiry in October 2024, Dave Morris revealed that in the 1990s

Starmer was himself spied on by John Dines. 'In the first eighteen months, Dines was exploiting Helen while they lived together by getting details of our confidential legal strategy following the private meetings we held with Keir Starmer,' Morris told the inquiry, as he explained that Starmer's legal advice was relayed back to the Special Demonstration Squad.

Surprisingly, Starmer's subsequent stance on the issue tends to suggest he has little sympathy with Helen Steel's plight. In October 2020, he whipped his MPs to abstain on the government's Covert Human Intelligence Sources (Criminal Conduct) Bill, regulating the future conduct of secret operatives and whether they are allowed to commit crimes to obtain information in the course of their work. Guidelines have banned intimate relationships like the one Dines embarked upon with Steel, yet this piece of legislation, which gained royal assent in March 2021, has fostered fears that it would make it harder for other women like Steel to unmask their own 'John Barker', the man who never was.

Some of Starmer's oldest political and legal friends have been perplexed by what they consider his illiberal position. One of them was the aforementioned John Hendy, with whom he had worked on legal cases in the 1990s and who now sits in the House of Lords as a Labour peer. 'I was very disappointed that he instructed the Labour MPs and peers to abstain on the Overseas Operations Bill and on the Covert Human Intelligence Sources Bill,' says Hendy. 'I think that sends the wrong message. I think the Labour Party should stand up for human rights, and I think as a human rights lawyer he should have led that. I presume he thought it was more politically advantageous, which is not a position of principle, is it?'

In February 2021, there were calls from some activists for him to give evidence to a public inquiry into undercover policing, which was set up by the then Home Secretary Theresa May in 2015. They said that he should explain if he was involved in the cover-up of any officers' behaviour while he was DPP for England and Wales between 2008 and 2013. What exactly Starmer knew about the existence and activities of 'spy cops' long before he became DPP also demands a full public explanation which has not, so far, been forthcoming.

By the time the initial McLibel case had been wound up in June 1997, some significant changes had taken place in Starmer's personal life. His long-term girlfriend, Angela O'Brien, with whom he had lived in one capacity or another for the best part of a decade, had moved out of the flat they owned together in Islington. It is understood that Starmer remained there until it was sold in August 1997, for £170,000. By then he was almost thirty-five years old, and he had struck up a relationship with the aforementioned Phillippa Kaufmann. She was four years his junior, and having belonged to the same set since the early 1990s, they had become close over a long period of time. Kaufmann is a well thought of barrister and built her career through specialising in cases relating to prisoners' rights, mental health, inquests and actions against the police. One friend of the couple says O'Brien was rather hurt by the situation.

Another friend adds that by this point in his life, Starmer was devoted to playing football for his team, Homerton Academicals, when he was not watching Arsenal; but football did not prevent him from socialising more widely as well. Several people have claimed that he had 'other girlfriends' besides O'Brien and Kaufmann. Intriguingly, they note that he has always been careful about remaining on good terms with these women. 'He was quite clever at keeping in contact with former girlfriends, so they didn't do anything unpredictable,' says one friend. 'He'd always return their calls.' After he and Kaufmann went public with their relationship, they didn't waste any time in taking things to the next stage, spending £262,500 on a four-bedroom house in Stoke Newington, north London, which they bought together in September 1997.

CHAPTER 7

DOUGHTY STREET

Throughout the 1990s, Doughty Street Chambers established itself as arguably the most forward-thinking and progressive set in London, committed to doing at least 10 per cent of its work pro bono. Initially, it occupied buildings at 10 and 11 Doughty Street, but by the end of the decade it had expanded, needing more space in order to accommodate its growing number of tenants. Its acquisitions included No. 54 in the same terrace. Next door, at No. 56, were the offices of *The Spectator* magazine. In July 1999, a new editor was appointed to the weekly title. This figure, made distinctive by his shock of blond hair, crumpled suit and plummy baritone voice, drew attention to himself in the street in a variety of ways, and Starmer would have been aware of his presence. He was, of course, Boris Johnson. By an amusing quirk of fate, thirteen years after being students in Oxford at the same time, and a little more than twenty years before they faced each other across the despatch box in the House of Commons as Prime Minister and Leader of the Opposition, Johnson and Starmer became what might be called professional neighbours. They remained so for six years, until 2005.

When Johnson was made editor in 1999, he doubled up as the motoring correspondent of *GQ* magazine, and it is in that context rather than for his *Spectator* editorials that he is best remembered by some Doughty Street barristers, who would see and hear him outside their window. 'I certainly knew Johnson was in the same street,' laughs one. 'These extraordinary cars that he had to review would turn up, and he'd be standing there trying to work out how to get into them.' Another Doughty Street member says he can recall almost colliding in his car with Johnson's 'badly ridden' bicycle 'more than once'. As well as staff who worked on *The Spectator*, a procession of the great and the good (and the not-so-good) of British journalism would file regularly into its offices at No. 56 Doughty Street to attend lunches put on by Johnson in the small dining room at the top of the building. Parties were also sometimes thrown on the premises. Starmer was not invited to these gatherings, yet he might have fitted in better at them than he would have assumed. *The Spectator* tended to reflect the libertarian views which its editor then held on sex, drugs, politics and life in general in a way that chimed with some of Starmer's own instincts – including in his attitude to the death penalty, one of the causes on which he has built his reputation.

Doughty Street's head of chambers, Geoffrey Robertson, has long believed that capital punishment is an outrage. By the time Starmer became a barrister, Robertson had spent years working on death-penalty cases, and he encouraged Starmer to develop his own interest in this area, tutoring him along the way. The reason they chose to devote time to this aspect of law is that, in a hangover from the days of the British Empire, the Judicial Committee of the Privy Council in London still hears death-penalty cases from various Commonwealth countries as well as UK overseas territories, Crown dependencies and military sovereign base areas. Although there appears to be an inherent contradiction in Britain, where the death penalty for murder was abolished in 1965, being the final arbiter on matters of life and death in corners of the globe where it once ruled, no replacement for this system has been agreed on. This gives British lawyers who are so inclined a genuine opportunity to defend those who face the death penalty. Another Doughty Street barrister with a long-standing interest in capital punishment cases, who is also credited as having been a mentor to Starmer, is Edward Fitzgerald. Blessed with a formidable intellect and great charisma, he is often spoken of within the Bar and across the judiciary as a legal giant of his generation. Rather appropriately, Fitzgerald is married to Rebecca Fraser, a granddaughter of the Earl of Longford, the late social reformer and Labour politician who spent much of his life backing unpopular causes.

Having talked to various lawyers while researching this book, it would be fair to say that Robertson and Fitzgerald are probably the two legal figures to whom Starmer owes most in a professional sense. The Labour peer Helena Kennedy was also his champion. It never does anybody any harm to have friends in high places, and Starmer is no exception. Yet the questions must be asked: why did this trio develop a soft spot for Starmer? And to what extent was their patronage warranted? Speaking on condition of anonymity, one person who knows Robertson and Fitzgerald says that they didn't just promote Starmer during his time at Doughty Street; they 'over-promoted' him by involving him in cases which enhanced his reputation, perhaps in the main because it suited them as much as it suited him. The upshot of this, in this person's opinion, was that Starmer 'began to believe the hype which went with his over-promotion'.

Robertson, Fitzgerald and Kennedy had all known Starmer since his days at 1 Dr Johnson's Buildings and found him to be competent and diligent. But was he in the top rank, as many newspaper profiles seem to suggest? This person says:

> I don't know why, but they picked Keir as a shining star and gave him preferential treatment. He was the blue-eyed boy. Take Ed Fitzgerald. He is a genuine human rights lawyer of

> the best kind, motivated by his Catholic beliefs, a really decent guy. He used Keir as a junior in lots of death-penalty cases. But I think you'd struggle to find one in which Keir appeared as the advocate, as opposed to junior counsel. He just used to sit behind Ed. All the puff about Keir's death-penalty work ignores the fact that he was mainly in trade for somebody else. I think they picked Keir because he could draft. He was a useful gopher. I also think Keir was politically manoeuvring. We all do that, figuring out how one case will generate more work. It's part of the prostitution of the Bar.

This may be a slightly harsh downgrading of Starmer's efforts in capital punishment cases in an overall sense, but the available court reports do suggest that it is broadly correct: Starmer tended to be the junior counsel rather than the advocate on his feet.

A second person with solid insights into Starmer's legal career agrees, saying:

> Although Keir wrote books about miscarriages of justice, he did not do much jury advocacy, and this shows. He does not 'do' passion very well. He has no orator's ability to use emotion or humour. His real ability as an advocate came from his writing down of his case for judges – so-called skeleton arguments – which were so persuasive that they tipped them in his favour before the hearing. Then he would flesh them out with polite, often low-key arguments which were persuasive and not rhetorical. He never had to raise his voice or his hand to make a good point. In the High Court and the appeal courts, this is an important skill. Less so in the House of Commons, although I've noticed he has been working better in the House on showing his emotions and trying the odd joke.

A third figure who saw him in action as an advocate comments more bluntly:

> Fundamentally, he's dull as hell. His submissions were timid. He was reluctant to take a difficult point that might be very significant. He tended to go down the path of least resistance. It was compromise rather than confrontation. It was all derivative and regurgitated. It was an attempt to make a virtue out of blandness. I have a horrible feeling part of his success was based on the idea that he looks the part subliminally. That's one of the tricks of the light with Keir. He looks like a matinee idol with that coiffed hair, but in reality he's like the deputy manager of the local branch of Barclays Bank.

And another legal figure from his Doughty Street days recalls:

> I always thought he was just a political wet, basically. For most of the time no one gave him responsibility. They just gave him bits and pieces to do. His practice was very run of the mill. The only interesting cases he did were as a junior to Geoffrey or Edward.

It is worth adding at this point that in August 2008, after twenty-one years at the Bar, it was calculated that although Starmer had appeared a grand total of seventeen times before the House of Lords and in the European Court of Human Rights, he had for the most part done so as junior counsel, perhaps reflecting an acceptance on his part that his powers of oratory have never been as impressive as those of other barristers.

Ken Macdonald, who preceded Starmer as DPP, first met him in the late 1980s, when they both worked as criminal barristers and moved in similar circles. Although they were never close friends, they did undertake a couple of cases together, and their paths crossed quite regularly. He broadly concurs that Starmer's abilities were chiefly to be found in the written rather than the spoken word. 'He's very forensic, clear, logical, rational and likes to take things in stages,' says Macdonald.

> That's how he was as a lawyer. The thing about Keir in a case was he was always very thoroughly prepared. He always knew the facts. He knew the law. And he would have a strategy. He would work out a case strategy in advance, and he would stick to it. I think what you see of him in politics is very similar to the way he was in law. He wasn't flamboyant. There were no great flights of oratory. There were no purple passages, none of that kind of stuff. It's a modern style of advocacy, actually. Giving great passionate speeches is a thing of the past. You have a much more conversational relationship with the court and the jury now. I'd say he was respected by judges because they thought he was smart and well-prepared and straight. He was never slippery. He didn't fall out with his opponents. He didn't push poor arguments. He didn't try to mislead a court about what the balance of the authorities was. He was very straight. He was clever and well-regarded as a barrister.

Yet another ex-colleague scoffs at this. 'He lacked the courage, vision and imagination that's necessary to make a great lawyer in the field of human rights law,' says this person.

> He always took the path of least resistance in trying to please the court rather than openly pushing points of genuine challenge. I can't think of a single case in the development of English human rights law in which he played a significant role. I may be wrong, but that was my experience.

• • •

Many will wonder what the motivation is for taking on cases in which a barrister appears to be defending the indefensible, by representing a murderer, for example. Edward Fitzgerald has represented a range of hated and controversial figures, including the child killer Mary Bell; the Moors Murderer Myra Hindley; and convicted terrorist Abu Hamza. Starmer's own death-penalty work has involved clients who were convicted of some equally shocking crimes. The simple answer as to why lawyers like Fitzgerald and Starmer take on such causes is, as noted in Chapter 5, the so-called cab-rank rule. When Geoffrey Robertson established the set in 1990, he was (and remains) adamant that every barrister should follow this rule, meaning that they must represent any client – regardless of their identity or the nature of the case – if the instruction falls within their field of practice and as long as they have the requisite experience and availability to do so. It is also undeniable that barristers like Fitzgerald and Starmer believe in the right to a fair trial. 'It would be terrible if we stopped defending people because they're unpopular,' Fitzgerald once said, adding that 'the legal process is an attempt to civilise our emotions of revenge. Anything that's against lynch law seems to me to be a good thing.' These are sentiments which undoubtedly trumped any desire on Starmer's part to make large sums of money. Had he wanted to, he probably could have done so, however. 'He did a lot of pro bono work,' says Macdonald.

> He did a lot of death-penalty work. He did a lot of low-paid work. He was clever enough to be anything he wanted to be. He could have been a commercial silk earning millions a year, but he chose the public law, civil liberties, human rights route, which is less well paid. It's not badly paid but it's not

> the commercial chancery law division at all. There were people who were real stars in the area. People like Ed Fitzgerald. You wouldn't say that he was in that league, but he was a successful, well-regarded public law barrister and a well-respected public law silk.

An ex-Doughty Street barrister backs this up. 'I'm sure he earned a lot compared to the national average, but not in barrister's terms,' he says.

> I think he did a lot which was unpaid because he believed in the cause, as did a number of people at Doughty Street. It had a very different attitude to other chambers. Barristers don't work for nothing, of course. Even a badly paid Doughty Street barrister earns far more money than most people. It's a relative thing. It's probably that he could have earned a lot of money rather than that he didn't earn a lot.

As a self-employed barrister, Starmer was also free to take on as much work as he wished, meaning he could work for long periods without a holiday if it came to it. With the legal aid budget having risen to £2 billion by 2009, a cost met by taxpayers, there certainly would have been opportunities for a barrister like Starmer to have kept the financial side of his life ticking over.

By the time the McLibel case had ended in 1997, Starmer had already embarked on various death-penalty projects. Some of this work required him to visit overseas territories. In order to practise abroad, he had to be admitted to a particular jurisdiction's Bar. One such application, to practise in Belize, ended in embarrassment for him. Records dating from October 1997 show that both he and Edward Fitzgerald were forced to appeal to the Supreme Court for an order to be enrolled as attorneys-at-law under the Legal Profession Act, as was necessary. Under this appeal, Fitzgerald was admitted; Starmer, however, was not. 'The case of Keir Starmer is different,' wrote the Supreme Court in its judgment. 'With an LL.B and a BCL from Oxford he clearly has received adequate training in law.' But, the judgment went on:

> With seven years of practice and appearances as junior in three appeals from Jamaica before the Judicial Committee it cannot be said that there is sufficient evidence of his competence to practise law in Belize. He has written a book on the legal protection of internationally recognised fundamental rights and freedoms, but this need not require any significant study and familiarity with Belize law. Accordingly, in the case of Mr Keir Starmer, I would dismiss his appeal.

It would be a further five years before he was admitted to the Bar of Belize, though in 1997 he was successfully admitted to the Bar of St Lucia and the Bar of St Vincent.

Alongside his own interest in natural justice, much of Starmer's death-penalty work came about as a result of his association with a London-based campaigning group called the Death Penalty Project, which was set up by two lawyers, Saul Lehrfreund and Parvais Jabbar, and which offers free legal representation to those on death row. Through this, Starmer travelled widely. He played a part in advising a class action in Uganda in 2005 which ultimately overturned the death penalty there and, it is claimed, saved the lives of 417 people. He was also involved in obtaining a Privy Council ruling in 2006 that the mandatory death penalty in the Bahamas is unconstitutional. This was achieved when he defended two convicted murderers, Trono Davis and Forrester Bowe, who had been automatically sentenced to death for their crimes. (Separately to his original conviction, Bowe was part of a gang that allegedly murdered a prison guard called Dion Bowles during a prison break in January 2006, shortly before the Privy Council ruling. Bowe died of natural causes in prison in 2014.) Starmer also advised legal teams in Malawi which campaigned to end the automatic death penalty for all death row prisoners in that country. The success of this was evident when, in 2007, the High Court of Malawi declared that the death sentences on all prisoners on death row were unconstitutional.

Not every death-penalty case ended so well as far as Starmer was concerned, however. In December 2001, a BBC newsreader called Lynette Lithgow Pearson was killed in Trinidad at the age of fifty-one, along with her 83-year-old mother and her 59-year-old brother-in-law. All had their throats slit. Daniel Agard and Lester Pittman were convicted of this triple murder. In 2003, the Privy Council ruled that Trinidad's mandatory death penalty for murder convictions was unconstitutional, but, in July 2004, it reversed this ruling, leading Starmer, who had been closely involved in the case, to comment:

> The majority in the Privy Council have taken a step wholly inconsistent with that court's usual, enlightened, approach to human rights. Those charged with implementing the criminal law in Trinidad and Barbados will now be forced to apply laws which are universally acknowledged to be inhuman. The constitutions of Trinidad and of Barbados were intended to be read so as to protect human rights, not to deny them. The ruling is bitterly disappointing both for those on death row and more generally for the development of the law in the Caribbean.

Nonetheless, Starmer continued to campaign against the death penalty. In September 2018, he visited Taiwan for four days to lobby against it. His trip, which included meetings with senior

Taiwanese politicians, was conducted with the support of the Foreign Office, a department which he got to know during some of the New Labour government's peak years, having served as a member of the Foreign Secretary's advisory panel on the death penalty between 2002 and 2008. This brought him into contact with those who held this post during those years: Jack Straw, Margaret Beckett and David Miliband.

During the 1990s and for most of the first decade of the twenty-first century, Starmer took on a wide range of work involving matters other than the death penalty. His well-publicised commitment to human rights law guaranteed that his practice attracted more high-profile and professionally satisfying endeavours of its own volition. In January 2020, he produced a video to announce his intention to stand for the Labour leadership. A significant portion of the film included commentary about his legal career. This was hardly surprising given that he was a lawyer for much longer than he has been an MP, but there is no doubt that he sought to make political capital by emphasising the cases which he took on behalf of the underdog. From the printworkers at Wapping in 1987 to the National Union of Mineworkers in 1992, to the McLibel case of the mid-1990s, many of what he considered his greatest legal hits were trumpeted in order to present the would-be leader in the most appealing light, as he declared, 'I have spent my life fighting for justice, standing up for the powerless and against the powerful.' Most candidates in his position would, of course, have done this as well, but it is interesting that some cases with which he has been associated – and which were Doughty Street's meat and drink as the 'go-to' chambers for this kind of work – were not mentioned in this film. To what extent their omission was deliberate is a matter for Starmer himself, though it is fair to say that many members of the public would not necessarily appreciate what the cab-rank rule is, nor, indeed, would every layman comprehend some of the more subtle legal arguments which help a lawyer to build a case for the defence. Nevertheless, it is worth going over some of these overlooked cases to gain a greater understanding of what Starmer's legal experience at the 'pink end' of the Bar has entailed.

In 2000, he was part of a team headed by Edward Fitzgerald which represented Khalid Al-Fawwaz, a London-based Saudi dissident who was fighting extradition to America on charges relating to the 1998 bombing of the US embassies in Kenya and Tanzania in which 224 people died. Starmer and his colleagues argued – unsuccessfully – that Al-Fawwaz's actions in connection to the bombings did not constitute a prima facie case of conspiracy. Al-Fawwaz appealed, the protracted appeal process enabling him ultimately to stay in Britain until 2012. The cost of such a legal fight was vast. In September 2001, it was estimated by officials at the Lord Chancellor's department that Al-Fawwaz, who had claimed political asylum in Britain in 1994 but who remained a Saudi citizen, had received £1 million in legal aid by that point alone. In retrospect, it is no wonder that Starmer did not enlighten viewers of his campaign video of the principled stand he helped to create on behalf of Al-Fawwaz. Many – and probably most – British taxpayers would not approve of the generosity shown to this man and his lawyers. On top of his massive legal bill, though, Al-Fawwaz was later found to have run the London office of the terror group al-Qaeda and used Britain as a base for arranging interviews with western media on behalf of its founder, Osama bin Laden. Al-Fawwaz is currently serving life in an American prison.

In January 2001, Starmer was part of a team that represented a group of armed prisoners who had escaped from HMP Whitemoor in Cambridgeshire in 1994. Prison officer John Kettleborough was shot in the ribs on the night of the breakout.

He survived. Years later, however, the absconders, including two former IRA prisoners, launched a legal battle for £50,000 each in damages over injuries sustained during the breakout. One of the IRA men was Gilbert 'Danny' McNamee, who had been jailed for the 1982 Hyde Park bombing. His conviction was later quashed. The other was Liam McCotter, who had been jailed in June 1988 for conspiracy to cause explosions. Both claimed they were unlawfully assaulted while being recaptured. They were granted legal aid to launch the proceedings against the Home Office, together with Andrew Russell, an armed robber. The action cost taxpayers more than £500,000. Ultimately, McNamee was awarded £5,000 and Russell was awarded £2,500 in damages. McCotter's claim was dismissed.

In June 2002, Starmer defended a man who was to feature in a BBC 2 documentary called *The Hunt for Britain's Paedophiles*. The man, whose identity is unknown, had pleaded guilty the previous year to offences involving possession and distribution of pornographic pictures of children and had been placed under a three-year community rehabilitation order with a condition of treatment. This resulted in his face being shown on camera for about three minutes when the documentary was being made. Claiming his client would be at risk of physical attack if his face were broadcast in an identifiable form, Starmer made an emergency application to the High Court asking for the man's face to be obscured. Ultimately, this was rejected by Mr Justice Ouseley.

Another brief that was absent from Starmer's campaign video came in February 2003, when he represented five asylum seekers in a test case at the High Court. There, it was decided by Mr Justice Collins that the Labour government's new policy of denying refugees food and shelter if they did not make an asylum claim in Britain as soon as reasonably practicable, and preferably on arrival at a British airport, was illegal. David Blunkett was the Home

Secretary who had introduced the new rule because of mounting concerns that Britain had become a soft touch for refugees, with at least 6,500 applications each month at an annual cost to taxpayers in welfare benefits alone of £1 billion. Blunkett was livid about the ruling at the time but was more sanguine when asked about it for the purposes of this book. 'This was where we'd tried to avoid people hanging about in the country, having a job and then claiming asylum,' Blunkett recalls. 'It was to try and stop people who'd clearly not declared they were refugees when they first arrived.' When asked about Starmer's involvement in the case, Blunkett says:

> The old adage is they [barristers] are like a taxi queue. They take the case that is top of the queue. And they always stick to that, right or wrong. We lost because Andrew Collins, who was the judge, was on a mission to determine that the judiciary should be able to strike down government actions on immigration. I felt exactly the same as I felt on a number of occasions when I lost a judgment in the eight years I was in Cabinet. I was cheesed off that that's the way our system works.

At the time of the judgment, Starmer gave an interview to *The Times* in which he was asked to explain the wider implications of the case. He said:

> First, there is the development of the notion of dignity and humanity in our law. It doesn't matter whether the foundation of that notion is the European Convention on Human Rights or the common law, it is simply unacceptable in a civilised society to prevent a vulnerable group of individuals from working, to exclude them from the welfare benefits system and then to

deprive them of a roof over their heads and of food. The other, wider, implication concerns the relationship between the government and the judiciary. Like many others, I was shocked at the personalised and ill-informed response of the government and some of the press to Mr Justice Collins's judgment.

In 2003, Starmer also represented Colin Richards, an armed robber who had held up two post offices in Essex before murdering a policeman, Acting Sgt Brian Bishop, at Frinton-on-Sea in August 1984. Richards was sentenced in 1985 on a tariff set at seventeen years which expired in September 2001. The Parole Board recommended him for release in November 2001, but he was not freed until August 2002, leading to him seeking compensation for the 'extra' period in which he was incarcerated. Ultimately, this was denied.

In March 2006, Starmer acted for Hilal al-Jedda, who held dual British and Iraqi nationality and who was suspected of recruiting terrorists to Iraq, where he was held in a British facility in Basra for eight months. He was also detained for helping a known terrorist travel to Iraq and conspiring with him to target coalition forces around Fallujah and Baghdad and was further thought to have conspired with an Islamist terror cell in the Gulf to smuggle detonation equipment into Iraq. In 2007, the House of Lords ruled his detention was lawful, but that ruling was later overturned by the European courts. It is noteworthy that in this case, Starmer was instructed by a firm called Public Interest Lawyers, which was run by a left-wing solicitor called Phil Shiner. Shiner made a fortune over a period of years by using legal aid to sue the Ministry of Defence over alleged misdeeds by British troops in Iraq. His reputation suffered lasting damage when he was struck off the roll of solicitors in 2017 after the Solicitors

Regulation Authority found him guilty of professional misconduct of a 'criminal standard'. He had claimed falsely that British soldiers murdered and tortured hundreds of civilians during the Iraq War.

In 2006 and 2007, Starmer represented three people in separate cases whose identities were not revealed but whose profiles attracted the attention of British authorities at a time of heightened concern for national security. One was a Tunisian asylum seeker who had a control order imposed for his membership of the Tunisian Islamic Front. The second was an Islamist extremist who attempted to travel to Iraq to fight against coalition forces. The third was an immigration case involving an Algerian national who was a follower of the radical Egyptian cleric Abu Hamza at the Finsbury Park Mosque (the latter of whom is now serving life in an American prison after being found guilty of various terrorism charges). Starmer also wrote a piece for the *Socialist Lawyer* in April 2007 which seemed to disapprove of the proposed deportation from Britain of another radical cleric, Abu Qatada, noting that

> the Special Immigration Appeals Commission ruled that it would be lawful, and no breach of Article 3 ECHR, for the government now to deport Abu Qatada to Jordan. Unsurprisingly, that decision was subject to immediate appeal. This flies in the face of the opinion of international human rights bodies and individuals worldwide.

As well as these cases failing to make the final cut of Starmer's promotional video, most of them share another characteristic: namely an adherence to the Human Rights Act 1998. The aim of this Act, which came into force in October 2000, is to incorporate into UK law the rights contained in the European Court of

Human Rights. Its introduction heralded a new legal landscape in which government departments strove to act in a way that was more progressive. One human rights lawyer says:

> I know the Act has had an awful reputation since then and is thought of as the source of all our ills, but then and now it's a very sensible piece of legislation. It has a more objective approach to problems. Until the Act, if a client came to you with a problem, you'd often have to say, 'I know it's unfair, but that's what the law says.' After the Act came in, you could look at the law and, if it produced an unjust result, find a way of penetrating under the body of law to ask yourself questions which the convention demands, like what is the proper balance between the rights of an individual and the rights of society.

Another lawyer, who is in practice as a criminal KC, is more scornful of this entire area of law. 'To call yourself a "human rights lawyer" is absurd,' he says.

> Any defence lawyer involved with defending people or involved with ensuring the rules of natural justice are complied with is in effect a human rights lawyer. All of us are involved in human rights – the human right not to be falsely convicted. Does that make Doughty Street a particularly 'human rights' set of chambers? I don't think it's any more 'human rights' than any of the more traditional sets. It's an American idea, but I suppose it's very nice if you want to talk up your credentials when applying for a Labour seat.

When you consider that the Human Rights Act has led to some highly controversial outcomes, it is hard to disagree. These include the rights of prisoners to give sperm to their wives or girlfriends for artificial insemination being upheld in 2009; the Asylum and Immigration Tribunal in 2007 allowing Learco Chindamo, the teenage killer of London headmaster Philip Lawrence, to remain in Britain despite being born in Italy because 'he has a right to a family life in Britain'; and, in 2004, nine Afghans who hijacked a plane which landed at Stansted Airport in 2000 being allowed to remain in Britain so as not to breach their human rights.

These more extreme examples apart, the late 1990s was a time of change in terms of engaging with the problems that the strict application of the law could create, and human rights was a cause which Starmer took up with energy. It became his specialism. In 1998, he published a book titled *Signing Up for Human Rights: The United Kingdom and International Standards*. That year he also accepted a fellowship of the Human Rights Centre at Essex University. In 1999, he published a 938-page book, *European Human Rights Law*, which one lawyer says archly he 'churned out surprisingly quickly'. That year he also became a member of the council of the campaigning group Justice, which was then run by his Doughty Street colleague and longstanding friend Helena Kennedy. (Incidentally, another board member was Sir Michael Tugendhat, a former High Court judge whose son Tom, a Tory MP, is a friendly acquaintance of Starmer.) In 2000, Starmer became chairman of the Human Rights Act Research Unit at King's College School of Law, London. He was also named the Liberty/Justice Human Rights Lawyer of the Year, being praised by the judges for his work in representing at the Privy Council convicted murderers awaiting execution. As the winner of the main individual prize, he was singled out for his detailed work on making human rights legislation accessible to lawyers and lay-people. There was no mention in the accompanying press reports that he had professional links to the bodies after whom the prize was named – Liberty and Justice – though perhaps there should have been.

In 2000, a new set of chambers was established in London. Called Matrix, it immediately attracted attention because Cherie Blair, wife of the then Prime Minister, Tony Blair, was among its twenty-two founding members. Matrix hit upon the idea of focusing its efforts on the new Human Rights Act, leading many commentators to conclude, perhaps cynically, that those involved were simply cashing in as the new law made its presence felt. As *The Times* reported shortly after the new set's creation:

> Matrix, led by star-studded names, which include the QCs Cherie Booth and Ben Emmerson, the guru on the new Act, is the first concrete spin-off in the profession to come from the forthcoming legislation. It is a clear sign that, despite the benefits the Act will bring – enabling people to pursue breaches of human rights in the English courts for the first time – it is also set to be a lawyers' bonanza.

Emmerson, who is a year younger than Starmer, was a member of Doughty Street Chambers when he left for Matrix. His expertise on the Human Rights Act was apparently derived from the fact that he had advised on its drafting, having spent much of his career taking cases to the European Court of Human Rights at Strasbourg, of which Starmer had less experience. Such was Emmerson's knowledge in the field of human rights that in the late 1990s, he was asked by the Lord Chancellor's department to teach other lawyers, civil servants and even judges in England and Wales about the implications of the new Human Rights Act. Emmerson joined Matrix with another recruit from Doughty Street Chambers, Tim Owen.

Starmer and his girlfriend, Phillippa Kaufmann, were also invited to defect from Doughty Street and join Matrix at this point. One of their former colleagues remembers: 'When Matrix was set up, they were keen to pinch our people. Keir was tempted but didn't go. Those who did go were quite a big loss to Doughty Street.' Another explains: 'When Matrix Chambers came along, with Cherie Blair and other luminaries, they made a big pitch for Keir. They lured two of our silks, but Keir rejected their blandishments. He wanted, he said, to position himself with pioneers rather than opportunists.' Who can say if Starmer came to regret this principled decision, however? For although he chose to remain at Doughty Street with Kaufmann, the pair separated the following year, with Starmer cashing in his £140,000 share of their house in Hackney and moving into a property in Kentish Town, north London, which was owned by Mark Adams, his friend from Reigate Grammar School. One source says his relationship with Kaufmann did not end entirely smoothly, with stories having circulated around chambers of him returning home late at night only to find the front door locked.

It is no exaggeration to say that in the 1990s and early 2000s, Starmer's personal life and professional life became more and more entwined in a way that other people might find suffocating. As described in Chapter 6, his relationship with Angela O'Brien had ended by 1997, and he subsequently took up with Kaufmann. After he and O'Brien had ceased to be an item, she struck up a relationship with one of Starmer's colleagues from Doughty Street Chambers, Hugh Barton, who was the same age and had the same kind of practice as Starmer. Around the time that Starmer and Kaufmann separated, O'Brien and Barton, who are married, moved to the north of England, where they still live happily. Then, even more awkwardly for Starmer, after he and Kaufmann parted ways in 2002, she began a relationship with another Doughty Street colleague of hers and Starmer's, Paul Brooks. Kaufmann and Brooks soon married and had two children. Many people would find it difficult enough that one ex-girlfriend had started seeing one of their colleagues, but for two exes to be involved with co-workers would be too much to bear. Yet Starmer seems to have coped. One person with knowledge of the situation says, 'I'm not sure why it ended between Keir and Phillippa Kaufmann, but there were no hard feelings as far as I know. Keir and Phillippa even continued to work on cases together.'

Starmer has explained that he subsequently dated Julie Morris, an employment lawyer, for three years. Friends who contributed to this book say that he was also close to another woman, Maya Sikand, who was in pupillage at Doughty Street in 1998. He has never spoken about her publicly. 'It was an open secret that Maya was having a relationship with him,' says one contemporary. 'I can remember sitting in a restaurant with some barrister colleagues when Keir sent her a text message and she passed her phone around and showed it to some of those present. She was smitten.' Some of Starmer's acquaintances remain unimpressed with this part of his life, however, with one being particularly scathing. This person says that Starmer and Sikand saw each other 'for years'. They both contributed to a legal textbook, *Blackstone's Criminal Practice 2009*, which was published in 2008. 'Maya still likes him a lot even though his treatment of her left a lot to be desired,' comments this second source. Sikand, who is a KC, has gone on to forge a successful legal career and has been a member of Doughty Street Chambers since 2020.

• • •

In March 2002, Starmer became a QC at the relatively early age of thirty-nine, joining the cadre of senior barristers who are considered the best in their field of practice. A few months later, he was mentioned in an *Observer* profile headlined 'The new legal crusaders', which focused on a group of ambitious lawyers under the age of forty-five with a 'burning desire for justice' who 'defend dissidents and terror suspects'. This article is also noteworthy for the following passage: 'Among them was Ben Emmerson, the dashing young advocate and colleague of Cherie Booth at the fashionable Matrix Chambers. Admirers say that if Colin Firth's human rights lawyer in the film *Bridget Jones's Diary* wasn't based on Emmerson, then it should have been.' These words solve a mystery which has portrayed Starmer in a very useful and flattering light for many years for no reason other than what appears to be sloppy journalism. Starmer was always happy not to disabuse people of the notion that *he* was the inspiration for Mark Darcy, who was created by Helen Fielding, the author of *Bridget Jones's Diary*. As we shall see, though, he never was.

What appears to have happened is that in April 2012, a decade after the *Observer* article was published, a *Sunday Times* journalist called Camilla Long went to interview Starmer. 'Just before my interview with Keir Starmer, the Director of Public Prosecutions (DPP), someone tells me that the chisel-jawed former human rights lawyer was the inspiration for Mr Darcy in *Bridget Jones*,' Long wrote at the time. 'I am not sure if this is true – but I can confirm he is every bit as awkward and tongue-tied as the fictional character.'

From then on, other journalists decided that it *was* true, and the myth held. Starmer never denied it, perhaps relishing the touch of glamour it gave him, though it does appear that he allowed his vanity to get the better of him. For example, in January 2020, during the Labour leadership contest, when ITV News asked him if the Darcy character was based on him, he answered: 'Everybody asks me this question when they should be asking

[Fielding] the question because she knows the answer and I don't. It's a rumour that's been doing the rounds for some years, but I honestly don't know the answer to it.' In the end, it was Fielding herself who explained the truth on *Desert Island Discs* in July 2020, making clear that Starmer played no part in her thinking up Mark Darcy.

While this may seem to be a trivial matter, one friend of Starmer says it is in fact rather revealing. The Starmer whom this person knows apparently paid attention when members of the opposite sex said he was good-looking. 'What's interesting is he knows full well he wasn't the model for Mark Darcy because he's never met Helen Fielding and has nothing to do with her,' says the friend. 'His answers were always designed to suggest it was true, but he knew it was bollocks.' The irony of all this is that in 2019, Hollywood actor Ralph Fiennes, who is a friend of Colin Firth, played Ben Emmerson – whose mention in *The Observer* in 2002 had kicked off the various Mark Darcy rumours – in the film *Official Secrets*. Emmerson was depicted in this thriller for the work he did in support of the GCHQ whistleblower Katharine Gun.

Becoming a QC in 2002 marked a new phase in Starmer's life and he threw himself into work as he took advantage of his enhanced professional standing. When he won his silk status – so called because of the silk gowns QCs wear – he was one of 111 barristers to do so. In those days, the Lord Chancellor's department picked the new silks under a system apparently based on merit, meaning that Starmer was ultimately anointed by the Lord Chancellor at the time, Lord Irvine of Lairg, who had been Tony Blair's pupil master in the 1970s. According to *The Times*, which carried a report about the new elevations, the Law Society, the solicitors' professional body, had attacked the QC system as a 'cartel that sustains a market in high fees', though this had little effect. The newspaper also revealed that the highest paid of the new QCs declared earnings of £705,000 a year, while the lowest paid reported a salary of £64,000, with the average salary of the new QCs being £268,688. Starmer would almost certainly have been earning a healthy six-figure sum by this stage, even if it was not as high as £705,000.

A few years previously, he had worked as a junior on an appeal case which had given him some valuable insights into the post-Belfast Agreement situation in Northern Ireland. This would, in turn, make him the ideal candidate for his first big publicly funded role, which he took up in 2003. In 1999, Starmer was part of a team that defended Private Lee Clegg, a paratrooper who had been convicted in 1993 of the 1990 murder of Karen Reilly. She was the eighteen-year-old backseat passenger in a stolen car which raced through an army checkpoint in Belfast at high speed. Clegg had opened fire on the joyriders with other members of his patrol. The driver, Martin Peake, aged seventeen, had also died. The case became a cause célèbre when Clegg was given a life sentence for Miss Reilly's murder and four years for attempting to wound with intent Mr Peake. Clegg appealed several times and was released on licence in 1995 by the then Northern Ireland Secretary, Sir Patrick Mayhew. This decision infuriated Republicans and Miss Reilly's family, who felt Clegg was shown leniency because he was a soldier. Widespread rioting in Republican areas across the province ensued. After his release, Clegg rejoined the army and launched a further set of appeals which resulted in the murder conviction being overturned in 1998. A retrial was held in March 1999 after new forensic evidence suggested one bullet entered the side of the car. At the retrial, Clegg was cleared of murder, but a conviction for 'attempting to wound' the driver, Martin Peake, was upheld. This gave rise to another appeal in which the lesser conviction was also quashed in January 2000.

According to Starmer's friend Mark Stephens, a solicitor who had instructed Starmer on many cases, some London lawyers threatened to stop giving him work because of his involvement in the Clegg case. 'He was heavily criticised at the time by the unthinking left of the legal village in London,' Stephens has recalled. 'Whereas Keir could see that [Clegg] had rights that were being infringed, and it didn't actually matter who was infringing rights – if you had rights that were taken away then you ought to do something about it. They didn't get that, and Keir did.' It is said that Starmer spent the best part of three months working on the case and would sometimes go to the British garrison to play football with the squaddies. He liked Northern Ireland in spite of its complications and liked to think he understood it. All this would later work in his favour.

Policing in Northern Ireland has long been a contentious issue. Under the terms of the Belfast Agreement of 1998, an independent commission was established under the former governor of Hong Kong, Chris Patten, which made a series of recommendations including the abolition of the existing police force, the Royal Ulster Constabulary. It was renamed the Police Service of Northern Ireland (PSNI) in 2001 and the PSNI Board was established that year. It is an independent public body made up of ten political and nine independent members whose job is to hold the PSNI to account on behalf of all communities in the province. In May 2002, the board held a meeting at which it was agreed that in order to monitor police compliance with the Human Rights Act, a human rights adviser would have to be hired. This paid position was never advertised. Instead, candidates with the requisite expertise were invited to an interview in January 2003. A three-year contract, which might be extended, was on the table for the right person. Starmer got the job, his experience as a human rights lawyer and his work as a consultant to the Association of Chief

Police Officers apparently being the chief reasons that he was chosen.

Initially, he was required to spend a day or two per month in Northern Ireland. He reported to Trevor Reaney, then the chief executive of the Northern Ireland Policing Board. He was the sole human rights adviser to the board, though from 2004 another lawyer, Jane Gordon, was hired as his assistant. Ian Paisley Jr, the son of the founder of the Democratic Unionist Party, the Rev. Ian Paisley, was at the time the member of the Northern Ireland Assembly for North Antrim. He was also a member of the PSNI Board who worked closely with Starmer. Paisley says:

> When Keir Starmer came on, we knew we had a job to do that was seen to be fair, seen to be impartial, that was able to appeal across the communities so we could say the PSNI is a perfectly legitimate force, and it's perfectly legitimate to serve us. We needed a defence line that allowed us to say, 'We acknowledge human rights issues, that's why we do this, this is how we police' and so on. We saw his role as providing the support to allow us to make the case about the human rights record of the police, so we could say here's our defence line, and he helped us provide that.

The job entailed Starmer attending a monthly meeting, giving briefings to the board, preparing board members for interviews and providing human rights training support on matters over which they had to hold the police to account. Paisley says:

> If the police did something and there was a question about it, we would know these were the probe lines we would have to go down to get satisfactory answers. We would hold the police to account by being a good critical friend and making sure they had growing community support.

Although the role was primarily a desk job, the police did take Starmer on patrol to give an insight into some of the issues they faced and to show the line that must be negotiated between the divided loyalist and nationalist communities. 'Every action has to be authorised by Gold or Silver Command and consistent with human rights regulations,' says Paisley.

> People like him, pushing a pen, looking at these things from the safety and comfort of an office is very different from being on the ground. I've seen it from all sides, and you get a real sense that it's a difficult and nail-biting job for those in command because of the split-second decisions they have to take.

Starmer has spoken of one close shave he experienced while he occupied this post. The Orange Order marches held on 12 July every year to mark the victory of William of Orange over James II at the Battle of the Boyne in 1690 attract large crowds and have in the past led to sectarian violence. 'I was on the ground sometimes outside the Ardoyne shopfronts in North Belfast on 12 July when the parades were happening, there were all sorts of things happening on the ground,' he recalled. 'We were there with our clipboards observing what was going on and suddenly golf balls were being thrown and there were petrol bombs and I was thrown in the back of a police van for safety.'

Situations like this cemented his awareness that a balance had to be struck in Northern Ireland. For this reason, Starmer was apparently scrupulous about keeping his counsel at all times and never talked about politics in Westminster or elsewhere. 'I only ever engaged with him professionally,' says Paisley.

> I had no social life with him. There was no after-work drinks party. I found him to be a consummate professional. I can't

> say he put a foot wrong in his engagement with us. He didn't engage in social chit-chat or show any inquisitiveness. He just did the job, which was perhaps unusual given the length of time he was there.

Asked whether he was well liked, Paisley is happy to confirm that he was. 'He was professional and reassuring in terms of how he did the job. I never heard a word of criticism about him from other colleagues of other parties or from independent members. So he kept his nose very clean and was scrupulous about that.' Paisley added that he had no knowledge of the Haldane Society trip to Northern Ireland which Starmer had led in 1991, referred to in Chapter 6. As previously mentioned, its subsequent report, 'Upholding the Rule of Law?', stated in its introduction: 'We call for British withdrawal [from Northern Ireland].' It remains unclear whether those who appointed Starmer knew about it either when they appointed him or at any point during the four years he held the PSNI Board job.

Yet his legacy is secure, as far as Paisley is concerned:

> In terms of hard policing and the force of hard policing, he gave us the tools and the arguments and the defence lines to allow us to say that water cannon are necessary or plastic bullets are allowed. They are still permissible today, as shown in the riots of April 2021. And all police officers in Northern Ireland carry a gun. The argument for retaining this was defended. I would say his lasting legacy is that you can have all of these accoutrements to policing provided they meet human rights guidelines efficiently, and he provided the board with the arguments to do that and the legal cover to do it. If the police had been using them without cover, I can imagine the board would have faced inquiries every day.

It was at this time that Starmer embarked on a new relationship with Victoria Alexander, a London-based solicitor eleven years his junior. She is the daughter of a Jewish accountant, Bernard Alexander, whose family came from Poland, and a Yorkshire-born doctor, Barbara Moyes, who converted to Judaism. She grew up in north London and went to the fee-paying Channing School for Girls in Highgate, where she is understood to have taken politics at A-Level and to have been left-leaning as a teenager. She qualified as a solicitor in 2001 and worked for the London firm Hodge Jones & Allen before later retraining in occupational health, in which capacity she now works in the NHS. She and Starmer met in 2005, apparently when she was preparing case files for him before he went into court. Starmer has recalled:

> The bundles of documents in front of me had to be 100 per cent accurate. I phoned up to check and said: 'This schedule, is it any good? Is it absolutely accurate?' She quite indignantly, quite rightly, said: 'Absolutely.' She says she then put the phone down and said: 'Who the fuck does he think he is?'

This encounter was the prelude to their first date at the Lord Stanley pub off the Camden Road in north London. They married in May 2007 on the Fennes Estate in Essex and started their honeymoon in Belfast before touring the whole island of Ireland. Aged forty-four, it is true to say that Starmer was fairly long in the tooth to be embarking on his first marriage, perhaps reflecting the rather complicated love life he had had up until this point. One who knows the couple says that they have a tight circle of friends in north London, many of whom are left-wing lawyers, but of Victoria they say: 'It's not clear if she realised when she married Keir that she was going to become a politician's wife.'

The couple, who are both vegetarian, began their married

life in the four-bedroom terraced house in Kentish Town which Starmer had acquired with a mortgage for £650,000 in April 2004. Within months of their wedding, there was a management shake-up at Doughty Street Chambers in which Starmer became joint head of chambers with Geoffrey Robertson in April 2008. By then, it had ninety barristers and Robertson needed somebody with whom he could share the organisational burden. Peter Thornton, who left to become Chief Coroner of England and Wales, had done the job previously, and Starmer replaced him unopposed. In the event, he would not be in this post for long, however. Having always wanted to be more than just a barrister, he soon had his sights set on an altogether different role, which just happened to be one of the biggest jobs in the public sector.

CHAPTER 8

THE CONTROVERSIAL PROSECUTION SERVICE

In February 2009, a businesswoman called Penelope Edwards placed an advertisement in the Encounters section of the *Sunday Times* which read: 'Amazonian professional, forty-one, intelligent, gorgeous, vivacious, enjoys swimming, travel, driving fast, seeks spontaneous, caring, well-spoken professional for loving relationship.' Perhaps surprisingly, Ms Edwards was not inundated with responses to this message from other lonely hearts, but within a couple of months one reaction did catch her eye. It was from a man who described himself as a 'successful barrister, fit, very spontaneous, looking for relationship'. She texted her phone number to the respondent and before long he rang her, introducing himself as Keir Starmer of the Crown Prosecution Service. They arranged a date. Not having heard of Starmer before, Ms Edwards hunted for a photograph of him online and considered him to be good-looking. As DPP, the third highest-ranking public prosecutor in England and Wales, he was also clearly very successful. When he showed up as agreed at a car park in Windsor on 19 April bearing a bouquet of flowers and a bottle of pink champagne, nothing seemed untoward, and they enjoyed lunch together by the Thames.

The relationship progressed rapidly over a very short space of time and might have become serious but for one thing: this man was not Starmer at all. He was, in fact, a Northamptonshire hairdresser turned serial conman called Paul Bint who had at that time more than 150 convictions to his name, having passed himself off previously as a banker, an aristocrat, a police officer, a ballet dancer and a property tycoon. Worse still for Ms Edwards, it later transpired that at the same time as he was seeing her, he had tricked another woman, Vivienne Walsh, into believing he was a criminal barrister called Jonathan Rees. His deception was discovered when he told a taxi driver he could not pay a £60 fare because his wallet had been stolen. He asked that the bill should be sent to his place of work. When no money was forthcoming, the furious driver went to the offices of the DPP to complain and had to be placated by the secretary of the real Starmer, who is the same age as Bint. From that point, the charade quickly disintegrated, and the wheels of justice began to turn swiftly. In November 2009, Bint was jailed for three years at Southwark Crown Court after being found guilty of fraud and theft.

Starmer has dined out on this rather surreal story ever since, often quipping publicly that when Bint was arrested, the question arose of whether he should be prosecuted. Starmer, being the DPP, realised immediately that he could not be party to this decision, though his sense of humour did allow him to ask jokingly whether Bint was pleading guilty, whether he was still claiming to be Starmer, and, if acquitted, where he – Starmer – would stand from a legal point of view. 'During the trial it was put to one of the women [Bint] had an affair with that he didn't look particularly like me,' Starmer also laughed on *Desert Island Discs*. 'To which, if I'm right in recalling, she said: "Well, everybody can have an off day."' It is certainly true that Bint resembles Starmer only faintly.

Some people have expressed surprise that Starmer should have been appointed to the exalted post of DPP. On paper, the man who was known for challenging government decisions on the grounds of human rights was not necessarily the natural choice to take on the responsibility of bringing to court most criminal prosecutions in England and Wales. So how did he come to take on this role, in which he was effectively ceasing to be a poacher and becoming a gamekeeper? Before answering this question, it is important to establish what the CPS is and what the responsibilities of the DPP are.

Until 1986, when the CPS was created, criminal prosecutions in England and Wales were brought by individual police forces or county solicitors. Its establishment meant that the business of prosecuting crime fell to regional CPS offices, each of which was split into specialist divisions, such as counter-terrorism, fraud, serious organised crime and so on. The CPS does not have the power to investigate crime. Instead, it considers evidence that has been gathered by police and other agencies and determines whether a suspect should face criminal charges. When deciding whether somebody should go to court or not, crown prosecutors must consider if there is sufficient evidence to provide a realistic prospect of a conviction and whether or not a prosecution is in the public interest.

Alongside this gatekeeping function, it has responsibility for preparing cases, for prosecuting them before a court and for reviewing them if new evidence materialises. As the head of the CPS, the DPP ranks behind only the Attorney General and the Solicitor General on the list of senior public prosecutors in England and Wales. The relationship between the DPP and the government is one of superintendence, meaning that the Attorney General answers for the DPP in Parliament but the DPP's decision-making is independent of the Attorney General. The Attorney General does have some powers of intervention, but they should be used only *in extremis*. The DPP is ultimately in charge of between 6,000 and 7,000 members of CPS staff working in offices around the country, who oversee an estimated 800,000 prosecutions every year, making the job as bureaucratic as it is legal. The DPP can also have some influence over the development of criminal justice policy, acting in concert with the Home Secretary and the Justice Secretary.

Starmer's route to this role began on 18 May 2008, when an advertisement seeking a new DPP appeared in the Appointments section of the *Sunday Times*. The same advert was subsequently placed in *The Times* and *The Lawyer*. Prospective candidates were given three weeks to apply. They had to supply a covering letter and a CV and complete a diversity form, and then submit to a round of interviews. Ken Macdonald was the incumbent DPP at this point, having been appointed in 2003. He was the first person to take on the job under Tony Blair's Labour government, and it is generally accepted that in doing so, he broke the mould. Until his elevation, the DPP had always been a career prosecutor. Macdonald, a longstanding criminal barrister, was best known as a defence lawyer. It was said that the Labour government had wanted to take a new approach to criminal justice when he was appointed, triggering accusations from some quarters of political interference. Whatever the truth of that matter, Macdonald effectively cleared the path for Starmer – or anybody else with limited prosecutorial experience – to succeed him. At the time that Starmer applied to be DPP, Labour was still in power, this time with Gordon Brown in Downing Street, and appointing another defence specialist would certainly be less controversial than it had been five years previously.

Details released under the Freedom of Information Act confirm that eighteen people applied to become DPP in 2008. One person with knowledge of the process says that the field was 'weak' and Starmer was quickly identified as being the pick of a poor crop. The £195,000 salary, which is relatively low by the standards of what can be earned by Britain's top legal minds, is one possible reason why the post did not attract higher-calibre individuals. Another is the fact that those who become DPP know that in taking on this job they are effectively bringing down the curtain on their career as a lawyer. One of Starmer's former colleagues says:

> It's not a job you take if you've got a good practice and you're enjoying yourself at the Bar. There's always a pay-off if you become DPP. Everybody knows it's a public service, but it's a miserable thing to do. So afterwards you either become a High Court judge or get a peerage. Keir would have got a peerage if he hadn't wanted to become Prime Minister. There was talk he might become Labour's shadow Lord Chancellor after he'd done his term as DPP, which would have put him in the Lords, but it was clear he didn't want that because he wanted to become Prime Minister, so he had to be in the Commons.

It is obvious that in accepting the job, Starmer knew it was a stepping-stone to Westminster.

Having sifted through the covering letters and CVs, the interview team invited all eighteen candidates to attend a technical interview. They were then whittled down to the four best contenders. One withdrew, leaving the remaining three to be evaluated by an occupational psychologist and to undertake a mock media interview. They then attended a final formal interview, with a selection panel comprising the then Attorney General Baroness Scotland; senior judge Sir Brian Leveson; the then permanent secretary to the Ministry of Justice Sir Sumantra Chakrabarti; and a fourth figure called Philip Oliver. Starmer was announced as the new DPP in July 2008, and he began the job three months later, shortly after celebrating his forty-sixth birthday. Recently married (his wife had by this point ceased to be a lawyer) and with his first child, Toby, only a few months old, this was the domestic backdrop to what was surely the most challenging and demanding work he had ever done to that point. His daughter, Lara, was born in November 2010, almost midway through his five-year contract as DPP, making further calls on his time and energy. Perhaps the only real perks of the job were that he had a car, a chauffeur and a generous pension.

'I don't know if anyone else encouraged him to apply for the post, but I was pleased when he expressed an interest in doing it because I thought he'd do it well,' says his predecessor Ken Macdonald, who now sits in the House of Lords as a crossbencher.

> It is highly burdensome. It's quite a powerful position; there's a lot of accountability to ministers, to the Prime Minister, to the government, to the public. All of that weighs on you to an extent. Apart from that, it's about running quite a large organisation of several thousand lawyers, who aren't the easiest people to manage. Running public organisations is frustrating at times. There are quite a lot of issues of morality and competence to deal with. You tend to get the blame when anything goes wrong. Some prosecutor could be sitting in Manchester making some stupid decision which two days later is on the front page of the *Daily Mail*, and you get the blame for it. That can be quite frustrating. You have to be able to take all of that. You have to develop a thick skin.

It says something about Starmer's cautious instincts that he opted to spend his first few months as DPP travelling the country to review the way the CPS functions. This certainly suggests that he entered this very prominent position in public life well aware of its potential pitfalls and concerned not to put a foot wrong. One figure who has followed Starmer's career closely has a rather more cynical interpretation of what he thought this might achieve, however:

> As soon as Keir was appointed, he immediately set about announcing he would visit every CPS area in the country on a listening tour, which struck me as a useless waste of time because that was not a systemised way of obtaining information, it was a way of trying to make himself seem popular. Ken Macdonald was loved by the CPS staff and no doubt Keir wanted to emulate that, but what a massive effort and what a massive waste of resources when he should have been checking the systems in a way that would enable issues to be brought to his attention – issues that needed his attention. You're not there to go around doing a roadshow. I thought that was odd.

This is, of course, just one point of view, but Ken Macdonald also acknowledges that Starmer adopted what might be described as a rather technical approach to the job. 'Keir was certainly interested in policy,' he observes.

> Keir's very interested in process. I think you can see that in his political life. He's very interested in how things work and how to make them work better, so he was much more focused as DPP than I was on the processes of decision-making: how were people making decisions; how can we get them to make decisions better? You tend to have one great theme as DPP. Mine was to try and get the CPS lawyers into court arguing their own cases rather than using independent barristers the whole time, because I thought that would make it a more exciting job and we'd be able to recruit better people. His was developing what he called 'core standards', so he was trying to work out what are the core standards that we should be applying

> in various stages of our work, and how can we guarantee that those standards are met. So his approach to the job was quite process-driven. It was similar to the way he did his cases – process-driven and careful and taking it stage by stage. I think you see that in his approach to politics quite clearly.

It wasn't just CPS staff whom Starmer wanted to get to know. Nazir Afzal, who worked as a director of the CPS in London in 2008, recalls Starmer asking him to go on a meet-and-greet-style outing shortly after he took on the DPP role. This was part of a strategy to make the CPS better known to the public. It eventually became clear to Afzal that the event to which he was invited had been organised by somebody who was already very well known to Starmer – and who had nothing to do with his work. For the purposes of this book, Afzal shared unpublished excerpts of an interview which he gave to a journalist in March 2021. He says:

> Within a couple of weeks of [Starmer] arriving in 2008, I got a call from him [Starmer] saying, 'Come with me, we need to go to this school and talk to them about the CPS.' I thought, 'Fine.' There was me geared up to go to this school in north London and expecting to talk to A-Level students about constitutional law or separation of powers and finding myself in a primary school with forty six- and seven-year-olds. The conversation was all about whether I sat in a police car, what's a good guy and what's a bad guy. Literally, it was at that level. But it was enriching to hear that conversation and the teachers were there. It was only afterwards that I learned [Starmer's] sister-in-law was a teacher at that school. She facilitated the engagement.

There was a more serious side to the listening tour, however. Afzal adds:

> I remember we spent most of 2009 travelling up and down the country. He was very keen to visit prosecution divisions and police colleagues everywhere. I remember arriving at Carlisle station visiting the police in Cumbria, for example, or in parts of Wales or wherever it may be. He did get around and every time he met with a prosecution team, he was keen not just to meet them; he would meet with the senior police team and also ask us to invite senior members of the community – victims' groups and local charities. And so, the conversation wasn't just focused on how we as prosecutors might do better; it was about what the relationship with the police was and what the relationship with the community was and where the gaps were. It might have been strange for him given he'd spent all his life in defence work and not prosecution work, but he rapidly understood that our work would be improved substantially by better engagement with the police and that clearly happened.

Starmer's record as DPP is a matter of public debate. For every lawyer or politician who would commend him for his time in the office, there is another who would point to an issue which raises questions about his decisions or those of the CPS. His instruction to CPS staff in 2009 to consider the Human Rights Act before they try to prosecute, for example, was regarded by many Conservative MPs as problematic because of the inherent risk in allowing criminals to escape justice on what could be a technicality.

What cannot be disputed, however, is that the DPP must assume responsibility for the heaviest cases, and in this regard Starmer's five years in the job now appear to have covered a fairly momentous period, with a wide range of complicated and very high-profile matters falling to him between 2008 and 2013, including the London riots of 2011 and the fallout from the highly contentious death of the newspaper vendor Ian Tomlinson. 'The case load is very interesting because you pick which cases you want to lead in and which cases you want to make decisions in,' says Ken Macdonald. 'So if you're a criminal lawyer that's a fantastic position to be in in terms of professional satisfaction.'

Be that as it may, Starmer also occupied the post during a change of government from Labour to the Tory-led coalition which was in situ from 2010. It put in place a round of sharp public expenditure cuts following the world financial crisis of 2008. The CPS was not immune. During Starmer's tenure, the CPS's budget was cut by 27 per cent, with the inevitable consequence that staff numbers were cut radically as well. None of this would have made his job any easier and might go some way to explaining why in March 2012, for example, it was revealed by the CPS's official inspectors that 63,000 criminal cases a year – or 7 per cent of the total – were wrongly dropped or unjustifiably brought to trial.

Dominic Grieve was the Attorney General from May 2010, meaning that he and Starmer worked closely together for most of the time Starmer was in post. He says their different political views had no impact on the way Starmer approached the job. 'The relationship of the Attorney General and the DPP is quite a complicated one,' says Grieve.

> The question, probably for both of us, was whether this was a relationship that was going to work well. And I quickly became very impressed by him in terms of his professionalism, and we had a very good working relationship. Bear in mind that it was a time of very considerable challenges, the biggest one of which was that the Crown Prosecution Service was being asked to make significant and substantial cuts, as everybody

> else was, following the formation of the coalition government. And he did that, in my judgement, showing considerable leadership and very considerable effectiveness, because we were obviously both worried that it would diminish the efficiency of the CPS. It was asked to carry out reforms that were going to have quite a profound impact on the morale of those people working within it, because it required the closure of offices; their amalgamation; changes to the way the work was carried out. And he carried that out with great efficiency.

Grieve says he and Starmer would meet on a monthly basis to discuss these cuts, giving Starmer valuable insights into the workings of Whitehall and government, which he would not have had if he had been a backbench opposition politician, for example. This suggests that he had an eye on the future. 'We'd also talk sometimes, of course, about other things, about casework and things of that sort,' Grieve recalls.

> But the truth was that the biggest challenge he was facing was this substantial paring down of the CPS without curbing its effectiveness. And while I think it can be said that we were all very lucky that it took place against a background of diminishing crime – or at least, put it this way, it wasn't rising, which it has done since – nevertheless, even when you take that into consideration, I think it was a considerable achievement on his part, and it was carried out with pragmatic realism.

Starmer also made it his business to meet journalists and other opinion formers from time to time. One such person recalls: 'Over lunch he was personable, charming, nice, easy to talk to, he had no side, and he was just straight. He wasn't like some people, who are terribly guarded. I wouldn't say he was suspicious of journalists. He didn't have that in-built hostility towards journalists. He was likeable.'

Given the volume of cases which are prosecuted by the CPS each year, it would obviously not be possible to examine every one of them, but it is worth mentioning a few of the better-known ones to illustrate their sheer range. For example, no sooner was Starmer in the job than he had to grapple with the highly emotive subject of assisted suicide. He chose not to prosecute the parents of a 23-year-old man called Daniel James who was paralysed while playing rugby and who subsequently visited a suicide clinic in Switzerland. Although the Jameses had taken their son to the clinic where he died in September 2008, Starmer said that there was no public interest reason to take the matter to court. This led him within months to introduce new guidelines ultimately indicating how families, doctors and nurses could escape criminal charges in similar situations. Inevitably, there was condemnation from opponents of euthanasia, and this was echoed by politicians who expressed worries that the DPP, a paid public official, had exceeded his authority by usurping the role of Parliament in fashioning the law as he saw fit. It is hard to imagine a public official having to engage with a more complex and ultimately personal question, and no politician, surely, would have envied him this task.

Another delicate matter Starmer dealt with early on involved the Conservative MP and shadow Immigration Minister Damian Green, who was arrested at his house in November 2008 as part of a police inquiry into Home Office leaks. Starmer was apparently given ten minutes' notice of this action. It emerged that Green was passed information which was considered embarrassing to the government about immigration and crime by a junior Home Office employee, Christopher Galley, some of which was given to a newspaper. In April 2009, a £5 million police investigation into the matter collapsed after the CPS decided there was insufficient evidence to prosecute either man because the information given to Green on the government's immigration policy was not secret and did not affect national security or put lives at risk. Bearing in mind this happened under a Labour government, Starmer did at least eventually demonstrate the kind of independent view that the office of DPP demanded, even if serious questions were asked on civil liberties grounds about why a serving politician in a country with a supposedly free press had been arrested in the first place.

Parliament appeared on Starmer's radar for a second time in 2009, when the *Daily Telegraph* obtained evidence that dozens of MPs had misused their expenses allowances to the tune of hundreds of thousands of pounds. In 2010, four Labour MPs and two Conservative peers were jailed for fraud. The CPS's decision to prosecute these men regardless of their political affiliation proved that Starmer was able to keep his own political views in check, as would be expected. Indeed, he has often boasted of this aspect of his time as DPP since becoming an MP.

As DPP, Starmer also earned himself a footnote in the Stephen Lawrence affair after personally applying to the Court of Appeal in 2010 for the original acquittal of one of those who had long been suspected of murdering Mr Lawrence in 1993, Gary Dobson, to be quashed. This meant that Dobson and another man, David Norris, could be tried again for the same crime after new forensic evidence surfaced. The case duly went to court, and in January 2012, Dobson and Norris were convicted of murder.

The following month, February 2012, Starmer tackled another high-profile case involving a politician, when he decided there was sufficient evidence to charge the Liberal Democrat Cabinet minister Chris Huhne and his ex-wife, Vicky Pryce, with perverting the course of justice. They had been under investigation for several months in relation to which one of them had been driving a car when it was caught speeding in 2003. Both were jailed in the spring of 2013.

Inevitably, however, there are cases dating from Starmer's stint as DPP which he would surely rather forget. In September 2010, he had to apologise to a woman for 'failings' in the trial of a man who was accused of sexually assaulting her. The woman, who was awarded £16,000 in damages, was wrongly blamed by a member of the CPS for the collapse of the case against her alleged attacker. And in December 2011, a police corruption trial collapsed, leaving taxpayers with a bill for an estimated £10 million. The officers had been accused of framing three innocent men for the 1988 murder of Lynette White, but during their trial it was established that potentially vital prosecution files had gone missing, forcing the judge to abandon the case. Such blunders in all probability rankle to this day the man who prides himself on being the master of his brief.

Another memorable case which ended badly for the CPS has been dubbed the 'Twitter Joke Trial'. In January 2010, Paul Chambers, twenty-eight, was intending to travel from England to Northern Ireland when he learned that Robin Hood Airport in South Yorkshire had been forced to cancel flights due to bad weather. Fearing delay, Chambers wrote on Twitter to his 600 followers: 'Crap! Robin Hood Airport is closed. You've got a week and a bit to get your shit together otherwise I am blowing the airport sky high!!' A week later, an off-duty manager at the airport found the message and reported it to airport security, who recorded it as 'not credible' as a threat. Nonetheless, protocol meant the police had to be informed, and Chambers was arrested at his office by anti-terror officers. He was charged with sending a 'menacing' message under the Communications Act 2003 and found guilty at Doncaster Magistrates' Court. He spent two years trying to appeal his conviction, during which he was locked in what has been described as a Kafkaesque nightmare.

As the case generated wider attention, comedians including Stephen Fry, Graham Linehan and Al Murray backed Chambers. Eventually, his conviction was overturned at the High Court in July 2012, raising serious questions from politicians and members of the public about why the case was ever taken so seriously. One figure with knowledge of this case claims that Starmer 'gave consent' and 'authorised the resistance of the appeal' through the CPS at the time. This case did force Starmer, in June 2013, to issue guidelines for the CPS on when to take legal action against those who breach UK communications laws on social media. He warned that a 'high threshold' should be applied by prosecutors when assessing social media communications, because of their volume and to prevent the legal system being deluged. In this, senior legal figures generally believe that he drew a sensible line in tackling what is theoretically an endless problem.

• • •

Two even more prominent cases with which Starmer is associated are worth examining more deeply on the basis that they help to inform us about his character and his success in the DPP post. The cases in question are the police operations known as Operation Elveden and Operation Midland.

Starmer was in post when the first prosecutions arising from the News International phone-hacking scandal involving the *News of the World* eventually began. Given that phone hacking involved hundreds of victims, it went to the heart of Rupert Murdoch's media empire and it was indefensible, this impropriety will obviously be remembered for many years to come. Yet the phone-hacking scandal itself led directly to another matter involving journalists, which can now be seen as a fairly hysterical over-reaction to the mood of the time and which did immense damage to all parties concerned. It related to allegations of inappropriate payments to police officers and other public officials. The police investigation which looked into this was given the codename Operation Elveden. It was launched on 19 June 2011 after officers ordered News International to hand over confidential emails containing details of the payments. This case remains a running sore to many in journalistic circles and beyond, and in light of Starmer's role in its outcome, it merits study.

Between July 2011 and September 2013, thirty journalists from News International and the Mirror Group were arrested or charged under Operation Elveden. After Starmer stepped down as DPP in late 2013, four more journalists were arrested. Most of the thirty-four individuals who were caught up in this tangled story worked for *The Sun*. It is worth stating from the outset that Starmer had previously been happy to court this newspaper, presumably because he knew it was the most widely read in Britain. In fact, according to one well-placed source, he even had a private lunch with its then editor, Rebekah Brooks, shortly after he was appointed DPP in 2008 and long before Operation Elveden was conceived. At that time, *The Sun* still supported the Labour Party, though this alliance ground to a dramatic halt in September 2009, when the newspaper announced that it had switched to backing the Tories with the brutal front-page headline: 'Labour's Lost It'.

It does not compromise this account to reveal at this point that, ultimately, not one of the thirty-four journalists arrested or charged under the guise of Operation Elveden has a conviction on their record. Yet the alarming truth is that many of them spent years on bail; they were put through gruelling court trials;

they were unable to work; and in some cases, their careers were ruined. At least two are known to have attempted suicide because of the stress they endured. The experience of a *Sun* reporter called Vince Soodin was not untypical and is worth recounting to give a sense of the type of treatment that was meted out. Soodin was arrested in a dawn raid in August 2012 for having written a story two years previously about a fox attacking a three-year-old at a school in Brighton. A police officer using a fake name had tipped off *The Sun* about this. Soodin was assigned the story and the tipster – whom Soodin never met – was paid £500. At 6 a.m. on 7 August 2012, eight police officers knocked on Soodin's door, went into his property, seized his belongings and those of his girlfriend, went through their clothes, underwear, diaries and any other item they deemed relevant, and then drove Soodin to a police station, where he was put in a cell. Later, he was questioned, released and re-questioned twice more. In August 2013, he was charged under an obscure thirteenth-century common law of conspiracy to commit misconduct in public office. He was suspended from his job and in September 2014 tried – like other Operation Elveden journalists – at the Old Bailey, a court usually reserved for the most serious crimes. The jury was hung.

The following year, he returned for a retrial but was told that the case against him had been abandoned and he could leave without a stain on his character. This was a result of the then Lord Chief Justice, Lord Thomas, quashing the conviction of another News UK journalist, Lucy Panton, shortly before. Defending press freedom and citing case law, Lord Thomas said that the trial judge in Panton's case, Charles Wide, had misdirected the jury by failing to tell them of the high threshold required for a conviction. Thomas also pointed out that jurors had to be satisfied that the defendants' conduct had harmed the public interest. Lord Thomas said, 'This is without doubt a difficult area of the criminal law. An ancient common law offence is being used in circumstances where it has rarely before been applied.' It appeared that the CPS had failed to make prosecution counsel and the trial judge aware of the latest developments in case law on misconduct. Lord Thomas added, 'The judge was entitled to far more help by the prosecution than he was given.' Soodin's agony was over, but it is astonishing to think that he was held on bail for 989 days. Many others suffered a similar ordeal.

It remains very difficult to understand why Starmer, who was ultimately at the helm of attempting to convict Soodin and twenty-nine others, should seemingly have been unaware for so long of the case law that Lord Thomas cited. The stories written by the journalists who were arrested concerned matters which fell squarely into the public interest. They included details of how British forces suffered kit shortages while at war, and of the authorities' soft treatment of the child killer Jon Venables after he was returned to prison for downloading child abuse images. It is somewhat ironic that the man who apparently expended considerable amounts of energy fighting for the rights of striking printworkers in the 1980s should, a quarter of a century later, have considered it appropriate to prosecute journalists working for the same company on what turned out to be a highly questionable basis. It is also strange that his much-vaunted liberal instincts seemed to evaporate when it came to dealing with these journalists, and that he was prepared to put in peril the important relationship between the state and the press.

On top of all this, the heavy-handed investigations and trials which sprang from Operation Elveden cost taxpayers something in the region of £20 million. The only justification for the exercise that the CPS can rely upon is that some of the journalists' public sector sources were eventually jailed. Perhaps the most notable is Bettina Jordan-Barber, a Ministry of Defence strategist who in 2015 pleaded guilty to conspiring to commit misconduct in public office after accepting £100,000 for assisting *The Sun* with a total of sixty-nine stories between 2004 and 2012. She was sentenced to twelve months in prison.

On 30 October 2016, three years after he had stepped down as DPP, Starmer was quizzed by the journalist Robert Peston about his responsibility for Operation Elveden during an edition of the television programme *Peston on Sunday*. He did not take the opportunity to apologise, instead claiming, somewhat disingenuously given that they were for the most part arrested and charged when he was DPP: 'Well, most of the prosecutions took place when I ceased to be DPP; I'm not the DPP, I didn't handle those cases and it's really not for me to comment on them.' He also said: 'I obviously have not had anything to do with those cases for three years now, so I'm not in a position to comment one way or the other.'

In January 2020, as mentioned in the previous chapter, Starmer released a campaign video as part of his bid for the Labour leadership which made much of his role in prosecuting journalists. In this short film, Rebekah Brooks, who has been the chief executive of News UK since 2011 and who was arrested under Operation Elveden, featured twice in library footage; Rupert Murdoch, the owner of *The Sun*, featured once as a voiceover intoned that Starmer had 'stood up to the powerful'. Was it mere political convenience that meant Starmer was prepared to leave it at that? Vince Soodin and countless others may be decent journalists, but in most people's eyes they would not be described as 'powerful'. Including images of Brooks and Murdoch in this film without their blessing was a curious decision on Starmer's part anyway. Not only is the position of DPP supposed to be non-political, raising questions about why Starmer was using his work as DPP for political purposes, but Brooks was never found guilty of any offence in relation to any matter connected with her work as a journalist.

Subsequent to all this, Starmer has tried to mend his fences with *The Sun*. According to several well-placed sources, after he became Labour Party leader, he even telephoned Victoria Newton, *The Sun*'s editor since February 2020, in an attempt to find some sort of modus vivendi so that both parties could move on. Given the events described, it is hardly surprising that Ms Newton was decidedly lukewarm when it came to responding to his overtures.

One source who has examined the Operation Elveden affair in detail believes there may have been a political dimension to the decision to prosecute so many *Sun* journalists. This source says:

> Gordon Brown was livid about *The Sun* turning its back on him and his well-known fury may have influenced the process of investigating the hacking. It wasn't against the law for these journalists to publish this information – even if they had to pay for it. The only law that was broken, if it was broken at all, was by the public officials for leaking confidential information. Even that may have only been a breach of employment conditions. It's a very grey area. I think that what Starmer did would have been the subject in any other circumstances of a furore. Say it happened to someone on the *Telegraph* or *Times*, for instance, I don't think this would have been buried in recent history in the way it has. Because it was *The Sun* and because of the association between it and its sister title, the *News of the World*, where the phone hacking took place, *Sun* journalists were tarred with the same brush. They are the unmentionables. These reporters were hung out to dry. I think Starmer is unfit for public office.

This account is given some credence by Tom Newton Dunn, who was political editor of *The Sun* throughout the phone-hacking saga. In May 2021, following the death aged seventy-seven of his former *Sun* colleague John Kay, Newton Dunn wrote that he believed political pressure was to blame for the pursuit of those journalists who were later found innocent. In his column in the *Evening Standard*, he wrote that Kay, who was charged under Operation Elveden and eventually cleared, had died a 'broken man' because of the toll it took on him. He further noted that Ed Miliband, who was the Labour Party leader when the scandal reached its height, devoted a considerable amount of his time to the wider matter of News International's practices. Newton Dunn opined: 'When the phone hacking scandal broke in 2011 … Miliband threw the kitchen sink at trying to bring down Rupert Murdoch's News International. Starmer – who was Miliband's protégé – came under pressure to investigate and prosecute News International journalists for pretty much anything.'

• • •

It was another of Rupert Murdoch's newspapers, *The Times*, that first brought to national attention while Starmer was DPP the appalling matter of the sexual exploitation of young girls in the north of England. This outrage came to light as a result of the sterling work of a reporter called Andrew Norfolk. From 2010, he began looking into evidence suggesting that gangs of mainly Asian Muslim men groomed and abused white teenage girls. It was a story he worked on for years, but some of his earliest reports concerning the town of Rochdale caught the eye of the aforementioned Nazir Afzal, himself a Muslim, who had been appointed the CPS's chief prosecutor for the north-west in the summer of 2011. In fact, Greater Manchester Police had heard about grooming in the Rochdale area in August 2008 when a teenage girl told officers that she had been raped by a group of Asian men. The girl gave police three pairs of her underwear, which was found to have traces of DNA from one of her alleged attackers, and after eleven months a file was sent to the CPS, but in July 2009 a CPS lawyer whose identity has never been revealed decided not to proceed. Afzal overturned this decision shortly after taking up his post and in May 2012 nine men from mainly Pakistani backgrounds were found guilty of grooming gang offences. Liverpool Crown Court heard the men had plied victims, some as young as thirteen, with alcohol and drugs so they could 'pass them around' and use them for sex. The case was seen as groundbreaking, paving the way for similar actions against gangs all over the country. Thousands of young girls had been subjected to unspeakable levels of abuse. Afzal later revealed that the original decision not to prosecute in Rochdale in 2009 was based on the victim's perceived lack of credibility. Bluntly, it had been assumed that a jury would not believe her. Unquestionably, Afzal deserves credit for going against the grain in the way he did, yet, as we shall see, it could be argued that this single decision by him had profound, if unintended, consequences.

'It might have been strange for [Starmer] given he'd spent all his life in defence work and not prosecution work,' says Afzal.

> But he rapidly understood that our work would be improved substantially by better engagement with the police and that clearly happened, and I think the best example of that was a little bit later when I was dealing with so-called grooming gangs and child sexual abuse in 2011 or thereabouts. We knew how impactful that work was, how the public were seeing what was happening or what was not happening, and once I'd

> prosecuted the Rochdale case in early 2012, then the world was looking down at authorities and saying, 'What are you going to do about this?'

Afzal says that from this point Starmer encouraged him to review similar cases that might have been dropped by CPS and to pursue the wider scandal of child sexual exploitation. To that end, he appointed Afzal to be his national lead on the subject. A panel consisting of Starmer, Afzal, various chief constables and other chief prosecutors invited police officers and police prosecutors from around the country to refer other past cases that were of concern to them. 'When we talked about the child abuse cases, [Starmer] was absolutely apoplectic about why children had been let down the way they'd been let down,' Afzal adds. 'Not just by us, but by every agency. And literally that became his priority for the whole of 2013. He let me do the media and so on, but internally he was absolutely determined to bring the change.'

For his part, Starmer did acknowledge in 2012 the issue of race as a common factor in these crimes, saying:

> In a number of cases presented to us, particularly in cases involving groups, there's clearly an issue of ethnicity that has to be understood and addressed. As prosecutors, we shouldn't shy away from that. But if we're honest, it's the approach to the victims, the credibility issue, that caused these cases not to be prosecuted in the past. There was a lack of understanding.

These sexual exploitation allegations were by no means the only ones to have cropped up during this time. It is at this point that Starmer's role in the Jimmy Savile scandal warrants analysis. He has repeatedly passed up the opportunity to provide the evidence that would prove decisively that, as DPP, he had no knowledge of

Savile having been under suspicion. It is for this reason that the episode continues to stalk him.

Savile died in October 2011 and, despite the best efforts of certain journalists, it was not until almost a year later that the allegations against him saw the light of day. Most notably, two well-informed staffers on the BBC2 programme *Newsnight* who had mounted an investigation as soon as his death was announced had uncovered a series of claims including that he had sexually abused minors on BBC premises. In December 2011, their explosive report was secretly axed by a BBC executive who has never been named. The story, involving one of the most famous men in Britain, was temporarily buried.

A year after Savile's death, in October 2012, ITV reported the full horror of the claims against him and the can of worms was forcibly opened. A national outcry ensued. Among new details to emerge at that stage was that two police forces – Surrey Police and Sussex Police – had investigated the elderly entertainer between 2007 and 2009 over accusations made by four women. The two forces had done so under the auspices of the Crown Prosecution Service, which had provided regular guidance and then assessed whether there was sufficient evidence to bring any charges. Ultimately, the CPS concluded in late October 2009, the month that Savile was interviewed by Surrey Police under caution, that no prosecution could be brought because none of the four complainants was willing to support any police action and the evidence against him was weak. This was probably the last chance that Savile could have faced justice and, in what ranks as one of the biggest blunders in recent criminal history, it was missed.

Starmer has always maintained that he, personally, was never aware when he led the CPS during Savile's lifetime that Savile had even been accused, let alone that the CPS had reviewed allegations against him and decided he could not be charged – even though he had been the DPP for nearly a year by the time that decision was made. Starmer has said, 'It never came close to crossing my desk and the local CPS lawyer who looked at the case did not even mention the decision to his immediate boss because, to him, it seemed routine.' How plausible is this explanation?

In considering this question, it is essential to go over the sequence of events. On 24 October 2012, Starmer made a statement acknowledging that the CPS was one of various public bodies that had allowed Savile to slip through the net. He said he had asked the chief crown prosecutor for the south-east, Roger Coe-Salazar, to 'consider the files' in relation to the four incidents that were referred to the CPS by the police in 2007 and 2008. Starmer said that Coe-Salazar had 'assured' him that the decisions that were subsequently taken were the right ones based on the information and evidence then available. In leaving it to Coe-Salazar to make this assertion, Starmer showed that he was perfectly happy for the CPS to mark its own homework. That day, Starmer also said, 'Out of an abundance of caution, I have asked for the papers in the four cases to be provided to my principal legal adviser, Alison Levitt QC, forthwith so that she can consider the decisions made and advise me accordingly.' In other words, Starmer was content for the CPS to mark its own homework for a second time – this time with Levitt wielding the red pen – when it came to this controversial matter.

Levitt's report was published in January 2013, but on close inspection it is clear that while it provided some worthwhile insights, it also posed questions that have never been resolved. She disclosed that in May 2007, a complaint was made to Surrey Police alleging that in the late 1970s Savile had sexually assaulted a girl aged fourteen or fifteen at Duncroft Children's Home. During Surrey Police's investigation, two more claims surfaced. One, dating from about 1973, accused Savile of sexually assaulting a girl aged around fourteen outside Stoke Mandeville Hospital. The other, again from the 1970s, was that Savile had suggested to a girl of about seventeen – also from Duncroft Children's Home – that she perform oral sex on him. Separately, in March 2008, Sussex Police looked into a claim that in about 1970 Savile had sexually assaulted a young woman in her early twenties in the back of a caravan in Sussex. In the course of their respective investigations, each police force came to know of the allegations the other had heard.

Levitt explained that an 'extremely experienced' CPS reviewing lawyer, whom she described as a 'rape specialist', had supervised the Savile matter when it was brought to the CPS's attention. Her report gave the impression that this lawyer oversaw the case entirely alone. Levitt interviewed this lawyer for the purposes of her report, but she did not name him in it. She granted him anonymity – a decision Starmer does not appear to have queried. This apparent right of anonymity was part of a pattern, for Starmer had not queried the decision not to name the CPS lawyer who had dismissed the Rochdale case in 2009 either. To this day, the identity of the CPS lawyer who acted in the Savile case remains secret. All that is known about him based on Levitt's report is that he worked in the CPS south-east office and that he had retired from the CPS by January 2013, when Levitt's report was published. Further enquiries for this book have established that he was a special casework lawyer in the rape and serious sexual offences unit (RASSO), a small division that mainly operated from offices in Guildford. I shall refer to him as the 'mystery lawyer'.

Significantly, Levitt stated that the mystery lawyer 'struggled to remember the details [of the case] after all this time'. It is surprising that Levitt was not more sceptical about his faulty memory of what was always going to be a high-profile case. But in view of his poor recollection of events, it is difficult to avoid wondering how reliable he was as a witness. Furthermore, Levitt does not appear to have asked him to explain whether he ever discussed the Savile matter with any of his CPS colleagues – including Starmer – over the thirty months that he took charge of the case. Shouldn't she have done so? And if not, how rigorous was she in her investigation of such a serious situation?

Police records show the mystery lawyer held three meetings with Surrey Police to discuss the case against Savile. The first was on 15 July 2008, fifteen weeks before Starmer became DPP. The next was on 22 January 2009, almost three months after Starmer became DPP. The last was on 31 March 2009 – five months after Starmer became DPP. Savile was interviewed by Surrey Police under caution at Stoke Mandeville Hospital, where he was a volunteer, on 1 October 2009 – exactly eleven months after Starmer became DPP. During this interview he denied the three allegations put to him and told officers the complainants were after his money. The mystery lawyer had a telephone meeting with Surrey Police a week later, on 8 October 2009. He then provided final written advice to the police on 26 October 2009 in which he said, 'On applying the evidential test, in the absence of statements from the victims, there was insufficient evidence to charge with any criminal offence.' On 28 October 2009, a police officer (whom, again, Levitt did not name) wrote to the four women involved telling them, 'The CPS have decided no further police action on this case.'

Levitt's report stated that the case files were returned to the police after it was decided no prosecution would take place. She explained that all trace of the Savile file was removed from CMS [the CPS's internal electronic case management system] and 'destroyed' on 26 October 2010 – two years after Starmer became DPP. This apparently happened in accordance with data protection policy. Since it was impossible to retrieve the CPS's own Savile file, some will wonder which 'files' Starmer referred to when he made his statement on 24 October 2012 declaring that his CPS colleague Roger Coe-Salazar had given the CPS a clean bill of health.

Levitt's report concluded that the decision not to prosecute Savile was made in good faith but that the police and the CPS had been overly cautious in their handling of the matter. Most egregiously, Surrey Police did not tell each complainant of the other complaints that had been made. And Sussex Police told its complainant that corroboration would be needed in order to charge Savile. Levitt did say she thought the mystery lawyer showed a surprising lack of curiosity when told by police that the complainants did not support the prosecution. She queried why he did not try to build a case. She also noted that had the complainants been given more information by the police at the time of the investigation – and if each one had been told that she was not the only woman to have complained – they would probably have been prepared to give evidence. The inference was that Savile could have ended up in court had the police and the CPS handled things differently.

Savile's assumed victims were expected to accept this slipshod approach and move on. So was the British public. But the fact is that two police forces investigated Savile for more than two years with the knowledge of the CPS and, in the case of Surrey Police, with the advice of the CPS both before and after they had interviewed him under caution. How likely is it that Starmer remained completely oblivious to this inquiry? It was active for the first year that he was DPP.

It should not be forgotten that Savile was not some unknown figure. He was one of the most famous men in Britain, a stalwart of the BBC and the charity world, a knight of the realm, and a sometime friend of the royal family who had once been trusted by senior politicians including Margaret Thatcher. He was, surely, a very likely subject of discussion within the CPS given the nature of the allegations against him.

How many CPS employees, other than the mystery lawyer, knew that the CPS was looking into this highly sensitive case between 2007 and 2009? Levitt's report did not say. Equally, who decided that Starmer, who had made a point of telling staff when he became DPP that his door was always open, and who attended regular meetings with CPS staff around the country, should be kept in the dark about the Savile investigation? It isn't even clear whether he first learned about the CPS's involvement before or after Savile's death. Levitt apparently failed to ask these basic questions. This turned out to be convenient for Starmer, but the public remains unsure about this undeniably murky business.

What is known thanks to Levitt's report is that entities other than the CPS *were* aware that Savile was under investigation. Levitt states that at intervals between 2007 and 2009 Surrey Police representatives informed Surrey County Council's children's services, the charity Barnardo's and West Yorkshire Police child protection unit that Savile was under suspicion. She further notes that in December 2008 Surrey Police created a 'blocked' record in relation to Savile that would allow this information to be made available to any forces or agencies carrying out a Criminal Records Bureau check. Again, many will find it curious that the police volunteered to each of these organisations what was going on but that somebody at the CPS considered it best that Starmer should remain ignorant. It is worth adding that certain journalists on *The Sun* were also aware that Savile was under investigation by 2008.

It should also be said that under Freedom of Information laws the CPS has revealed that the then chief crown prosecutor for Surrey, Portia Ragnauth, 'had ultimate responsibility for the decision making of all the lawyers in her Area, and she was therefore responsible for that [charging] decision'. Former colleagues stress that Ms Ragnauth must know the identity of the mystery lawyer, though she has never revealed it. She continues to work for the CPS and at the time of writing was a specialist prosecutor in the proceeds of crime enforcement team. She did not respond to requests to comment for the first edition of this book, and in January 2025, the Crown Prosecution Service wrote to my researcher, Miles Goslett, warning him not to contact Ms Ragnauth about it because the Civil Service Code prevents civil servants from speaking to the media without permission.

Plainly, this matter continues to dog Starmer. As recently as December 2023, *The Guardian* published a report headlined 'Keir Starmer was not told about dropping of Jimmy Savile case, say sources'. This article again emphasised his lack of knowledge of the mystery lawyer having ruled out a prosecution in 2009, a year after Starmer became DPP, as though this was in some way acceptable. Yet this piece – which was presumably designed to remove any lingering doubt about his role in the Savile episode – was not definitive, for the sources on which it relied were unnamed. One of them insisted:

> Keir knew nothing about it. We had a lawyer with a file with Jimmy Savile written on it … The reviewing lawyer was told there were several victims but that none of them were willing to attend court, so he closed the case. The reviewing lawyer should have asked for advice.

Another anonymous source added, 'If you think Keir is a control freak now [in 2023], that has its roots in the Savile case and his early days in the CPS. That's when he realised how hard he needed to work to ensure consistency across a large organisation.'

If Starmer really didn't know what was going on at the CPS at the time, why wasn't he better informed? Doesn't his lack of awareness raise questions about his grip? He is on record as saying he takes 'full responsibility for every decision of the Crown Prosecution Service when I was Director of Public Prosecutions'. But how can the public be reassured that he *didn't* know anything about the Savile affair? His defence appears to rely solely on the testimony of the mystery lawyer, who has by his own admission an incomplete recollection of events.

Any trawl online shows that, to this day, many voters consider Starmer to be personally responsible for Savile escaping justice. In the final analysis, Starmer could have gone a long way to clearing up this mess years ago – for example by asking the mystery lawyer to make a sworn statement naming everybody at the CPS who knew of and dealt with the Savile case between 2007 and 2009. For reasons best known to himself, however, he has not yet done so. It should be added that in December 2024, Starmer made Alison Levitt a Labour peer.

Savile is not the only person who has come back to haunt Starmer's record as DPP. In September 2024, scores of women claimed they had been sexually abused by the late Harrods owner Mohamed Al Fayed, including five who described being raped. It turned out that Al Fayed had been questioned in 2008 about the sexual harassment of a fifteen-year-old schoolgirl. Starmer was the DPP in February 2009 when the CPS said that no charges would be brought because there was 'no realistic prospect of conviction'. When this news surfaced in 2024, a Downing Street spokesman said, 'Keir did not handle this case.' He then used the same phrase Starmer had used when denying all knowledge of the Savile affair years before: 'It did not cross his desk.' Again, however, there were questions about why Starmer was not better versed in what was going on at the CPS when he ran it, not least because his personality is one that shows a clear need for control. One startling pattern that can be seen from these examples is the anonymity that has been granted by the CPS to each of its lawyers who was associated with poor decision-making – whether in the Fayed case, the Rochdale case in July 2009 or the Savile case in October 2009. Many will argue that their identities should be known by the public.

• • •

In January 2013, Starmer issued a public apology and called the Savile case a 'watershed moment' in which the 'approach of the police and prosecutors to credibility in sexual assault cases has to change'. By the time he had completed his term as DPP in the autumn of 2013, the waves created by the Savile scandal led to sexual abuse being pushed somewhere near to the top of the news agenda and staying there. While it may be true that he was not personally responsible for the CPS's decision in 2009 not to prosecute Savile, there is no doubt that this failure occurred on his watch and was therefore, ultimately, his responsibility. This was the background to his acceptance of an invitation in December 2013 to chair a taskforce advising the Labour Party on transforming the rights of victims in the criminal justice system. The proposals it eventually produced were to have been introduced by then Labour leader Ed Miliband had he won the 2015 election; but as Miliband never became Prime Minister, this work resulted in Starmer sponsoring the Victims of Crime Bill instead, a Private Member's Bill which he introduced to Parliament in October 2015.

When it was announced in 2013 that Starmer had taken on this job, he gave an interview to *The Guardian* in which he said:

> Our criminal justice system is riddled with assumptions about how victims behave and most of them are misplaced. My main concern is that the more vulnerable you are as a victim or a witness the less able the criminal law is to protect you. We saw this as we unpicked the child sexual abuse cases – both the Rochdale grooming cases but also the [Jimmy] Savile cases. Victims did not have the confidence to come forward; when they did come forward they had all sorts of assumptions made about how they were going to behave. Then there was the journey through the courtroom itself.

It was clear that under Starmer's plans, the rights and feelings of victims were to be put first, and he gave interviews and made speeches throughout 2014 to promote this ideology. The then Met Police chief, Bernard Hogan-Howe, would later reveal that Scotland Yard's policy of immediately believing every allegation of sexual abuse made by victims was founded on a report written in 2014 by the Chief Inspector of Constabulary, Tom Winsor, which stated: 'The presumption that a victim should always be believed should be institutionalised.' Winsor is said to have been influenced by Starmer's policy. So, too, was Starmer's successor, Alison Saunders, following Starmer's departure as DPP in October 2013. However well-intentioned all this was, it did not take into account the twisted mind of a man called Carl Beech.

In October 2014, the Metropolitan Police opened a triple-murder and historical sexual abuse investigation which they called Operation Midland. It was launched after a series of alarming accusations made by a man who was given the nom de plume

'Nick'. He claimed that he and others were the victims of what became known as the 'VIP paedophile scandal', in which members of the establishment had raped, tortured and murdered children in the 1970s and 1980s. 'Nick' – whose real name was in fact Carl Beech – told police that he had been physically and sexually abused at parties attended by various prominent individuals in London and elsewhere. He named the former Prime Minister Sir Edward Heath; the former army chief Lord Bramall; former MPs Harvey Proctor and Lord Janner; former Home Secretary Lord Brittan; former head of MI6 Maurice Oldfield; and former head of MI5 Michael Hanley as being among the perpetrators of these supposed crimes. Beech also said he had witnessed Mr Proctor murdering two children, one of whom he identified as Martin Allen, who disappeared in London aged fifteen in November 1979. Beech even gave police a penknife, which Mr Proctor had purportedly threatened him with, and told officers: 'I hope there will be enough evidence to see [Proctor] in court.'

Infamously, on 18 December 2014, Detective Superintendent Kenny McDonald told the BBC that 'Nick' had been interviewed at length by 'experienced detectives' from the child abuse command and an investigator from the murder command. 'They and I believe what Nick is saying to be credible and to be true ... so yes, we do believe what Nick is saying,' McDonald stated.

Operation Midland now ranks as one of the biggest police scandals of recent years. The Met spent £2.5 million investigating Beech's claims before turning its inquiries onto this alleged whistleblower himself. After indecent images were found on electronic devices he owned, it transpired that he was in fact a paedophile. He was also a fantasist. Operation Midland was closed in 2016 without any arrests having been made. In 2019, Beech was convicted of twelve counts of perverting the course of justice and jailed for eighteen years. In light of the trouble to which Starmer went to advance the idea that all victims must be believed, the fallout from this extraordinary case continues to trouble him as much as it does the Met. In March 2021, six former Home Secretaries wrote to *The Times* urging the incumbent Home Secretary Priti Patel to open an investigation into Operation Midland, specifically in relation to the procedure by which search warrants are issued. Lord Baker of Dorking, Lord Clarke of Nottingham, Lord Howard of Lympne, Jack Straw, Lord Blunkett and Lord Reid of Cardowan said that they are 'acutely conscious of the need to maintain public confidence in the police'. They added that they agree with Sir Richard Henriques, the retired High Court judge who reviewed Operation Midland, that 'confidence in the police and the Independent Office for Police Conduct has been seriously damaged'. When Starmer was asked about this on LBC on 22 March 2021, he acknowledged that Midland went 'very, very wrong' and said there needs to be some 'basic accountability', but he seemed sceptical of the idea that there should be an inquiry. Others, plainly, would disagree.

Among them is the criminal barrister Daniel Janner QC, son of the late Lord Janner, who was falsely accused by Beech. Mr Janner has known Starmer since the 1990s via their legal careers. Though he would not claim to know him well, he certainly has strong feelings about what he regards as the complicated situation that Starmer had a hand in creating. 'We're both benchers of Middle Temple as it happens,' says Janner.

> We took silk on the same day. I wouldn't say he's a friend but a work colleague. There's absolutely no doubt that the genesis of the false allegation industry which reached its height with the Carl Beech trial emanated from the approach of Keir Starmer in relation to his determination that all victims are to be

> believed. He denies he had that policy. But Harvey Proctor has gone into some detail showing how this *was* his view. He made speeches which show he shifted the way police approach victims. And the shift was this approach that all victims are to be believed. If you go from that stance, you will find it leads to fantasists and those who are chasing money. My issue is it put the police in a very difficult position because it was coming from the prosecuting authority down through the police, and what on earth are they meant to do? And it leads to the madness we had with Carl Beech. He made false allegations against many, including my father, who was meant to have allegedly raped him in the Carlton Club. Then you get an appalling DPP who wasn't up to the job, Alison Saunders, who comes in and carries that policy forward. It was a Starmer policy.

In the case of Lord Janner, nine High Court cases were brought against him. When the Janner family made it clear that they would not pay any compensation to any alleged victims, 'the entire lot collapsed like a pack of cards', says Daniel Janner. He adds:

> If there was anything in it, the lawyers would have disputed it. It emanated from Keir Starmer, and it shows a complete lack of judgement. That's what's disturbing about it. There were nine separate claims against my father and then his estate when he died, and the entire lot were either dismissed or withdrawn. So of course I feel angry and resentful about it, but this is serious stuff. My impression of [Starmer] as DPP in respect of this policy is that he not only lacks judgement but it has an appalling knock-on effect, and he's very rigid. The rigidity of his approach led unquestionably to the unravelling of Operation Midland.

So strongly did Janner feel about Starmer's lack of suitability to remain in public life that he wrote to *The Times* in January 2020 urging Starmer to pull out of the leadership race on the grounds that the prospect of him becoming opposition leader was 'unacceptable in a just society'.

The former Tory MP Harvey Proctor, who was also falsely accused by Beech, remains deeply aggrieved by Operation Midland as well. He, too, blames Starmer personally for his plight. 'Starmer began his political career which was based on a "believe the victim" policy,' Proctor claims.

> As DPP he was concerned with the insufficient number of convictions for rape and sexual abuse which were detrimental to his reputation and his role as DPP and on his potential future political career. He made it clear as DPP, and subsequently as a politician, that 'victims' should be believed and supported. He placed them at the heart of the criminal justice system. He was the head of the CPS when it took a decision not to prosecute Jimmy Savile for historical child sexual abuse in 2009. By way of attempted redemption, he gave speech upon speech to promote the 'believe the victim' strategy. It was such pressure and 'political' challenges that in November 2014 led Tom Winsor of Her Majesty's Inspectorate of Constabulary to instruct the Metropolitan Police Service and all police constabularies that [the view that] 'a victim should always be believed' should be institutionalised. Starmer initiated the undermining of centuries of British justice that people should be judged innocent until proven guilty. We will never know the full extent of the suffering Starmer has caused to others.
>
> His policy reached its zenith in Operation Midland with many but not all being led to question Starmer's stance. The

> direct impact on my life of this wrong-headed policy was to lose me my job, my reputation and my home. There continues to be unresolved family difficulties and the irreparable loss of friendships. Emotionally and financially, I am not in the same position I used to be. I was falsely accused of serial child murders and sexual child abuse and the torture of children. My home and my office were illegally searched by eighteen Met Police officers. I now know the search was illegal as the Met Police misled district judge Howard Riddle into granting the search warrants. Riddle himself has confirmed that he was misled, and distinguished former High Court judge Sir Richard Henriques has backed up this claim. Such alleged criminality requires proper investigation. The consequence for me was that effectively I felt my life had been extinguished. Sir Keir has not apologised to me or taken any personal responsibility. He has not communicated with me in any way. I believe Sir Keir Starmer is not fit to be Prime Minister and he should not grace the benches of the House of Commons.

Ironically, it is now clear, of course, that the House of Commons was the very institution on which Starmer had his eye at the point he stood down as DPP in October 2013. By then, he had earned the unbending respect of the sitting Attorney General, Dominic Grieve, with whom he'd had to work closely. They got on so well that Grieve gave a speech at Starmer's leaving party, heaping praise on him as 'one of the most successful directors of recent years'.

CHAPTER 9

'ONE OF THE STARMERS SHOULD BE AN MP'

Keir Starmer is often described as being an intensely ambitious man, yet it is arguable that this trait is at least in part a consequence of the hopes and dreams of other members of his family, which were foisted upon him. As we have seen, his parents longed for him to do well at school and then to study a subject at university that would lead him directly to a profession. Yet by – supposedly – naming their eldest son after Keir Hardie, the first Labour Party leader, they were not just making a political statement; they were also acknowledging a desire that had existed within the wider Starmer clan for many years. The evidence for this comes from a letter written in December 2014 by Starmer's father, Rodney. One of the recipients of this round robin letter was kind enough to share it for the purposes of this book. After the main body of the typed text, under the heading 'PS... Stop Press...' Rodney Starmer expressed to friends his delight that his son had just been elected as Labour's prospective parliamentary candidate in the safe Labour seat of Holborn & St Pancras. He then wrote:

> Keir lives, works and the children go to school in the constituency. We are very pleased and wish him well. My dad, Bert, said many years ago that one of the Starmers should be an MP.

> He thought it would be my brother Dennis but that was not to be. Bert was the only Radical in his generation of Starmers.

Who can say why Starmer's grandfather, a mechanic, seemed so fixed upon a Starmer making it to the House of Commons? What is easier to imagine is that Keir Starmer himself was aware of Bert's dream. After all, if Rodney Starmer was prepared to share this anecdote with friends, he must have told his son about it sometime beforehand.

Starmer returned to private practice as a barrister in late 2013, after his five-year contract as DPP had concluded, but it was obvious that he did not intend to confine himself solely to the law for much longer, telling friends he did not want to take a seat in the House of Lords, as he could have done as the ex-DPP, but instead wanted a frontline political career. What was very much to his advantage was the fact that, under the Fixed-Term Parliaments Act 2011, everybody knew that the next general election would be held in May 2015, giving him a date he could work towards.

Starmer's acceptance of his friend Ed Miliband's invitation in late 2013 to chair a Labour Party taskforce on victims' rights, as referred to in Chapter 8, all but made public his intention to move into politics. Yet before he could do so, there was another, more pressing, matter to tackle. As Starmer well knew, it is customary for retiring male DPPs to be honoured with a knighthood, but he had to decide whether he would go against his progressive instincts by accepting a title which he would keep for the rest of his life, and which would allow his wife to be addressed as 'Lady Starmer' to boot. He had already joined the ranks of the establishment by becoming DPP, but would there be any consequences for him politically if he cemented this status with a knighthood? What would his Labour-supporting parents and friends say? One who knows him well says he certainly wrestled with the problem. 'Keir has always been cautious,' says the friend.

> Some advised him not to take a knighthood, for the sake of his Labour career, but of course he did. They all do – even Republicans and left-wingers, who are told it's expected of them when for example they become judges. He prefers not to use it, but it probably provides a certain reassurance to Middle England.

The Cabinet Office has refused to confirm who nominated Starmer for his knighthood. All it did reveal under Freedom of Information laws was that the State Committee considered his nomination and that its members in 2013 comprised Dame Mary Marsh, Baroness Bottomley, Dame Suzi Leather, Elizabeth McMeikan, Dr Diana Walford, Dr Suzy Walton, Sir Paul Jenkins and Sir Bob Kerslake. Having been vetted and cleared, he would have been advised about a month before it became public that he was to be honoured 'for services to law and criminal justice'. The statement announcing this was published in the 2014 New Year Honours list, which was released to the press on 30 December 2013, and the investiture took place at Buckingham Palace on 12 February 2014. He asked his parents to join him at the palace, where he was knighted by the Prince of Wales, and his father later wrote to tell friends about the occasion. Explaining that they set off for London at 6 a.m. for the 10 a.m. ceremony, they were accompanied in their car by a Great Dane called Chip, which they had taken in as a rescue dog the previous year.

Rodney Starmer described himself and his wife as 'the proudest parents there', having seen their son kneeling before Prince Charles. He even wrote a short account of his career, culminating with the knighthood, which was published in the newsletter of the Barn Theatre in Oxted, one of his favourite haunts, in 2014. Starmer has always maintained that his relationship with his father was distant, and this belief is backed up by Bruce Reed, the theatre's chairman. Reed says, 'It's interesting, because it was many years before any of us knew of the existence of Keir Starmer. It wasn't until he became Director of Public Prosecutions [in 2008] that Rod said, "Hasn't my boy done well?" I thought, "Boy? What boy is this?!"' This suggests that, like many men of his generation, Rodney Starmer perhaps had some difficulty showing his emotions, leading to a less fulfilled relationship between father and son than either side wanted. It also gives credence to the notion that Keir felt that being recognised at Buckingham Palace might be more important to his parents than it was to him. That would explain why he has always been reticent about using the title. In 2015, he told his local newspaper: 'I've never liked titles. When I was DPP, everyone called me director and I said, "Please don't call me director, call me Keir Starmer." It's a very similar battle now.' Similarly, the parliamentary authorities only refer to him as plain 'Keir Starmer' in all official communications, at his request. Of course, accepting an honour and then refusing to use it does leave him open to accusations of what Boris Johnson has called 'cakeism', that is to say, having your cake and eating it. It also puts him in direct contrast to other big Labour Party figures. For example, Tony Benn, a politician whom Starmer is known to admire, famously renounced his hereditary peerage in 1963, albeit so that he could take his seat in the House of Commons, whereas Starmer actively collected his title.

Bill Bowring, who worked closely with Starmer at the Haldane Society in the 1980s and 1990s, believes that Starmer might not be as resistant to joining the establishment as he would have people believe. Bowring comments:

> I don't think he would have been shocked if you'd told him in 1990 that he would one day be a QC, a former DPP and a knight. I think one of Keir's faults, which has come out from time to time, is his wanting to insist how working-class he is, when he's absolutely plainly not. I mean, if you're a QC and former DPP, you've left your working-class roots far behind. That's a weakness of his, to go on about it. He's become very middle-class. I think he finds the aristocratic end of the Tory Party very disagreeable. I think he thinks being Sir Keir Starmer QC is really as far as he wants to go in the establishment. But he is establishment; of course he is.

Just before his inclusion in the New Year Honours list was announced, news spread that he was sizing up his local parliamentary seat in north London, Holborn & St Pancras. Encompassing most of the London Borough of Camden, it has long been considered one of the safest Labour seats in the country and, given its proximity to Westminster, is highly desirable from a practical point of view. It contains pockets of poverty as well as of prosperity and stretches from Covent Garden in the south to Hampstead Heath in the north, and from Primrose Hill in the west to Islington in the east. It had been held by the former Labour Cabinet minister Frank Dobson since its creation in 1983. Dobson's majority at the 2010 election had been a rock-solid 9,942.

This speculation may not have been welcomed by Starmer, but it was perfectly true. He had been quietly cultivating the seat, and in this he had the support of Dobson himself. A close friend of the late MP says, 'I remember talking to Frank about Keir. Frank was always very keen that Keir should succeed him. He had known him for quite a while, he really liked him, he thought he was impressive, and he never thought anyone but Keir should take over the seat from him.' Starmer also enjoyed the backing of the then Labour leader Ed Miliband, who happened to live in the constituency and who moved in the same circles as Starmer. He, too, had privately given Starmer his blessing. As noted in Chapter 8, Miliband was determined to hold Rupert Murdoch and his newspaper empire to account over the phone-hacking scandal, and some even believe Starmer's decision as DPP to sanction the prosecution of journalists from Murdoch's stable pleased Miliband so much that he was even happier to support his political ambitions.

The rumours that Starmer was limbering up to launch a bid for the seat were well known when, in June 2014, the 'Heathman' column in one of the constituency's papers, the *Hampstead and Highgate Express*, began to list the number of local events Starmer had appeared at despite Dobson still officially being the MP. 'The 51-year-old [Starmer] would neither rule himself in or out of any future Labour parliamentary race when Heathman spotted him at a presentation evening for pupils at William Ellis School in Highgate Road last Thursday,' the paper reported.

Starmer further sought to boost his credentials as a community-minded man by taking a position in June 2014 with the London-based charity Kids Company. It was run by Camila Batmanghelidjh, who once claimed to be a 'psychiatrist', and its chairman of trustees was the BBC executive Alan Yentob. Since the early 2000s, it had been astonishingly successful in persuading central government departments to give it more than £42 million of public money, allegedly to help deprived inner-city children. Thanks to its well-oiled PR machine, it was also feted by rock stars and celebrities, becoming a fashionable and very well-supported cause in the process. Yet getting involved with Kids Company was arguably an ill-judged decision on Starmer's part, however well-intentioned. He presents himself to the public as a forensically minded barrister, but it is clear that he did not undertake sufficient due diligence before hopping on board this enterprise. The fact that he has never discussed his association with the charity publicly all but proves he knows this.

On 24 June 2014, Starmer took to Twitter to announce that he felt it a 'privilege' to be asked by Batmanghelidjh to become chairman of a child protection taskforce operating under the umbrella of an initiative called 'See the Child. Change the System'. It was billed by the charity as 'a Kids Company campaign to rethink children's social care and mental health services'. At the point Starmer took up this post, the coalition government run by David Cameron and Nick Clegg was in its twilight, and there was a genuine belief among some senior employees at Kids Company that the then Labour leader, Ed Miliband, would become Prime Minister after the next general election in May 2015. As Starmer had strong links to Miliband, securing him for this role was considered a coup for Kids Company, as it would potentially provide a direct line of communication to Downing Street. Since Kids Company said it needed £1.5 million to start work on 'See the Child. Change the System', Starmer's worth to the charity was obvious.

Although a press conference was held to announce that Starmer had joined this Kids Company project, nothing of any consequence happened for several months in relation to it. Then, in February 2015, questions began to be asked about Kids Company itself, starting with an article in *The Spectator*. The magazine pointed out that the charity had made a series of claims which were so far-fetched as to be unbelievable, including in its own annual reports, which stated that the number of people it helped in 2010 was 16,500, a figure which had more than doubled to an astonishing 36,000 the next year. *The Spectator* raised concerns about Kids Company's spending habits, its accountability, its transparency and about what appeared to be an unusually cosy relationship between Batmanghelidjh and the then Prime Minister, David Cameron. Other media outlets took an interest in the story, matters escalated, and by the summer of 2015, the charity was forced to close down amid a raft of accusations about its apparently serial misuse of public money and allegations concerning sexual abuse, which were later dropped. Starmer's initiative had quietly sunk without trace by this point, meaning that he escaped any association with one of Britain's best-known charities exploding in what was a very public scandal. He must have counted himself lucky that 'See the Child. Change the System' never got off the ground properly under his stewardship. This was one failure of his with which he could be pleased.

• • •

In mid-July 2014, Frank Dobson finally announced at a constituency meeting his intention to stand down at the next general election, firing the starting gun for the competition to succeed him and represent one of Labour's strongholds in the capital. Starmer's campaign was already under way but had been forced to operate in the shadows until this point. Out of respect for Dobson and the integrity of a contest, which had to be seen to be open and fair, he had necessarily but covertly begun to assemble the support and financial backing he would need to mount a credible campaign. Dobson's statement removed this cloak of secrecy and allowed him to become an even more visible figure in the constituency. Bill Bowring recalls that Starmer left no stone unturned in his quest to become an MP. Even though Bowring had not had much to do with Starmer for several years, he received a call and was invited to help. 'He lobbied me and others relentlessly at the time he was going for Frank Dobson's seat,' remembers Bowring.

> He was on to me for anyone I knew who could possibly be lobbied to vote for him in the local Labour Party. I know people in St Pancras, people in particular who were on the Haldane executive who live in the constituency, and he was very keen that I should ask them if they'd be supporting him, which was fair enough. I strongly suspect they did.

Within a couple of weeks, Starmer was able to confirm that he was ready to put his name forward to stand as a parliamentary candidate, as long as Labour did not run an all-woman shortlist. Although the area had never had a female MP before, it appears Starmer knew by this point that a shortlist excluding men was not on the cards. Apart from anything else, he would hardly want to lose credibility so early in his career as an aspiring politician by announcing he was entering a competition which it would be impossible for him to win. He told the *Camden New Journal* on 31 July:

> It would be an honour for anyone to succeed Frank Dobson. It will now be for the party to agree the process and timetable but if it is an open shortlist I intend to seek selection from members of Holborn & St Pancras, my home for over fifteen years. Our constituency needs an MP who will continue Frank's principled campaigning, fight to get the Tories out of power and be able to influence a future Labour government. I believe I can bring my experience as a human rights lawyer, DPP and campaigner to do that. I am only too aware of the impact that politics has on the daily lives of all of us.

As a result of his networking efforts, he was able to inform the paper that he had already received 'strong support' for his candidacy from local party members and others, including the former chairman of the Equality and Human Rights Commission (EHRC), Trevor Phillips; the Labour peer Helena Kennedy (whom he had known for twenty years by this point); another Labour peer, Joan Bakewell; and the former Labour Cabinet minister Tessa Jowell. 'I am also grateful to have trade union support from Aslef,' he added. Given that King's Cross, St Pancras and Euston railway stations are all in the constituency, securing Aslef's support was certainly important.

Starmer was not the only person who was interested in succeeding Dobson, of course, and it would not be accurate to surmise that Ed Miliband's tacit approval of his candidacy made it a foregone conclusion that he would do so. For example, Sarah Hayward, then the leader of Camden Council, also signalled her intention to stand. Soon, others expressed an interest in joining the race, though Hayward was always regarded as Starmer's principal threat. As summer turned to autumn, however, one undeniable fact which pointed to Starmer having received some preferential treatment did dawn on his competitors. It became clear that Labour high command was in no hurry to find Dobson's replacement. Even in September – two months after Dobson had said he would quit – party chiefs were suggesting it might be November before the lucky man or woman would be named.

What lay behind this relaxed attitude? The Labour Party's own rules. These state that nobody can be selected as a prospective parliamentary candidate until they have been a party member for a minimum of a full year. As DPP, Starmer was meant to be politically neutral and was therefore not allowed to belong to a political party. For this reason, he had only been able to rejoin the Labour Party after having ceased to be DPP on 1 November

2013. Mutterings were soon heard that the selection contest was being delayed solely for Starmer's benefit. These grumbles were arguably borne out by the protracted timetable eventually decided upon. The contest would not open in earnest until 29 October, with all candidates needing to submit their papers by 10 November and the final selection taking place on 13 December. If these arrangements really were part of a fix that was weighted in Starmer's favour, it says much about the Labour Party at that time that they were put in place for a man who had no formal political experience whatsoever.

In 2014, there were about 1,200 local party members who would be eligible to vote in the contest. Ultimately, Starmer had to appeal to them. He was brilliantly placed to do so, thanks to having cultivated a public image as a high-profile barrister and then as DPP. Securing an interview with the *Evening Standard* was, for example, far easier for him than it would have been for his rivals. Indeed, in early September, he invited a *Standard* reporter to Doughty Street for a wide-ranging chat about his political aspirations, in which he trotted out familiar, though, as already established, somewhat dubious lines. For example, he said: 'I had a very traditional Labour background ... My dad worked in a factory all his life.'

Despite being willing to charm anybody and everybody who might be of use to him in his quest for a seat in Westminster, he was not above putting some people's noses out of joint. One barrister, Jon Holbrook, says that Starmer accepted an invitation to speak at the Battle of Ideas law debate being held in London on 18 October. Almost four weeks before the debate was to be held, on 23 September, Starmer wrote to Holbrook pulling out of the event, citing professional duties. 'I am really sorry,' he wrote to Holbrook, 'but a case of mine has been moved and now starts on Monday 20 October, and the only time the client can meet to go through some critical evidence is Saturday 18 October. Alas I will have to withdraw from the battle of ideas event.'

Holbrook takes up the story: 'I had no problem with him doing so – we were not, for example, paying him – save that he chose not to tell us the real reason when making his excuses,' he says.

> He claimed [his absence] was due to a professional legal commitment meaning that he had 'to go through some critical evidence' on that Saturday. Surprise, surprise on the morning of Saturday 18 October he tweeted how great it was to have met Sadiq Khan at the TUC march that was taking place that day. It always struck me as the actions of a weak man. If he had simply said to us, as organisers, 'I'm sorry, I now realise that, particularly as an aspiring Labour MP, I need to attend the TUC march and rally' I would have entirely understood.

On 12 October, those who had declared were invited to a warm-up event in Camden Town to address branch members from four wards in the constituency on a subject of their choice. Starmer chose to speak about 'Why Labour needs a values-based approach to 2015', a topic which, in retrospect, was not guaranteed to set anybody's pulse racing. On 29 October, however, he raised his game significantly by publishing a glossy leaflet featuring more than 100 prominent people who had come out to back him. They included Doreen Lawrence, the mother of murdered teenager Stephen Lawrence; Fiona Millar, journalist and partner of Tony Blair's former spin doctor, Alastair Campbell; and Ken Livingstone, the former Mayor of London. The former Foreign Secretary, David Miliband, was also happy to be named as an endorser on the leaflet. He and his younger brother, Ed, had fallen out after both of them had a tilt at the Labour leadership four years previously, yet by gaining the elder Miliband's support, Starmer was seen to be above this unseemly sibling rivalry. Robert Latham, a wealthy Doughty Street barrister who has turned out to be pivotal when it comes to bankrolling Starmer's political aspirations, was also on the list, as was Labour Party worker Ben Nunn, who became Starmer's director of communications when he assumed the leadership in 2020. Starmer put his rivals in the shade with this leaflet and the number of backers he had secured, but not everybody approved of it. One party member even complained to the *Camden New Journal* that its mere existence confirmed Starmer and his team had been working the seat long before anybody else and 'surely before Frank Dobson had even announced he was going'.

By the time nominations closed, twenty-four people had put their names forward, illustrating a clear competition in those wishing to represent this plum constituency. Each submitted a personal statement. Starmer's, in which he called himself 'a national voice for local people', made great play of his familiarity with the constituency but contained at least two arguable assertions. 'I am local,' he wrote. 'I have lived in Kentish Town for fifteen years and worked in Holborn for twenty-five years.' This was arguably misleading. As far as records show, he had lived in Kentish Town since his relationship with Phillippa Kaufmann had broken down just twelve or thirteen years previously; and although he had worked in Doughty Street, which is in Holborn, from 1990 until 2008, thereafter he was based at the CPS office in Westminster until 2013, raising questions about where the 'twenty-five years' figure came from. The rest of the one-page statement covered his family, his legal career, his work on Labour's criminal justice strategy and his ambition to serve as a constituency MP.

On 18 November, the first of the neighbourhood branch meetings took place, where nominations were made for the final selection contest. Every branch had to nominate two candidates, at least one of whom had to be a woman. Branches were able to add a third name if an ethnic minority candidate had not been chosen in the first two votes. More nomination meetings in other branches followed. Starmer did well, as predicted, sailing through to the final round of candidates, who were interviewed by a ten-member committee of senior Holborn & St Pancras Labour Party figures and then whittled down to a shortlist of five to compete in a final hustings on Saturday 13 December. Alongside Starmer and Sarah Hayward were hospital consultant Dr Patrick French; former Camden Council leader and human rights lawyer Raj Chada; and West Hampstead councillor Angela Pober.

On the eve of that final meeting, Starmer received the endorsement of an elder statesman of the Labour Party in the form of Neil Kinnock, who praised his 'courage, integrity and principles'. It was further proof of Starmer's single-mindedness that he was able to wheel out such a big gun at this late stage. A few days later, at St Pancras Church, all thoughts of spending the afternoon Christmas shopping or watching Arsenal play at home were put aside by hundreds of party members, who queued round the block to be able to have their say in selecting the person who they knew, barring a freak result, would almost certainly be their next MP. By this point, more than 200 postal votes had been cast, yet each candidate still had to perform well in front of the membership in order to secure a majority of the rest.

Local journalist Richard Osley, the deputy editor of the *Camden New Journal*, who was present, noted in his blog:

> When his turn came to speak at the final hustings, Sir Keir talked about his family: his six-year-old son who was desperate for this selection campaign to end, and a deeply personal story about the NHS. He talked about how immigration should be celebrated in an answer to one question, and fudged another about his thoughts on the coalition.

In Osley's opinion, Starmer did not speak as well as another candidate, Raj Chada, but by then it was probably too late anyway. Having as an MP a figure with a profile as high as Starmer's was seemingly enough to satisfy the appetites of most people present. Frank Dobson, who was officiating, announced after just one round of voting that Starmer had scored a sizeable majority of votes, though the exact number has never been made public. After making a short victory speech, in which he urged everybody present not to hold an inquest into which candidate each had voted for, he repaired to the bar of the Premier Inn in the Euston Road for a celebratory drink before hosting his closest friends and advisers at home. Amusingly, one aide contacted Osley that night and asked him – not for the first time – to stop using Starmer's knighthood when writing about him, presumably because of fears it might alienate voters. Osley took the view that this request simply meant he was duty-bound to use the title more often when writing about Starmer in the *Camden New Journal*.

After Holborn & St Pancras Labour members had had their say, ending the party's suspiciously long five-month wait to select a candidate to succeed Dobson, there was not an enormous amount of time left for Starmer to 'nurse' the constituency before the election. Just before he was selected, he claimed to dislike the type of campaigning which focused on his personality, telling the *Hampstead and Highgate Express*: 'I want to get on with the real job of winning the next election. I don't find the self-promotion of this process a comfortable experience.' Despite this professed reservation, he still found the time to give interviews to the national press. Within a week of his nomination, he told *The Guardian* why he had chosen politics over the law, predicting that

> 2015 is going to be a defining election. If I'm right, then the next ten years are going to be really tough and – this isn't meant to

> sound arrogant – but I think if I do have skills and experience that might help, I don't really think I can walk away from it.

The *Sunday Times* was also invited to Doughty Street Chambers for a chat with the aspiring MP a few days after he was named as the candidate. Having inherited a constituency that was his to lose, there were no serious obstacles in Starmer's way as election day loomed. Still, he campaigned hard in the seat, sometimes with Frank Dobson's help, perhaps spurred on by the fact the leader of the Green Party, Natalie Bennett, posed a potential threat, as did the Conservative candidate, Will Blair. It was only when his mother died less than two weeks before polling day that his progress was interrupted. A large funeral attended by almost 150 people was held. Josephine Starmer was seventy-five years old and, despite her crippling illness, had overcome the odds to lead a much fuller life than any medical professional had ever believed possible. What was no doubt a personal tragedy to Starmer was that his mother did not live to see him win a parliamentary seat and enter the Commons.

CHAPTER 10

CORE GROUP PLUS

On 7 May 2015, Starmer was elected the Member of Parliament for Holborn & St Pancras with nearly 53 per cent of the vote and a majority of 17,048 – an increase in the Labour haul of more than 7,000 since the previous election in 2010. At the age of fifty-two, he had made it to Westminster at the first attempt. Bert Starmer's wish had finally been granted.

Nevertheless, the new member was disappointed. In defiance of most polls and to the surprise of David Cameron himself, the Conservatives swept to victory with an overall majority for the first time since 1992. As in other similar seats, left-leaning voters punished the Liberal Democrats for going into coalition with the Tories, boosting Labour's local support and giving Starmer what he called the 'delusion' that his party was on course to win. 'In those final weeks on my patch, it looked as if we were getting better results, so the exit poll was crushing,' he later said.

The new MP had hardly had time to get his feet under his new desk in Parliament's Portcullis House when a clamour arose for him to take a further giant leap in his political career. The comment pages of *The Guardian*, often considered Labour's house journal, began to feature serious discussion of the idea that Starmer should stand in the contest to replace Ed Miliband, who had announced his resignation as Labour leader the morning after the party's drubbing.

'Who better than the new MP Keir Starmer, former Director

of Public Prosecutions and human rights lawyer, to help stop the UK joining Belarus outside the European Court of Human Rights?' asked veteran columnist Polly Toynbee. Lord Myners, who had been a minister in Gordon Brown's government, said he was underwhelmed by the current contenders – former frontbenchers Andy Burnham, Yvette Cooper, Liz Kendall and Mary Creagh, and a left-wing perennial backbencher called Jeremy Corbyn – and that he 'would like to see someone really quite radical. I would like to see Keir Starmer, who has only been a Member of Parliament for a week, but he's got a real background, he's done a proper job.' Could the party really consider such a new candidate? 'Many people would say no. But goodness me, wouldn't that electrify the campaign?'

A grassroots movement also sprang into being. Under the rather cumbersome title 'Sir Keir Starmer QC KCB for Labour Leader', a group of online devotees set up a Facebook page urging their hero to put himself forward, attracting hundreds of followers within a few days. The fact that Starmer had not responded to the group's tweets and emails did not discourage them. 'Silence speaks volumes,' said Narice Bernard, a disenchanted Labour supporter who helped found the campaign. 'He hasn't said he'll stand, but he hasn't said he won't. It's clear that when someone goes into politics at his stage of life they do so for a very good reason – they want to make a difference.' The crusade was not factional, Bernard stressed. 'I suspect he is from the left of the party, but it's not about left and right, it's about leadership.'

Starmer put a stop to the speculation after a few days, tweeting 'V flattered by #keirforleader initiative and thanks for so many supportive messages but Labour needs s/one with more political experience.'

Having decided against a run on his own account, Starmer had to choose among the real candidates to lead the party. He backed

Burnham, a former Health Secretary, who was initially the bookies' favourite to succeed Miliband. Once considered a Blairite, Burnham was regarded as being in the centre-left mainstream of the party. His leadership manifesto pledged to restore the 50 per cent tax rate on high earners that had been abolished by the Tories, to renationalise the railways and to raise the minimum wage. However, he said he would scrap Labour's commitment to a mansion tax, describing the idea as 'the politics of envy'. Burnham believed Labour had lost because 'a sense has built up that we aren't in favour of people getting on. That is toxic. We need to get back to communicating simple policies that will make a real difference to people.'

Candidates needed the support of at least thirty-five MPs to make it onto the ballot, and Burnham received sixty-eight nominations, more than any of his rivals. This counted for nothing with the Labour membership, who four months later elected Corbyn with 251,417 votes, nearly 60 per cent of the total and more than three times as many as second-placed Burnham. Incidentally, according to one source, Rodney Starmer was an enthusiastic supporter of the new leader and remained so until his death in 2018. 'Rodney stood up at a meeting of his local Labour Party in east Surrey and read out a speech proposing Jeremy Corbyn for leader in 2015,' says this person. 'He later became very angry at the various plots being organised against Corbyn by members of the Parliamentary Labour Party.' It remains an open question whether he knew that his son was involved in at least one of these.

• • •

However preposterous, the experience of being touted for the leadership within days of his election underlined how high expectations were for Starmer by the time he arrived in Parliament.

In his former role, he had been within the orbit of the political world. He had worked closely with ministers, given evidence to parliamentary committees and become a public figure in his own right, making decisions on controversial issues at the heart of national debate. Even so, politicians who dealt with him as DPP were astonished that he made the move into full-time politics.

In his early months in Parliament, Starmer eased the transition by sticking to familiar policy territory. In his maiden speech on 28 May, during a debate on home affairs and justice, he used the presence of four surviving Magna Carta manuscripts in the British Museum, located in his constituency, as a hook to attack government plans to replace the Human Rights Act with a British Bill of Rights:

> As we now celebrate the 800th anniversary of Magna Carta, let us affirm the principle that human rights apply to everyone equally. Any proposed British Bill of Rights inconsistent with that principle will not be worth the paper it is written on and will face widespread opposition, not least from me on behalf of my constituents in Holborn & St Pancras.

Following tradition, Starmer also paid tribute to his long-serving predecessor. 'Although I doubt I will clock up thirty-six years, I intend to follow in Frank Dobson's footsteps – albeit my jokes are likely to seem tame when compared with his, and I might give the beard a miss.' (Dobson's jokes were indeed notorious. The late former Conservative minister Alan Clark recorded in his diaries that they were 'so filthy that really they're unusable, even at a rugger club dinner'.)

In July he began a short stint on the Commons Home Affairs Select Committee, chaired by Labour MP Keith Vaz. Only four meetings were held during his membership: hearings on the migration crisis at Calais and the prevalence of new psychoactive substances, and sessions with Metropolitan Police Commissioner Bernard Hogan-Howe and Home Secretary Theresa May. He asked Hogan-Howe about body-worn police cameras, expressing the hope that they would soon be used by all London police officers. Given the opportunity to grill May, he chose the perhaps obscure topic of Ofcom's role in dealing with broadcasters disseminating extremist content – and in particular, the balance between the need to tackle extremism and the broadcasters' right to freedom of expression under Article 10 of the Human Rights Act.

One major departure from Starmer's preference for criminal justice matters was HS2, the proposed new high-speed railway linking London with Birmingham and the north of England, terminating at Euston station. The building works would mean years of disruption for Starmer's constituents, 17,000 of whom lived within 300 metres of the planned construction work, and the demolition of hundreds of homes. In a debate in September 2015, he spoke of the impact on local residents, businesses and the environment of a programme that could last twenty years. The Bill was passed, but Starmer voted against, defying the Labour whip for the first time.

Early in the new parliament, MPs were faced with the question of how much they ought to be paid. After the expenses scandal of 2009, whose worst offenders Starmer had prosecuted as DPP, the matter was put into the hands of the Independent Parliamentary Standards Authority (IPSA), which recommended in June 2015 that MPs' salaries should rise from £67,060 to £74,000 – an increase of 10 per cent at a time when pay remained frozen in much of the public sector. Some MPs voiced opposition to the proposal, including Starmer's constituency neighbours Tulip Siddiq in Hampstead & Kilburn and Catherine West in Hornsey & Wood Green, but Starmer declined to do so. He said he accepted that any increase was hard to justify in the prevailing economic climate, but 'having overseen the prosecution of a number of MPs for expenses fraud, I firmly believe that any decision should be taken by IPSA, an independent body, without lobbying by MPs one way or the other'.

The IPSA proposal was implemented, taking Starmer's salary from one third of what he had earned as DPP to just under three eighths. He did not have to make do with that, however. According to the Register of Members' Interests, between the 2015 and 2017 elections, Starmer earned a further £45,490.62 for legal work on top of his parliamentary duties, plus an extra £1,609.22 for six articles in *The Guardian*.

His clients included the Government of Gibraltar, who paid £9,480 for twenty hours' work in December 2015, leading to speculation that he had advised the territory on how to 'nobble' Brexit as the UK prepared for its referendum. Starmer was unable to deny this, maintaining that 'legal advice is confidential and privileged', but Gibraltar itself later spared his blushes by issuing a statement that 'his advice was sought in relation to non-political matters affecting prosecutions and procedures relating thereto. Both instances were entirely unrelated to the UK or Gibraltar's membership of or exit from the European Union.' Another customer was the prestigious law firm Mishcon de Reya, whose in-house learning and thought-leadership academy he advised for six hours a month from June to September 2016, for a monthly fee of £4,500. This non-parliamentary work made him one of the highest earners on the Labour benches.

• • •

That summer's leadership campaign was not the only event that would signal the direction the Labour Party was taking. After eight years in the job, Boris Johnson was to stand down as Mayor of London at the following year's election. The clear favourite to be selected as Labour's candidate was the Blairite Tessa Jowell, who, as Culture Secretary, had led the city's successful bid to host the 2012 Olympics. Starmer, however, backed Sadiq Khan, the MP for Tooting and former Transport Minister, who was considered well to the left of Jowell. The two men knew each other well, Khan having been a solicitor specialising in human rights law before entering politics. 'Sadiq made his name rooting out injustice and righting wrongs,' wrote Starmer in the *New Statesman*. 'He was never afraid to take on powerful vested interests in the government, the police or the prison service. This is precisely what we need in a mayor.' Five years later, Khan would return the favour.

• • •

As Parliament prepared to return in September, Corbyn assembled his first shadow Cabinet. As well as left-wingers like John McDonnell and Diane Abbott, appointed shadow Chancellor and shadow International Development Secretary respectively, the team included more moderate figures such as Hilary Benn and Lucy Powell, who led on foreign affairs and education. When more junior frontbench appointments were announced a few days later, Starmer was named as a shadow minister in Labour's home affairs team, leading on security, immigration and asylum.

Inevitably in the competitive world of politics, there was a degree of envy at Starmer's rapid promotion. 'There is always resentment for people who end up on the front bench from others who don't,' observes a colleague. 'What they said was, he's just an automaton lawyer, he hasn't done the hard yards. But actually, that was a mistake; he was very political. He understands politics inside out.'

According to Burnham, now the shadow Home Secretary and effectively Starmer's boss, the new spokesman had not displayed any of the self-importance that might have come with his former status. 'The fact he was a former DPP and came to work in my shadow Home Office team with no airs and graces says a lot about Keir Starmer,' he said later.

One of Starmer's first actions was to introduce a new law on the rights of victims of crime. This was an issue on which he had long campaigned, as mentioned in Chapter 8. The way victims were treated ought to lead to a 'pause in the oft-repeated mantra that we have the best criminal justice system in the world', the former DPP had written in 2014. His Ten-Minute Rule Bill – under which MPs can make the case for new legislation in a speech lasting up to ten minutes – included measures giving victims the right to appeal against a decision to stop a criminal investigation and establishing a duty to report suspected child abuse in regulated professions like healthcare and teaching.

Despite attracting cross-party support, the proposal went the way of most Private Members' Bills and failed to attract enough backing to make progress in Parliament. Many of its provisions were attached as amendments to the government's own Policing and Crime Bill the following year, but protocol meant that despite his expertise in the subject, Starmer was barred from speaking in the debate since he was by then shadowing a different department. ('That's the rules,' he said. 'I'm not grumbling.')

Otherwise, Starmer's nine months in the shadow home affairs post were dominated by three issues, each of which had previously been difficult territory for Labour. The first of these was the Investigatory Powers Bill, known to its critics as the 'snoopers' charter', which would govern the security services' ability to access private communications, including internet records. Alert to the risk of seeming to hamper the fight against crime and terrorism, Starmer went out of his way to strike a constructive note. He welcomed the Bill as a necessary step given advances in communications technology but emphasised the need to balance public safety with concerns about personal privacy and abuse of power.

'I spent five years prosecuting some of the most dangerous terrorists in this country, so it would be quite difficult for people to pin the charge of being soft on terrorism on me,' Starmer said. 'The public do want to be properly protected, and that is my position and the party's position. It's a case of getting the balance right, and that doesn't mean we simply yield to everything the security services, law enforcement or the government says it wants.' On the other hand he noted, 'If there's not a new act, the security services will continue to use powers exposed by Edward Snowden [the former CIA operative who leaked details of government surveillance programmes] but without the safeguards that we now think are appropriate. You need the powers, but they've got to be properly administered.'

As DPP, he told the Commons, he had worked with the security services on cases 'that involved some of the most serious and grotesque crimes, and I shared the anxiety of tracking down individuals before they committed unspeakable crimes. For me, that has always made a compelling case for retaining some communications and personal data.'

While proposals for bulk data collection certainly amounted to an intrusion of privacy, he said in a BBC interview:

> The question is whether it can be justified. Privacy is a right, it's a really important right, but it's not an absolute right. The question is, is any invasion necessary, and is it proportionate? … I've seen this from both sides of the argument. I spent twenty years as a human rights lawyer, taking on cases for people who

> had had their human rights invaded. I then spent five years as Director of Public Prosecutions working with the security and intelligence services. We do need these powers but there must be the right safeguards.

Labour abstained at the Bill's second reading stage in March 2016, arguing that the proposals did not offer tough enough safeguards against unwarranted intrusion. By the third reading in June, however, the government had offered significant concessions – for which Starmer received a good deal of the credit – including greater privacy protections, stronger judicial oversight, a commitment that interception warrants could not be issued because of legitimate trade union activity and an independent review of the use of bulk data. Now Labour officially backed the legislation, to the consternation of civil rights campaigners and some in the party.

Two Labour MPs were conspicuous by their absence at the vote. One was Corbyn, the party leader. The other was Diane Abbott, who went on to condemn the new law as a 'serious erosion of our rights and liberties' after she succeeded Burnham as shadow Home Secretary later in the year. 'I tried to raise these points in the course of the final debates,' she said, implicitly criticising Burnham and Starmer for their approach.

The second big issue to confront Starmer in his new role was the mounting crisis as huge numbers of refugees crossed the Mediterranean, especially from Syria, in the hope of a new life in Europe. While still a backbencher, Starmer had criticised the government for failing to uphold Britain's 'long and proud tradition of helping those most in need'. Along with neighbouring constituency MPs West and Siddiq, he wrote to the PM calling for more of the migrants who had found their way to Europe to be housed in Britain. 'Just 1,000 Syrians, at the very most, will be granted asylum under our schemes – a fraction of the tens of thousands whom Germany and others have helped,' they wrote. 'We must also take our fair share of those affected by this crisis.'

As Labour's spokesman, he backed ministers' refusal to accept a mandatory quota of migrants under the EU's scheme. But while he welcomed the government's move to accept 4,000 refugees a year over the course of the parliament, he was not satisfied, complaining, '4,000 refugees represents less than 0.5 per cent of the refugees entering the EU this year. That is not good enough.' While it would be for the government to decide on the right number, Starmer noted: 'It has been suggested that if every city or county in Britain took just ten refugee families, we would be able to help perhaps 10,000 individuals.'

Starmer implied that Britain itself had some responsibility for the situation that had prompted millions to leave their homes. 'Following the decision to extend our military action in Iraq to Syria we now have an even greater moral responsibility to provide a fair and humane response to those fleeing persecution in both countries,' he asserted. 'Yet by limiting our response to just 20,000 Syrian refugees over the next five years, the government has failed this test of moral responsibility. More should be done, and quickly.'

In January 2016, Starmer visited camps in Calais and Dunkirk where migrants had gathered in anticipation of what they hoped would be an onward journey to England. He described the 'truly appalling' conditions in a debate shortly afterwards. The Dunkirk camp was

> basically a forest in which there is a swamp. On the ground is mud, water, urine and everything else that one would expect to find mixed in when there are no toilets or running water. In the middle of that, on any piece of semi-firm soil, are pitched

> flimsy tents. I do not think that anybody could go in any capacity to those camps and not come back a changed person.

The plight of refugees and the treatment of asylum seekers in Britain became a regular theme of Starmer's interventions at the despatch box. He rejected the argument that welcoming more migrants in Britain would create a 'pull factor' by encouraging more to make the hazardous journey; opposed plans to remove state support from young migrants in the UK when they turned eighteen if their asylum application was rejected; and pressed the government to change its stance of refusing to take asylum seekers who had already reached European countries. He supported the successful Dubs Amendment – named after its proposer, Labour peer Lord Dubs – under which the government would transfer 480 unaccompanied asylum-seeking children from Europe.

Though he later commended programmes for settling asylum seekers in the UK and praised the minister responsible for refugees, Richard Harrington, for his work, he concluded:

> In twenty years' time chapters in history books will be written about this moment in world history, in European history and in our own history, and I have concerns that – on reflection and looking back – our response will be judged as reluctant and limited, and in comparison with others not fair and not proportionate.

Sincere as it presumably was, the position Starmer expounded on refugees and asylum seekers was the one that might traditionally have been expected from Labour: generous, and in the eyes of many voters perhaps too generous. Critics of the party's policy asked in what sense people seeking to enter the UK could still be said to be fleeing persecution if they were already in France; where extra asylum seekers were to be housed given Britain's well-known shortage of social housing; and why those like the shadow minister who were pushing to receive more migrants never seemed to be offering their own spare rooms for the purpose.

Nevertheless, Starmer's long-held position on asylum did not make it any easier for him to pursue another of his objectives: to change perceptions of Labour on the broader question of immigration. The issue had become a major concern for voters in Labour's later years in government and was widely held to have contributed to the party's defeat in 2010. While the Conservative-led coalition government had failed to meet its target of bringing annual net migration below 100,000 – not least because of the EU's freedom of movement policy, which, as long as the UK remained a member, made it impossible to restrict migration into the UK from the twenty-seven other member states – Labour still lagged behind the Tories in public trust on the issue.

At the beginning of 2016, Starmer launched a three-month listening tour of the UK in order to help construct a new approach. 'Many Labour voters and supporters are worried about migration and their concerns must be our concerns,' he said. On his travels he would be 'listening to the arguments and seeing for myself both the advantages and the challenges that migration brings in different places.' Starmer accepted that his party had sometimes tried to avoid the issue. 'I do accept that many in the Labour Party have not really wanted to have the difficult conversations with people about immigration,' he said in Oldham, an early stop on his expedition. 'What Labour can't do is start with the assumption that there are some views we don't want to hear or are somehow not legitimate.'

Given Starmer's strong support for EU membership and the commitment to free movement that came with it, it is unclear how radically he would have been prepared to shift Labour's position. Either way, the exercise bore no fruit in terms of policy, for two main reasons. First, the immigration question was soon engulfed by the Brexit referendum campaign, in which the debate over free movement would play a major part.

The second reason was that responsibility for the policy passed to Abbott, who, as with the Investigatory Powers Bill, took rather a different view from Starmer and Burnham. She dismissed the idea that Labour should adopt a firmer stance on the issue in response to public opinion, writing later that year that 'Labour cannot outdo UKIP or this government on immigration. It should not try. It should pursue its own principled immigration policies which recognises [*sic*] the large benefits of immigration along with some costs.' In any case, it seems unlikely that any dramatic policy overhaul would have been sanctioned by Corbyn, who had said during the leadership campaign that Britain should celebrate its high levels of migration and described Labour's 2015 manifesto commitment to control immigration as 'appalling'.

• • •

Two further contentious issues confronted Starmer in his first year as an MP. In September 2015, he found himself in the minority in his own party, as well as in Parliament as a whole, when he voted to legalise assisted suicide. Under the Assisted Dying Bill, on which all MPs were given a free vote with no instructions from party whips, people with less than six months to live would have had the option of being prescribed a lethal dose of drugs, provided each case was approved by two doctors and a High Court judge.

During the debate Starmer recounted at length, and to the frustration of some fellow MPs, how and why he had drawn up the existing guidelines during his time as DPP. These stated that the criminal law should rarely, if ever, be used against those who assisted loved ones to die at their request, provided the patient had reached a voluntary, clear, settled and informed decision, but that no such stipulation could be made for doctors and nurses under existing legislation. We had therefore 'arrived at a position where compassionate amateur assistance from nearest and dearest is accepted, but professional medical assistance is not unless you have the means of physical assistance to get to Dignitas', he told Parliament. 'That, to my mind, is an injustice we have trapped within our current arrangements.' Despite Starmer's arguments, the Bill was defeated by 330 votes to 118.

The other controversial issue was that of whether to approve the government's plan for airstrikes against ISIL in Syria in December 2015. The day-long Commons debate included the unusual spectacle of two frontbenchers from the same party making an impassioned contribution on opposite sides of the debate. While Corbyn censured what he described as 'an ill-thought-out rush to war' and said that 'only a negotiated political and diplomatic endeavour' would bring an end to the Syrian crisis, shadow Foreign Secretary Hilary Benn won a rare standing ovation on both sides of the House for his speech declaring, 'We are here faced by fascists ... What we know about fascists is that they need to be defeated.' This, he said, was why socialists had joined the fight against Franco in the 1930s and the entire House had stood against Hitler and Mussolini. 'My view is that we must now confront this evil. It is now time for us to do our bit in Syria. And that is why I ask my colleagues to vote for the motion tonight.'

Starmer steered between the two poles. 'I am not a pacifist and I would back a lawful, coherent and compelling case for the use of military force by the UK against ISIS,' he wrote shortly before the debate. But although he believed there was a sufficient legal basis for the action, 'I am driven to the conclusion that the strategy outlined by the Prime Minister is flawed.' In the debate, he said:

> I am not against airstrikes per se, and I accept that it is difficult to see how territory can be taken from Daesh [as ISIL/ISIS were also known] without them. In my view, however, airstrikes without an effective ground force are unlikely to make any meaningful contribution to defeating Daesh, and there is no effective ground force.

The Commons backed airstrikes by 397 to 223, but like Corbyn and most Labour MPs, Starmer voted against.

• • •

Starmer had quickly established a reputation inside and outside Parliament, but politically he was an enigma. He made no secret that he was a Corbyn-sceptic, even telling the 2015 Labour conference: 'JC is not the messiah, he hasn't got all the answers, and if you touch him you're not healed.' Beyond that, even close colleagues found him hard to place on the political spectrum. In early interviews, he fended off attempts to probe the question: 'People want to be paid properly for the work they do … People want to live in secure housing they can afford – that's not about left and right, it's basic fairness and dignity,' he told *The Guardian* during the 2015 campaign. 'I do not need to have a label in order to make my mind up,' he said on another occasion.

After the election, he regularly made clear that he had no time for the tendency of some in the party to pursue doctrine at the expense of victory, telling the *New Statesman* he would

> reject wholeheartedly any notion of a Labour Party that is not committed to returning to power at the first opportunity. Of course that needs to be principled power. But standing on the sidelines looking for the purest ideology is a dereliction of duty for any Labour member.

In a lecture to the Fabian Society, he spoke of a feeling within Labour that by the 2015 election the party had 'lost its way and turned into a pale imitation of itself. This was not a simple left/right divide; both those on the left and those on the right of our party were yearning for Labour to be more radical, more confident and, above all, more ambitious.' All true, no doubt, but a formulation that avoided placing himself anywhere on the scale.

The working assumption was that he belonged somewhere in the amorphous soft left of the party, but some in the leader's team concluded that he was more moderate than that, and probably somewhere to the right of Ed Miliband. Despite this ideological divergence, Starmer and Corbyn got on reasonably well. They developed a functional working relationship, though interactions tended to be professional rather than pally. Both disliked confrontations. The Corbyn team was impressed with Starmer's discipline in sticking to lines that had been agreed by the shadow Cabinet.

This benign judgement became embarrassingly public when a document emerged in which Labour MPs were assessed for their fidelity to the socialist project and its leader. Ever alert to nuances of loyalty, opposition and betrayal, Corbyn allies had drawn up a list placing colleagues in one of five categories: Core Group, Core Group Plus, Neutral But Not Hostile, Core Group Negative and Hostile.

Some frontbench figures, including the Chief Whip Rosie Winterton and shadow Minister for Mental Health Luciana Berger, were labelled Hostile, as was Sadiq Khan, by now the party's London mayoral candidate. Starmer, however, found himself listed as Core Group Plus, placing him – at least in the eyes of the dossier's author – in Corbyn's loyal outer circle.

There were competing versions of how the list found its way into the public realm. One was that several filing cabinets were left in a parliamentary corridor after a clear-out in the leader's office; another was that the document was left in a Westminster pub. A spokesman for Corbyn denied reports that the list had been drawn up by the leader's staff, but MPs on the list told reporters they believed it was 'kosher'.

Whatever its provenance, the list was a gift for Cameron, who had a field day at Labour's expense at Prime Minister's Questions. It was also a source of amusement to Corbyn critics on the Labour benches (John Spellar pinned a 'Core Group Negative' badge to his lapel, and another MP demanded an immediate upgrade to Hostile). The fact that it had diverted attention onto Labour's divisions away from the government's travails infuriated many in the party.

But the episode also demonstrated how adeptly Starmer had managed to gain the trust of the Corbyn operation without fully sharing its objectives. The dynamics of that relationship would be critical in the aftermath of the political earthquake that followed soon after.

CHAPTER 11

REMAINIAC

Seventeen months after his arrival in Parliament, Keir Starmer found himself at the forefront of a debate that would for more than three years dominate not just politics but, it often seemed, much of national life. Its outcome would change British politics for ever.

Together with most of his party, Starmer supported the 2015 legislation for a referendum on Britain's EU membership in the early stages of its passage through Parliament. He abstained at the final reading, again in common with other Labour MPs. By the time the campaign got under way, Jeremy Corbyn was leader and Starmer had taken up his post as a shadow Home Office Minister. Starmer's contributions to the campaign therefore focused on crime and security: he argued that EU criminal justice measures were crucial in the fight against organised crime, people trafficking, cybercrime and terrorism. He took the opportunity of restating his credentials as a former DPP. 'Anybody who's been involved in this on a practical, operational level recognises the risks here,' he told *The Independent*. 'It's a risk to the safety of people in this country.' Such warnings were dismissed as part of the Remainers' 'Project Fear' by the Leave campaign, which argued that collaboration with agencies in other countries would continue outside the EU, and that Europe's open borders were in fact the bigger threat to Britain's security. Whatever the merits of Starmer's argument, they did not prevail.

'Devastating result,' he tweeted the morning after the referendum. 'Now we must face the future with united determination to mitigate the impacts and heal the deep fractures in our society.' For Starmer and a large number of Labour colleagues, that future had to begin with the removal of their party leader.

Corbyn's performance during the campaign had been a lamentable disappointment to many on the Remain side, who felt his support had been half-hearted at best. He took little part in day-to-day campaigning and in his interventions seemed more preoccupied with the EU's need to reform than with its achievements. His failure to rally Labour voters to the cause in greater numbers infuriated senior figures in the party, but it also terrified them. Following David Cameron's resignation as Prime Minister the morning after the referendum, many feared a snap general election. With a leader so demonstrably unable to mobilise Labour support at the ballot box, they reasoned, the prospects for such a contest were not good.

That weekend, Corbyn sacked his shadow Foreign Secretary, Hilary Benn, when the news broke that he was encouraging colleagues to agitate for a change of leadership. Nineteen further shadow Cabinet members quit, along with a number of more junior frontbenchers, including Starmer.

His letter to Corbyn is worth reproducing in full, since it reveals perhaps more than he intended:

> Dear Jeremy
>
> It is with deep regret that I am writing to resign as shadow Immigration Minister.
>
> As soon as you were elected leader, I recognised and respected the mandate you had from members and undertook to serve and support you. To that end, I accepted the shadow

Immigration post and have worked hard to deliver results for you and the party.

I have never spoken out publicly against you and I do not intend to do so now.

However, the EU referendum result was catastrophic for the UK, for our communities and for the next generation. We now face a very different future.

The challenge of leadership in this context is very different to the challenge only a year ago. It is clear that we need a much louder voice on the critical issues of renegotiating the UK's place in the world and mitigating the damaging impact of our exit from the EU.

In the last few days I have maintained my support for you, notwithstanding my reservations. However, the resignations across the shadow Cabinet and the shadow frontbench yesterday materially change this. It is simply untenable now to suggest that we can offer an effective opposition without a change of leader.

In the circumstances, I am duty bound to resign.

I do so with great sadness and deep regret.

Yours sincerely,

Keir Starmer QC MP

At first glance the letter seems simply polite. Whether out of courtesy or in order not to burn bridges, he avoided being unduly critical: unfortunately, new circumstances mean we need a new leader. But on closer reading, it is non-committal to a fault. Starmer took the shadow home affairs job because he respected Corbyn's mandate, not because he endorsed what he was trying to do (not that he would ever say so 'publicly'). He had reservations but maintained his support, which he was ultimately withdrawing because all these other resignations made the situation untenable. In other words, he had not joined the frontbench team because he supported Corbyn, but he had not left it because he didn't. (He later offered another explanation: he resigned because of Corbyn's suggestion the day after the referendum that the government immediately invoke Article 50 of the Lisbon Treaty, the mechanism to begin the two-year departure process – a position on which Labour soon backtracked. 'When he said that, I felt he was in a fundamentally different place from me in terms of how we fight for the future of our country,' Starmer said.)

The next day, Labour MPs overwhelmingly passed a motion of no confidence in Corbyn, who declared the vote 'unconstitutional' and refused to resign. In the subsequent leadership contest, Starmer was one of 172 MPs to nominate Owen Smith, who had resigned as shadow Work and Pensions Secretary after the referendum and emerged as the sole anti-Corbyn candidate. In a prelude to the long debate that would follow, Smith said that as leader he would press for a further public vote on the terms of Britain's EU exit.

But if Labour MPs longed to see the back of Corbyn, party members felt the opposite: at the end of July, they re-elected him with a landslide 62 per cent of the vote. With the leader clearly at odds with most of his parliamentary party, a long summer of infighting ensued.

Eager to build a team that could offer some semblance of competence and unity, Corbyn and his advisers – and especially his close ally the shadow Chancellor John McDonnell – were keen to have Starmer back in a high-profile position. Encouraged by the low-key nature of his resignation and the absence of hostility in his letter, they began to sound him out about the idea of joining the shadow Cabinet.

During the negotiations, it emerged that Starmer had two

potential career moves in mind. One was to take over as shadow Home Secretary following Burnham's departure from the front bench to stand as Mayor of Greater Manchester. The other was to become shadow Brexit Secretary. The latter job was confirmed in the reshuffle that September.

As the leader of a pro-EU party, the Eurosceptic Corbyn had good reason to want an ardent Remainer in the Brexit post. 'The Corbyn political operation was smart enough to understand that it was leading a seriously Remain party, and it had a seriously pro-Remain spokesperson in Keir,' says one experienced Labour Kremlinologist. 'And that was a big advantage to them because he could shield them from everything they thought privately. They wanted him out there sending pro-Remain mood music.'

The situation also presented Starmer with a big decision: should he stay put on the back benches or get back in the game by joining the team of a leader whom he had recently judged unsuited to the challenge of the times and unable to offer effective opposition? Unlike most of the colleagues who had quit in June, he decided to return. 'Brexit is so important, it would have been neglect of duty to simply sit it out,' he later explained. With Corbyn re-elected, 'the right thing to do is to get behind the leader, and do the best job you can, and that's all I'm trying to do'.

But another reason was in play. Starmer told colleagues at the time that he believed the next leader of the Labour Party would come from within the shadow Cabinet – a line which caused resentment among some former frontbenchers, who felt it was a mistake to legitimise Corbyn's leadership. 'He realised that he was trading a little bit of credibility to get into the shadow Cabinet to try and influence the future,' says one who knows him. 'He'd weighed it up.'

Those around Corbyn were also certain that this would have been part of Starmer's calculation: the successor would be chosen by a largely Corbyn-supporting membership who would look more favourably on a figure who had tried to make the project work than one who had stayed on the sidelines. Indeed, Diane Abbott, whose position on Brexit was close to Starmer's, distrusted his motives and would regularly warn the Corbyn team that he was out to topple the leader. She would later confirm this in a BBC interview, saying she had been 'suspicious of him' and believed 'he had a project of his own to become leader of the Labour Party. I blame his mother for calling him Keir.'

Whatever his own ambitions, Starmer could not quite bring himself to voice unambiguous support for the man at the helm. Asked by the BBC's Andrew Marr the weekend after the reshuffle if he thought Corbyn would make a good Prime Minister, the new shadow Brexit Secretary replied: 'Well look, we've had a leadership election, Jeremy won that, we accept it and we respect it.' That word again. 'Of course we want a Labour government, of course we want to support Jeremy to that end. He's won the membership, he now needs to win the country – he knows that, we know that and we need to work together on that.'

At the same time, Starmer was not entirely trusted by the Corbyn team. Sir David Lidington, who as Chancellor of the Duchy of Lancaster in incoming Prime Minister Theresa May's Cabinet was closely involved in the Brexit saga, remembers inviting Starmer to his office.

> I wanted to have a chat, to try and see, 'where are you coming from on this?' But he wasn't allowed to come and see me one to one. They sent minders with him. He came into my office with Seumas Milne and somebody else, who sat there. It was like having a meeting with the Russian ambassador when he's got somebody from the FSB in the embassy to take a note of what he says. I saw Seumas sort of looking from one to the other of

> us, and I always felt that when the revolution came, in Seumas's mind, both of us were going in front of the firing squad, it was just a question of sequence.

Starmer's opening move in his new job was to write to David Davis, the Secretary of State for Exiting the European Union, demanding that Parliament be given a vote on the government's Brexit plan before triggering Article 50. The letter also contained no fewer than 170 questions about ministers' intentions – a question for every day until 31 March 2017, the government's Article 50 target date, which suggests that the missive was more a political ploy than a genuine attempt to throw light on the subject. The range and detail of the questions also signalled Starmer's strategy of bringing lawyerly investigation to bear on every aspect of Brexit. To his detractors, it suggested he would focus on minutiae as a pretext for obstructing the effort to give effect to the referendum result.

Starmer's prosecutorial approach was rewarded with an early victory in Parliament. Davis had argued that getting the best deal with the EU would mean keeping the UK's negotiating position confidential, but the Scottish Nationalists, the Liberal Democrats and a number of Conservatives had supported Starmer's stipulation that MPs be allowed to vote on the government's opening terms. While the referendum result had to be accepted and respected, he told the Commons: 'That is not the end of the matter. The next question, and one that is increasingly pressing, is: on what terms should we leave the EU? That question was not on the ballot paper.' The argument was challenged by Brexiteers – former Conservative leader Iain Duncan Smith urged Davis to 'resist the temptation to take advice from a second-rate lawyer who doesn't even understand the parliamentary process', a jibe for which he later apologised – but ministers judged that on this question, opinion in Parliament was with Starmer. The government accepted a motion that 'there should be a full and transparent debate on the government's plan for leaving the EU' and that MPs must be 'able properly to scrutinise that plan for leaving the EU before Article 50 is invoked', though in a way that respected the referendum result and did not undermine the government's negotiating position.

Pro-Europeans quickly decided they had found their champion. Laudatory media profiles began to appear, hailing Starmer as 'Britain's last Remaining hope' and 'the real Leader of the Opposition'. At a private event in Parliament, Starmer was seen to wince when someone greeted him as 'the man who'll make sure we stay in the EU'. The government benches also knew they were in for a hard time: 'You can't pretend he's not a serious person,' remarked a Conservative MP. At a time when the government had only a slim majority and many Tories were worried about Theresa May's plans, the shadow Brexit Secretary had become one of the most consequential political figures in the country.

The role of the Commons – and, by extension, the influence of the shadow Brexit Secretary – was further enhanced in January 2017, when, in a case brought by investment fund manager Gina Miller, the Supreme Court ruled that the government could not trigger Article 50 without authority from Parliament. It fell to Starmer to respond to the Bill the government subsequently introduced, which he conceded was 'very difficult' for the Labour Party. 'We lost the referendum,' he solemnly intoned.

> Yes, the result was close … Yes, technically the referendum is not legally binding. But the result was not technical; it was deeply political, and politically the notion that the referendum was merely a consultation exercise to inform Parliament holds no water … Had the outcome been to remain, we would have

> expected the result to be honoured, and that cuts both ways ... as democrats we in the Labour Party have to accept the result. It follows that the Prime Minister should not be blocked from starting the Article 50 negotiations.

Starmer, along with Corbyn and most of his party, voted with the government to allow the Brexit process to begin, but not before extracting another concession from ministers: a commitment that the final agreement with the EU would have to be approved by both Houses of Parliament with a 'meaningful vote' – a phrase coined by Starmer – before it was concluded. With the government having also agreed to publish an official document setting out its plans, the shadow Brexit Secretary declared another success for his attritional approach.

'Just to be clear,' he told the Commons,

> nagging away, pushing votes and making the argument over three months, we have got a white paper, and it is important. Nagging away and making the arguments, we have got commitments about reporting back. Nagging away and making the arguments, we have got a commitment to the vote at the end of the exercise.

As would become clearer in the months that followed, 'nagging away' was not universally regarded as a laudable pursuit; one person's accountability and perusal looks to another like obstruction and delay.

With the Brexit process officially under way, attention began to focus on the terms of Britain's withdrawal and the substance of the country's future relationship with the EU. In her Lancaster House speech in January, setting out her negotiating priorities, Theresa May had ruled out membership of the single market and customs union, with no jurisdiction for the European Court of Justice, and declared that if the EU was not prepared to reach what the government considered an agreement, Britain would leave without one: 'No deal is better than a bad deal.'

In a speech of his own at Chatham House at the end of March, Starmer set out six tests that any deal would have to meet before Labour would support it. The agreement would have to ensure a 'strong and collaborative' future relationship with the EU; deliver the 'exact same benefits' as membership of the single market and customs union; ensure the 'fair management of migration'; defend 'rights and protections and prevent a race to the bottom'; protect national security and 'our capacity to tackle cross-border crime'; and 'deliver for all regions and nations of the UK.'

But while Starmer claimed that his tests were intended to protect 'core progressive values', others pointed out that one in particular was designed to be unachievable: it was, almost by definition, impossible that Britain could enjoy the 'exact same benefits' outside the single market as it did as a member. This observation was not confined to commentators and opponents: it was shared by Labour's international trade spokesman, Barry Gardiner, who, at a private event for a think tank a few months later, cheerfully declared it to be 'bollocks'. Labour knew very well that

> we cannot have the exact same benefits and actually it would have made sense – because it was the Tories that said they were going to secure the exact same benefits – and our position should have been to say they have said they are going to secure the exact same benefits and we are going to hold them to that standard.

Starmer's relationship with Gardiner was fractious at the best of times. Gardiner was always instinctively closer to Corbyn's approach to Brexit than Starmer's, and their overlapping responsibilities had led to something of a demarcation dispute at the time of Starmer's appointment. The two scrapped regularly in meetings. Colleagues recall that on one trip to Brussels, the pair squabbled all the way out and all the way back, continuing their row in the pub afterwards.

Now Starmer was furious. He complained to Corbyn, who duly took the miscreant Gardiner to task ('We've had a conversation with him. It's quite clear he does support our strategy,' Corbyn later asserted). The shadow Brexit Secretary arguably had good reason to be cross. A form of words emphasising collaboration, rights and fairness was supposed to be something that any Labour MP could sign up to. The six tests had been designed not just to give Labour licence to vote against any deal that might emerge but to hold together a parliamentary party that was almost as divided on the issue as the Conservatives.

It was not the first occasion on which colleagues had raised Starmer's ire. He had been incensed when, in November 2016, McDonnell had said in a speech that 'Labour accepts the referendum result as the voice of the majority, and we must embrace the enormous opportunities to reshape our country that Brexit has opened for us' – a much more positive line than that agreed by the shadow Cabinet's Brexit subcommittee. Since the referendum, senior Labour figures had tried Starmer's patience by airing starkly conflicting views on practically all aspects of Brexit, including immigration and free movement, the future trading relationship and the desirability of a second public vote.

The party was forced to clarify its position when Theresa May unexpectedly called an early general election for 8 June 2017. May's plan had been to capitalise on the Tories' double-digit poll leads and expand her majority in Parliament in readiness for the forthcoming battle over the terms of Brexit. Her gamble was that former Labour supporters who had voted Leave in the referendum would swing behind the Tories as the only party fully committed to honouring the result.

Labour refused to accept her strategy. The party's manifesto promised that a Labour government would take Britain out of the EU and would 'seek to unite the country around a Brexit deal that works for every community in Britain'. They would replace Conservative plans with 'fresh negotiating priorities that have a strong emphasis on retaining the benefits of the single market and the customs union'. EU nationals living in Britain would have their rights guaranteed immediately, but freedom of movement would end.

Starmer was at pains to emphasise that Brexit itself was not at stake in the election. In an interview early in the campaign, he said Labour could not 'look like we are trying to rub out the result of the referendum'. Though he had wanted to remain, 'I accept the referendum was a referendum that was for real … I'm not prepared now for the Labour Party not to genuinely accept the result. We asked for a decision and we got it.'

All this made it difficult for May to sustain the argument that the election was all about defending the referendum decision. With both main parties apparently committed to going through with Brexit, voters focused on other issues – not least the Tories' hurriedly conceived plan to reform funding for social care, which triggered a mid-campaign U-turn that called into question May's claim to offer 'strong and stable leadership'.

Starmer spent most of the campaign knocking on doors with Labour candidates in marginal constituencies, where he claimed to find little discussion of Brexit. 'It's come up far less than I had thought it would, and that's across the country,' he reflected during a stop in the Midlands. 'It was billed as a Brexit election: in the end, it's an election that's turned into "What sort of Britain do you want to live in?" And therefore there's a lot of talk about the health service, about public services, about tax – about the basic deal between government and people.'

However, Starmer was notably circumspect about the Labour manifesto as a whole, with its programme of nationalisation, tax hikes and spending increases. 'I think what's really important about this manifesto', he said,

> is that it's opened a space for an honest discussion about the investment we need in infrastructure, in people, in skills, in the health service, in public services, and it's set out what we need to pay for it. That's a debate that I think we've all shied away from for a very long time in all political parties. And that's a debate that needs to be had.

If May's judgement that a bigger majority would be needed to get a Brexit deal through Parliament was ultimately proved right, her 2017 gamble failed to pay off. Far from boosting her majority, the voters removed it altogether, returning a hung parliament with the Conservatives as the largest party, and forcing the Prime Minister into a deal with Northern Ireland's Democratic Unionists to keep the government in place. Labour gained an extra thirty seats, with Starmer's own majority increasing by more than 13,000 to just over 30,000. Safe to say his hand in marshalling the opponents of May's Brexit plans had been strengthened.

• • •

With attention largely focused on other issues, the Brexit policy in Labour's manifesto had been enough to get them through the election, but it did not end the ambiguities in the party's position. In the weeks following the election there was confusion over the single market and the customs union, with Starmer contradicting Corbyn and McDonnell by holding out the possibility of continued membership after Britain's EU withdrawal.

In a sign that Starmer was beginning to win the internal arguments within the shadow Cabinet, he announced at the end of August that Labour would seek a transitional deal with the EU on the existing terms of membership: 'That means we would seek to remain in a customs union with the EU and within the single market during this period. It means we would abide by the common rules of both.' In her Florence speech the following month, Theresa May set out her own plan for an implementation period in which Britain would remain in the single market and customs union for two years. Starmer's proposal went further, saying this phase should be 'as short as possible, but as long as is necessary' – which suggested that under Labour, Britain could be following Brussels rules and paying into the EU budget for years after its departure in March 2019 – and that remaining permanently in a customs union with the EU was a 'possible end destination' for Labour. The party's uneasy truce was ratified when its autumn conference endorsed the policy. But as official negotiations with the EU intensified, the government's travails put Labour's internal disagreements in the shade.

There is no need to repeat here the long and tortuous battle within the government ranks that resulted in the Chequers compromise, the subsequent Cabinet resignations and the eventual conclusion of the Withdrawal Agreement that was put before Parliament early in 2019. Three developments are more pertinent to us: the forces most hostile to Brexit winning the upper hand within Labour; the blocking of Theresa May's deal; and the ultimate outcome for Britain and Europe. Starmer's role was pivotal in all three.

The Starmers' family home, 23 Tanhouse Road in Oxted. It was bought with a mortgage in 1963, shortly after Starmer's birth, and his parents lived there for more than fifty years. His father plied his trade as a toolmaker in various workshops nearby.

© Bagshaw & Hardy

Starmer attended Reigate Grammar School from 1974 until 1981. Via Margaret Thatcher's reforms as Education Secretary, it became a private establishment in 1976. Starmer's fees were covered by Surrey County Council. Ironically, despite his ambivalent attitude to private education, he supported the school long after he had left it.

© Ian Capper, CC BY-SA 2.0

Music was prominent in Starmer's life as a schoolboy. He played the flute, piano and recorder and studied at the Junior Guildhall School of Music in London. He was also a member of various orchestras including this one, pictured, which performed at the Lord Mayor's Show in London in 1980.

Starmer captained the 1st XI football team in his final year at school. Their performances were mixed, but sports coach Graham Best says Starmer was skilful and 'a good leader both on and off the field'. Now in his sixties, Starmer still plays football when time allows. He is also an Arsenal season ticket holder. His diary is even annotated with the date of every fixture.

Starmer, pictured with friends from the University of Leeds, which he attended between 1982 and 1985. Some there knew him as the 'King of Middle-Class Radicals'.

Class of 1985. Starmer, on the far right in the fourth row, claims he did not know the difference between a solicitor and a barrister when he arrived to study law at Leeds. His relationship with one tutor, Clive Walker, is thought to have been pivotal to his professional legal career.

Starmer, pictured in the third row from the front, eight places from the left, as a student at St Edmund Hall, Oxford. He did the BCL course in 1985–86. One friend at Oxford was the future Labour Cabinet minister David Miliband.

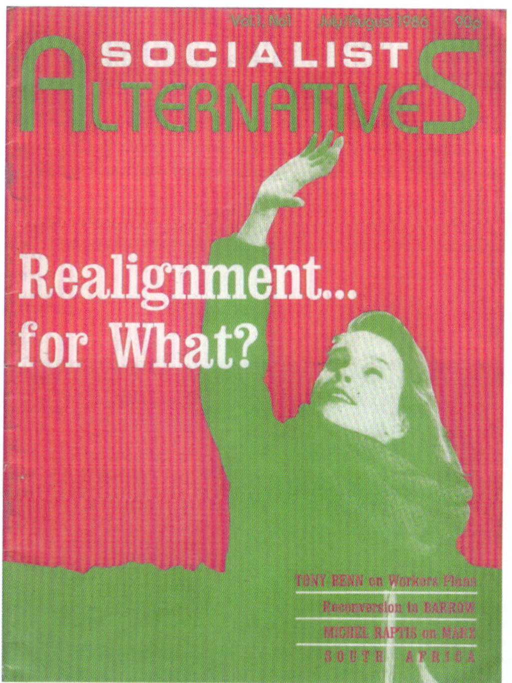

The first issue of *Socialist Alternatives*. The periodical was at the centre of Starmer's life from 1986 to 1987. Contributor Richard Barbrook says Starmer was 'the guy who got the magazine done'. Drugs were apparently smoked at editorial meetings, though Starmer is not thought to have indulged.

Phillippa Kaufmann, with whom Starmer lived from 1997 to 2001. His love life has certainly been complicated, with two ex-girlfriends marrying colleagues of his from Doughty Street Chambers.

Starmer was made a Queen's Counsel in 2002, aged thirty-nine. In 2005, he said taking silk was 'odd, since I often used to propose the abolition of the monarchy'.

Starmer with his wife, Victoria, and his parents, Josephine and Rodney, on his wedding day in 2007. His relationship with his father was distant, but he adored his mother.

Starmer was the Director of Public Prosecutions from 2008 until 2013. Decisions he took at the Crown Prosecution Service made him enemies who maintain he ruined their lives, including the former Tory MP Harvey Proctor. Questions remain about the CPS's handling of sex abuse allegations against Jimmy Savile and Mohamed Al Fayed. In 2025, the child grooming gang scandal returned to haunt him as well.

Starmer, pictured with his wife, Victoria, after being elected to the House of Commons for the first time in 2015. It has been observed that he does not routinely wear a wedding ring, though he did on this occasion.

Starmer served – often uneasily – as shadow Brexit Secretary under Jeremy Corbyn for more than three years. Some in Labour circles blame his anti-Brexit stance for Labour's crushing 2019 electoral defeat. Others say he was practically mute on the heated topic of antisemitism, which plagued the party.

Starmer and his deputy, Angela Rayner, 'taking a knee' in June 2020 in solidarity with Black Lives Matter. His progressive views have always been prominent. In 2020, he signed up for 'unconscious bias' training. And, asked by the BBC in 2021 if it was transphobic to say only women have a cervix, he answered: 'It is something that shouldn't be said. It is not right.'

Millionaire businessman Lord Alli seemed the ideal appointment as Labour Party fundraiser in 2022. But his motives were questioned when it emerged that he had bought Starmer and his wife tens of thousands of pounds' worth of clothes and spectacles. When it was discovered in August 2024 that he had been given a highly prized Downing Street pass, a full-blown scandal erupted from which Starmer has never fully recovered.

Lord Hermer KC is one of Starmer's oldest and closest friends, yet many were surprised when he was appointed Attorney General in July 2024. His respect for international law and list of past clients meant he became one of the Cabinet's most controversial figures during Starmer's first year in government.
© Mark Kerrison / In Pictures via Getty Images

Morgan McSweeney is considered responsible for masterminding Starmer's rise, first to Leader of the Opposition and then to 10 Downing Street. Within 100 days of Labour taking power he had replaced Sue Gray as chief of staff. Some wonder when he will start grooming a potential successor as PM, who, like McSweeney, might be expected to come from the right of the party.
© Tayfun Salci / ZUMA Press Wire / Alamy Stock Photo

Sue Gray was forced out of her post as chief of staff by younger rivals who found her divisive and briefed against her. She is said to have hated the 'blokey' atmosphere in Downing Street, where many conversations were based around football. Her departure was a humiliation for Starmer, but he still rewarded her with a peerage.
© Stefan Rousseau / PA Images / Alamy Stock Photo

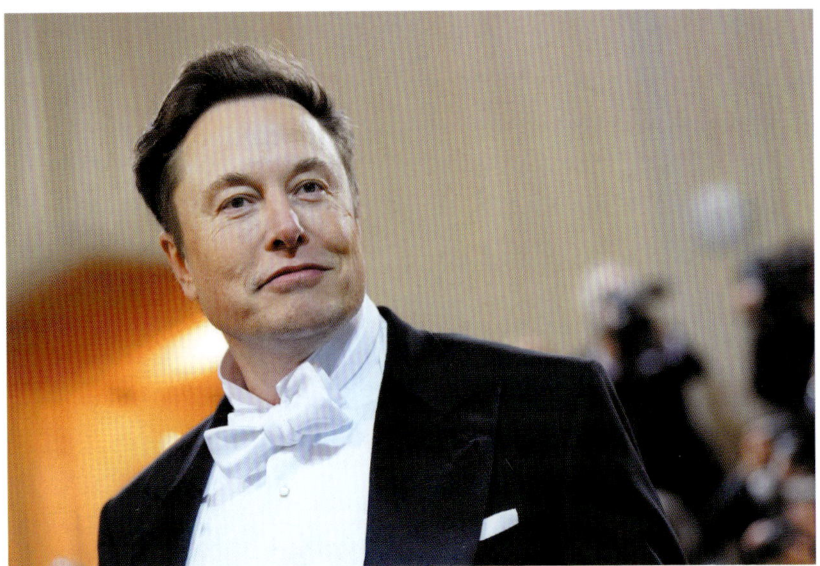

Elon Musk, the richest man in the world, played a surprisingly prominent role in Starmer's political life during the opening months of his premiership, rarely missing an opportunity to lambast him or his policies. With well over 200 million followers on X, formerly Twitter, Musk's influence is astonishing – and potentially wounding, as Starmer can attest.

© Kristin Callahan / Everett Collection / Alamy Stock Photo

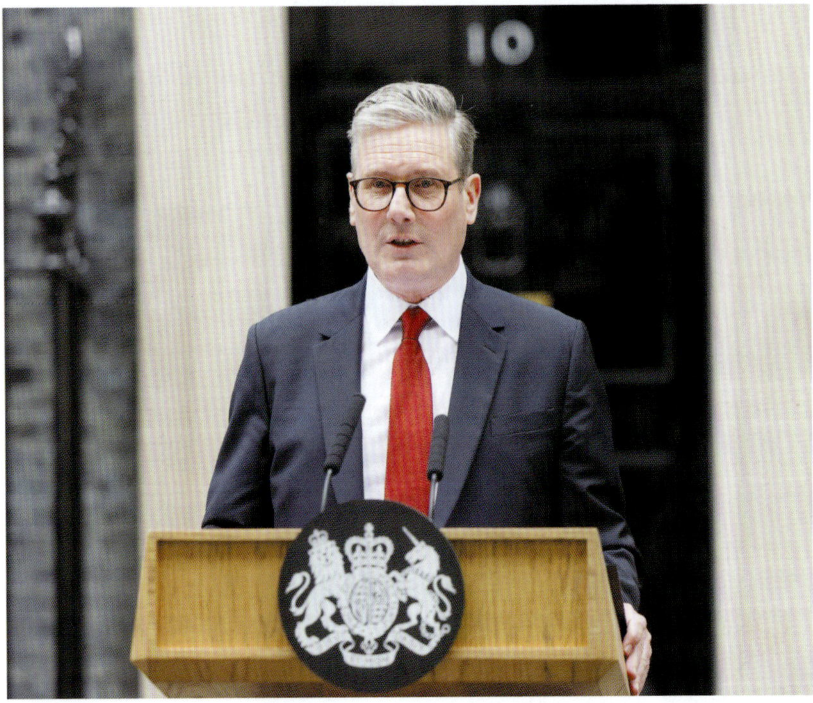

Starmer giving his first speech to the nation as Prime Minister on 5 July 2024. His unease was noticeable. In the seven minutes that he spoke, he glanced down at his notes 158 times, an average of once every two and a half seconds.

© Kirsty O'Connor / 10 Downing Street / Pictorial Press / Alamy Stock Photo

In January 2018, the shadow Cabinet's Brexit subcommittee met to discuss a proposal that the party should support a permanent customs union with the EU. Starmer had been advocating the policy internally for several weeks and had presented a paper on the issue to the leader's office. Corbyn's team were worried that the idea would tie Britain too closely to the EU and look to Leave voters like a further dilution of Labour's commitment to honour the referendum result. At the meeting, to Starmer's surprise, participants were given numbered copies of an alternative paper aimed at deferring the issue and rejecting a Norway-style model which would leave the UK as a rule-taker and therefore fail to acknowledge voters' wish to 'take back control'. When Corbyn began to read aloud, Starmer interrupted, raging that the new paper was an insult to him and his team and had been 'sprung on us with no discussion, no consultation, no prior notice'. He would not be willing to defend this position in the media, he said.

'Jeremy started speaking, and Keir just said "enough", this was completely outrageous,' said one who was present. Starmer was so incensed that some in the room feared he might resign. 'He looked close to telling them to shove it,' said another witness. 'I think Jeremy was slightly surprised at how angry Keir was.'

Others present backed Starmer's approach, and at the end of the meeting the leader's office paper was quietly collected and never seen again. A compromise was brokered whereby the leader would go along with Starmer on customs provided the policy also called for Britain to be exempt from certain single market rules on competition and state aid – rules which Starmer supported but Corbyn had always disliked.

The episode was just one flashpoint in a continuous tussle between the shadow Brexit Secretary and the team around the leader. A colleague recalls that Starmer would regularly 'grind them down with utter, deep application of logic, challenging a position and dissecting it with laser-beam analysis. Not just the forensic barrister but very deep drilling down into policy heft.'

Resisting the influence of more Brexit-friendly figures like Unite general secretary Len McCluskey, party chairman Ian Lavery, shadow Cabinet Office Minister Jon Trickett and senior Corbyn aides Karie Murphy and Seumas Milne became an unrelenting task. 'He'd get Jeremy in the room to agree a position, and then Jeremy's people would unpick it over the next few days, and he'd have to get Jeremy back in the room,' says one close observer. 'The fact that he got in the room in the first place is a testament to the fact that he just wouldn't relent. He was very, very patient and resilient. You've got to give him credit for the political grind, which few do give him credit for.'

Close Corbyn allies, on the other hand, felt Starmer sometimes irritated colleagues with his lawyerly approach and tendency to intellectual arrogance, often giving the impression that he felt he was the only one who really understood the nuts and bolts of the issue. Some also felt Starmer tried to run Brexit policy almost as a parallel operation: rather than working collaboratively, he would stay in a bubble with his staff and feed into the wider team only when necessary. Despite this semi-detached approach, however, members of the Corbyn team doubt that Starmer ever really came close to resignation. They reasoned that he would not readily have relinquished such a prime spot within Labour's Remain-backing majority and the broader liberal establishment, especially given his evident ambitions in the longer game.

Some believe Starmer's thinking on Brexit could have been influenced to some degree by his membership of the Trilateral Commission, a non-governmental group which serves as a talking shop for liberal internationalists. Founded in 1973 by the American banker David Rockefeller, it seeks to foster relations between Europe, North America and the Asia Pacific region. In April 2018, Starmer was listed as a member of the Trilateral Commission along with his friend David Miliband, the former Foreign Secretary who is now the handsomely paid head of the International Rescue Committee, a New York-based charity. During that year, the Trilateral Commission held meetings in Singapore, Beijing, California and Ljubljana, though it is not clear which of these gatherings Starmer attended, if any. Some within Labour circles are suspicious of Starmer's association with the group, seeing it as a vehicle to promote the interests of international financial elites.

Once Labour's position on customs was agreed, there were efforts on the Labour benches to soften the party's position still further. One group of younger pro-European MPs, including Chuka Umunna and Chris Leslie, derisively dubbed 'the shinies' by more jaded colleagues, argued that Labour should support an amendment to the Brexit legislation committing the government to joining the European Economic Area (EEA), thus keeping Britain in the single market but obliging adherence to many EU rules, including free movement of people. The party split three ways on the issue, with ninety Labour MPs defying instructions to abstain when the issue came to Parliament. Many of Starmer's colleagues believed he, too, would have backed a form of continued single market membership if Corbyn had not been implacably opposed.

'Almost everybody in the Labour Party has a view on Brexit,' Starmer said that spring. 'But almost no two people have the same view. They all give me their opinions all the time in texts, in emails, in one-to-one conversations, in groups.' While two thirds of Labour voters backed Remain, two thirds of Labour MPs represented seats that voted to leave, which inevitably led to differences of opinion. Starmer's view had been informed by his 'strong belief that we cannot allow the Labour Party to divide and break up on this issue. We have got to hold the party together, and of course that means there are huge challenges.'

That is not to say that the shadow Brexit Secretary was a neutral arbiter between the various Labour views. Those close to the leadership noted that whereas he had initially been disciplined in sticking to an agreed line, Starmer became bolder in pushing the boundaries of Labour's position as time wore on. This was particularly true when it came to the debate over a second referendum. Deputy leader Tom Watson had sparked excitement by remarking at the end of 2017 that while Labour had not called for another public vote, 'when you're in complex negotiations on behalf of the nation you shouldn't rule anything out'. Corbyn, asked about his colleague's observation, replied: 'He did indeed say that, but our position is that we are not advocating a second referendum.' When it was later put to him that he was not saying he would never support another ballot, he said: 'We are not calling for one either.'

At this stage, Starmer was publicly resistant to calls for a further vote. At a meeting of the Parliamentary Labour Party in January 2018, he told colleagues that while he understood why people argued for a second referendum, there were serious practical problems, as well as

> something more fundamental than that. If we sit here as a party aspiring to govern then we have got to recognise that if we spend all that time looking back in grief about what many of us didn't want to happen, thinking, 'How do we rub it out?' then we are unable to do what we need to do, which is to fight for the [final deal] that reflects what we stand for.

In a talk at University College London a few weeks later,

Starmer went further, telling students that having campaigned to get people to vote in the referendum,

> I'm not going to go back to those people and say, 'Now you've given me a result I didn't want I'm going to ignore it.' I think that would be really, really dangerous … I think it's absolutely right that if we do have a referendum, we abide by the result.

The official line, reiterated by McDonnell, was that 'all options are open' but that Labour's preferred route was to win a general election and change Brexit policy from within government. In March, Owen Smith breached this compromise position with an article in *The Guardian* arguing that 'we have the right to ask if Brexit remains the right choice for the country. And to ask, too, that the country has a vote on whether to accept the terms and true costs of that choice once they are clear.' Smith's stance was applauded by pro-Remain Labour colleagues, and his immediate sacking from the shadow Cabinet failed to end the debate.

Later in the summer Barry Gardiner went off-script again: telling people they were 'stupid enough' to make the wrong decision 'undermines the whole principle of democracy in this country', he argued. This drew another swift response from Starmer, who explained again that another referendum remained a possibility. If the deal was voted down, 'Parliament then decides what happens next and, in those circumstances, in my experience in the last few years, keep your options on the table, not off the table'.

By the time London Mayor Sadiq Khan called in September for 'a public vote on any deal or a vote on a no-deal, alongside the option of staying in the EU', pressure was growing among grassroots members for an official shift in Labour's policy. Constituency parties and unions submitted more than 100 motions for debate at the autumn conference calling for a second referendum.

A YouGov poll found that 86 per cent of Labour members wanted a referendum once negotiations were concluded.

The idea worried some Labour strategists, who feared such a policy would alienate both Leave voters and Remainers who wanted to get Brexit over with. It would also give potential Conservative rebels in Parliament a reason to back May's deal.

After much backroom wrangling, including a Sunday night meeting lasting into the early hours, the party thrashed out a form of words the leadership could live with: 'If we cannot get a general election, Labour must support all options remaining on the table, including campaigning for a public vote.' Starmer, who was instrumental in persuading activists in the meeting to accept the compromise, subsequently regarded it as a point of honour not to allow any slippage from the referendum commitment.

Exactly what the public would be voting on the second time around was left deliberately vague.

As the conference unfolded over that week, Starmer's intervention was decisive. On the Monday morning, McDonnell told ITV's *Good Morning Britain* that any such referendum would determine 'whether you accept the deal or not, or whether you send people back to negotiate a proper deal', not whether to stay in the EU after all. This echoed Len McCluskey, who had said the previous day: 'The referendum shouldn't be on "Do you want to go back in the European Union?" The people have already decided on that.'

Starmer contradicted this, saying the motion did not tie Labour to any position on the question in a second referendum. To the consternation of Corbyn's office but the delight of delegates, the shadow Brexit Secretary underlined the message in his conference speech the following day. 'It is right that Parliament has the first say … but if we need to break the impasse, our options must include campaigning for a public vote.' He then added a line that had not been cleared by the leader's office and did not appear in the official text: 'And nobody is ruling out Remain as an option.'

This was a defining moment. The new stance, coupled with the policy of remaining in a customs union, widened the gap between the government and opposition approaches to Brexit and set the backdrop for the political battle that would follow. The tumultuous ovation in the hall cemented Starmer's status as the hero of Labour's anti-Brexit activists. And his extemporised departure from the agreed line in the full glare of a party conference confirmed colleagues' suspicions that he saw himself as Labour's next leader.

Back in Westminster, to the nation's mounting exasperation, combat over Brexit resumed. The shadow Brexit Secretary made his presence felt in the proceedings. Whether he was doing so in the name of constitutional accountability or to frustrate Britain's departure from the EU at every turn was in the eye of the beholder.

In the two and a half years between the referendum and the debates on Theresa May's deal, Starmer engaged the government in a long series of parliamentary skirmishes on subjects ranging from the procedure for invoking Article 50 to the wisdom of fixing Britain's exit date in statute. He also used an arcane procedure known as a Humble Address, under which Parliament could vote to compel publication of confidential papers. In this way he forced the government to release civil service assessments on the impact of Brexit on different sectors of the economy and the Attorney General's legal advice to the government on the protocol to prevent a hard border in Northern Ireland in the absence of a deal.

In the Commons, ministers occasionally vented their frustration at what they saw as blocking tactics. Brexit Minister Steve Baker accused Labour of using a strategy of 'demoralisation and delay' as a ruse to overturn Brexit. David Davis complained that Starmer's speeches were 'becoming rather repetitive – they are always crowing and carping'. Davis's successor, Dominic Raab, dubbed Starmer 'the prince of process' as he was always arguing about 'protocol and procedure' rather than the substance of Brexit itself. After another Starmer lecture on the shortcomings of the government's plans, Raab archly observed from the despatch box, 'I gently say to the opposition that it is not entirely clear that it is Labour's overriding objective to give effect to the referendum.'

Unsurprisingly, Labour was preparing to vote against May's agreement with the EU well before it was concluded in November 2018. Shadow Foreign Secretary Emily Thornberry had become the latest frontbencher to provoke Starmer's ire when she told a Chatham House event in March 2018 that the deal was likely to be so vague that Labour might end up supporting it: 'If past evidence of the last few months is anything to go on, it's going to be a "blah, blah, blah" divorce,' she said. 'If you hold up "blah, blah, blah" to the six tests, it will probably pass it.' Starmer was once again reported to be 'furious' about the deviation from the agreed line, which he insisted had not changed. The shadow Brexit Secretary was adamant that his party was prepared to oppose the deal, even though it would mean Labour MPs walking into the same lobby as hardline Tory Brexiteers.

From the moment it was tabled, the prospects of May's Withdrawal Agreement winning parliamentary approval looked slim – not least because of the contentious Northern Ireland 'backstop'. This specified that in the absence of a future trade deal, the whole UK would remain in a single customs territory with the EU, and Northern Ireland would stay in some aspects of the single market. Though the arrangement was intended to be temporary while alternatives were agreed, the UK would not be able to leave the backstop without EU agreement. A statement from Brussels that the backstop scenario would in practice last for the shortest possible time was not enough to convince MPs, who on 15 January 2019 voted down the deal by 230 votes, the biggest government defeat for over a century. All but three Labour MPs voted against the agreement. Starmer declared during the debate that Labour believed the deal was not in the national interest: 'It does not come anywhere near to meeting our tests, it will make the country poorer and more divided and it will not protect jobs and the economy.'

By the end of March, the May deal had suffered two further heavy defeats. The EU had granted an extension to the Article 50 departure deadline to 12 April, but the prospects of agreement in Parliament by this time looked remote. The Withdrawal Agreement had been opposed both by those Conservative MPs who thought it tied Britain too closely to the EU after Brexit and by those who wanted to remain more closely aligned; a move in either direction would risk losing support from one wing or the other. Labour was in a similar position, with some MPs eager to get Brexit over with and a much larger group wanting a second referendum. Parliament held a series of 'indicative votes' on a wide range of Brexit propositions – including a customs union, EEA membership, a confirmatory public vote and revocation of Article 50 in the event of no deal – with the intention of revealing what kind of Brexit proposition could find a majority. In a demonstration of the prevailing political gridlock, every one of them was rejected.

After a seven-hour Cabinet meeting on 2 April, May announced that she would seek a further Article 50 extension to 30 June and invited Corbyn to take part in cross-party talks in an attempt to agree a unified approach. Following an initial meeting between May and Corbyn in Downing Street, the talks were continued in the Cabinet Office by a wider team from each side.

Starmer led the Labour delegation, which included McDonnell; shadow Business Secretary Rebecca Long-Bailey; shadow Environment Secretary Sue Hayman; and Corbyn advisers Seumas Milne and Andrew Fisher. As the main discussions wore on, however, it became clear that official agreement was unlikely on any terms that would get through Parliament. On 17 May, Corbyn ended the talks, saying they had gone as far as they could. Seven days later, May announced that she would resign as Conservative leader the following month and step down as Prime Minister once the party had chosen a successor. Her parting thought: 'Compromise is not a dirty word.' The window of opportunity for a cross-party compromise on Brexit, always narrow, had closed.

Starmer was by this point looking to the future. Since March 2019, he had been attending regular Monday morning meetings of the Arlington Group, named after Arlington Road in Camden, where his colleague Jenny Chapman lived. The purpose of these gatherings was to prepare Starmer for the next Labour leadership contest. Others in attendance included MPs Nick Smith – who is married to Chapman – and Steve Reed plus Tom Kibasi, who ran the left-wing IPPR think tank at that time.

• • •

The Brexit Party swept to victory in elections to the European Parliament; the Conservatives came fifth, and Labour was knocked into third place behind the pro-Remain Liberal Democrats. Boris Johnson became Prime Minister, beating Jeremy Hunt in the Tory leadership contest on a promise to leave the EU on 31 October, 'deal or no deal'. Parliament passed a law requiring the PM to seek a further extension if no deal was agreed by 19 October; twenty-one Conservative MPs who backed the move were expelled from the parliamentary party. Johnson announced a five-week prorogation of Parliament, a move later ruled unlawful by the Supreme Court. After unexpectedly cordial talks between Johnson and Irish leader Leo Varadkar, the government agreed a new deal that would scrap the unpopular backstop, taking the whole UK out of the customs union but leaving Northern Ireland following some EU rules, meaning some checks would be necessary on goods between Northern Ireland and Great Britain but not on the Irish border. Commitments on continued alignment with EU regulations were scrapped from the Withdrawal Agreement and moved to the non-binding political declaration on the future relationship, which now envisaged a free trade agreement rather than any closer association – a harder Brexit than May had proposed. When the new deal was put before Parliament on 19 October, effectively the new deadline day, MPs instead voted to delay approval and force a third Brexit postponement. Johnson reluctantly complied and ten days later, at the fourth time of asking – once the EU had agreed to push the departure date to 31 January – Parliament agreed to his motion for a general election.

It was during this dramatic period, with any prospect of Labour backing a Tory deal having vanished, that the party's anti-Brexit forces began to dominate. Labour's performance in the European Parliament elections, in which it won just 14 per cent of the vote, inspired senior figures, including Emily Thornberry, Shami Chakrabarti and Diane Abbott, to call for a shift in the party's position towards a second referendum in any circumstances.

Starmer led the charge, tweeting: 'It's no use trying to hide from these very disappointing results. We need to reflect hard and listen to our members, supporters and voters. The only way to break the Brexit impasse is to go back to the public with a choice between a credible Leave option and Remain.' Crucially, McDonnell, who had by now developed a close alliance with

Starmer over Brexit policy, also signalled a shift in his position. The shadow Chancellor said that since at this point the Tories looked unlikely to back an election given their own recent drubbing at the hands of the Brexit Party, 'our only option now is to go back to the people in a referendum'. Some Labour MPs in Leave-voting constituencies disagreed – Glòria De Piero warned that reversing the 2016 result 'would be an effective ending of Labour's historic coalition of working-class, middle-class, city and non-city voters' – but Corbyn agreed to move. 'It's clear that the deadlock in Parliament can only be broken by the issue going back to the people through a general election or a public vote. We are ready to support a public vote on any deal,' he wrote to MPs.

A further step was taken during the Conservative leadership contest, when Corbyn challenged the final two contenders to put any deal to a referendum. 'In those circumstances, I want to make it clear that Labour would campaign for Remain against either no deal or a Tory deal that does not protect the economy and jobs.'

Starmer's immediate priority was to prevent a no-deal Brexit – something Johnson, unlike his predecessor, seemed perfectly willing to countenance. A plan to pass a vote of no confidence in the government and install the opposition leader as caretaker Prime Minister was abandoned when it became clear the other parties would not accept the idea of Corbyn in No. 10. An alternative was needed.

Much of Starmer's summer holiday in Devon was spent climbing a hill in search of a mobile phone signal and 'standing in the rain with one or two disinterested sheep' while co-ordinating tactics with allies across Parliament. Informal contacts between Starmer and discontented Tories had been going on for more than two years, but at this point the tempo changed significantly, according to those involved. The threat of a no-deal exit, as well as suspicions that Johnson would prorogue Parliament and thereby thwart moves to prevent it, had brought into the picture a number of Conservative MPs, including former ministers, who had never previously rebelled. In mid-August, MPs from all parties met formally in Westminster, some breaking their holidays, to agree the strategy for what became the Benn Act – proposed by former shadow Foreign Secretary Hilary Benn and dubbed the 'Surrender Act' by Johnson – which forced the Prime Minister to ask the EU for a further delay.

'By that stage, Starmer had the upper hand,' says one former Labour MP. 'Corbyn had almost lost interest. All Corbyn wanted was a way out, a general election.' Starmer's next battle was over the stance Labour should take when such an election arrived. After talks with union heavyweights at the TUC conference in July, Corbyn announced a new approach: in government, Labour would negotiate a new deal with the EU and put it to a referendum alongside the option to remain. Which side the party would officially take in such a referendum was still an open question.

Once again, there was pressure for the party to go further: this time to oppose Brexit altogether. Watson urged members to sign the 'Remain Declaration', calling on Labour to become 'the party of Remain'. Resistance continued from those around Corbyn, but the shadow Brexit Secretary was firmly on the side of the Remainers. If it came to another referendum, he said in an interview that summer, 'I would campaign for Remain because I don't think there's a deal that is as good as the deal that we've got.' Internally, he pushed as strongly as he could for Labour to commit to supporting Remain in any subsequent referendum. All talk of respecting the 2016 result had been abandoned.

As in previous years, the issue came to a head at the Labour conference in September. As well as a statement of the official policy from the party's National Executive Committee and a supportive motion proposed by party members, delegates debated an alternative proposition, also backed by dozens of constituency parties, that would have committed Labour to 'reflect the overwhelming view of its members and voters' and therefore 'campaign energetically for a public vote and to stay in the EU in that referendum'.

Though he did not explicitly call for delegates to back the Remain motion, Starmer left little doubt as to his position. At a People's Vote rally during the opening weekend of the Brighton conference, he declared that in a referendum, 'I will campaign for Remain alongside millions of other people in this country, because it's not just a technical question of whether you want to be in or out of the EU, it's about what sort of country we want to be.' In an interview afterwards, he said a majority of Labour members wanted to remain, and 'we've got to listen to what they've got to say about it'.

Winding up the impassioned debate from the conference platform, Starmer reminded the party whom they had to thank for the evolution of its policy. 'Last year I stood before you and said nobody was ruling out the option of Remain,' he said. 'We've come a long way.' While he respected those who took a different view, 'You know where I stand on the question of Remain. I've said many times that I will campaign for Remain.' He announced that an incoming Labour government would legislate for a public vote immediately upon taking power and hold it within six months. Labour now had a simple message: 'If you want a referendum, vote Labour. If you want a final say on Brexit, vote Labour. If you want to fight for Remain, vote Labour.'

Amid chaotic scenes and a heavily disputed show of hands, the motions endorsing the party's official line were carried and the pro-Remain policy narrowly defeated. Starmer admitted he was disappointed by the result. 'What Jeremy's trying to achieve, in fairness is – given the divisions across the country – somebody's got to be prepared to say: "We'll have a referendum to find a way through and I'll stay above that" ... I personally think it's better to campaign for Remain and that's what I've said.' In practice, though, this is what would happen. Starmer went on:

> I have got a pretty clear idea of where the members are on this, and therefore I think it is very likely that the members will want us to campaign for Remain. We campaigned for Remain in 2016, we are currently campaigning for Remain against any Tory outcome, and it seems to be obvious where the members are on this.

By this time, there were so much resistance to Corbyn's leadership within the Parliamentary Labour Party that plotting against him had become, for some MPs, an extension of their day job. One such person recalls a secret meeting at the Covent Garden penthouse flat of Lord (Waheed) Alli, the Labour peer and businessman, in the autumn of 2019. The scheming had nothing to do with Brexit, however.

> It was just before the 2019 election was called. Everyone there was appalled by the antisemitism in Labour. We were trying to work out how we were going to get rid of Corbyn. Keir wasn't there, but that's because he wasn't part of the antisemitism group. [Labour MP] Peter Kyle led the meeting. He set it up with Lord Alli. There were at least thirty or forty people there. Every one of us spoke. The irony is, nobody mentioned who Corbyn's successor should be. Nobody mentioned Keir. Peter Mandelson and Margaret McDonagh were there too. I remember thinking they seemed to know their way around the flat very well. Lord Alli himself was very quiet. He didn't even stay for the whole meeting. We just used his apartment. He had laid on full catering.

In November, with the election campaign under way, Labour's election manifesto duly spelled out the party's position on Brexit:

> Labour will give the people the final say on Brexit. Within three months of coming to power, a Labour government will secure a sensible deal. And within six months, we will put that deal to a public vote alongside the option to remain. A Labour government will implement whatever the people decide.

The Labour deal would include a permanent customs union and close alignment with EU rules – neither of which would amount to Brexit at all in the eyes of many Leave voters.

During the campaign, Corbyn confirmed the position he would take, or rather decline to take, in a referendum campaign. 'I will adopt, if I am Prime Minister at the time, a neutral stance so I can credibly carry out the result of that to bring our communities and country together rather than continuing an endless debate about the EU and Brexit,' he told a BBC *Question Time* audience.

Compared to the crisp Conservative slogan – 'Get Brexit Done' – Labour's policy became an object of derision among the electorate. In research conducted by this author, voters mocked the prospect of Labour ministers going to Brussels to negotiate a new deal and then coming home to campaign against it. They found the idea of a Prime Minister remaining neutral on such a fundamental question simply ridiculous. Many former Labour voters were appalled that the party had, as they saw it, done everything in its power to prevent the 2016 result from being honoured and was now seeking to reverse it.

Starmer, however, was already looking to the future. By the time the election was called, he had assembled an informal team of advisers including Claire Ainsley, then director of the Joseph Rowntree Foundation think tank and author of *The New Working Class: How to Win Hearts, Minds and Votes*, and Morgan McSweeney, the head of Labour Together, a Blairite activists' network founded in 2015 and run with the Labour MPs Lisa Nandy, Jon Cruddas and Steve Reed. The Labour donors Sir Trevor Chinn and Martin Taylor bankrolled the operation, which was dedicated to developing Labour for a post-Corbyn age. Starmer had also begun to hold dinners with journalists where discussion would range well beyond his Brexit brief – a sure sign that his horizons had shifted.

On 12 December 2019, Boris Johnson's Conservatives won the general election with an eighty-seat majority. Labour lost sixty seats, its worst performance since 1935. Jeremy Corbyn announced his resignation. On 23 January 2020, Johnson's Withdrawal Agreement became law, and eight days later the UK left the European Union.

• • •

Insiders say it would be unfair to blame Starmer for the untidy policy Labour took to the people in 2019, given the array of views within the party and even within the shadow Cabinet. 'He's sufficiently aware to know that something that you need a flowchart to understand is bad policy,' as one colleague puts it, but there had to be a position for Labour to unite around. Some suspect he had strong reservations about Corbyn's decision to agree to an election. But by contributing to the impasse in Parliament, and with his outspoken support for holding a new referendum and remaining in the EU – a stance that infuriated many Labour voters in Leave-voting constituencies and confounded colleagues on his own benches who would have preferred the party to back a deal when it had the chance – Starmer surely helped to create the circumstances of Labour's rout. Yet even if, as many in the Labour Party think, his own personal ambition helped explain his pursuit of the referendum-and-Remain policy, his efforts had not been in vain.

CHAPTER 12

UNDER NEW MANAGEMENT

Shortly before six o'clock on the morning of Friday 13 December 2019, *The Guardian* website published a shortlist of Labour MPs who it believed might stand to succeed Jeremy Corbyn as party leader. With the final election results just in and the scale of Boris Johnson's stunning victory at the polls clear, six names were mooted: Starmer, Emily Thornberry, Rebecca Long-Bailey, Angela Rayner, Jess Phillips and Lisa Nandy. *The Guardian*'s instincts would prove almost entirely accurate. Five of the six on its list did indeed throw their hats into the ring. Only Rayner decided not to do so, opting to contest another elected position, the deputy leadership, instead. A further candidate, Clive Lewis, would join the leadership race, though his bid was soon scuppered.

At his own count in Islington in the early hours, Corbyn had acknowledged that his party's woeful performance signalled the end of his four years in charge. He would not lead Labour into the next election, he said, but he would not resign immediately either. Instead, he requested that the party embark on a 'process of reflection' – with him in charge – while it chose a new leader. Many within Labour and outside it thought this ill-advised and self-indulgent. They believed Corbyn's continued presence at the top of a battered organisation, which had lost sixty MPs and now had just 202 members in the House of Commons, prevented it from making a clean break with the immediate past. Yet Corbyn would not be moved.

Four days after the election, on 16 December, Frank Dobson's funeral was held at St Pancras Church in Starmer's constituency. Among the hundreds of people who gathered to pay their respects were many of Labour's best-known figures, including Corbyn, Tony Blair, Neil Kinnock, Ed Miliband, Jack Straw, John McDonnell, Andy Burnham, Sadiq Khan and Emily Thornberry. As Dobson's successor, Starmer was invited to give a spoken tribute. One attendee remembers that other mourners were less than impressed. 'He talked about his selection and how he'd got to know Frank, and it just didn't strike the right note,' this person recalls.

> It was a funeral. It wasn't a political event. It was a church. And he referred to Frank being an atheist, and I thought that was a bit simplistic. Frank was extremely interested in religion, he was a trustee at York Minster, he was very well read in religion, and he knew a lot about it. I felt sorry for the priest who had to pick up from there. I remember Chris Bryant saying afterwards, 'Keir seemed to talk mostly about himself,' and I thought that captured it rather well.

The starting gun to mark the beginning of the contest to succeed Corbyn had been fired, and those who wished to replace him were preparing their campaigns. Remarkably, Starmer apparently decided to use the funeral for these purposes. 'After the funeral we all tottered off to the big hotel next door,' reports the same source.

> It was very nice, actually. There were vast quantities to drink, but it was a very highly charged event because it wasn't just

> that Frank had died and had a lot of friends, we had also just lost the election. So it was a sort of wake for something in the party as well as a wake for Frank. These two sad events came together. But I remember Keir was lobbying people in the queue going in and running down Emily Thornberry. He was doing a bit of canvassing. I thought that wasn't quite the thing.

Party rules dictated that each candidate would be required to secure the blessing of 10 per cent of the party's MPs or MEPs – this was set at twenty-two MPs or MEPs – by 13 January. If they managed to clear this hurdle, they would need to add to this support from at least 5 per cent of Labour's constituency parties or other affiliated groups, such as trade unions, by 15 February. Those with sufficient backing to make it onto the final ballot paper would then face a vote by full party members, union affiliates and registered supporters, a group which numbered 784,181 eligible voters. The new leader would be announced on 4 April. In between, there would be hustings and televised debates around the country. The contest would be a marathon rather than a sprint. Starmer had already been bolstering his links with colleagues.

One former Labour MP remembers:

> Keir came late to politics. He'd gone straight to the front bench in 2015, but to many of us he was an outsider. The generation below him knew each other from the National Organisation of Labour Students. So he had to ingratiate himself with them. It was Jonathan Ashworth's clique of Ellie Reeves, who was Ashworth's girlfriend for a long time, and Stephanie Peacock, who is now Ashworth's girlfriend, plus Vicky Foxcroft and Louise Haigh. Rachel Reeves was part of it as well, though she never used to go out with them at night. Their roots go deep in the party and he had to get their networks to vote for him.

Thornberry, Lewis, Nandy and Phillips declared their candidacies first. Then, on 4 January, Starmer showed his hand with a three-pronged approach. First, he released a video online in which 'ordinary' Labour supporters waxed lyrical about his record in the law and politics over the previous three decades. That day he also visited the Brexit-backing town of Stevenage in Hertfordshire. He rounded off his campaign launch by writing a piece for the *Sunday Mirror*. Under the headline 'It won't be a decade before Labour wins a general election if we unite', he spelled out his objectives as the candidate who could bring Labour's pro- and anti-Corbyn factions together. These included continuing 'the moral fight against poverty, inequality and injustice', and campaigning for 'peace and justice around the world with a human rights approach to foreign policy and international relations'. His slogan was 'Another Future Is Possible' and many people appeared to agree, for he was the bookmakers' clear favourite to succeed Corbyn from the start. The last candidate to announce their bid was Rebecca Long-Bailey, a Corbynista who had been the shadow Business Secretary since 2017. She made her pitch in an article published in *Tribune* magazine on 6 January.

In an early indication of how one-sided the contest would turn out to be, Starmer had gained the backing of forty-one MPs – almost twice the number required to get onto the ballot – within four days. He also won the endorsement of the trade union Unison, which had 1.3 million members. Comprising a wide range of public sector employees, Unison had backed Corbyn's leadership bid in 2015 and it was considered vital in helping to select the next Labour leader. Announcing its support for Starmer, its general secretary, Dave Prentis, commented:

> We believe – if elected by the membership – Keir Starmer would be a leader to bring the party together and win back

> the trust of the thousands of voters who deserted Labour last month. Keir has a clear vision to get Labour back to the winning ways of the past. He is best placed to take on Boris Johnson, hold his government to account and ensure Labour can return to power.

Usefully for Starmer, given the continued presence of the party's left-wing Momentum faction, he also recruited Simon Fletcher, Corbyn's former chief of staff and the man behind Corbyn's successful leadership bid in 2015, as his strategic adviser. Morgan McSweeney, representing the right wing of the party, became Starmer's campaign manager. McSweeney, who was by then in his early forties, had been born in County Cork in the Republic of Ireland before moving to London aged seventeen to attend university. He had joined the Labour Party in 2001 and worked his way up the ranks until, in 2015, he helped to run Liz Kendall's unsuccessful leadership bid.

Starmer launched his campaign formally at the Mechanics Institute in Manchester on 11 January, delivering a speech in which he said factionalism had to go if the party was to recover. He said Labour needed to be a 'very effective opposition' against Boris Johnson, describing him as 'a man of no principles, no moral compass, who will go anywhere to stay in power'. Yet he was careful to recognise Corbyn, saying he

> made our party the party of anti-austerity, and he was right to do so. He made us the party that wanted to invest more heavily in our public services, and he was right to do so. We must retain that. We build on that and don't trash it as we move forward.

Starmer knew that worshipping at Corbyn's altar was obligatory if he was to get enough votes to lead the party himself.

On 13 January, Lewis withdrew, unable to muster enough support among the parliamentary party. The remaining five candidates each had sufficient backing to make it to the second round. The first hustings took place in Liverpool on 18 January. The event was dominated by the issues which had caused such division within the party over the previous few years, namely antisemitism and Brexit. Then Phillips, with twenty-three MPs supporting her – just one more than the threshold required – withdrew on 21 January, leaving a field of four. For Starmer, the contest was brought to an abrupt halt in early February when his mother-in-law, Dr Barbara Moyes, died in hospital following an accident. He had to step away from his political commitments to be with his family, and missed a hustings event held in Nottingham at which the Labour MP Jim McMahon stood in for him. Other candidates might have been concerned at not being able to appear at this event, yet Starmer's absence had little, if any, effect on his campaign. As the short-priced favourite, his lead always seemed unassailable. On 15 February, Thornberry was eliminated from the race after failing to achieve enough support from local constituency parties. This left Starmer – who had by this point secured the backing of eighty-eight MPs (42 per cent of the parliamentary party) – to fight it out among the wider membership with Long-Bailey and Nandy.

There were several obvious differences between the three remaining candidates. Most obviously, Starmer was the only man. As there had never been a female Labour leader before, this mattered. He was also seventeen years older than Long-Bailey and Nandy, both of whom were forty. This generational difference undoubtedly convinced them that they might be able to appeal to younger members more easily than Starmer, but being older allowed Starmer and his team to play the 'experience' card, presenting him as someone who had already held high public office as DPP. His near thirty-year career in the law also allowed him to outgun his rivals financially. During his campaign, Starmer attracted donations of just over £700,000 in cash and services, significantly more than the other candidates. The vast bulk of this money – £580,000 – came from thirty-five individual donors. Various small businesses came up with just under £50,000, while three trade unions – Unison, USDAW and Community – bankrolled Starmer to the tune of just over £80,000 in cash and practical support.

His old friend and colleague Helena Kennedy was instrumental in helping with these financial efforts, organising one highly lucrative event at Doughty Street Chambers where many legal figures dug deep. One, Robert Latham, a Doughty Street human rights lawyer, gave him £100,000. This sum was matched by Lord Alli, who was made a Labour peer in 1998 and who was close to Margaret McDonagh, the Blairite former general secretary of the party. As we have seen, Alli's Covent Garden flat had been used for secret Labour meetings during the Corbyn era. Helena Kennedy also hit the phones for Starmer, regaling Labour members with tales of his legal achievements and overall competence.

Just before the first of four televised debates was held, in the second week of February, Starmer announced the ten pledges on which he would focus if he were leader. He based these promises on 'the moral case for socialism'. The first covered 'economic justice', in which he would increase income tax for the top 5 per cent of earners and reverse cuts in corporation tax. The second area was 'social justice', in which he said he would abolish universal credit, 'defend our NHS' and axe university tuition fees. His third vow related to 'climate justice'. His fourth pledge concerned 'promoting peace and human rights'. By this, he said he meant 'no more illegal wars' and a review of arms sales. The idea of 'common ownership', in which public services including 'rail, mail, energy and water' are in public hands, was his fifth promise. His sixth guarantee was to 'defend migrants' rights', including a promise to 'defend free movement as we leave the EU'. The seventh pledge was to 'strengthen workers' rights and trade unions'. Next, he said he would promote the 'radical devolution of power, wealth and opportunity', including scrapping the House of Lords. 'Equality' was pledge number nine and 'effective opposition to the Tories' was the final promise. In this, he said he would provide 'forensic, effective opposition' in Parliament and would 'never lose sight of the votes "lent" to the Tories in 2019' while swearing to take 'robust action to eradicate the scourge of antisemitism' and to 'maintain our collective link with the unions'.

On the surface, some of the items on this political shopping list probably appeared reasonable or even appealing to moderate Labour members. Yet on closer examination, they incorporated a nakedly left-wing agenda which might potentially generate support from the more extreme element of the party too. Renationalisation, the extension of union power and significant tax increases were all things of which Jeremy Corbyn would approve. At the same time, the 'no more illegal wars' statement was clearly designed to prove that Starmer was cut from very different cloth to Tony Blair, whose decision to join the invasion of Iraq in 2003 lingered long in the memory and had turned him into a hate figure.

At the time, some pointed to his youthful ideology as evidence that Starmer genuinely held a desire to take Britain as far to the left as Corbyn had intended to had he won power. In retrospect, most observers could see that the pledges looked much more like a ruse to secure the Corbynista vote, become leader and then return Labour to the centre ground ahead of the next general election.

What was commonly agreed even in 2020 was that Starmer's

politics are in many ways ambiguous, with neither the hard left nor the centrists necessarily claiming him as one of their own in any distinct sense. Immediately after Starmer became leader, James Schneider, Corbyn's former head of strategic communications, wrote:

> Keir Starmer is not a ghoulish neoliberal, reactionary authoritarian, or a lover of war, but he isn't a socialist. Hard to place, he appears to be on the progressive end of social reformism, the nicest possible part of the establishment. He has no strong allergy to being near socialist ideas, but they aren't to his taste or style.

Starmer, in fact, does refer to himself in public as a socialist – though, as has been pointed out by others many times before, Labour is not and never has been a socialist party per se; rather, it is a party which has socialists in it.

Perhaps the only real difficulty that Starmer encountered during the campaign related to the money his team received from friends and supporters. He had a 28-day window in which to declare each donation in the House of Commons Register of Members' Financial Interests. Yet some rivals concluded that he was being slippery by taking advantage of this allowance, pointing out that some of his funding might not be publicly known by the time members cast their vote. Starmer breached no rules by taking his time to publish the names of his donors, but the MP Jon Trickett, for example, who backed Rebecca Long-Bailey, thought it was below the belt. 'Delaying publishing donations until the vast majority of people have voted is entirely undemocratic,' he said.

On 4 March, Starmer and Long-Bailey gave journalist Andrew Neil separate interviews which were broadcast on the BBC.

Neil challenged Starmer about the donations. Yet so, too, did Long-Bailey when she spoke to Neil. She told him: 'I think there's always an assumption that you don't get nothing for nothing in this world. And those who donate to your campaign will expect to be repaid in some way in the future.' She also slated Starmer for having what she thought was a vague set of policies, despite his having published his list of ten pledges. 'I don't know what Keir's policy ideas are, if I'm honest,' she said.

> I know he says he wants to adopt the same values that the [Labour Party] has, but what does that mean in practice? I hope that he keeps to our values and our principles. I think we need to see more detail. We need to see more meat on the bone in terms of what Keir believes in – and indeed about all of the candidates.

As the campaign neared its conclusion, the *New Statesman* published a 5,000-word interview of Starmer which included on the record quotes from friends including Gavin Millar. It was almost certainly crafted with Starmer's help as he edged closer to the finish line untroubled by either of his younger rivals. In it, he revealed himself to be more 'metrosexual' than perhaps anybody realised, as he confessed to 'moisturising nightly'. He also spoke of his wife's Jewish faith, a product of her father, a Polish Jew who emigrated to Britain and married her mother, who converted. 'It's very important that [my children] understand the history of their granddad,' Starmer said. 'Occasionally on a Friday night we'll have prayers with him.' Although he was careful not to criticise Corbyn's leadership during the contest, remarks such as this hinted that he was prepared to acknowledge that antisemitism had contributed to Labour's catastrophic loss in 2019, and he clearly wanted to purge it from the party.

Perhaps more revealingly, he harked back to his days on *Socialist Alternatives*. When asked if he was still a red–green, he shot back, 'Yeah!' Showing that his political instincts were far closer to Corbyn's than many realised, he added:

> I don't think there are big issues on which I've changed my mind. The big issue we were grappling with then was how the Labour Party, or the left generally, bound together the wider movement and its strands of equality – feminist politics, green politics, LGBT – which I thought was incredibly exciting, incredibly important. Broadly speaking, I think the Labour Party has done that very successfully.

By the morning of Saturday 4 April, Britain was in lockdown because of the Covid-19 crisis. The planned conference which was to be held in London to announce the new Labour leader was cancelled. Instead, the party relayed the result over its social media feeds. Starmer won in the first round, having received 275,780 votes (56.2 per cent of the available vote). Rebecca Long-Bailey was a distant second with 135,218 votes (27.6 per cent). Lisa Nandy trailed in third place with 79,597 (16.2 per cent). Starmer also achieved the most support from both the constituency parties and affiliates, having secured 374 constituencies and fifteen affiliates. Long-Bailey ended with the backing of 164 CLPs and seven affiliates. Nandy had clocked up seventy-two constituency parties and four affiliates. In a pre-recorded speech which was distributed online, Starmer spoke of the 'honour' of his victory. In words that would come back to haunt him, he also said: 'I want to pay tribute to Jeremy Corbyn, who led our party through some really difficult times, who energised our movement and who's a friend as well as a colleague.' But, inevitably, the moment was bittersweet as he was also forced to acknowledge that public life had 'all but come to a standstill'. The matter of the new Labour leader's identity suddenly appeared to be rather trivial in comparison to a potentially lethal disease which threatened millions of people around the world. Just as had been the case when he became DPP, Starmer had competed among a relatively weak field of candidates and won. Now he had to try to restore morale and order to his divided party before embarking on the matter of readying it for the next election. In this, he would be accompanied by his new deputy leader, Angela Rayner, who had also been voted into her post that day with just over half of the available votes.

Having become Leader of Her Majesty's Opposition after just five years in Parliament, the next task confronting him was to try to rebuild the Labour Party into a credible government in waiting.

• • •

Jeremy Corbyn's people had left the Leader of the Opposition's office in a shambles, strewn with paper and even discarded clothes. Old letters and draft speeches were crammed into drawers, cupboards and crates or simply left lying around. A printed email chain detailing a plot to depose former deputy leader Tom Watson after the election before last was found in a desk. The whole mess was consigned to the shredder.

The metaphor for the job that faced the new tenant was too perfect. Starmer had taken over a party that was divided, disorganised and demoralised and the voters' verdict on it had been stark. It was time to start again.

The job of recreating Labour began with the appointment of Starmer's frontbench team. John McDonnell and Diane Abbott resigned before they were pushed, while fellow Corbynites Jon Trickett, Ian Lavery and Richard Burgon were relieved of their duties along with Barry Gardiner, the new leader's old antagonist.

The return of Ed Miliband, Lord Falconer and David Lammy – who shortly afterwards joined Starmer as an unpaid associate tenant at Doughty Street Chambers – also suggested a change of direction from the Corbyn years. But the reshuffle hardly amounted to a wholesale clear-out: of the thirty-two members of Starmer's first shadow Cabinet, twenty-five had served on Corbyn's front bench at the 2019 election.

Some Labour figures welcomed this as a sign that Starmer would try to unify the party's competing tribes rather than wage war on the defeated left. The splits of the previous five years had been brought painfully into focus by the leak of an 860-page dossier, compiled in the last months of Corbyn's leadership, claiming to document evidence of a 'hyper-factional atmosphere' in party HQ, which had supposedly impeded the handling of disciplinary complaints, particularly those relating to antisemitism. The report even stated that 'some employees seem to have taken a view that the worse things got for Labour the happier they would be, since this might expedite Jeremy Corbyn's departure from office'. The document had been compiled as evidence for the Equalities and Human Rights Commission, which was conducting an inquiry into Labour's approach to antisemitism, but would not now be submitted.

The leak sparked a fresh outburst of infighting. Twenty-nine left-wing MPs – including four members of Starmer's new frontbench team – called for the document to be published in full, while opponents of Corbyn condemned it as an attempt to divert blame for the handling of antisemitism complaints away from the leadership and onto party staff.

Starmer tried to calm the situation, ordering a review into how the document came to be commissioned and leaked while stressing the need for unity. 'We have to stop the factionalism in our party. We have to create a different culture,' he told members in a video call. 'If we carry on taking lumps out of each other we are heading for a loss at the next general election.' Nevertheless, the dossier row highlighted what would become a persistent tension: maintaining a united party on the one hand and showing voters that Labour had changed on the other.

Though always politically active, Starmer had not spent his life steeped in Labour's internal politics. Since his selection as a parliamentary candidate, however, he had become acquainted with the sectarian struggles that preoccupy many of its members at all levels, from the smallest ward of a local constituency party to the shadow Cabinet and the National Executive Committee. Even in Holborn & St Pancras, elections to minor committee posts had often turned into ferocious ideological struggles. Camden Momentum, the local branch of the left-wing group set up to support Corbyn's leadership, urged Labour members to vote against Starmer in the leadership election, claiming he was making an 'opportunistic tilt to the left' despite failing to 'engage with, encourage or welcome the left at the local level'. Controlling the Labour Party's levers of administrative and organisational power would be crucial and, on this front, he was able to make early progress.

Centrist candidates swept the board in by-elections to the NEC that took place alongside the leadership contest. Together with the leader, deputy leader and three frontbench representatives, this meant there was already a 'Starmerite' majority on the ruling body that had recently been dominated by the left. The value of this was quickly seen when it approved David Evans, Starmer's preferred candidate, to take over as the party's general secretary following the resignation of Corbynite Jennie Formby. Evans quickly launched a review of Labour's organisational structure, bringing in Bob Kerslake, former head of the civil service, to lead the project.

If the party's internal mechanics seem to outsiders to be bewildering, impenetrable and irrelevant, they are an inescapable part of life inside Labour. One who is familiar with their mysteries says the importance of these apparently humdrum developments should not be underestimated:

> Most leaders have to wait several years for an NEC majority or a general secretary of their choosing. Corbyn didn't get his until after his 2016 re-election as leader. Blair had to negotiate almost every single general secretary there ever was between the different factions, and I don't think he ever got his first choice. Whereas Keir, right off the bat, managed to push through his first choice. And that speaks to the efficacy of the political operation around him.

An ally adds:

> There were so many different parts of the party that were preparing for life after Corbyn that there was always going to be energy that could be tapped there. And critically, he's just not that interested in the internal workings of the Labour Party to have spent a whole lot of time with a spreadsheet thinking about who he needed to speak to and who he needed to get on board. His politicking in that respect was far more natural and probably more effective for that.

Colleagues say Starmer also brought a new level of discipline to proceedings. 'All the meetings, which had previously been a shambles, are now being run properly,' said Falconer. 'The Corbyn Cabinet was full of people intervening on topics which had fuck all to do with the topic they were talking about, and high levels of abuse or obsequiousness. That doesn't happen any more.'

On one issue in particular, Starmer was determined to show an early and conclusive break with the past. In his victory speech in April, he had described antisemitism as 'a stain on our party' and promised to 'tear out this poison by its roots and judge success by the return of Jewish members and those who felt that they could no longer support us'. The words echoed those of Chief Rabbi Ephraim Mirvis, who wrote during the general election campaign that 'a new poison – sanctioned from the top – has taken root in the Labour Party'. Shortly after his election, Starmer called Mirvis to mark Yom Hashoah, the day when Jewish communities commemorate the victims of the Holocaust. Mirvis tweeted:

> Thank you to Sir Keir Starmer for his personal call today to convey his solidarity with the Jewish community as we mark Yom Hashoah. I welcomed hearing directly of his commitment to take the necessary action to root out antisemitism from the Labour Party as a top priority. It is heartening that the task of rebuilding the Jewish community's trust in the Labour Party has begun.

Determined to match words with action, Starmer sacked Rebecca Long-Bailey for sharing online an interview given by the actress Maxine Peake, in which Peake claimed police techniques that had led to the killing of George Floyd in Minneapolis had been 'learnt from seminars with Israeli secret services'. Long-Bailey had commented: 'Maxine Peake is an absolute diamond.' The decision infuriated the left, but Starmer was unrepentant, saying it had been wrong to share an article containing antisemitic conspiracy theories. 'I've made it my first priority to tackle antisemitism and rebuilding trust with the Jewish community is a number one priority for me,' he added. Jewish groups welcomed the decision and Labour MP Margaret Hodge, who had been among Corbyn's sternest critics, tweeted: 'This is what a change in culture looks like. This is what zero tolerance looks like. This is what rebuilding trust with the Jewish community looks like.' Starmer underlined his commitment to the Jewish community when, in July 2020, Labour agreed to pay substantial damages and offered an unreserved apology to seven former employees who sued the party for making false and defamatory comments about them after they slammed the leadership's handling of antisemitism complaints in a BBC *Panorama* programme broadcast a year earlier.

More Jewish leaders recognised the change of approach. Lord Triesman, Lord Mitchell and Lord Turnberg returned to the Labour Party, having left over antisemitism under Corbyn. The former Chief Rabbi Lord Sacks, who had previously described Corbyn as an antisemite who had 'given support to racists, terrorists and dealers of hate', said the party was 'doing better' under Starmer. 'The first thing is they have acknowledged the problem and its scope. And the second thing is that the leader has shown that he is willing to take responsibility. And thirdly he has reached out to the Jewish community in a way that the Jewish community feel very reassured by.'

A critical test came in October, when the EHRC published its report into the party's handling of antisemitism complaints during the Corbyn era. Starmer had always intended this to be the defining moment at which the party could deal absolutely with the issue, acknowledge past failures and begin to restore its reputation. The Commission's findings were unequivocal and devastating. It concluded that the Labour Party was responsible for three breaches of the 2010 Equality Act relating to harassment, political interference in antisemitism complaints and failure to provide adequate training to those handling such complaints. The body said its analysis pointed to 'a culture within the party which, at best, did not do enough to prevent antisemitism and, at worst, could be seen to accept it'.

Starmer said, 'I found this report hard to read. And it is a day of shame for the Labour Party. We have failed Jewish people, our members, our supporters, and the British public.' He accepted the report in full and without qualification and promised a culture change within the party, adding that if there were still those 'who think there's no problem with antisemitism in the Labour Party, that it's all exaggerated, or a factional attack, then, frankly, you are part of the problem too, and you should be nowhere near the Labour Party either'.

In response to the report, Jeremy Corbyn wrote: 'One antisemite is too many. But the scale of the problem was also dramatically overstated for political reasons by our opponents inside and outside the party, as well as by much of the media.' He was immediately suspended from the Labour Party – a decision taken by the general secretary, David Evans, which Starmer made clear he supported. 'I can't tell you how disappointed I was,' he said later. 'Because the words he used, what he said, coming from the former leader of the Labour Party in response to that report were just about as bad as you can get.'

Though Corbyn was readmitted the following month, Starmer decided to withhold the Labour whip from him until he apologised for claiming that the scale of antisemitism had been exaggerated. 'I'm the leader of the Labour Party, but I'm also the leader of the Parliamentary Labour Party,' Starmer tweeted in explanation of his decision. 'Jeremy Corbyn's actions in response to the EHRC report undermined and set back our work in restoring trust and confidence in the Labour Party's ability to tackle antisemitism.' It escaped nobody's attention that in his acceptance speech, Starmer had referred to Corbyn as 'a friend as well as a colleague'. Had he been telling the truth?

The left's response was fierce. Corbyn began legal action. Former party chair Ian Lavery said the refusal to let the former leader sit as a Labour MP looked like 'a vengeful, divisive, provocative sort of move from Keir Starmer' who was conducting a 'personal and political vendetta' and behaving as though the party was 'a tin-pot dictatorship'. Len McCluskey bewailed 'an act of grave injustice which, if not reversed, will create chaos within the party'. Momentum condemned the decision and a number of constituency Labour parties passed motions of solidarity with Corbyn. The simmering row also prompted a 'digital walkout' from an online NEC meeting by thirteen left-wing members, who were also cross at the leadership's support for appointing moderate Margaret Beckett as its chair in preference to the hard-left Ian Murray of the Fire Brigades Union, the former vice-chair whom they considered next in line. Howard Beckett, assistant general secretary of the Unite union and no relation, incongruously raged: 'Today the entire left walked out of the NEC. We won't stay silent on Keir Starmer's factionalism any longer.' Margaret Beckett was elected unanimously in their absence.

In an interview for the Limmud Festival of learning in December, Starmer spoke again about the Jewish heritage of his wife's family. Victoria's father had been born Jewish and had roots in Poland, while her mother, who had recently died, had converted to Judaism. Starmer said that they were bringing up their two children 'to recognise the faith part of their grandfather's family, and it's very important. Just carving out that tradition, that bit of faith on Friday is incredibly important, because we get together, and we do Zoom prayers now.' Though by no means a secret – he had spoken about it earlier in the year during the leadership campaign – the fact of Starmer's Jewish family ties came as news to many people, including some close colleagues.

In the early months of his leadership, then, Starmer had set a new tone on antisemitism, dealt with transgressions and in so doing begun to rebuild relations with the Jewish community. But all this raised a question which was regularly asked by his opponents: if Starmer so deplored Labour's record on the issue under Corbyn, why did he spend four years in his shadow Cabinet?

The question was put to him directly at the Limmud Festival. 'I thought it was better to stay and try and change things; others thought it was better to leave,' he said. 'I thought it was better to make the arguments that needed to be made in the shadow Cabinet. I took the view that if you are in a party you stay in and fight for change; other people took a different view.'

Some colleagues insist that Starmer did challenge the leadership on the issue. He pushed for the party to adopt the International Holocaust Remembrance Alliance's widely recognised definition of antisemitism, which had been resisted by Corbyn allies, and to establish a streamlined complaints procedure that would allow members to be summarily suspended or expelled for extreme breaches of the rules. 'He got criticised for not speaking out loudly enough, but he challenged Jeremy on it at the shadow Cabinet, and it was contrary to his personal political interests at the time to do it, so fair play to him,' says one colleague.

Other Labour MPs were sceptical, however. One who was in Parliament at the time recalls colleagues pleading with Starmer to speak out against antisemitism, to no avail. This person says:

> I remember [Jewish MP] Margaret Hodge speaking at a PLP meeting, quoting some of the revolting messages she'd been sent, and Keir said and did nothing. And when [Jewish MP] Louise Ellman had just resigned in October 2019, [Jewish MP] Ruth Smeeth was crying and she said at a PLP meeting, 'Keir, you're the most senior person here … I am begging you to say something about this.' He didn't say a word then either. Barry

> Gardiner was so outraged he printed out some of the messages Margaret had received and left them on the desks of shadow Cabinet members so that they could see what was going on. And again, Keir didn't say a word. Given his wife is Jewish, this was very surprising.

Still, expelling a former leader and sacking a prominent frontbencher were considered proof of Starmer's determination to rid the party of one of the most toxic features of the Corbyn years. Showing that the party had changed in other respects would be a much harder slog. While Starmer himself was manifestly a different kind of leader from his predecessor, rescuing the Labour brand would mean putting clear red water between the new leadership and the old regime.

Again, the mission was complicated by the awkward fact that Starmer had spent four years in Corbyn's senior team, effectively campaigning to make him Prime Minister – a connection which Labour's opponents were determined to exploit for all it was worth. When Starmer asked at Prime Minister's Questions in July about the threat Russia posed to Britain's national security, Johnson retorted that the new Leader of the Opposition had 'sat on his hands and said nothing while the Labour Party parroted the line of the Kremlin, when people in this country were poisoned on the orders of Vladimir Putin.' Starmer replied that he had spoken out strongly against the Salisbury attack of 2018, in which an assassination attempt by Moscow operatives upon a former Russian military officer resulted in the death of a British woman. Starmer said at the time that he believed responsibility lay with Russia, a stance that differed from that of Corbyn, who questioned the conclusion that Putin's government was responsible and even suggested a sample of the nerve agent used in the attack be sent to Russia so the Kremlin could confirm whether or not it was theirs. Corbyn's response had dismayed many of his own MPs and confirmed many voters' doubts about the approach a Labour government would take to security and defence. Starmer tried to dismiss Johnson's attack – 'In case the Prime Minister has not noticed, the Labour Party is under new management' – but he knew that moving on from the Corbyn era would take more than a slogan.

'Let's be brutally honest with ourselves,' he told his first Labour conference as leader. 'When you lose an election in a democracy, you deserve to. You don't look at the electorate and ask them: "What were you thinking?" You look at yourself and ask: "What were we doing?"' Being serious about winning meant dealing with the things that had driven people away from the party. 'Never again will Labour go into an election not being trusted on national security, with your job, with your community and with your money.'

He saw that this was not primarily to do with Labour's policies so much as its values. Many voters, including former Labour voters, believed that the party had come to see the world in a completely different way from them. Episodes like the response to the Salisbury attack suggested a reluctance to stand up for Britain. Corbyn's refusal to sing the national anthem at public events like the Battle of Britain memorial service and his equivocal attitude to terrorists – he had talked about inviting 'friends' from Hezbollah and Hamas to Parliament, among many other incidents – were a disturbing sign for many former Labour voters. There was a widespread feeling that Labour under Corbyn treated longstanding supporters outside its metropolitan enclaves with disdain, and even seemed to dislike the country it claimed to want to govern.

Starmer soon set about the long task of trying to change this perception. 'I'm really proud of my country and I wouldn't be leader of the Labour Party if I wasn't patriotic,' he said on a 'Call Keir' video meeting with voters in Bury soon after becoming leader.

> In the Labour Party we should be proud of being patriotic. We're all working, knocking on doors in the rain or shine, to try to put in place a team that can go into government to improve the country we live in because we love the country we live in. I don't think we should shy away from that.

The new patriotism strategy scored an early hit in the shape of a front-page splash in the traditionally Conservative *Sunday Telegraph* on the seventy-fifth anniversary of VE Day in May 2020, in which Starmer wrote in praise of the generation who had 'protected our country in its darkest hour'. The piece, which was accompanied by a photograph of a saluting, medal-bedecked old soldier, also noted the effect of the coronavirus crisis in care homes, the debt the country owed to key workers and the need to tackle longstanding injustices, but in a way that would have been unthinkable under the party's previous leader.

To Westminster observers, this manoeuvre signalled a new level of ambition and professionalism.

But despite this promising early success, the interaction of patriotism, values and history soon proved difficult territory for Starmer. The Black Lives Matter protests that followed the killing of George Floyd also in May 2020 were an early example. Asked during a radio phone-in whether he approved of protesters in Bristol pulling down a statue of the slave trader Edward Colston and dumping it in the harbour, Starmer said:

> It shouldn't have been done that way. Completely wrong to pull down a statue down like that. Stepping back, the statue

> should have been taken down a long, long time ago. We can't, in 21st-century Britain, have a slaver on a statue … The statue should have been brought down properly, with consent, and put, I would say, in a museum.

The following day, in common with a number of other public figures and left-leaning politicians, he 'took a knee' in support of the BLM movement. It should be said that he chose to do this days after twenty-seven police officers were injured in violent Black Lives Matter protests in London. Two officers were seriously injured. One of them, a policewoman, suffered a broken collarbone, a broken rib and a collapsed lung after a protester threw a bicycle at her horse, causing it to bolt.

Rather than take a knee in public, Starmer tweeted a photo of himself and his deputy leader Angela Rayner kneeling on the floor of an empty meeting room in Parliament with the caption: 'We kneel with all those opposing anti-Black racism. #BlackLivesMatter.' The approach suggested an attempt to balance the sensibilities of left-wing activists with the views of the wider public, who were much more sceptical about BLM and its aims. Soon afterwards, the attempt came to grief.

Asked in an interview what he thought of BLM's calls to 'defund the police', Starmer was unequivocal:

> That's nonsense, and nobody should be saying anything about defunding the police. I would have no truck with that. I was Director of Public Prosecutions for five years, I worked with police forces across England and Wales, bringing thousands of people to court, so my support for the police is very, very strong and evidenced in the joint actions I've done with the police. There's a broader issue here, the Black Lives Matter movement, or moment if you like, internationally, is about

> reflecting something completely different, and it's reflecting on what happened dreadfully in America just a few weeks ago and acknowledging that as a moment across the world. It's a shame it's getting tangled up with these organisational issues, with the organisation Black Lives Matter.

This pronouncement chimed with what the public might have expected from a responsible political leader: acknowledgement that a serious issue had been brought into focus but rejection of a protest movement's more extreme demands. The left took a rather different view. BLM tweeted: 'As a public prosecutor, Sir Keir Starmer was a cop in an expensive suit', and some Labour MPs criticised his choice of words: '#BlackLivesMatter isn't just a moment, it's a movement,' said Streatham MP Bell Ribeiro-Addy. 'It's clear that if we want to see real change, it's going to take sustained pressure from below.' His old adversaries at Camden Momentum urged the NEC to pass a vote of no confidence in the leader. An endorsement from Nigel Farage ('Heartily agree with @Keir_Starmer's condemnation of the Black Lives Matter organisation') did nothing to reassure his critics.

Starmer then expressed contrition for the language he used. 'I meant "moment" as in "a defining moment", a turning point, and I genuinely think that reflects the sentiment that many, many black community leaders have expressed in recent weeks,' he said, adding:

> I was absolutely not pandering to a racist vote. I was trying to recognise the significance of what was happening and express a determination that it should be a turning point, and to join with those across the Black Lives Matter movement who desperately do want it to be a turning point ... If people thought it meant something else, then of course I regret that.

A caller on his LBC phone-in show suggested his comment might be 'indicative of unconscious dismissive language and attitudes' of the kind that feed structural racism in society and asked if he would consider taking unconscious bias training. Starmer said he was introducing such training for all Labour Party staff and he would take the course himself. Asked by host Nick Ferrari if he thought he needed it, he replied:

> I think everybody should have unconscious bias training. I think it is important. There is always the risk of unconscious bias, and just saying, 'Oh well, it probably applies to other people, not me' is not the right thing to do, so I'm going to lead from the front on this and do the training.

The implication of his remarks – that all voters need instruction to overcome their inherent racism – would not have been lost on those who heard them.

The response to Starmer's comments on BLM was nothing to the row that followed the leak of an internal document recommending that the party associate itself with the union flag. Based on research by a branding agency called Republic, the presentation stated that 'belonging needs to be reinforced through all messengers' and that 'communicating Labour's respect and commitment for the country can represent a change in the party's body language'. Among other advice on restoring economic credibility and regaining the trust of voters, it suggested that 'the use of flags, veterans, dressing smartly at the war memorial etc give voters a sense of authentic values alignment'. The recurring theme of patriotism, together with interventions such as a political broadcast in which Starmer promised to 'rebuild our country' while standing next to the flag, suggested the advice was already being acted upon.

The backlash from the left to what became known as 'the flag memo' was immediate and ferocious. Clive Lewis, a black MP who had served as shadow Business Secretary under Corbyn, said, 'It's not patriotism; it's Fatherland-ism. There's a better way to build social cohesion than moving down the track of the nativist right.' Social media was awash with condemnation of Labour's supposed embrace of nationalist bigotry, and a barrage of comment pieces in left-leaning papers demanded to know what the point of the left was if it was going to walk and talk like the 'far right'. Other commentators, by no means confined to the right, mused upon the left's apparent disdain for the flag and the history of Britain, and wondered how deep the Starmerite conversion to patriotism really went.

Perhaps most damning of all was the verdict of a member of staff at Labour HQ, who said of the leadership: 'They don't believe any of this stuff; they're saying whatever they think will get them votes.'

When opportunities arose for Labour and its leader to display their attitude to national security, the resulting message could perhaps be described as ambiguous. In September 2020, Starmer ordered his MPs to abstain on the second reading of the Overseas Operations Bill, which was designed to protect British soldiers and veterans from prosecution over actions taken while serving abroad. Critics of the bill were concerned that it might deny justice to victims of alleged torture and war crimes, and – given Starmer's earlier work as a human rights lawyer – many were surprised at his stance on the issue. Nineteen Labour MPs defied the instruction and voted against, including three frontbenchers who lost their jobs as a result. Thirty-seven members of the Holborn & St Pancras Labour Party wrote to the *Camden New Journal* to vent their displeasure at their MP's stance and remind him that his leadership election platform had included a commitment to 'no more illegal wars'. Two months later Starmer and his party changed tack and opposed the legislation at its final stage in the Commons.

In October, the leadership faced an even bigger rebellion over the Covert Human Intelligence Sources Bill, also known as the 'Spy Cops' Bill, which gave legal protection to undercover agents forced to commit crimes while on secret operations. Thirty-four Labour MPs voted against the legislation despite again being whipped to abstain – a directive which allowed Conservative Home Secretary Priti Patel to say, 'Their leader may have changed, but Labour still can't be trusted on national security.'

There were also tentative efforts to move away from the Corbynite approach to the economy. Starmer's suggestion that the government should 'look at the idea of a wealth tax' was swiftly abandoned despite support for the idea from the party's left. He told the Confederation of British Industry conference in November that he wanted a new partnership between Labour and business, saying he was 'under no illusion about the work we have to do if we're to win back your trust … When a business is failing it is often because the management is failing. The Labour Party is now under new management.'

These attempts by Starmer to change some of the more electorally damaging perceptions of his party's brand caused consternation in parts of the left. As we have seen, the Haldane Society of Socialist Lawyers banned Starmer from membership on the grounds that he was 'demonstrably not a socialist'. Some in the Labour movement began to complain that since the leadership contest little or nothing had been heard of his ten pledges, which had been carefully calibrated to secure the support of a membership still largely loyal to Corbyn.

One such figure was Unite leader Len McCluskey. 'The fact is that Keir Starmer ran on a radical programme, some might say a Corbyn programme, and of course I keep this to hand,' he told an interviewer from *The Observer* in August 2020, flourishing Starmer's campaign leaflet. 'For me, he has to recognise that the ship he is sailing, if it lists too much to the right, then it will go under.' As for the union's status as Labour's biggest donor, 'It would be a mistake if anybody took Unite for granted.' Two months later, its executive voted to cut funding to the party by around £150,000.

Some senior party figures saw this as a small price to pay for a bit of distance between the Labour Party and one of the most outspoken supporters of Corbyn's socialist policies.

But the left remained vocal enough to remind outsiders that the Labour Party as a whole had not been transformed overnight by Corbyn's departure. Starmer's own deputy, Angela Rayner, undermined the new message of statesmanlike moderation by shouting 'scum' at Conservative MP Chris Clarkson during a speech in the Commons, earning a stern rebuke from the Deputy Speaker, Eleanor Laing. Labour MPs including Diane Abbott and Dawn Butler spoke out in support of the blockading of newspaper presses by the protest group Extinction Rebellion. A Labour Party report titled 'Remaking of the British state: for the many, not the few', commissioned under Corbyn but not made public until ten months into Starmer's leadership, proposed the abolition of the honours system and gallantry medals for the military; reparation payments to former colonies; the scrapping of trade union laws; and the disestablishment of the Church of England. Labour MP Nadia Whittome declined to condemn protesters in Bristol who injured police officers and set police vehicles on fire while demonstrating against the Police, Crime, Sentencing and Courts Bill, while sixteen Labour city council candidates signed an open letter blaming the police for 'excessive force'.

In the early months in the job Starmer had managed to show

that he was not like Jeremy Corbyn. But this left another question: who was he? Answering this and persuading voters that Labour was a serious alternative government would be hard enough at the best of times – let alone during a global pandemic.

CHAPTER 13

CAPTAIN HINDSIGHT

Starmer's victory speech, delivered in front of closed window shutters in his north London home, marked the beginning of a year in which he would not address a public event in person or shake a single voter by the hand. During a public health crisis in which lives were being lost, this misfortune barely registered on the scale of human hardship, as he readily acknowledged. Even so, lockdown had created the worst possible campaigning conditions for a new political leader needing to introduce himself to the country.

He had planned to launch his leadership with a nationwide tour of former Labour seats in order to reconnect with those parts of the electorate who had turned their backs on the party. Instead, he made do with a series of town hall-style meetings on video calling platforms, during which he would listen to voters' views and answer their questions. As isolated workers all over the world were finding, such virtual engagements were better than nothing but no substitute for genuine human interaction. This was a major drawback for the Starmer project, which would depend on grasping – and being seen to grasp – the reasons for the breakdown of Labour's relationship with its former heartlands.

Confined to their homes, shadow Cabinet meetings took place via Zoom at 9.30 every Tuesday morning. Starmer broke up long days in front of his screen or on his phone by jogging. He also set aside some time to work on the autobiography he had begun drafting. But as well as limiting his contact with potential voters, the restrictions made it harder to cement relationships with his colleagues in Parliament. Starmer was constrained not just physically but politically. In his living-room victory address, he acknowledged that the government faced a huge responsibility, saying:

> Whether we voted for this government or not, we all rely on it to get this right. That's why in the national interest the Labour Party will play its full part. Under my leadership we will engage constructively with the government, not opposition for opposition's sake. Not scoring party political points or making impossible demands. But with the courage to support where that's the right thing to do.

Unusually for a new party leader, the first order of business was not to begin plotting against his main opponent but to ring him to discuss how they could work together. Starmer spoke to Boris Johnson by telephone soon after arriving in his new office on 4 April 2020, the two agreeing to meet the next week in Downing Street to discuss how best to tackle the Covid crisis. The appointment could not be kept. The following day, Johnson was admitted to hospital having tested positive for the virus. After a week, including three nights in intensive care, Johnson was discharged to recuperate at Chequers. Looking haggard, he released a video thanking the NHS for saving his life and praising nurses and doctors for looking after him 'when things could have gone either way'.

With 1,000 deaths per day being attributed to Covid-19, Starmer sensed correctly that there was no public appetite for party politics. Nor did he disagree with the thrust of the government's approach: those who questioned the policy of extended lockdowns were to be found on the Conservative benches, not

Labour's. Instead, he chose to focus on the question of competence, asking detailed questions about ministers' handling of the situation and the basis of their decisions.

Yet Johnson's illness, and his fiancée Carrie Symonds delivering their baby, Wilfred, at the end of April, meant that Starmer had to wait until he was a month into the job to confront his opposite number at Prime Minister's Questions. He opened their long-awaited encounter by welcoming Johnson back to Parliament and congratulating him on the arrival of his son. Then came the punch:

> When the Prime Minister returned to work a week ago Monday, he said that many people were looking at the 'apparent success' of the government's approach, but yesterday we learned that, tragically, at least 29,427 people in the UK have now lost their lives to this dreadful virus. That is now the highest number in Europe and the second highest in the world. That is not success, or even apparent success, so can the Prime Minister tell us: how on earth did it come to this?

Interrogating the figures on deaths in care homes, the rate of testing, the abandonment of contact tracing and the supply of personal protective equipment for NHS staff, he accused the government of being 'slow on lockdown, slow in testing, slow on the supply of PPE'.

Starmer's performance pleased the critics. Laura Kuenssberg, then BBC political editor, described the clash as 'the lawyer versus the showman'. Joe Murphy, her counterpart on the *Evening Standard*, went further, writing:

> The word 'forensic' is the one that everyone will use about Sir Keir's silky performance at the despatch box. It was indeed. Yet

> the word doesn't actually begin to capture the quietly terrifying force of a skilled former chief prosecutor assembling all the evidence and nailing it piece by damning piece to the accused.

Starmer's early outings as Labour leader helped to draw a contrast with both his opponent and his predecessor. The journalist Andrew Neil tweeted that it was 'clear that the United Kingdom now has a functioning, probing, measured, informed official opposition. The government will need to raise its game.'

Johnson himself mentioned Starmer's lawyerly credentials at every opportunity, whether because he believed it would be an effective line of attack with voters or simply because he thought Starmer would find it annoying. For example during one bad-tempered exchange over school reopening plans in June, the PM declared:

> The right hon. and learned Gentleman still cannot work out whether he is saying that schools are not safe enough or that we should be going back more quickly. He cannot have it both ways. It is one brief on one day and another brief on the next. I understand how the legal profession works, but what the public want to have is some consistency.

In those early days, the public seemed to like what it saw of the new Leader of the Opposition. By June 2020, YouGov found more voters thinking Starmer was doing a good job than those who felt the same about Johnson, and that people were more likely to agree than disagree that Starmer looked like a Prime Minister in waiting. Labour's polling deficit against the Conservatives, which had stood at twenty-four points when Starmer took over, had almost closed by the early autumn. But this success was short-lived. In principle, the idea that the country needed a decent opposition holding the government constructively to account during the crisis was surely correct. In political terms, it would prove a much harder strategy to implement than it sounded.

Starmer and his party supported the government's overall approach: lockdowns, school closures and generous financial support for jobs and businesses. After the emergency provisions in the Coronavirus Act were passed in one day without a vote in March 2020, Labour under Starmer did not oppose their renewal six months later and voted to extend them in March 2021.

This, however, left plenty of scope for him to criticise. The supply of PPE, the arrangements in care homes, the calculation of official mortality figures, the test and trace programme, the support for self-employed people and new job starters, the school reopening plans, the procurement contracts for safety equipment, the NHS capacity planning for winter, the exit strategy from lockdown and the immigration surcharge for NHS and care workers from overseas (on which he was able to claim the credit for a change in policy) were all subjected to Starmer's scrutiny, among much else. His reproaches were usually delivered more in sorrow than in anger, but there was an echo of Brexit-era Starmer: assurances of support on the overall destination but quibbles about every single step along the way.

His repeated complaint that the government had been slow in making every major decision – lockdown, testing, PPE, an exit strategy – developed into a kind of mantra as the weeks wore on. He mentioned it in interviews he gave. To large parts of the public, this began to sound more like carping from the sidelines than constructive opposition. Even non-Tories were often inclined to give the government the benefit of the doubt as it battled to contain an emergency in unprecedented circumstances. Few thought Labour under Starmer would be handling the situation any better.

His approach certainly vexed Johnson. At PMQs on 8 July

2020, he replied to a question from Starmer on the spread of infections in care homes by saying:

> The reality is that we now know things about the way the coronavirus is passed from person to person without symptoms that we just did not know. That is why we instituted the care home action plan on 15 April. That is why we changed the procedures. Perhaps he did know that it was being transmitted asymptomatically – I did not hear it at the time. Perhaps Captain Hindsight would like to tell us that he knew that it was being transmitted asymptomatically.

The moniker – coined by Johnson's PPS, Alex Burghart – would be used frequently to characterise the Labour leader as an armchair critic who enjoyed the luxury of retrospective complaint without the responsibility of making decisions based on limited information.

But while some began to see Starmer as a nit-picking opportunist, many on his own side felt he was giving the government too easy a ride. His observation in PMQs that the expansion of critical care capacity in the NHS had been an 'amazing piece of work' resulted in a storm of protest on Twitter from those who blamed the government for Britain's escalating death toll. Alastair Campbell, Tony Blair's former press secretary, wrote that the opposition should 'show no mercy' in challenging ministers, even during a crisis.

Starmer ordered his MPs to abstain in Commons votes on the 'rule of six' for private gatherings, a 10 p.m. curfew for pubs, and the tier system, under which different restrictions would apply to different parts of the country depending on the local prevalence of the virus. This decision brought predictable scorn from

Johnson, who declared that 'Captain Hindsight is rising rapidly up the ranks and has become General Indecision'.

Starmer was also regularly criticised for demanding new measures when the government was already widely expected to announce them at any moment. A glaring example came in January 2021, when interviews in which he called for a new national lockdown and the closure of schools within the following twenty-four hours were broadcast after government sources had briefed the media that exactly such an announcement was imminent. Starmer's office said the interviews were recorded before the move was confirmed, but the charge remained that his position was always that the government should be doing more of what they were doing anyway, but faster: questions about the effectiveness of restrictions or the wider consequences of lengthy lockdowns went unasked by the official opposition.

Nevertheless, Starmer did occasionally take the opportunity to give the government a good kicking. During the first lockdown, when millions were prevented from travelling even to visit sick relatives or attend funerals, Johnson's chief adviser, Dominic Cummings, was accused of breaking the law by driving his family from London to his parents' home in County Durham so that their young son could be looked after while both he and his wife were ill. The incident provoked a furious reaction from much of the public and the media – including right-leaning newspapers – and from some Conservative MPs, as well as the government's opponents. Starmer said: 'If I were Prime Minister, I'd have sacked Cummings,' and raged that it looked like 'one rule for the Prime Minister's advisers, another rule for everybody else'. Combined with recent blunders over the easing of restrictions and slow progress on testing and tracing, it saw public approval of the government's management of the crisis plummet. 'I am putting the Prime Minister on notice that he has got to get a grip and restore public confidence in the government's handling of the epidemic,' Starmer warned. 'There is a growing concern the government is now winging it. At precisely the time when there should have been maximum trust in the government, confidence has collapsed.'

He adopted a similar tone of outraged indignation after Johnson's last-minute cancellation of plans to ease restrictions over the 2020 Christmas break, under which up to three households would have been allowed to meet indoors for the first time in months. Starmer, who had called unsuccessfully for a 'circuit-breaker' lockdown to check a rise in Covid cases earlier in the autumn, demanded a review of the festive relaxation, prompting the Prime Minister to say in the Commons: 'I wish he had the guts to just say what he really wants to do, which is to cancel the plans people have made and to cancel Christmas.' Three days later, on 19 December, Johnson announced that the spread of a new variant of the virus had forced him to reverse the decision and introduce new, tougher rules for much of the country. Having warned of such an outcome, Starmer said that the measures were necessary and that he supported them, but he did note – many felt entirely accurately – 'We have a Prime Minister who is so scared of being unpopular that he is incapable of taking tough decisions until it is too late.'

If Starmer was sometimes able to articulate people's frustration over incidents like the Cummings debacle and the Christmas U-turn, the pandemic's unrelenting dominance of the news made it even harder than usual for an opposition party to win attention for its own agenda. A rare opportunity came with the leader's speech to Labour's online party conference in September 2020, in which, as previously noted, he said Labour had deserved to lose the election. He also declared:

> In 1945, Attlee had to build a society fit to reward the sacrifices of the war. In 1964, Wilson had to make the 'white heat of technology' work for working people. In 1997, Blair wanted to extend the new era of opportunity to everyone. In the seventy-five years since the historic victory of 1945 there have only been three Labour winners. I want to be the fourth.

As the second wave of the pandemic gathered pace during the autumn of 2020, however, such promising themes were soon submerged in the all-Covid news cycle. By the turn of the year, left-leaning commentators and some in Parliament began to wonder aloud when Starmer would begin to set out a compelling vision of Labour as an alternative government. 'It's all tactics, no strategy,' said one Labour MP. 'Keir and his people are not political and they're making increasing missteps because they don't have an analysis about where they ultimately want to get to.'

Labour advisers briefed friendly media sources that there was, in fact, a plan. Starmer was approaching his leadership in phases: having established himself as a serious figure at the head of a constructive opposition, he would now begin to set out Labour's priorities.

In his New Year speech, he promised 'a decade of national renewal' and pledged that, if in power, he would not rely on the 'big government chequebook' to fix the country's problems. Co-opting the famous Brexit slogan, he also vowed to make the centrepiece of his first King's Speech a 'Take Back Control' Bill, which would 'evolve new powers over employment support, transport, energy, climate change, housing, culture, childcare provision and how councils run their finances'.

In February 2021, in what was billed as his most important speech to date, he set out his own broader analysis, designed to rival the narrative that had helped the Conservatives win and consolidate power a decade earlier. While David Cameron and George Osborne had successfully claimed that their policies represented a return to sound economic management after years of Labour overspending, Starmer argued that the pandemic had disproportionately affected the UK because Tory austerity had weakened the foundations of British society, and that the post-Covid reconstruction presented an opportunity for change. The core of his speech was a proposal for British Recovery Bonds, through which savers would be able to invest in the country's recovery, along with state-financed start-up loans for 100,000 new small businesses: 'An example of the active, empowering government I believe is needed if we're to build a more secure economy.'

But such interventions failed to gain traction, and the idea of British Recovery Bonds soon sank without trace. Criticisms resurfaced, boosted, as we have already seen, by the row over the notorious 'flag memo'. As can sometimes happen in politics, the theme of Starmer's lacklustre leadership gathered momentum and became self-perpetuating as more commentators chimed in with a long list of personal and political complaints. It was not just newspaper columnists who went for him. Labour MPs and even shadow Cabinet members also grumbled regularly to reporters about their leader's shortcomings. The overriding question on people's lips was: is Starmer up to the job?

In early February, the Socialist Campaign Group, comprising left-wing MPs, unions and party members, demanded an emergency conference to discuss what it called the leadership 'crisis'. Critics pointed to evidence from NEC elections suggesting that membership had fallen by just under 57,000 – about 10 per cent, or nearly 250 a day, to 495,961 – since Starmer became leader. The party's finances had also taken a hit: cash received totalled just over £15 million during his first year in charge, compared to £21.8 million during Corbyn's opening twelve months.

Some in the party were also distressed at the abandonment of what they still considered a fruitful campaign issue: Brexit. In December 2020, Starmer had whipped Labour MPs to vote for the deal Boris Johnson and the EU had reached on Christmas Eve, arguing that while a better deal should have been negotiated, Parliament now faced a binary choice:

> A thin deal is better than no deal, and not implementing this deal would mean immediate tariffs and quotas with the EU, which will push up prices and drive businesses to the wall. It will mean huge gaps in security, a free-for-all on workers' rights and environmental protections, and less stability for the Northern Ireland protocol.

Party loyalists explained that the issue had to be put to bed: they could not hope to win back lost voters while still apparently refusing to accept their decision on EU membership, emphatically confirmed at the 2019 election. Starmer later signalled that he would not seek to restore freedom of movement – discarding one of his ten leadership election pledges – saying any Labour government would inherit the agreement as it now stood. 'I don't think there's scope for major renegotiation,' he said. 'We've just had four years of negotiation. We've arrived [at] a treaty and now we've got to make that treaty work.' Thirty-seven MPs defied his order to back Johnson's deal, and many wanted to continue the battle. Exeter MP Ben Bradshaw, a centrist, was representative of this view. He said Starmer had been right to focus on Covid but added 'it is not going to be sustainable not to talk about Brexit for very much longer. Otherwise, what's the point of being the opposition?'

How far such criticism was justified ceased to matter. The idea that Starmer's leadership was struggling became an established fact, an embedded part of the political narrative. He was also facing more tangible misfortunes. In October 2020, it was reported that he had collided with a Deliveroo cyclist while driving his Toyota RAV4 SUV to his tailor in Kentish Town. The injured party was taken to hospital to have his arm patched up. Luckily, for Starmer, the police decided to take no action.

A more politically embarrassing moment came in February 2021 when an exchange at PMQs led Starmer to initiate a stand-up row with Johnson in the Commons voting lobby. In response to a question on coronavirus travel restrictions, Johnson said: 'If we had listened to the right hon. and learned gentleman, we would still be at the starting blocks, because he wanted to stay in the European Medicines Agency [which had taken much longer than the UK medicine regulator to authorise Covid vaccines] and said so four times from that despatch box.'

Starmer hit back furiously: 'Complete nonsense. Don't let the truth get in the way of a pre-prepared gag: the Prime Minister knows that I have never said that, from this despatch box or anywhere else, but the truth escapes him.'

Conservative MP Mark Francois happened to be sitting behind Johnson. 'I said to him, "Did he say it?" and Boris said, "Yes,"' Francois recalls. 'So I texted my researcher and said, "PM certain he said it. Find the quote!" He found the extract from Hansard.' Francois then made a point of order at the end of PMQs, declaring that Starmer had indeed said, on 31 January 2017, 'Why would we want to be outside the European Medicines Agency, which ensures that all medicines in the EU market are safe and effective?' After the session, Francois says,

> I walked out of the chamber to the Members' Lobby. As I came out, I saw the PM and Trudy, his PPS, standing with Starmer basically wagging his finger at him very aggressively, red in the

> face, and he's almost shouting at him. And he's saying, 'I never said that; that's wrong.' The PM stood his ground. He didn't overreact. He just said, 'Look, Keir, check the record.' Denis Healey's first law of politics is 'When you're in a hole, stop digging.' Keir Starmer was in the cab of a JCB. It's lucky for Keir nobody took a photo.

Back in his office, Starmer watched the exchange again and realised what had happened. As his spokesman later explained, he had 'misheard' and thought Johnson had said he wanted to join the EU vaccination programme. 'Keir accepts that, on this occasion, the Prime Minister was referring to old comments about the European Medicines Agency, and Keir admits he was wrong and made a mistake in his response.' It crowned a terrible week for Starmer, which also saw the leaked flag memo.

Perhaps the biggest obstacle to Labour's attempts to gain ground on the government was altogether out of Starmer's hands. By November 2020, a taskforce established by Johnson and overseen by the venture capitalist Kate Bingham had secured 350 million doses of vaccines under development. On 2 December, Britain became the first country in the world to approve the Pfizer-BioNTech vaccine, and the first inoculations took place six days later. Two more vaccines, from AstraZeneca and Moderna, were approved by early January 2021. By Starmer's first anniversary as Labour leader, some 27 million people had received at least one dose, making the UK's programme one of the most successful in the world. Polls found that close to nine in ten voters approved of the scheme, a remarkable score for any government endeavour.

The success of the vaccine rollout eclipsed Starmer's continued criticism of the government's handling of the pandemic. More seriously for Labour, it blunted the party's whole political attack on Johnson's Conservatives, whom they sought to portray as incompetent.

Added to this was the fact that the Conservative Chancellor, Rishi Sunak, was spending – albeit reluctantly – on an unprecedented scale and Johnson's government had committed to 'levelling up' previously neglected parts of the country. Labour's habitual anti-austerity message was now redundant.

Starmer was not without his defenders. His allies were at pains to emphasise the progress he had made given the battering the party had received at the 2019 election. Having inherited what one senior aide described as a 'burning skip of a party', the new leader's task effectively combined Tony Blair's reinvention of Labour in the 1990s with David Cameron's rebranding of the Tories after 2005. 'If we'd been a car, we'd have been scrapped,' said one shadow minister. Voters had begun to lose trust in Labour before they had even heard of Jeremy Corbyn; a swift transformation of the party's fortunes was never realistic. Yet although Starmer represented a return to mainstream politics, most people were simply not that interested in what the opposition had to say, especially when they were willing the government to conquer Covid – a government which under Johnson's premiership still felt relatively new, despite the Conservatives' decade in office.

Even so, there was no escaping the fact that the more the voters saw of Starmer, the less impressed they seemed. The 48 per cent of the electorate who told YouGov that they thought he was doing his job well in the summer of 2020 proved to be a peak. That number declined steadily over the autumn, falling to 26 per cent by April 2021. Nearly twice as many said they thought he was doing badly. Overall, the Conservatives had once again opened a consistent lead in the polls.

The state of the parties was soon tested not in opinion surveys but at the ballot box. In May 2021, elections were held for councils, mayoralties and police and crime commissioners, as well as for the Scottish Parliament and the Welsh Assembly. The stakes were raised when Mike Hill, the MP for Hartlepool, stood down over allegations of sexual harassment, triggering a by-election in a formerly solid Labour seat which the party had held by a small margin in 2019. Yet Hartlepool was an overwhelmingly Leave-voting constituency, and plenty of observers scratched their heads when Paul Williams, a Remainer, was imposed as the candidate without an open selection process having taken place. Seasoned politicos smelled danger.

Launching his party's national campaign, Starmer proclaimed that 'every vote for the Labour Party is a vote for nurses' pay, for NHS staff' – arguably an odd choice of theme, since none of the hundreds of council or mayoral candidates up for election in May would have any power over such questions were they to be elected. For several weeks, though, the Tories themselves seemed eager to supply the opposition with extra material. It emerged that David Cameron had privately lobbied ministers and senior civil servants to give Greensill Capital, a firm in which he had an interest and which subsequently collapsed, access to a coronavirus bailout scheme. It was also reported that Johnson had said he would rather see 'bodies pile high in their thousands' than take the country into a third lockdown before agreeing to do so the previous autumn. And Dominic Cummings, who had left his role as Johnson's chief adviser in November 2020, claimed Lord Brownlow, a Conservative donor, had paid £58,000 towards the cost of refurbishing the PM's Downing Street flat before being reimbursed by Johnson, a loan which he had failed to declare.

Starmer did his best to capitalise, switching the focus of Labour's message to 'the return of Tory sleaze'. It didn't work. A visit to the wallpaper department of the Manchester branch of John Lewis to highlight the story that Johnson had spent £840 on a single roll was roundly ridiculed, while, gallingly for Starmer, YouGov gave the Conservatives an eleven-point lead, even though more than half of respondents said they considered the Tories 'very sleazy and disreputable'.

To cap it all, Starmer was thrown out of licensed premises while campaigning in Bath. The humiliating moment was captured by a Sky News camera crew as Rod Humphris, the Labour-voting landlord of The Raven, ejected him after lambasting his passive stance on lockdowns and mask-wearing. 'Get out of my pub!' Humphris shouted at a visibly chastened Starmer. 'That man is not allowed in my pub!' The confrontation seemed to sum up the fortunes of an increasingly beleaguered politician.

When the election results came in, the Conservative Party had performed best in England, gaining eleven additional councils and 234 new councillors. Labour lost control of ten councils and lost 326 councillors. More remarkably, the Conservative candidate, Jill Mortimer, won Hartlepool with a 16 per cent swing from Labour and a majority of 7,000, marking only the second time since 1982 that a governing party had gained a seat in a by-election. Elsewhere, the Tory Mayor of Teesside was re-elected with nearly three-quarters of the vote, and his counterpart in the West Midlands was returned to office comfortably. Labour wins in mayoral contests in London, Wales, Bristol, Liverpool, Manchester and the West of England could not disguise the party's latest thrashing.

In his ritual TV interview the next morning, Starmer looked rattled, perhaps even slightly manic. 'We have changed as a party, but we've not made a strong enough case to the country. We've lost that connection, that trust, and I intend to rebuild that and do whatever is necessary to rebuild that trust,' he insisted. Quite what that would entail was unclear even to him. 'Changing the things that need changing,' he said. 'That is the change that I will bring about.' Some commentators wondered if the party's outlook under him was just too narrow. Others questioned whether he was the right man to lead Labour. A few even asked if Labour itself had a future. Starmer told those closest to him that he was going to resign the leadership. After several hours of soul searching, he was talked down by his wife and his chief of staff, Morgan McSweeney.

A reshuffle ensued, the most significant element of which was the advance of Rachel Reeves to the post of shadow Chancellor. In her capacity as chair of the Labour Party and national campaigns co-ordinator, Angela Rayner had – officially, at least – been in charge of the disastrous local elections operation. Starmer's working relationship with Rayner had become increasingly strained, a situation not helped by their very different personalities, and he concluded this was an opportune moment to demote her. In doing so, he hoped to stamp his authority on the party. He misjudged the situation badly.

When Rayner heard from the press on the afternoon of Saturday 8 May that she had been sacked, she and Starmer met in his office, where a lively argument developed. Rayner's position was soon bolstered by MPs on the left including Jon Trickett and Diane Abbott, who publicly questioned Starmer's decision. John McDonnell went on television the next morning to accuse Starmer of using Rayner as a scapegoat. He told the BBC that Starmer's style of running the party was 'very centralised' and that in reality he had personally 'controlled' the election campaign.

There were other problems for Labour to contend with that weekend. The *Sunday Times* political editor Tim Shipman posted two tweets and two retweets about Baroness Chapman, Starmer's political director and one of his most trusted confidantes. In his first tweet, Shipman observed that loyalty to Chapman appeared to be the 'most important commodity as far as Labour high command is concerned this evening'. Then he retweeted a tweet that included the phrase: 'Who is this woman? What has she got on Starmer?' Shipman's second tweet, which was attributed to an unnamed Labour source, claimed that Chapman had been banned from Starmer's house 'on the orders' of his wife, Victoria. Shipman was quickly advised that his online activity would have consequences. Although he deleted the messages, he was pursued through the courts and in February 2022 he had to apologise to Chapman and pay her a substantial sum for the false suggestion of a secret adulterous relationship with Starmer.

With Labour engaged in an unedifying mini civil war straight after the May 2021 local elections, and because Rayner had her own power base within the party, Starmer was forced into the humbling position of having to promote her. Following their argument, she would henceforth have four job titles to her name: deputy Labour leader, shadow First Secretary of State, shadow Chancellor of the Duchy of Lancaster and shadow Secretary of State for the Future of Work. Mocking Starmer's feebleness a few days later, Boris Johnson warned him during a Commons debate that 'the more titles he feeds her, the hungrier, I fear, she is likely to become'.

That was not all. As Starmer sat on the front bench listening to those words, he would also have been able to mull over the recent sacking of his close parliamentary aide Carolyn Harris, after she was caught using the WhatsApp messaging service to brief against Rayner. There was more. Tony Blair produced a blistering response to Labour's poor showing at the polls, attacking Starmer in the pages of the *New Statesman* in a piece headlined 'Without total change Labour will die.' Where was the 'compelling economic message', Blair demanded, as he warned Labour was being defined by the 'woke' left. He said that Starmer was 'struggling to break through with the public' and the party needed to embark on a 'total deconstruction and reconstruction. Nothing less will do.' Not to be outdone, Rayner told the BBC that Starmer had not yet managed to capture the attention of the electorate. 'What I heard on the doorstep is they [voters] didn't know what Keir Starmer stood for. So that's what I think our challenge is,' she said damningly. ITV News was also given the benefit of Rayner's analysis, as she explained that Labour 'got the tone wrong' during the elections and sounded 'patronising' to voters. Next on her list was Politico's *Westminster Insider* podcast. She told its interviewer that even she might have voted for the 'authentic' Boris Johnson, adding that Starmer does 'cheese me off'.

A public relations drive was called for. In mid-May 2021, ITV announced that Starmer had agreed to give a lengthy interview to Piers Morgan, host of the chat show *Life Stories*. The programme, broadcast in early June, was unrevelatory save for Starmer refusing fourteen times to say whether he had ever taken recreational drugs. The closest he came to admitting guilt was to acknowledge that he 'had a good time' at university.

Two more Westminster by-elections followed. By now, it was taken as read that bad results would hasten Starmer's exit from the top of the Labour Party. The first ballot, on 17 June, was held at Chesham & Amersham after the death of the Conservative MP Cheryl Gillan. The Tories were not expected to lose the seat, but it was assumed that Labour would put in a credible performance, having secured 7,000 votes at the previous general election. When the Liberal Democrats trounced both main parties, with a swing against the Tories of more than twenty-five points, there was amazement in some quarters. The result disconcerted Johnson, but Starmer was arguably wounded more deeply. Labour had polled only 622 votes – 1.6 per cent of the total cast – despite having more party members than that in the area at the time. Its candidate, Natasa Pantelic, came fourth and lost her deposit.

Tracy Brabin's election as Mayor of West Yorkshire meant another testing by-election two weeks later in her former constituency of Batley & Spen, where Labour's majority was a beatable 3,500. Diane Abbott said it would be 'curtains' for Starmer if the seat was not held. Kim Leadbeater, the younger sister of the late Labour MP Jo Cox, who had had been murdered five years previously, was eventually persuaded to stand despite having little political experience in her own right. She squeaked home, defeating the Tory candidate, Ryan Stephenson, by 323 votes. Fate decreed that Starmer would survive.

In between these contests, he revamped his backroom team. Having already had to dispense with the services of Carolyn Harris, his other close aide, Baroness Chapman, ceased her duties as political director. This was unsurprising since many in Labour blamed her for the Hartlepool fiasco. Ben Nunn, Starmer's communications director, quit at the same time and was replaced by Matthew Doyle, a former adviser to Tony Blair. Most significantly, Morgan McSweeney relinquished his role as chief of staff and moved into Labour headquarters to become the party's campaign director. He was replaced by Sam White, son of the *Guardian* journalist Michael White, who had previously been an aide to the Labour Chancellor Alistair Darling. Meanwhile Deborah Mattinson, a pollster who had worked for Labour in the Blair–Brown era, became head of strategy. These appointments reflected the fact that Starmer had begun turning with increasing regularity to Blair, his former spin doctor Alastair Campbell and the former Cabinet minister Peter Mandelson for advice.

On the eve of Labour's annual party conference, held in Brighton in late September, the Fabian Society think tank published 'The Road Ahead', Starmer's 12,000-word tract setting out his plans for returning to power. In it, he predicted that the pandemic had changed the way people lived and worked, perhaps for ever. 'I believe we are living through a time when the individualism that prioritises personal entitlement, moral superiority and self-interest is receding in society's rear-view mirror. In its place, we have the chance to build something more secure, more fair and more just,' he wrote. He was openly ridiculed by some Labour MPs – particularly on the left – who thought the exercise pointless as it had no prospect of appealing to working-class voters. His old foe John McDonnell dismissed it as 'banality after banality' and 'the Sermon on the Mount written by focus group'. It generated little attention otherwise.

At the conference, Starmer enjoyed mixed fortunes. He scraped a win on a contentious vote on changing Labour leadership rules, which doubled – from 10 per cent to 20 per cent – the number of MP nominations required for candidates taking part in future leadership ballots. The unions and their most devoted MPs were furious, fearing no truly left-wing candidate would ever be leader again, but Starmer decided it was worth the risk, reassured that no Jeremy Corbyn-type figure would likely be able to challenge him in future. His victory was undermined by the fallout of Angela Rayner's anti-Tory rant at a fringe meeting, however, where she was recorded accusing the Conservative Party of being 'scum, homophobic, racist, misogynistic, absolute pile of [inaudible], banana republic, vile, nasty, Etonian [inaudible] piece of scum.'

When Starmer was asked about this petulant outburst on *The Andrew Marr Show* on BBC1 the next morning, he replied, 'Angela said those words, she takes a different approach to me. It's not language that I would have used.' He divulged that he would discuss the incident with her but said he would not force her to apologise. Adam Fleming, a BBC reporter, seized on his defence. 'Keir Starmer is not able to say to Angela Rayner, "You should apologise for these comments" even though he himself would not have made them,' Fleming pointed out. 'Is that because he doesn't have the strength to do that? Because she has her own mandate directly elected by the party?' These questions went unanswered. Starmer was under pressure to deliver what some felt needed to be the speech of his life. Despite the presence of hecklers, his performance was considered sufficient to keep his mounting problems at bay. He even managed a quip at the Prime Minister's expense. 'My dad was a toolmaker,' he said. 'Although, in a way, so was Boris Johnson's.'

Relations between Starmer and Labour's left wing remained tense, but he was saved to some degree that autumn by ructions in the Tory Party. In early November, Owen Paterson, a former Cabinet minister who sat on the back benches, resigned his seat after he was found to have breached lobbying rules. The affair attracted more media attention than it might have done thanks to Boris Johnson's misguided attempt to change parliamentary rules in an effort to save Paterson's career. For this, Johnson was attacked by MPs from all parties. Opinion polls immediately moved in Labour's favour as mutterings of 'Tory sleaze' began to stick. Pressures between Johnson and his Chancellor, Rishi Sunak, also revealed themselves. And these troubles were underscored by a leak to the BBC questioning Johnson's overall performance. 'There is a lot of concern inside the building about the PM,' an anonymous Downing Street source told the broadcaster. 'It's just not working. Cabinet needs to wake up and demand serious changes, otherwise it'll keep getting worse.'

On 29 November, Starmer announced another shadow Cabinet reshuffle. Wes Streeting was promoted to the health brief while Bridget Phillipson was put in charge of education. A promotion was also accepted by Yvette Cooper, who returned to the front bench as shadow Home Secretary. Nick Thomas-Symonds, one of Starmer's best friends in Westminster, was told to make way for her. Pat McFadden, a minister under Gordon Brown, became shadow Chief Secretary to the Treasury. And Ed Miliband, the former party leader who had been so important in helping to smooth Starmer's route into politics, became shadow Climate Change Secretary. Starmer praised him as 'a powerful, internationally well-respected voice on the issue'. These moves were designed to take the party closer towards the fabled centre ground of politics – so much so that, for a while, Starmer seemed reluctant even to say the 's' word. When asked during an interview with the *i* newspaper whether he was a socialist, he would not answer directly. 'What does that mean?' he replied, before adding, 'The Labour Party believes that we get the best from each other when we come together, collectively, and ensure that we give people both opportunity and support.' His diffidence made people wonder whether he had any faith in his own political proclamations.

The press soon worked out that Angela Rayner had been kept in the dark about the reshuffle. Starmer had simply not bothered to tell her, laying bare their fractious relationship. He hoped the injection of fresh blood would shore up Labour's position. What he could not have realised was that his political fortune was about to turn for reasons which had less to do with his own skills or popularity, or those of his colleagues, and much more to do with the Conservative Party's peculiar knack for self-destruction.

The next day, 30 November, the *Daily Mirror* ran the first article in what became known as the Partygate scandal series. 'Boris Johnson "broke Covid lockdown rules" with Downing Street parties at Xmas,' the newspaper revealed about the gathering, which had been held at No. 10 a year before, in December 2020, when most of Britain had been in lockdown. 'Officials knocked back glasses of wine during a Christmas quiz and a Secret Santa while the rest of the country was forced to stay at home.' A Downing

Street spokesman said: 'Covid rules have been followed at all times.' Yet the claims were not comprehensively denied.

ITV then picked up the baton, having been handed footage, also dating from December 2020, of Allegra Stratton, a government spokeswoman, giving a mock press conference in which she joked about a party having been hosted in Downing Street during that period. At the next scheduled Prime Minister's Questions, on 8 December 2021, Labour MP Catherine West asked Johnson if there had been a party in Downing Street on 13 November 2020. Johnson replied, 'No, but I am sure that whatever happened, the guidance was followed and the rules were followed at all times.' Such a definitive answer would turn out to be an error. At the same session of PMQs, Starmer raised the Stratton video, asking Johnson if he had the 'moral authority' to lead the country. Johnson replied that he had asked Simon Case, the Cabinet Secretary, to 'establish all the facts and report back as soon as possible'. Three hours later, Stratton resigned. Some felt she was carrying the can to contain a gathering scandal. It was too late, however. Days later, Case was accused of attending one of the parties he was meant to be investigating. He had to recuse himself from his own inquiry. He was replaced by a senior civil servant named Sue Gray. She would be kept busy, as other Partygate claims materialised involving public servants attending events in official buildings during the lockdown of 2020.

Other affairs also preoccupied Boris Johnson at this point, specifically the Omicron variant of coronavirus, which was considered by government scientists to be deadly. He announced his intention to introduce what he called 'Plan B' measures to curb its spread – in effect a second successive Christmas lockdown. These proposals were put to a parliamentary vote on 14 December. Ninety-nine Conservative MPs rebelled, making it the largest revolt of Johnson's thirty months in power. As he had been previously, Starmer was in favour of the restrictions and the legislation only passed thanks to Labour backing it. Johnson's woes deepened two days later when Owen Paterson's constituency of North Shropshire, which he had held with a majority of 23,000, was lost in a by-election to the Liberal Democrats on a swing of 34 per cent. When Rishi Sunak explained to him why the science around Omicron was wildly off-target, and why no Christmas lockdown would be necessary, Johnson paid attention. After consulting the Cabinet, the lockdown plan was aborted. Johnson took the credit for this welcome U-turn, but Sunak's in-depth research – courtesy of his global banking contacts – had been key to it. Sunak was vindicated when the forecast of up to 6,000 Covid-related deaths per day was later calculated to be out by a factor of twenty. It is notable that Starmer had never even questioned these putative figures, cementing in the minds of many his reputation as a man of cautious rigidity who was content to believe whatever the experts said.

From then on, Johnson's hold on power only became shakier. New Year opinion polls gave Labour a clear lead – a position that would be maintained until October 2024. When presented with the choice between Labour and the Conservatives, the public's preference for Labour was, to many, hardly surprising considering even some of Johnson's own team were beginning to scatter. Lord Frost, the Brexit Minister, resigned a few days before Christmas in protest at the introduction of vaccine passports, tax rises and the projected cost of Johnson's net zero policies. As the Cabinet continued to argue about the wisdom of Johnson's plan to raise National Insurance contributions by 1.25 per cent from April, Christian Wakeford, the backbench Conservative MP for Bury South, defected to Labour on 19 January. And five days later, Lord Agnew, the Business Minister, bowed out while at the despatch box in the House of Lords, blaming the government's 'lamentable' record of presiding over more than £4 billion of fraud in the Covid business schemes.

All the while, Partygate stories seeped into the public consciousness. First it was disclosed that in May 2020 – during the first lockdown – Johnson's principal private secretary, Martin Reynolds, had invited 100 staff to a gathering in the Downing Street garden. Johnson told the Commons at PMQs in mid-January that this had been, technically, a 'work event'. Then separate allegations appeared about another event in the No. 10 garden in May 2020 – this time illustrated by a photograph of Johnson and his fiancée, Carrie, sitting with staff on the terrace, enjoying a bottle of wine and some cheese. Some Tory MPs began calling for Johnson to resign. Starmer joined them. Labour extended its poll lead, hitting 40 per cent for the first time since July 2018. When further Partygate details came to light, this time involving two functions in Downing Street the night before Prince Philip's funeral in April 2021, Johnson was on the ropes.

On 25 January, the Metropolitan Police announced a criminal investigation – codenamed Operation Hillman – into whether those attending parties in Downing Street had broken the law. This had been considered necessary after Scotland Yard received evidence from Sue Gray's inquiry. On the same day, it was reported that a surprise party to mark Johnson's fifty-sixth birthday had been held in a Downing Street stateroom on 19 June 2020. Public anger at ministers flouting their own rules was palpable. Starmer, sensing this, said that he believed Johnson had broken the law.

By the end of January, Sue Gray had finished her investigation, but because the Metropolitan Police had begun its own inquiry, only a summary of her findings was published. They included 'failures of leadership and judgement' and insights into a culture of excessive drinking at work. Gray examined sixteen events, of which a dozen were being investigated by police. By this point Johnson had become paranoid that his own MPs were limbering up to defenestrate him. On 31 January, he went to the Commons to apologise for what Gray had discovered, but even that backfired. As he and Starmer sparred verbally, Johnson complained that during his five years as Director of Public Prosecutions Starmer had 'spent most of his time prosecuting journalists and failing to prosecute Jimmy Savile'. As detailed in Chapter 8, this remark was not without foundation – not least because Starmer had said years before that he took responsibility for all of the CPS's failings between 2008 and 2013. Yet in a show of how unpopular Johnson had become, his words were portrayed by some media outlets as having been so offensive that he was effectively forced to apologise for having uttered them. The fact that the CPS under Starmer had handled the Savile episode so badly was of secondary importance.

In March 2022, the Met began fining Downing Street officials who had breached lockdown rules, confirming that Johnson had technically misled Parliament when he had spoken about the issue in December 2021 – among the most serious charges a Prime Minister can face. On 12 April, Johnson received a £50 fine for breaking Covid regulations by attending his surprise birthday party in No. 10. This made him the first Prime Minister to have been found to have broken the law while in office. Starmer appeared to have the moral high ground all to himself. By then, Russia had invaded Ukraine – a foreign war which quickly had a substantial effect on raising UK energy prices – and inflation had reached a new thirty-year high of 6.2 per cent. In July 2022, it breached 9 per cent. Natural Tory supporters were left depressed by Rishi Sunak's Spring Statement that March, with the tax burden on course to be the highest since the Second World War.

With reports of squabbling and backbiting in the Tory ranks, voters began to wonder whether life under a Labour government could be any worse.

Yet while Johnson fought to keep his premiership from being knocked off course, Starmer's political life had not been entirely free from complication. In tandem with the Partygate scandal, Labour had to deal with a similar controversy known as Beergate, in which Starmer and Angela Rayner were the chief protagonists. The year before – in the spring of 2021 – a photograph had been published in *The Sun* showing Starmer, on the evening of 30 April, standing in an office at Durham Miners' Hall with a bottle of beer in his hand, chatting to some colleagues. The office – which was taxpayer-funded – was used at the time by a Labour MP called Mary Foy. Starmer was in the area campaigning during the local elections and had eaten a curry with some colleagues in Foy's office. Lockdown restrictions banned people from socialising inside with somebody from another household. Durham Police were alerted contemporaneously, but they concluded there was nothing to investigate.

More than six months later, in January 2022, when Partygate dominated the news agenda, the *Daily Mail* republished the photograph of Starmer drinking beer in Foy's office in Durham. He was accused of 'brazen hypocrisy' for his criticism of Johnson's lockdown 'partying'. The picture of Starmer was a still taken from thirty-four seconds of video footage filmed by a Durham University student called Ivo Delingpole. Four Labour figures could be seen in the footage. Nearby was a fifth person – an unidentified woman whose back was to the camera. Labour used the same defence that Johnson had tried to rely on, namely that Starmer was at a work 'meeting', had paused to have something to eat and then returned to work. It was put to Labour that Angela Rayner was also present, but a Labour spokesman categorically denied this. In early February 2022, Durham Police again looked into whether any breach had occurred and, again, concluded there was none.

Two months later, however, Labour belatedly admitted that Rayner had in fact been at the Durham event. The party claimed that its previous denial of her attendance was a 'mistake'. Starmer told reporters, 'Whether Angela Rayner was there or not makes absolutely no difference. There was no breach of the rules, the matter's already been looked into. I know what's going on here. We're a few days away from local elections, and Conservative MPs are trying to throw as much mud as possible.' He said there was a 'huge contrast' between the Durham event and lockdown parties in government buildings – for which the police had already issued dozens of fines. How Starmer could have forgotten that Rayner was with him in Durham, and why neither he nor Rayner volunteered straight away that she had been there, has never been explained. In this opaque environment, some senior Tories became convinced that the presence in Durham of other politicians who were close to Starmer had been withheld from the public.

On 6 May 2022, the local elections took place. Durham Police confirmed that day that new evidence 'into potential breaches of Covid-19 regulations relating to this gathering' meant that an investigation was being conducted. It turned out that seventeen people had been present. A copy of Starmer's schedule was published. It showed that the plan had always been for him and his team to eat together that night. The relevant entry read: '20.40 – 22.00 Dinner in Miners Hall with Mary Foy.' On 9 May, Starmer announced that he would resign as Labour leader if he received a fine. He took four legal opinions before issuing his statement. Rayner made an identical promise. Did their threat to quit politicise the situation? Many thought so, for Durham Police's decision would in effect concern the future of Britain's official opposition, not merely whether the Labour leader and deputy leader had breached lockdown rules. By then, the local election results were known. They were a mixed bag for Labour, which gained 108 seats. To little surprise, the Tories lost 487 seats, principally in the south. This left the Liberal Democrats as having performed best, adding 224 new seats. Labour did take overall control of the most councils, though, including Wandsworth, Westminster and Barnet in London, all of which had been Tory-run for decades.

On 8 July 2022, Durham Police concluded that the gathering Starmer and Rayner had attended in April 2021 was 'reasonably necessary for work purposes' and that no fixed-penalty notices had been issued over it. Starmer and Rayner were cleared, though Starmer later told his journalist friend Tom Baldwin that the episode had left him 'angry and humiliated'. Be that as it may, many members of the public remain sceptical of the outcome of Beergate – just as they dispute Starmer's claim not to have known that Jimmy Savile was under police investigation when he ran the CPS.

None of this apparent murkiness bothered executives in the publishing industry, however. In April 2022, Starmer received an advance of £18,450 from HarperCollins to produce the volume of autobiography he had begun writing two years previously. At the time, publishing director Arabella Pike said:

> In his book Keir Starmer will go back to his early life to trace the origins of his politics and the influences that have shaped him as a leader. It will make a fierce argument for the vital role of respect and integrity in political life as he sets out his vision for Britain's future. We are delighted and excited to be publishing.

The book – in this form, at least – would never see the light of day.

• • •

The day before the Beergate story concluded, Boris Johnson resigned as Tory leader and Prime Minister following a historic mass resignation of his ministers in protest at his handling of a series of scandals. His eventual replacement, Liz Truss, took up her post on 6 September. Two days after that, it was announced that the Queen had died. After a period of mourning for the late monarch, Chancellor Kwasi Kwarteng unveiled his mini-budget on 23 September. It axed the cap on bankers' bonuses; ditched plans to raise corporation tax from 19 per cent to 25 per cent; cut the basic rate of income tax by 1p; and abolished the 45 per cent top rate of tax which kicked in at earnings of £150,000. Many Tories were thrilled at what appeared to be a return to the party's natural economic habits. However, because Truss had already promised to freeze energy bills at an average of £2,500 per year for two years – costing the public purse between £120 billion and £150 billion – alarm spread rapidly through the markets. With no mini-budget forecast by the Office for Budget Responsibility having been published, sterling plunged by 3.5 cents to reach its lowest level against the US dollar since 1985, closing that day at $1.09. Truss's credibility never recovered. She sacked Kwarteng on 14 October and reversed most of the planned tax cuts, but it was no good. She resigned on her forty-fifth day in office.

Within a week she was replaced by Rishi Sunak. This left Starmer in the dizzying position of facing his third Prime Minister in as many months. Unlike his predecessors, Sunak was at least prepared to engage proactively with Starmer, ringing him on his first day in Downing Street so that they could exchange personal contact details. When they spoke, both men were aware that the Conservative brand had been wrecked by Partygate and by Truss's chaotic spell in government. In their hearts, they knew there was every chance that they would swap places after the next general election. Starmer had two clear years to prepare for office. Suddenly, his little-noticed 2020 conference speech, in which he aspired to be the fourth Labour leader since the war to win a general election, looked less a distant dream and more an approaching reality.

CHAPTER 14

SIR FLIP-FLOP

In the months leading up to Sunak's arrival as the latest Conservative Prime Minister, Labour had been going through a high turnover phase of its own. Hundreds of members had been thrown out of the party for a range of wrongdoings – often related to antisemitism – and thousands of Jeremy Corbyn's supporters had torn up their membership cards. This made the job of expunging the hard left from Labour's candidate lists easier. Luke Akehurst, a member of the National Executive Committee and secretary of Labour First, which represents those on the right of the party, was instrumental in filtering prospective MPs, drawing up shortlists on which local members would vote. He was seen as Starmer's 'enforcer'. As a man in his early fifties who had long sat on the right of the party, he was suspected of denying left-wingers the chance even to make it through to the final round of voting in individual contests. Yet so determined was he to avoid another rout at the ballot box that he stood firm, using the skills he had acquired at the BBC and the communications firm Weber Shandwick to great effect.

Akehurst was helped in overseeing candidate selection by a fixer in his mid-thirties called Matt Faulding. He was on the payroll of the Labour peer Lord Alli, the man who had donated £100,000 to Starmer's leadership campaign in 2020, until being 'loaned' to Labour on secondment. Faulding worked in conjunction with Labour official Matt Pound. Under Faulding and Pound, due diligence tests were introduced and social media posts trawled in order to prevent Corbynites from slipping through the net. The message was clear: only sensible progressives were welcome in Starmer's Labour Party. Some on the left regarded this as an authoritarian purge, entrenching a sense of mistrust in the leader and the somewhat limited, centrist organisation that was being fashioned under him. His cheerleaders said he didn't care. Winning the next election was his only goal.

There remains a deep scepticism among many in Labour regarding what they see as the continuing weeding out of the left, though. One source says:

> Thousands of members have been suspended after social media searches. People say stupid things, but this operation to go through these things looking for cause for complaint about the mainstream and centre-left Labour people comes from the right of the party. It's always the same pattern. It's to get the left out. It takes a lot of organising. The officials have to be sympathetic, if not actually colluding. It all seems to go the same way.

Others question the rise of two centre-right groups, Labour First and Labour Together. There are subtle differences between them, with the trade union-orientated working class gravitating towards the former and the intellectual middle class coalescing around the latter. 'It's all about getting approved candidates into parliamentary seats,' explains a Labour veteran.

> There have always been different outfits within the Labour Party. What's new about these groups is the money and the staff, which seem to have a universal reach that didn't exist in Labour before. Where does the money come from? There's a lot of it. My view is that the people really leading this stay in

> the shadows. We don't know who is funding it, but it's murky. It began before Starmer was leader, but it's been ramped up under him. The energy put into it and the methodical way it's being done is exceptional. All the fingers point in the same direction: upwards. And if such an operation were not wanted, it could be stopped very quickly from above.

There is evidence of this purge having been applied to certain sitting MPs who were considered unhelpful to the leadership. The best-known casualty was the Corbynite shadow Transport Minister Sam Tarry, who happened to be the occasional boyfriend of Angela Rayner. When a round of national rail strikes was called in the summer of 2022, Starmer tried to maintain a neutral stance and encouraged his shadow Cabinet colleagues to do the same. Certainly, he said, none of them should join a picket line. Yet Rayner defied him, tweeting on the first day of the walkout, 'Workers have been left with no choice. No one takes strike action lightly. I will always defend their absolute right to do so for fairness at work.' After Starmer subsequently admitted that for 'pragmatic rather than ideological' reasons he had abandoned his pledge to renationalise the railways – one of several promises he made on winning the leadership in 2020, most of which had by then been cast aside – Tarry joined the strikers at Euston Station. From there, he told *Channel 4 News*: 'If I lose my job for standing shoulder-to-shoulder with rail workers, then so be it.' The next day, Starmer called his bluff, cutting Tarry from his frontbench team. In October 2022, members of Tarry's Ilford South constituency voted to deselect him as their MP.

Starmer's dismissal of Tarry, four months after he had ordered a group of left-wing backbenchers to remove their names from an anti-NATO Stop the War letter following Russia's invasion of Ukraine, reflected his determination to continue moving Labour back to a mainstream centre-left position. Yet that wider ambition came at a price, as internal struggles flared up. When the summer rail strikes were called, Andy Burnham, the Mayor of Greater Manchester, defended rail workers' rights and challenged Starmer to explain what Labour stood for. 'There can't be much further delay now in saying, "This is what we are about" so that people can get the sense of where the next Labour government would go,' Burnham told the BBC impatiently. 'That really does have to happen at the annual conference in Liverpool. I would have said it should have started more last year.'

Starmer's apparently muddled perspective was also evident that summer when another shadow minister, Lisa Nandy, visited a picket line of BT workers. Arguably, Nandy's visit proved that the strikes posed far greater difficulties for the Labour leader than for the government, which – being against industrial action – at least had a clear line to follow. Even shadow Cabinet ministers spoke of a 'breakdown in discipline' over Starmer's attitude to the walkouts. This confusion angered the many moderates on the front bench because of their union backgrounds. But alongside these tensions was a growing perception that Starmer was dreary and plodding. He had become known by some newspaper columnists as 'the nasal knight' on account of his slightly gluey oratory. It was felt that a leader with more personality would have been able to unite his colleagues when it came to an issue such as strikes. During a press conference in Gateshead, he was even asked by ITV News if he was 'too boring' to be the next Prime Minister. He shot back: 'The only thing that's boring is opposition!'

His situation was not helped that August when he was found to have breached the MPs' code of conduct for failing to register on time eight interests with the parliamentary authorities, including free tickets to football matches worth more than £2,000 and the sale of eight acres of land in Surrey which had netted him approximately £400,000. He apologised and issued a statement saying, 'My office and I have carried out a review of the process to ensure that this does not happen again.' In fact, he would find himself back in the dock over a similar issue two years later – with more serious ramifications.

The Labour conference in September 2022, held in Liverpool, is remembered predominantly as being the first such event to open with a rendition of the national anthem. Not every observer was convinced by this show of patriotism, noting that it had been necessary for lyric sheets to be handed out to attendees. Cynics remembered, too, that Starmer, by now sixty, had previously called for the abolition of the monarchy. Was his sudden burst of enthusiasm for King Charles III genuine? Or was this a ruse to win round centrist voters in time for the next election? In fact, that week the spotlight shone more intensely on the government than on Labour thanks to the effects of Kwasi Kwarteng's mini-budget, which had recently been announced. Even though it triggered a spike in mortgage rates, leaving the nation reeling, it was noteworthy that Starmer and his deputy could not make more of Tory woes. When Rayner was asked by journalists about Kwarteng having cut the basic and top rates of income tax, she said she would reverse both decisions if in power. Half an hour later, Starmer told Sky News that he backed the income tax cut on the basic rate from 20p to 19p in the pound. As with the strikes, a fundamental difference at the top of the party was on display. How united was Labour, commentators pondered. Was its lead in the polls in fact a negative one – merely the product of the Conservative government's disarray?

The following month, Truss's brief tenure in No. 10 led Starmer to make additional changes to his top team. He did this, he said, on the basis that a general election could be called by Sunak at any time. Sam White was removed as chief of staff after just over a year in the job. Officially, his departure was due to a merger between the Leader of the Opposition's office and Labour headquarters. Although Labour was by then riding high in the polls, with a consistent lead of ten points or more, White was blamed by some for Starmer's poor handling of the Beergate row. His departure strengthened the hand of Morgan McSweeney, who was responsible for election campaign planning. Marianna McFadden, a former New Labour official and the wife of the frontbench MP Pat McFadden, was drafted in as deputy campaign director. She joined from the Tony Blair Institute, where she had been 'head of insight'.

By the time Jeremy Hunt, the new Tory Chancellor (and the fourth MP to hold the post that year), delivered the Autumn Statement on 17 November, inflation had hit 11.1 per cent and taxes were forecast to rise by £25 billion. The causes of this turbulence were easily identifiable – chiefly the £400 billion coronavirus bill and the consequences of the war in Ukraine – but in another blow, the Office for Budget Responsibility stated that the UK had entered a recession after the economy shrank over two successive quarters. It was anticipated that living standards would fall by 7 per cent over the following two years. With £30 billion of public expenditure cuts on the horizon, 40,000 illegal immigrants having crossed the Channel by boat in the first ten months of the year, record levels of legal immigration and Tory Party infighting having reached the status of a spectator sport, the battered government's popularity was freefalling. My own polling from the time showed that fewer than one in ten voters regarded the Tories as competent, while Labour were more trusted on nearly every key policy issue, including traditionally Tory areas such as immigration and crime.

Starmer enjoyed further exposure when he won the *Spectator* Politician of the Year award at the end of November and by mid-December he was able to look back on some successes at the ballot box, usefully underscoring his party's poll lead. Of the five Westminster by-elections that took place in 2022, Labour held three seats with big swings away from the Conservatives and also retook from the Tories the Red Wall constituency of Wakefield. The Lib Dems snatched the other seat – Tiverton & Honiton – from the Tories, cutting the government's majority further. Progress showed itself in other ways, too. Just before Christmas, a Labour business conference at Canary Wharf attracted large numbers of executives who believed that Starmer was the favourite to become the next Prime Minister. He and Rachel Reeves had strengthened their working relationship by attending scores of these breakfast-time meetings with industry leaders that year. At each, they promised to observe fiscal rules that were not traditionally associated with a self-declared socialist leader. Reeves's desire to promote enterprise was considered genuine. Glowing write-ups in the press duly appeared. Surprisingly, the fact that nobody in the shadow Cabinet had any serious private sector commercial experience to speak of was overlooked. The attempt to reposition Labour as the party of business was widely judged to be working.

The public sector was a different matter. Far from feeling Christmas cheer, the country was close to what appeared to be a general strike. Civil servants, nurses, teachers, paramedics, postal workers and rail workers all planned industrial action over pay which threatened a winter of paralysis. Fearful that inflation would become embedded in the system if mass strikes took place, Sunak worked on legislation requiring unions to offer a minimum service when any strike was held. When the Bill was unveiled in January 2023, Starmer said that as Prime Minister he would repeal it if it were passed. This marked quite a contrast to the indecision he had shown over industrial action six months earlier. It was voted into law in July 2023.

In the first few days of January 2023, Sunak also announced a five-point plan for the year to come. His stated aims were to halve inflation; grow the economy; reduce debt; cut NHS waiting lists; and pass laws to act against illegal immigration or – in plain English – 'stop the boats' from crossing the English Channel. He made these pledges, he said, because he saw them as the most urgent problems facing Britain. Starmer delivered his own New Year speech twenty-four hours later, promising to modernise central government and give communities the chance to control their economic destiny. It was well received, his task made easier by the fact that, unlike Sunak, he was not addressing problems that had occurred over the period when his own party had been in government.

The impetus was clearly with Starmer. That month he and Reeves attended the World Economic Forum at Davos. While taking part in a panel discussion, he hit out at Sunak's absence, jibing that 'our Prime Minister should have showed up'. Later, when asked by a journalist whether he preferred Davos or Westminster, he opted for the former. 'Westminster is too constrained,' he said. 'Once you get out of Westminster, you engage with people that you can see working with in the future. Westminster is just a tribal shouting place.' Some parliamentarians found this casual dismissal offensive, but, as a late entrant to British politics, perhaps Starmer's preference for the rather more glamorous international political circuit was unsurprising.

He continued to ride the wave of optimism that was building. In February, the Equality and Human Rights Commission took Labour out of special measures, a state it had endured for the previous two years after its report found 'serious failings' under Jeremy Corbyn including the 'unlawful harassment' of Jewish members. This was a crucial moment for Starmer to demonstrate that under his stewardship the party had cleaned up its act. He wrote a piece for *The Times* acknowledging the 'evil' of antisemitism, promising not to be complacent about the danger it posed and assuring everybody that he knew there was still work to do to restore trust. He also used a speech that week to state that Corbyn – who had sat as an independent MP since 2020 – would not be allowed to stand as a Labour candidate at a future general election. This decision was endorsed by the NEC in a vote the following month.

There were howls of indignation from the left, but the louder they were, the more Starmer felt justified in having cast aside his predecessor. He appeared to get a little carried away, however. Despite having publicly referred to Corbyn as a 'friend' in his acceptance speech on becoming Labour leader in 2020, he began to deny that he had ever regarded him as such, saying on LBC radio that he was never a friend 'in the sense that we went to visit each other or anything like that. I worked with him as a colleague.' Few were convinced by this revisionist view, but soon afterwards came some surprising front-page news concerning a figure whom Starmer clearly regarded as more politically simpatico than Corbyn anyway: Sue Gray, the career civil servant who had investigated the Partygate affair. She had agreed to become Starmer's chief of staff. Conservative MPs in general and Boris Johnson loyalists in particular were incandescent. They claimed this was proof that Gray had never been an impartial Whitehall figure but had instead pursued the governing party in the manner of a Labour stooge, ensuring Johnson's downfall. Starmer was insouciant. He let it be known that having Gray on his team was simply a further sign that he was readying himself for government. She was given permission to take up her post in September 2023 after a period of enforced leave.

In the early part of 2023, Labour morale was boosted further when the pro-EU businessman David Sainsbury gave the party

£2 million, his first donation since 2016. This sum reportedly wiped out the party's debt, which had been exacerbated by falling membership, as it began preparing for a general election that had to be held by January 2025. The topic of money was not restricted to Labour, incidentally. In March 2023, Sunak published three years of his personal tax summaries. These showed that he had earned £4.7 million between April 2019 and April 2022 and paid a total of £1 million in tax at an overall effective rate of 22 per cent. Spotting an opportunity to contrast himself and the Prime Minister, Starmer followed suit. The summary he published showed that in the tax year 2021/22 he made a capital gain of £85,466 – incurring tax of £23,930 – after his sister sold a house in Surrey which he had helped her to buy seventeen years previously.

However, less than a week after the budget, in mid-March, a piece of legislation titled Pensions Increase (Pension Scheme for Sir Keir Starmer QC) Regulations 2013 was unearthed by the Tories. This unusual law, courtesy of Starmer's post as Director of Public Prosecutions, guaranteed his pension was increased once a year to keep pace with rising prices and exempted him from paying the tax that was usually imposed on pension pots worth more than £1 million. In the budget, Jeremy Hunt had proposed abolishing the existing standard lifetime pension allowance – which attracted tax after hitting £1.07 million. Starmer objected, calling it a policy 'for the richest 1 per cent', and was among 176 Labour MPs to vote against it. Inevitably, charges of hypocrisy rang out.

Starmer found himself further on the defensive in the spring of 2023. That January, Sunak ordered the Secretary of State for Scotland, Alister Jack, to block the SNP's contentious Gender Recognition Reform Bill. This legislation would have given anyone in Scotland over the age of sixteen the ability to change gender without a medical diagnosis. A few days later, a rapist called Isla Bryson, who had been convicted of attacking two women when named Adam Graham, was sent to a women's prison in Scotland after changing gender while waiting to go on trial. When the story broke, the public was scandalised and Bryson was moved to a men's prison.

While it is impossible to say whether Starmer would have blocked Scotland's Gender Reform Bill if he had been able to do so, he had made his position on the wider transgender rights question clear by then. In December 2020, he attended the Pink News awards and pledged to fight for LGBT equality. 'The GRA [Gender Recognition Act] is in desperate need of reform to introduce self-declaration for transgender people,' he said. Six months later, he made a Pride month video saying, 'We're committed to updating the GRA to introduce self-declaration for trans people.' In September 2021, he was asked by the BBC if it was transphobic to say that only women have a cervix. He answered, 'It is something that shouldn't be said. It is not right.' In March 2022, he was asked repeatedly on LBC radio whether a woman can have a penis, but he would not give a straight answer. In September 2022, while visiting the Tapa military base in Estonia, he said, 'Trans women are women.' And in early April 2023, in an interview with the *Sunday Times*, he eventually settled on the notion that '99.9 per cent of women haven't got a penis.' The implication is that he believes one in 1,000 women do have male genitals. Even if this is his genuine belief, one well-placed source says that some of his closest female colleagues in Parliament, including Rachel Reeves and Bridget Phillipson, comprehensively disagree with him. 'Rachel and Bridget don't share his views,' says this person. 'They are very secret about it because they're fearful of the consequences. The trans lobby would call them terfs [trans-exclusionary radical feminists] if it knew their true feelings.'

Within a week of talking to the *Sunday Times* he was on the back foot for a second time after the Labour Party rolled out a series of online adverts attacking Sunak personally by portraying him as soft on crime, among other things. One of the strangest examples read: 'Do you think adults convicted of sexually assaulting children should go to prison? Rishi Sunak doesn't.' Below these words was the claim that, under the Tories, 4,500 people convicted of sexually assaulting children 'served no prison time'. The project misfired badly. Not only had Sunak not even been an MP in 2012 when the sentencing guidelines the ad referred to were passed, but Starmer had been Director of Public Prosecutions at the time and had sat on the sentencing council which decided that not every sex offender should go to prison. Labour grandee David Blunkett called it 'gutter politics'. The Tories retaliated, labelling Starmer 'Sir Softy' as newspapers published stories about his own questionable record. Notably, he had been among a group of MPs to sign a letter to the Home Office in February 2020 calling for a halt to the deportation of foreign criminals. Calls like this were seen in a different light when twenty-five Jamaican nationals were taken off one such flight that month having been granted a reprieve, with some lodging human rights claims. One beneficiary was Fabian Henry, who had been imprisoned in 2013 for attacking a seventeen-year-old girl twice and for abducting and having sex with a fifteen-year-old. As of 2023, he was still living in Britain despite the Home Office's attempt to return him to Jamaica. The attack on Sunak had turned into a self-inflicted wound for Starmer.

This row came just a few weeks after Labour had tried in vain to block the Illegal Migration Bill. It was introduced by Home Secretary Suella Braverman in March 2023 to change the law so that anybody entering Britain illegally could be deported immediately to their home nation or to a third-party state such as Rwanda, to which Britain had already paid £140 million for this purpose. Labour's opposition to Braverman's Bill – on moral grounds, the party said – was interpreted by some as indicative of Starmer's relaxed attitude to this thorny issue. Yet some Labour MPs privately knew it was a problem. By then, about £40 million of taxpayers' money was being spent weekly on the accommodation of at least 50,000 new illegal arrivals in hotels all over the country.

Even though Starmer's recent record was not glittering, there was some surprise when the Labour-friendly *Guardian* produced a scathing assessment of his character and policies when marking the third anniversary of his leadership in early April 2023. In a downbeat leading article opining that the 'party remains a mystery to voters', the newspaper observed that Starmer was seen as 'dull' and complained that, though he had tried hard, he had failed to 'capture the mood of the country' as he had 'no coherent strategy'. It noted that he had wheeled out a dozen slogans since becoming leader, 'each one more meaningless than the last'. It went on: 'No one knows what Sir Keir or his party clearly stand for – apart from attacking its left flank.' It rounded off by saying, 'Instead of building the party to fill a gap in politics and give Labour a distinctive electoral appeal, Sir Keir gambled that the Tories would implode. That bet has not paid off.' *The Guardian* believed that the Tories were, in fact, getting their act together by, for example, extending state-sponsored childcare provision.

It was particularly galling for Starmer that this brickbat was hurled only six weeks after he had set out the five 'missions' that he said would be at the centre of a future Labour's government's first-term programme: achieving clean energy; delivering the highest growth in the G7; safeguarding the NHS; breaking down barriers to opportunity for all; and securing safer streets. Yet in giving his leadership the thumbs-down, it was reckoned

The Guardian was only echoing the sentiments of most of those who had listened to the speech he had made in Manchester when unveiling these vague ambitions. It was, by common consent, light on detail, with not a word about immigration, for example. If such a thing as Starmerism existed, nobody on *The Guardian* had a clue what it was. One former Labour colleague speaks of the back of Starmer's neck 'turning pink' whenever he is agitated. This blast of friendly fire certainly caused his skin to flush.

A further complication then arose when the left-wing MP Diane Abbott wrote a letter to *The Observer* in which she was seen to have downplayed suggestions of prejudice against Jewish people. Abbott apologised, but the whip was withdrawn and an investigation launched. Starmer tried to turn the incident to his advantage, emphasising Labour's 'zero tolerance' towards antisemitism and saying Abbott's suspension showed 'how far the Labour Party has changed'. Yet had it really, if one of its most senior MPs had to be punished in this way?

That spring, Starmer gave up on the idea of writing an autobiography and instead handed over his pen and notebook to Tom Baldwin, a former journalist who in 2011 became director of strategy to the then Labour leader Ed Miliband. Baldwin had been helping Starmer with his memoir already, but it was decided it would be better if he produced an officially sanctioned biography of the Labour leader instead. In choosing Baldwin for this task, Starmer certainly displayed debatable judgement. It is worth setting out why.

It should be said at the outset that Baldwin – a close confidant of Tony Blair's notorious spin doctor Alastair Campbell – is well known to me. I was on the receiving end of his deceit and hypocrisy when he was a political reporter on *The Times* around the turn of the millennium. Back then, the newspaper had lost its way, though happily it has long since returned to being a reputable publication. At that time, Baldwin seemed also to have swerved off course, being prone to heavy drinking and cocaine abuse. I cannot speak for any current peccadillos. Although the events I am about to outline occurred some time ago, I have not forgotten them – and neither has the man who spent a year in a federal prison in the United States thanks to the incompetence and indifference that underlay the story Baldwin had written.

In June 1999, *The Times* launched what quickly became a vendetta against me. I was then the treasurer of the Conservative Party. Initially, the newspaper's stories focused on far-fetched claims about the size of the financial donations I had made to the Tories, and whether those donations had breached the party's rules (which they hadn't). Before long, my business and charitable interests came under scrutiny. Then I was falsely accused of money laundering and drug running. Through a freelance British reporter, Baldwin's employer, News International, bribed a US government employee to search a huge Drug Enforcement Administration database. Some meaningless references to me were found. The same database contained mentions of Princess Diana, the English National Ballet and Sir Denis Thatcher. Baldwin took every liberty imaginable with a few insignificant gobbets of information and wrote a speech about me which he gave to a Labour MP called Peter Bradley to read out in the chamber of the House of Commons, thereby using parliamentary privilege to air lies and false allegations based on the stolen material. Before Bradley spoke, Baldwin tipped off his friends on other newspapers to ensure maximum reputational damage would be inflicted on me. I had no doubt that his actions, and those of Bradley, were an abuse of parliamentary process. Baldwin was at the heart of the catalogue of falsehoods about me which *The Times* published. He wrote many of the baseless articles which were used to try to destroy my name. This twisted campaign only came to an end when

I sued the newspaper. By way of settlement, its proprietor, Rupert Murdoch, personally agreed to publish a front-page retraction of the allegations.

Yet the paper was careless in protecting the US Drug Enforcement Agency analyst who was Baldwin's source for this material, a man called Jonathan Randel. In January 2003, Randel was sentenced to a year in an Atlanta prison for taking unclassified information from agency databases and files and giving it to the freelance reporter who was helping *The Times*. Following Randel's conviction, the Assistant US Attorney responsible arranged to come to London, intending to interview a number of *Times* journalists, including Baldwin. *The Times* was in those days defended by an in-house lawyer called Alastair Brett. He sought protection for Baldwin from the US Department of Justice by seeking legal advice on how to avoid answering questions. And where did he go for help? To Doughty Street Chambers, set of Keir Starmer, the future biographical subject of Tom Baldwin.

• • •

In May 2023, voters cast their ballots in hundreds of England's district councils, metropolitan boroughs and unitary authorities. By then, the government's problems were growing. Quite apart from coping with the daily responsibilities of power, the faltering economy, the NHS backlog and the consequences of the Ukraine war, Sunak had to try to hold together a hostile parliamentary party, all while dealing with local difficulties. These included Dominic Raab standing down as Deputy Prime Minister after an inquiry concluded that he had bullied civil servants; the BBC chairman, Richard Sharp, quitting his post after apparently breaching public appointment rules by failing to declare his links to an £800,000 loan made to Boris Johnson; and the independently wealthy

Sunak himself trying to shake off the perception that he did not understand the lives of ordinary people.

The expectation that the Tories would do badly in the local elections was easily met when they lost 1,061 council seats and surrendered control of forty-eight councils across both the south and the north. Labour and the Liberal Democrats made substantial gains, picking up 537 seats and 407 seats respectively. Labour secured control of twenty-two new councils, overtaking the Tories as the largest party in local government for the first time since 2002.

No elections were held in Wales or Scotland, nor in London or any other big cities, but the next morning Starmer announced, 'We are on course for a Labour majority at the next general election.' His words were thought by some political scientists, such as Sir John Curtice, to be premature. It was pointed out that these results, if repeated at a general election, would bring about a hung parliament in which Labour held 312 seats – well short of the 326 needed for an overall majority. Still, Tory hopes of securing a fifth term in office at the forthcoming general election were fading fast. Between July and October 2023, six by-elections were held following the resignations of five Tory MPs – among them Boris Johnson – and one independent MP, Margaret Ferrier, being subject to a recall petition by her constituents. In these contests, Labour sustained its reputation as the incoming government by gaining four new seats. The Lib Dems picked up one seat while the Tories narrowly held Uxbridge, where Johnson had been the MP. For Sunak, it seemed as though the walls were closing in.

Starmer felt emboldened to support certain deeply unpopular Tory policies, such as the two-child benefit cap, which restricts most parents from receiving welfare payments for a third child. After he told the BBC that he would keep the measure in place if elected, his colleagues were stunned into fury. There was greater

Labour unity on the issue of illegal immigration. Starmer's mantra was to 'smash the [people-smuggling] gangs', but he said he would not follow Tory plans to stop those arriving by small boat from claiming asylum in Britain. In time, he promised that the Rwanda scheme would be axed if he was in power – even if it was seen to work and even though more than £300 million had been promised by Britain to Rwanda. Ultimately, he said, he wanted to reach an EU-wide returns agreement in which Britain accepted quotas of immigrants from the bloc and sent back illegal arrivals. To that end, talks with the French President, Emmanuel Macron, opened.

Starmer went into the Labour conference in Liverpool that October knowing it was likely to be the last before the next general election. There, just as he began his speech, he was interrupted by a protester who had managed to bypass his security detail, get onto the stage and sprinkle what turned out to be glitter onto his shoulders while shouting political slogans. It was unnerving for the Labour leader, but he collected himself while the man, later identified as 28-year-old Yaz Ashmawi, was muscled away. 'If he thinks that bothers me, he doesn't know me,' Starmer said to roars of approval. Not every problem could be batted away so easily, though.

On 7 October – three days before he delivered his conference speech – the Middle East had been shaken to the core after Hamas terrorists slaughtered, raped and tortured at least 1,200 people in Israel. It marked the largest number of Jews killed in a single day since the Holocaust. Hundreds more were taken hostage and held in Gaza. Within this horror lay a major test for Starmer. It wasn't just that he had to show he was different from Jeremy Corbyn, who had once called Hamas 'friends'. It was also that, in this most complicated and protracted military and political conflict, Labour has historically been sympathetic to the Palestinians, not least because of the party's support among British Muslim voters.

Initially, Starmer's reaction was robust. He was applauded for saying during his conference speech that Labour supported a two-state solution but that 'Israel must always have the right to defend her people'. The next day, however, in an interview with LBC, he was asked by the presenter Nick Ferrari what, in his opinion, would be a 'proportionate' response to the attacks. His answer would cause him immense problems. He said, 'I'm very clear, Israel must have that, does have that right to defend herself. And Hamas bears responsibility.' Ferrari then asked, 'A siege is appropriate? Cutting off power, cutting off water, Sir Keir?' To this, Starmer answered, 'I think that Israel does have that right. It is an ongoing situation. Obviously, everything should be done within international law. But I don't want to step away from the sort of core principles that Israel has a right to defend herself and Hamas bears responsibility for these terrorists.'

Footage of the interview was circulated rapidly, firing up huge numbers of voters, particularly British Muslims, and enraging councillors and parliamentarians. Starmer has always maintained that he was tired when he spoke to Ferrari and that his second answer was a continuation of his answer to the first question he was asked, as opposed to his endorsing the idea that Israel had a right to cut off power and water in Gaza. Yet the damage was done. He lost several of the following weeks to internal rows. While attempting to soothe tempers, he remained resolute, backing the government by refusing to call for a ceasefire. Senior Labour figures such as London Mayor Sadiq Khan, Manchester Mayor Andy Burnham and Scottish Labour leader Anas Sarwar pleaded with him to change his mind, but he held firm, using a speech at the Chatham House think tank on 31 October to say a ceasefire would not be 'the correct position now'. Instead, he called for 'humanitarian pauses' to allow the 'urgent alleviation of Palestinian suffering'.

Two days later, more than thirty Labour councillors quit the party over Starmer's stance and leaked audio surfaced of Sarwar accusing Starmer of lacking 'empathy' and 'humanity'. Compounding the situation for him, that same day it was noted by prominent media outlets that on the morning of his Chatham House speech, Starmer had worn a poppy on the lapel of his suit jacket. Hours later, he recorded a video to mark the start of Islamophobia Awareness Month, and sharp-eyed viewers realised that the poppy had been removed. It was immediately assumed by some that he had taken off this symbol honouring the armed forces as a way of placating the Palestinian cause. Simon Danczuk, a former Labour MP, was representative of this view as he accused him of 'removing your poppy when you're trying to win Muslim votes'.

The disagreeable mood spilled over into a Commons vote on 16 November in which Starmer suffered a significant rebellion. Fifty-six Labour MPs backed a Scottish National Party motion calling for an immediate ceasefire. Ten frontbenchers – none of them shadow Cabinet members – resigned that night after Starmer made clear that anybody defying the party line by calling for a ceasefire would lose their job. He showed pragmatism afterwards as he said, 'I regret that some colleagues felt unable to support the position tonight, but I wanted to be clear about where I stood, and where I will stand … No government would allow the capability and intent to repeat such an attack [as that on Israel] to go unchallenged.' Behind the scenes, though, the awkwardness was palpable. One Labour MP at the time says that Starmer began to distance himself from his colleagues. 'The parliamentary party realised he'd changed his mobile phone number and he didn't even tell the wider party what the new number was,' this person remembers. 'It was in December 2023. It was really odd. Only the inner circle had the new number.'

In early December, a diversionary tactic was deployed. Starmer managed to make waves by writing an article for the *Sunday Telegraph* in which he paid tribute to Margaret Thatcher for 'effecting change' and 'setting loose our natural entrepreneurialism'. He used the piece to suggest that he was her natural heir. The bait was taken. With a general election on the horizon, his words were seen as an attempt to appeal to fed-up Tory voters who were considering switching to Labour, and he was condemned by various commentators for his apparent cynicism. Not only were Thatcher's policies at odds with his socialist instincts, they said, but who could forget his self-declared loathing of the philosophy of Thatcherism? When he went on to deliver a gloomy New Year address in early January 2024, referring to Britain as a 'downtrodden country' thanks to successive Conservative governments, the *Daily Mail* contrasted his pessimistic stance with Thatcher's vision, reminding readers that she had once said, 'We want to govern because we can do better, not because we couldn't possibly do worse.' His invocation of Thatcher's politics was further confused in mid-January when he gave an interview to ITV in which he criticised her, saying, 'What she did was a clarity of mission and purpose. But actually what she did was very destructive.' He was clearer about one of Labour's former leaders, however, using the same interview to claim that he had never believed Jeremy Corbyn would be Prime Minister – despite serving in his shadow Cabinet during the elections of 2017 and 2019. 'I didn't think the Labour Party was in a position to win the last election,' he announced. Having been effusive in his praise for Corbyn so many times between 2016 and 2020, it did not take long for evidence to surface which made a mockery of his retrospective dismissal of his former boss. Starmer's announcement to the BBC on 26

February 2019 that Corbyn would make a 'great Prime Minister' was just one example that was held against 'Sir Flip-Flop', as he had become known by some Westminster sketchwriters.

Publications that might have been expected to show Labour greater support, such as the *i* newspaper, began to lay out Starmer's policy U-turns, including reversing his pledge to renationalise key industries; changing his mind about scrapping university tuition fees; ditching plans to raise tax for the highest 5 per cent of earners; and reneging on his idea to end outsourcing in the NHS. Then, in early February, there was significant embarrassment when he was forced to disown Labour's £28 billion-a-year green investment pledge. Having been conceived in 2021, this was arguably the party's flagship idea, though exactly how it was to be funded was never fully explained. The vast sums of money were to have been spent on electric battery manufacturing, offshore wind, tree planting and home insulation. Discarding the scheme was the most embarrassing volte-face of his leadership up to that point. Environmental groups were furious, but, supposedly under pressure from Rachel Reeves, Starmer had to admit that reality had bitten. He knew that maintaining such an expensive plan would undermine Labour's pitch as an economically responsible government in waiting. Even so, it escaped few people's attention that only two days before ditching the policy, he had said it was 'desperately needed'. Was Labour in flux or was it ready for office? The Conservatives thought they knew the answer. Their website began selling novelty flip-flops bearing Starmer's image for £16.99 a pair.

An opportunity for voters to inspect his moral standards came about during the Rochdale by-election campaign that month, following the death of the Labour MP Tony Lloyd. With a majority of more than 9,000 votes, Labour had been expected to retain the seat until the *Mail on Sunday* obtained a recording of its candidate, Azhar Ali, saying at a Lancashire Labour Party meeting that Israel had allowed the 7 October attacks to happen in order to give it the 'green light' to invade Gaza. Ali had also said Starmer had 'lost the confidence' of MPs by refusing to condemn Israel's attacks on Gaza. Remarkably, given the antisemitic tone of these conspiratorial comments, Labour said it would continue to campaign for Ali, thereby placing charges of hypocrisy at Starmer's door. The next day a fuller version of the recording was published in the *Daily Mail* in which Ali was heard blaming 'people in the media from certain Jewish quarters' for the suspension the previous October of Labour MP Andy McDonald for having said, 'We will not rest until we have justice. Until all people, Israelis and Palestinians, between the river and the sea, can live in peaceful liberty.' Sixteen days before the poll, Labour had to jettison Ali. As nominations for the election had closed, he couldn't be replaced, meaning the party did not field a candidate in a constituency it should have held. (George Galloway, of the Workers Party, clinched the seat on 29 February.) In its analysis, the BBC poured scorn on Starmer, asking, 'Why was the story allowed to run for almost 48 hours?' It added that by seeming to dither he had left himself open to the impression that he was 'politically inept'.

Such criticism was tempered to some degree by two Labour gains in Westminster by-elections on 15 February at Wellingborough and at Kingswood, both previously held by the Tories. Yet the episode certainly undermined Starmer's message that he had rooted out anti-Jewish sentiment from his party. Most troublingly for him, tensions were being stoked weekly during pro-Palestine demonstrations in London that had sparked reports of intimidation towards Jews. Why had Starmer been happy for a bigot to represent Labour, the party which had supposedly changed?

He was still nursing the wounds he had received over the

Rochdale fiasco when he fell under suspicion in Westminster for related reasons, angering dozens of MPs from various parties in the process. A routine Opposition Day debate on 21 February had been allocated to the SNP and its representatives had tabled a motion calling for an 'immediate ceasefire' in Gaza. Although the subsequent vote would not be binding, Starmer feared that certain backbenchers would fall into line with the SNP, thereby breaking the Labour line and weakening him. Memories of the previous October's parliamentary rebellion, when fifty-six Labour MPs defied his authority, were raw. By convention, the Commons Speaker, Sir Lindsay Hoyle, should only have taken a vote on the SNP's motion and then on the government's amendment but – highly irregularly – Labour also tabled an amendment to the SNP's motion, calling for a ceasefire but using different language with more caveats. Hoyle allowed a vote to be held on it as well. Soon it transpired that Starmer had held a private meeting with Hoyle to lobby him to accept Labour's amendment. In sanctioning this, Hoyle was accused of bending parliamentary rules to spare Starmer further trouble, though this was denied at the time. It remains a shady episode. While the decision was Hoyle's as Speaker, many MPs on all sides believe Starmer placed Hoyle in a difficult position in which, ultimately, he was seen to have sacrificed his impartiality. Indeed, some consider Hoyle lucky to have kept his job. Ninety-five MPs signed a motion of no confidence in him.

A subject that some felt raised equally troubling questions about Starmer's judgement came into view at the end of February following the publication of my unauthorised biography of Angela Rayner, *Red Queen?* The book established that Rayner and her husband, Mark Rayner, claimed to live in separate houses in Stockport, Greater Manchester, for the first five years of their marriage – and that during this period Angela Rayner's brother,

Darren, claimed he lived with Mark Rayner and his sister's children. Although the electoral roll confirmed these unorthodox arrangements, multiple neighbours at both addresses strongly disagreed. They said that Angela Rayner had – as most people would assume – lived with her husband and her children in their marital home. Her brother, neighbours said, had in fact lived in Angela Rayner's own house which she had bought before she got married. What is more, when Angela Rayner re-registered her sons' births in October 2010 – a month after her wedding – their new birth certificates stated that she lived with her husband. Her handwritten signature proved as much. Because a birth certificate is a public document, available to any member of the public who wishes to access it, this was easy enough to obtain.

Further research showed that Rayner had bought her own house in 2007 under the right-to-buy scheme with a £26,000 discount and sold it in 2015 at a £48,500 profit. As she oversaw Labour's housing policy, and because she had talked openly about her plan to cut right-to-buy discounts for others if Labour won the next election (without advertising the fact that she had benefited from the scheme herself), this was a matter of public interest. Had she breached electoral law? What about her council tax status?

Reports about what became known as Raynergate featured in most newspapers for fourteen consecutive weeks, propelled in part by a police investigation that was eventually dropped. Throughout this saga, Rayner said she had taken independent advice about her property and finances that cleared her of any wrongdoing – but she refused to publish it or even to say from where it had come. Many found it telling that whenever Starmer was asked by journalists about the advice Rayner said she had received, his lawyerly instincts came to the fore. His stock answer was that he had not seen the advice and so could not comment on it.

This bureaucratic reaction may have been acceptable to him, but it appeared farcical that a Prime Minister in waiting was unable – or unwilling – to challenge his deputy over an issue relating to a Labour policy in which the police had become involved. Was he forced to go along with Rayner's bizarre account for fear of upsetting her? Or was the legal advice open to doubt? Once again, questions about his principles and leadership were asked but never satisfactorily answered. Rayner went to some lengths to conceal certain facts from the public, seemingly with Starmer's blessing. But why did she feel the need to do this? And why did Starmer support her in it?

It is worth adding that on 30 May 2024, Rayner gave an interview to Beth Rigby of Sky News in which she claimed she had re-registered her sons' birth certificates in 2010 because her husband, Mark, wanted everybody's name and address to match up for the purpose of 'family records'. She said, 'There was no fiddle or anything like that. It was purely because he wanted this record for his children.' Yet until she gave the Sky News interview, Rayner had said repeatedly during the controversy that until 2014 she had lived at a different address to the one recorded on the birth certificates. This suggests that either her electoral roll entry was false or she falsely completed her sons' birth certificates to show them living at a different address to hers – potentially an offence under Section 4 of the Perjury Act 1911. After enquiries, the police took no further action. At no point did Rayner ever suggest that she was registered at two different addresses at once. Was Starmer aware of this discrepancy – and if not, why not?

A culture of secrecy within Labour had also shown itself when it came to managing allegations against sitting MPs, a handful of whom were suspended between 2021 and 2023 following rule changes that were passed at the Labour conference in 2021. The case of Nick Brown, who had been in the Commons since 1983, stands out as a notable example of these arcane practices. In September 2022, Brown was suspended from the parliamentary party and forced to sit as an independent after an unspecified complaint was made against him. A Labour investigation was launched. No details of the allegations leaked, but in December 2023, Brown resigned his Labour membership, denying any wrongdoing and calling the disciplinary process 'a complete farce'. When, in April 2024, Tory MP Mark Menzies resigned the whip over lurid allegations (denied by Menzies) that he had misused campaign funds, Starmer asked why it took the Conservative Party 'so long to act and whether they've reported this to the police, who it seems to me should be involved'. But in asking this, was he displaying false virtue? Harry Cole, the political editor of *The Sun*, wrote of his surprise at Starmer's stance in light of Labour's handling of 'the disturbing allegations of criminality made about their former Chief Whip Nick Brown two years ago'. Fascinatingly, Cole went on:

> Legal reasons prevent me from sharing the details yet, but they are of the most serious nature and there would be genuine public outcry were they to ever see the light of day. At no point did anyone in Labour HQ pick up the phone to the rozzers, so spare me the faux outrage. Instead, Labour hid behind an opaque internal process that resulted in Brown announcing he would stand down at the next election and allowing the whole sorry saga to be brushed under the carpet… for now.

Nick Brown must be considered innocent until proved otherwise, of course. When contacted for the purposes of this book, he declined to comment. Yet, as with the mystery over what and when Starmer knew of the CPS's handling of police inquiries into Jimmy Savile between 2007 and 2009, or the truth of Angela

Rayner's housing arrangements, the same questions apply when it comes to Brown, about whom he has said nothing publicly. What, if anything, did Starmer know of the allegations against Brown? When did he first hear of them? And if they were as serious as some have suggested, why was Starmer content for the matter to be dealt with internally and not by the police?

There is even a suggestion that Brown was targeted by figures on the right of the party. It had not been forgotten that in 2021 he had tried to help Jeremy Corbyn in his doomed bid to be reinstated to the Labour Party. One well-placed source says:

> Party leaders are inveterate micro-managers, whether they're Labour or Tory. It's in the nature of the office. They become remote and compensate for that by trying to find out what's going on. In Labour there has been a pattern when it comes to MPs being suspended: an accusation has arisen, it's anonymous, the MP has had no right to know who their accuser is, and they've had to accept it. It's inconceivable that Starmer wouldn't have been made aware of the details of Nick Brown's case. As an ex-DPP, it's the area he's familiar with. He handles it with authority. It would have been very difficult for him not to be aware of these allegations, even if he then delegated.

And a former member of Labour's NEC observes:

> Nick Brown was an MP and whip for so long that he knows everything about the party. He was very fair. He couldn't have been anything other than fair, having served as Chief Whip under Blair, Brown, Corbyn and Starmer. But he knows where the bodies are buried. I have wondered whether he was removed in order to get him out of the way.

By the time of the local elections on 2 May 2024, Jeremy Hunt had delivered what would turn out to be his final budget as Chancellor. The main announcement was a 2p National Insurance cut – the second in less than six months – which would save employees hundreds of pounds per year. Hunt also adopted two of Labour's key ideas, introducing from April 2025 a new non-dom tax regime for UK residents whose permanent home is overseas and extending a windfall tax on oil and gas companies. The government believed this would shut down potential lines of attack from Labour. If Starmer, who had just marked his fourth anniversary as leader, felt wrong-footed, he hid it well. 'We will look at the government's spending plans, we will adapt our funding plans accordingly, but let me be equally clear: everything in our manifesto will be fully funded, fully costed and we will set that out in due course,' he promised.

If the Tories hoped the budget would save them at the ballot box, they were to be disappointed. They lost 474 councillors – almost half the number of seats they were defending – and gave up control of eight authorities. Labour gained 186 councillors, though its vote share was down marginally. It did, however, lose control of Oldham council after Muslim voters turned on the party over Starmer's position on the Palestinian cause in Gaza. Any discouragement this may have given rise to was offset by the party recapturing Blackpool South in a Westminster by-election held on the same day. It was the twenty-second by-election to take place since the humiliation of losing Hartlepool to the Tories three years previously. Labour had either held or gained thirteen seats in those contests and lost only one, Rochdale.

On 8 May, just before PMQs began, there was shock in Westminster when the Tory MP for Dover, Natalie Elphicke, defected to Labour. Another Tory MP, Daniel Poulter, had done the same on 27 April, but Elphicke's desertion was considered more significant. And yet arguably it did not quite have the effect Starmer had desired, for it raised fundamental questions about his principles and political judgement. First, Elphicke was a right-wing Tory who had been openly critical of Starmer's immigration policy the previous year, saying he could not be trusted because '[Labour] really want open borders'. Since then, she had praised Sunak for 'showing that with grit and grip he can turn the small boats crisis around'. Was her newfound respect for Starmer genuine? There were also questions about her personal conduct. In 2020, her husband, the former Tory MP Charlie Elphicke, was found guilty of sexually assaulting two women. She stood by him, saying he had been punished for being 'charming, wealthy, charismatic and successful – attractive and attracted to women. All things that in today's climate made him an easy target for dirty politics and false allegations.' She had then inherited his Commons seat in a manner not everybody considered to be open and democratic.

Had Starmer thought carefully enough before welcoming his latest MP into the fold? The defections of Elphicke and Poulter were undoubtedly problematic for Sunak, not least because both had made clear they did not intend to stand for Parliament at the next election, making their eleventh-hour desertions all the more brutal. Yet Labour MPs were highly sceptical. Was this just more evidence of Starmer's opportunism in seeking to become the next Prime Minister? One audience member on the BBC programme *Question Time* asked why he was adopting Tories instead of reinstating his own MP, Diane Abbott, who remained suspended more than a year after the whip had been withdrawn.

Proceedings in Westminster on 22 May began unusually. Shortly before PMQs started, the Tory MP Craig Mackinlay walked into the Commons chamber. He had not been seen there for months, having contracted sepsis the previous September. His hands and feet had been amputated and replaced with prosthetic limbs. He was applauded by every MP present, even though clapping in the chamber is forbidden, before tributes were paid to him by the Speaker and by Sunak. When it was Starmer's turn to say a few words, he struck an odd note by saying to Mackinlay, 'Thank you for meeting me privately this morning with your wife and daughter, so I could personally convey my best wishes to all of you.' If the meeting had been private, some wondered, why did Starmer feel the need to mention it publicly? Mackinlay was humble in his acceptance of everybody's words, but he reserved his warmest wishes for Sunak. 'He has been with me throughout,' he said. 'He has not advertised it, but he has been to see me multiple times. To me, that shows the true depth of the character of the Prime Minister, and I thank him for that.'

By this point, the Rwanda Bill had been passed after more than a year of political and legal wrangling instigated by the Labour Party, and the nation's inflation rate had fallen back to the Bank of England's target of 2 per cent – its lowest since July 2021. Having seen these pledges fulfilled, Sunak decided to call an early general election. He caught most people off guard – even in his own party – as he stood outside a rain-lashed 10 Downing Street just after five o'clock that afternoon to announce he was going to the country.

Labour's average poll lead over the Tories was an astonishing twenty-two points. To even the most optimistic Tory supporter, it seemed inconceivable that it could be overturned. The more interesting question was whether this vast gap was attributable to the Tories' recent record in government or whether Labour's near-certain victory was a positive reflection of Starmer's leadership coupled with a belief in his vision for restoring Britain's fortunes.

CHAPTER 15

ALL CHANGE

A perennial question is why Rishi Sunak decided to hold the 2024 general election in July rather than in November, as had been anticipated. Insiders say that as well as the positive reasons already outlined – the Rwanda legislation having passed and the rate of inflation having returned to 2 per cent – there were at least two negative motives. First, Sunak believed that the number of small boats crossing the Channel would increase over the summer. And secondly, on 22 May, all the available intelligence suggested that Nigel Farage was unlikely to return to frontline politics via Reform UK during the six-week campaign, potentially improving Tory chances at the ballot box.

Labour strategists were delighted by the timing. Having fought the local elections less than three weeks earlier, their party machine was still warm, making it far easier for politicians and activists to return to the fray. Furthermore, they considered the Tory election slogan – 'Clear plan, bold action, secure future' – to be complicated when measured against the single word on which Labour decided to sell itself, 'Change'. Indeed, close analysis has led the Labour Together think tank to deduce that Labour won the election for two reasons, both connected to this slogan: most voters believed that Labour under Starmer *had* changed; and most Britons wanted a change of government.

Securing this political transformation did not come cheap. To that end, in 2022 the businessman Lord Alli, who had been given a peerage by Tony Blair in 1998, had been appointed Labour's chief fundraiser. The Tory government had almost doubled the limit on how much each party could spend to £35 million, no doubt believing it could outgun Labour. Alli regarded the higher ceiling as a gift in itself. He set about his task with relish, hosting dinners for would-be donors and using his well-maintained contacts book to drum up support from those who had not previously written substantial cheques to the party or had not done so for some time. Between 30 May and 4 July, Labour declared more donations than every other party combined, adding just over £9.5 million to its war chest. More than £8 million of that figure came from just ten sources, including the supermarket heir Lord (David) Sainsbury, ex-Autoglass boss Gary Lubner and the sculptor Antony Gormley.

Significantly, the trade unions gave less money to Labour than they had done in the previous three elections. Unison donated £1.49 million and six other unions contributed less than £1 million between them. But Unite, one of the biggest unions, with 1.4 million members, closed its wallet entirely. This was quite a snub considering it had given Labour £3 million to spend on the 2019 campaign. It also refused to approve the party's manifesto, believing it offered insufficient guarantees when it came to protecting workers' rights and jobs in the oil and gas sectors. Its scepticism probably wasn't such a surprise to the Labour leadership, though. Unite's leader, Sharon Graham, had been warning Starmer since 2023 that he could not take the union's support for granted. Only a radical agenda that transformed British industry and society permanently would do, she said. She made clear her belief that the programme of fiscal responsibility laid out by Rachel Reeves had led to 'inertia'. Yet Starmer and the team around him had no appetite to worry about a lack of union money, as their predecessors would have done. They were fixated on victory, and concluded their best bet was to say and do as little as possible, exercise caution and allow the dysfunctional Conservative Party to win the election for Labour. Showing that momentum was with him, Starmer spent much of the campaign visiting seats that had Tory majorities of at least 8,000 and, in some cases, almost twice that.

During the opening ten days, Sunak made a series of policy announcements, including on income tax cuts for pensioners and ending 'Mickey Mouse' university degrees. As individual ideas they were perfectly well received, but they made little impact. Another – the introduction of mandatory National Service at eighteen – was also met with interest by many who were aware of it, but ultimately it fared badly. Its chances were not helped by Steve Baker, a minister in Sunak's government, complaining that the idea had been 'sprung on candidates'. Some polling that I carried out during the first week of the campaign chimed with the potency of Labour's 'safety first' approach. Voters knew the Tories seemed to have been running a more energetic effort than Labour – 65 per cent of those canvassed had seen a story generated by the Conservatives, compared to 54 per cent who had seen one from Labour – yet Labour maintained a substantial lead. On 27 May, a letter signed by 121 businessmen was circulated to illustrate that Labour was now seen as the party of business. In fact, it did not stand up to scrutiny. No serving FTSE 350 executives had signed it. Some of the signatories were Labour members. Others had retired from the world of commerce altogether. The public didn't seem to mind.

By then, Starmer had apparently rediscovered his enthusiasm for the left, describing himself as a 'socialist' who was on the side of 'working people' and who 'always puts the country first and party second'. Emphasising the 'change' theme, he used his first major speech to talk about growing up during the 'hard times' of the 1970s in small-town Surrey.

> I know there are countless people who haven't decided how they'll vote in this election. They're fed up with the failure, chaos and division of the Tories, but they still have questions about us: has Labour changed enough? Do I trust them with my money, our borders, our security? My answer is, yes, you can, because I have changed this party, permanently.

He also spoke of how he 'knows what that feels like to struggle with bills'. Later that day when he visited Brighton, however, it was noted by *The Sun* that he was wearing a hooded jacket made by Sandro, the Paris fashion brand, which cost £519. Journalists began combing his entry in the MPs' register of financial interests and noticed that in April he had accepted £16,200 of 'work clothing' from Lord Alli. On 22 May, he had also recorded that Alli had bought him £2,485 worth of glasses. Starmer had always kept his distance from Sunak, believing it made it easier to caricature him as an 'out-of-touch' rich Tory. Yet here was evidence that he was not averse to enjoying expensive things that were out of reach to most of the working people whose votes he sought. When, a couple of days later, he flew to Scotland in a private jet to give a speech on Labour's green energy policies, he was branded a hypocrite. Even *The Guardian* felt moved to report on his mode of transport.

A key moment in the electoral battle came on 3 June, when Nigel Farage belatedly confirmed that he would, after all, stand as the Reform UK candidate in Clacton. He also announced that he would lead the party after Richard Tice agreed to step down. Labour's high command knew that one likely outcome of Farage's presence on the ballot paper would be to squeeze the national Conservative vote still further. It was music to their ears. But by then, Labour was itself recruiting last-minute candidates before the 7 June deadline after a string of MPs announced they were retiring in circumstances that were not altogether straightforward. One person who was encouraged by party bosses to stand down but refused says, 'They wanted us to make way for Starmer's favourites. Everybody who agreed to retire was promised a seat in the Lords. But of course here we are months on and some of those seats in the Lords haven't materialised.'

In the ensuing scramble, the NEC appointed contenders directly rather than local parties making the decision. There were strange goings-on at Brighton Kemptown after the incumbent Labour MP, Lloyd Russell-Moyle, was suspended on 28 May. He was told of this news in a telephone call from Starmer's office. The Labour Party had agreed to look into an eight-year-old non-criminal complaint that had already been investigated, and which Russell-Moyle has described as 'vexatious', making it impossible for him to be a candidate. Into his place stepped Chris Ward, who had been Starmer's speechwriter since 2015 and who was mocked by some in the shadow Cabinet for being one of Starmer's 'blue-suited boys' (also known collectively as 'Wrong Direction').

Others who were lucky enough to be chosen to stand at the last moment included Luke Akehurst, Starmer's 'enforcer', who had played a key role in removing dozens of Corbynites as prospective parliamentary candidates over the previous few years. He was given the Labour-friendly seat of North Durham. Josh Simons, the director of the Starmerite think tank Labour Together, was parachuted into the seat of Makerfield. Heather Iqbal, a former adviser to Rachel Reeves, was handed Dewsbury & Batley. James Asser, the former co-chairman of LGBT+ Labour, found a berth at West Ham & Beckton. And Georgia Gould, the leader of Camden Council, whose father, Philip, was a key Blairite, was chosen to stand in Maida Vale. Other beneficiaries included Torsten Bell, a former Labour Party aide who ran the Resolution Foundation, a favourite Labour think tank. He was picked at Swansea West. Alex Barros-Curtis, who led Starmer's legal and finance team during his 2020 leadership bid before becoming Labour's executive director of legal affairs, was selected for Cardiff West.

There was deep cynicism when it became clear how the cards had fallen for those who were close to Starmer. Critics remembered his words from 2020 when he declared that selections for candidates must be 'more democratic and we should end NEC impositions of candidates. Local party members should select their candidates for every election.' He had also said that 'there should be no power without accountability, and true accountability requires transparency'. Beth Winter, a former Corbynite Labour MP in Wales, took to Twitter to express her displeasure. 'In his leadership campaign, Starmer promised to end imposing candidates. He broke that promise. The imposition of candidates in Cardiff West & Swansea West cuts local members out of the process. It is an insult to Party members, an insult to Wales, and an affront to democracy.'

Other Labour figures in Wales were furious about Bell and Barros-Curtis being foisted upon voters because neither of them had any known connection to the principality. One told the website Nation.Cymru, 'The UK party … have all angles stitched up. It is very depressing for those of us who have been in the party for decades.' The elevation of Barros-Curtis was regarded as particularly extraordinary because a few days later, it was announced that Labour had dropped a complicated legal case which ended up costing the party more than £3 million. Barros-Curtis was identified as having been the driving force behind this expensive adventure, though he must have acted with the agreement of Starmer. The action dated from April 2020 – the second week of Starmer's leadership. It concerned an 860-page internal Labour report which had been commissioned during the Corbyn era and was originally intended to be submitted to the Equality and Human Rights Commission (EHRC) when the party was being investigated for antisemitism. Labour's then general secretary Jennie Formby decided that the report – which claimed that racism, sexism and bullying were common throughout both wings of the Labour Party – should not be sent to the EHRC. It was leaked to the media, however. Nine individuals who were named in the leaked report as having made complaints about antisemitism then sued the Labour Party for failing to protect their data and invading their privacy.

Labour, in turn, launched a counter case against five Labour employees – including two of Corbyn's top advisers, Seumas Milne and Karie Murphy – accusing them of having conspired to leak the report in order to destabilise Starmer's leadership. Another member of this quintet was Georgie Robertson, daughter of Geoffrey Robertson, Starmer's close colleague at Doughty Street Chambers. This legal wrangle remained active for four years until Labour abandoned it immediately after Barros-Curtis's nomination for Cardiff West. When the case was dropped, one anonymous Labour MP told the *Daily Telegraph*:

> The parachuting of Alex Barros-Curtis into a safe Labour seat is a disgrace now we know what he is responsible for. This Starmer-appointed official has spent millions of pounds of the Labour Party's money dragging former party employees through the courts for four years, pursuing a pointless and failed political vendetta.

One of Corbyn's former advisers, James Schneider, added, 'The case cost Labour millions of pounds and trapped five former party staffers in cruel legal limbo. It should never have been allowed to happen.' Coming at the start of an election campaign in which the spotlight was trained most on the governing Conservative Party, this embarrassing saga did not receive the attention it might have done. One well-placed source says, 'Starmer should consider himself lucky that the electorate didn't realise to what degree he himself was involved in this case. It wasn't just Alex Barros-Curtis.' Another source comments that Labour's fundraisers were 'furious' that Starmer did not put an end to the doomed action years before. 'Potential donors found it very off-putting that their money might be used to pay lawyers' bills,' says this person.

At the same time, Corbyn again showed himself to be a thorn in Starmer's side by announcing that he was to stand as an independent candidate in Islington North, the seat he had held since 1983. Starmer had hoped that he had ended Corbyn's political career. He was wrong. Arguably more damaging for Starmer was the tussle over the future of Corbyn's political soulmate Diane Abbott, who had been suspended as a Labour MP in April 2023 after suggesting that Jewish, Irish and Traveller people experience prejudice but not racism. Starmer's dislike of Abbott showed itself in the length of time it took for her to be allowed to stand for Labour in Hackney North, which she had represented since 1987. On 28 May 2024, it was confirmed that the whip had been restored to her. However, some newspapers were briefed that she would be banned from standing as a Labour candidate. It took a further three days for Starmer to announce that she was, in fact, free to represent the party. He did so only after Angela Rayner told journalists that she knew of no reason why Abbott should not stand. In the intervening seventy-two hours, Starmer had needlessly created a story on which the media had feasted.

In fact, Abbott had been conflicted about whether to stand at all. Her allies believed Starmer hoped she would not so that the seat could be handed to one of his favoured associates. But when she realised she was being blocked, her resolve to serve another term in Parliament was strengthened. A spokesman for Momentum, the group set up to support Corbyn's leadership, was gleeful at Starmer's acquiescence. 'You come at the queen, you better not miss,' they mocked. 'Diane Abbott has been bullied and abused her whole career. Starmer tried to force her out. She held firm – and won. This is a huge victory.' The ineffective handling of the Abbott question pointed to tensions behind the scenes. Stories began to swirl about the uneasy working relationship of Labour's campaign director, Morgan McSweeney, and Starmer's chief of staff, Sue Gray. Those difficulties would only intensify.

The election operation was tightly managed from Labour HQ by McSweeney plus national campaign co-ordinator Pat McFadden and his wife, Marianna. They decided that a limited number of Labour politicians would give broadcast interviews. Other than Starmer and McFadden himself (who also chaired three meetings per day), the principal players were Rachel Reeves, Wes Streeting, Darren Jones, Bridget Phillipson and Jonathan Ashworth. Angela Rayner was sent on a nationwide road trip on a Labour battle bus. The Conservatives made clear their wish for six head-to-head TV debates between Sunak and Starmer, one each week until polling day, but Labour officials were prepared to commit to only two. 'I can do one debate or 100, I know what Sunak is going to say,' Starmer told the BBC by way of explanation. 'But I want to talk for as long as I can to voters directly and take my message to them and hear from them.' This was perhaps not surprising from a man who had always been open about his dislike of Prime Minister's Questions, particularly given that an election front-runner is always less inclined to take the risk of a set-piece debate. According to one source, a well-known TV actor who supported him but cringed every time he gave a speech approached Starmer's office that spring offering to help smooth out his 'syncopated adenoidal delivery', but a junior colleague politely declined the invitation. The tactic of keeping Starmer away from the TV cameras was potentially risky in view of an Ipsos poll that came out soon afterwards. It found that half of voters did not know what he stood for.

The first head-to-head debate, on ITV on 4 June, involved some predictably terse exchanges between Sunak and Starmer over tax and immigration. It was also revealing of some deeper truths about both men's personalities. At one stage they were asked whether they would use private healthcare if a relative needing surgery was stuck on an NHS waiting list. Without hesitating, Sunak said, 'Yes.' But Starmer caused astonishment by saying, 'No. I don't use private health. I use the NHS.' Did this well-off, middle-aged politician really mean to say that he would be content for one of his relatives to suffer so that his socialist instincts would remain intact, commentators wondered? Some branded him heartless. Sunak drew applause as he repeatedly attacked Labour's plans for the economy, insisting that under Labour taxes would rise by £2,000 per year. It took Starmer a long time to react to this accusation with any vigour. According to one person who was in the TV studio, it even had to be pointed out to him that he had failed to respond to the charge. 'Starmer is remarkably diffident on the economy,' says this eyewitness.

> When Rishi Sunak kept going after him about the tax rises, Starmer wouldn't engage and I remember at half-time during

> the ad break, someone from his team came up to him and said, 'You've got to get into this.' He then crowbarred his rebuttal of the £2,000 tax rise into an answer about net zero. You could tell he was lacking in confidence on the economy.

The next day, in Portsmouth, Starmer was asked by reporters why he had taken so long to counter Sunak's tax claim. He said that Sunak had been 'lying'. It was a serious charge to level at the Prime Minister, but there was no mistaking that the tax row had injected some life into a hitherto dull contest. Labour did indeed appear to be rattled over their tax plans and the story led the news. Things might have stayed that way were it not for Sunak's catastrophic blunder. On 5 June, he attended a national D-Day event in Portsmouth and then on 6 June – the anniversary of the Allied landings – he went to Normandy for a British commemoration. Under pre-agreed plans, he left France before foreign politicians including Joe Biden and Emmanuel Macron gathered on Omaha Beach for an international ceremony that afternoon, his team believing it was little more than a photo opportunity. As the Prime Minister flew back to London to give an interview to ITV, David Cameron, the Foreign Secretary, represented him. Without realising it at the time, Sunak's decision to leave had consigned to oblivion whatever chance the Tories had of capturing the agenda. Media coverage portrayed him in the most negative light possible. His early exit was considered indefensible.

Starmer was also in France that day and in contrast to the Prime Minister he stayed for both events, taking advantage of the situation to pose for photographs with the President of Ukraine, Volodymyr Zelenskyy, among others. When news of Sunak's absence filtered through to reporters, Nigel Farage was the first to condemn him. 'The Prime Minister has ducked out of the international D-Day event to fly back to the UK to campaign,' he tweeted. 'I am here in Normandy in a personal capacity because I think it matters. Does he?' Farage was followed by politicians from all sides. When Starmer was asked to comment, he struck a moderate tone: 'For me, there was only one choice, which was to be there, to pay my respects, to say thank you and to have the opportunity to speak to those veterans.' Sunak, he added, 'will have to answer for his choices'.

The fallout from this public relations disaster perhaps obscured the fact that the Conservatives were not the only ones who had to field tricky inquiries about absences, however. That week, restless journalists had begun to ponder the whereabouts of Starmer's wife, Victoria. She had not been seen since the election was called. On 11 June, the *Daily Telegraph* published a piece titled 'Why Keir Starmer's wife is being kept off the campaign trail'. A Labour source told the paper, 'It's the children. They have got teenagers who are completely freaked out by the idea of being in Downing Street or in any way being in the public eye.' The source also pointed out that pro-Palestine activists had been causing problems for the family.

Twenty-four hours later, the *Daily Mail* published a similar article asking, 'Why is Sir Keir Starmer's wife not accompanying him on the campaign trail?' It was a question the paper could not answer, but it is surely significant that the following week – on 19 June – three people were found guilty at Westminster Magistrates' Court of public order offences for their involvement in a pro-Palestinian demonstration outside the Starmers' home. The court was told that in April 2024, members of the group Youth Demand had hung a banner outside the house that read 'Starmer stop the killing' and surrounded it with red hand prints. Pairs of children's shoes were also put in the front garden to represent the children killed in Gaza. These had been found by Victoria Starmer and she had given evidence against Youth Demand.

Who can say what, if any, effect the coverage about his wife had on Starmer? And yet he certainly appeared unsettled around this time. On 12 June, the Conservatives became embroiled in an unhelpful story concerning allegations that bets had been placed on the timing of the election by various people including a small number of MPs and seven police officers who – potentially – had insider knowledge of it. Yet on the day the story broke it was Starmer, who was in Grimsby for the Sky News leaders' event, who seemed tetchiest. This was the halfway mark of the campaign and, while being interviewed by the channel's political editor, Beth Rigby, he was accused by one audience member of being a 'political robot'. When he then spoke about his father having been a toolmaker, some audience members laughed. Starmer carried on, but he looked uncomfortable – cross, even. The next day, when asked by Christopher Hope, the political editor of GB News, about his reaction to the jeers, he unburdened himself.

'My dad worked in a factory all his life,' he told Hope.

> He felt people disrespected him. It hit a nerve last night because he felt that … when someone said, 'What do you do for a living?', he would say, 'I work in a factory,' and there'd be a pause where nobody knew quite what to say. And he felt really disrespected. It caused him in his life to withdraw from social engagements. So when someone laughed last night, my dad would have turned in his grave. If you're laughing at someone because they work in a factory, that is the one thing that I think had a massive impact on someone like my dad – the disrespect – and it's in me. You can see I'm angry about it, frustrated, because I will never allow that sort of disrespect for working people to be any part of my plans, any part of the Britain that I want as the future. So I will proudly tell anybody who will listen that my dad worked in a factory. He was a toolmaker. A

> very good toolmaker. He loved his trade. And my mum was a nurse, and she loved being a nurse. And we didn't have a lot of money. I'm proud of what my parents did. I don't like it when people laugh at my dad because he worked in a factory.

The reason that audience members in Grimsby laughed that night almost certainly had nothing to do with snobbery at all, of course, and Starmer had no proof that it did. He seemed unable or unwilling to consider that some people might simply have been amused by his mentioning his father's line of work yet again. Some of them might even have been familiar with Tom Sharpe's satirical novel *Ancestral Vices* in which the protagonist, Walden Yapp, tries to make friends with the local workers in a small town by doing the very same thing. '[Yapp] made a start by telling them his father had been a toolmaker … The news was greeted with a lack of enthusiasm he found quite remarkable and in some cases with what he could only judge to be looks of genuine alarm.'

In truth, Starmer had discussed his father's toolmaking on so many occasions over the previous five years that it had become something of a running joke. Moreover, as shown in Chapter 13, Starmer himself had used his father's trade for comical purposes during his 2021 Labour conference speech when he quipped, 'My dad was a toolmaker. Although, in a way, so was Boris Johnson's.' His admission of anger that night in Grimsby suggested his own feelings ran deeper. Did he bear the emotional scars of bullies who had mocked him during his childhood? Had he simply missed the point? Or was something else wrong?

On 13 June, Labour's manifesto was published. Two things about it were immediately striking. It contained no fewer than thirty-three photographs of Starmer; and the phrase 'working people' was used twenty times, notably in relation to a promise not to increase 'National Insurance, the basic, higher, or additional rates of Income Tax, or VAT'. Who were 'working people', though? Labour was vague about its definition for five days, until Starmer was pressed during an interview on LBC. He said it referred to those who 'earn their living, rely on our services and don't really have the ability to write a cheque when they get into trouble'. Not everybody was convinced, and it heightened fears that pensioners and savers might be dragged into any tax-raising measures that a Labour government chose to implement. It certainly did nothing to quell suspicions that tax rises would be at the top of Labour's first budget, should it win power. Starmer gave an interview to *The Guardian* assuring voters that he was telling the truth. 'I'm not going to write five years' worth of budgets three and a half, four weeks before an election,' he said. 'But I am going to say we're fully costed, fully funded, and that none of our plans require tax rises over and above the ones we've already set.' Paul Johnson, the director of the Institute for Fiscal Studies think tank, predicted that if Labour won, taxes would have to increase.

The manifesto focused on five 'missions', listed as a desire to deliver economic stability; make Britain a clean energy superpower; crack down on anti-social behaviour; reform childcare and education; and cut NHS waiting times. Another striking guarantee was the recruitment of 6,500 new state school teachers by adding VAT to private school fees – though, worryingly given the context, the reasoning behind this measure featured a spelling error, as it was explained that the new teachers would 'prepar [*sic*] children for life, work and the future, paid for by ending tax breaks for private schools'. A central plank of Labour's programme for government was its claim to be 'the party of wealth creation'. It promised to 'kickstart economic growth to secure the highest sustained growth in the G7 – with good jobs and productivity growth in every part of the country making everyone, not just a few, better off'. Yet this was illogical. Britain had no control over the economic performance of the other six countries in the G7. Therefore it was a promise that it had no power to deliver.

This statement also confused some who had heard Starmer describe himself as a socialist just two weeks earlier. Even though socialism can be difficult to define explicitly outside of Marxism, it is generally recognised as a politico-economic system with egalitarianism, and a desire to redistribute wealth, at its core. Did Labour really want everybody in Britain – including the highest earners – to be better off? Or was the plan in fact that private enterprise should pay ever greater amounts of tax in order to finance new Labour projects like Great British Energy? This publicly owned company would, it was hoped, work with energy companies, local authorities and co-operatives to install thousands of onshore wind, solar, and hydropower projects to 'deliver power back to the British people'. The manifesto also outlined £8.5 billion in tax rises, compared with £17 billion of tax cuts being offered by the Tories. When asked if taxes would be hiked further or spending would be cut if growth did not materialise – or if the fiscal rules would be changed – Starmer said, 'You won't see any plan that takes tax measures over and above what we have already set out.' Economists were clear that this would leave room for Labour to tinker with other kinds of levies, including inheritance tax or capital gains taxes.

A renewed drive for net zero and closer ties with the EU were also on the table. So was a promise to launch no fewer than fourteen 'reviews' into everything from defence to education and pensions. And a plan to allow sixteen-year-old children to vote was also mentioned in the manifesto. If enacted, this would enfranchise Starmer's son, Toby, who turned sixteen in 2024. Starmer's protection of him has extended to him asking newspapers not to name him in print, despite his birth certificate being publicly available to anybody who wishes to see it. Many will see the irony in Starmer believing those of his son's age are old enough to vote in a general election, helping to determine the future of the country, but too young to be identified in a newspaper article.

Another eye-catching pledge concerned ticket touts. 'Access to music, drama and sport has become difficult and expensive because of ticket touting. Labour will put fans back at the heart of events by introducing new consumer protections on ticket resales.' That spring, there had been a storm over ticket scams relating to concerts that the American singer Taylor Swift was about to give in London, so addressing this problem was seen as a potential vote-winner. As if on cue, on 22 June, Starmer attended a Taylor Swift concert himself at Wembley Stadium. '"Swift" campaign pitstop,' he wrote on Twitter, sharing a picture of himself with his wife at the concert. If this was meant to show that they were everyday people who enjoyed the same activities as millions of voters, it was to backfire badly within a couple of months.

That day, *The Guardian* published a 5,000-word interview with Starmer in which some of his other cultural tastes were put to the test. Its journalist Charlotte Edwardes, who had tailed him for weeks between April and June, was left disappointed. She managed to elicit that Starmer does not have a favourite novel or poem (though, oddly, he said on *Desert Island Discs* in 2020 that his favourite book was the Scottish novel *A Disaffection* by James Kelman). Neither, apparently, does he dream at night. She noticed that during her weeks-long investigation of him 'his suits get sharper; he acquires new specs; more clay is swept through the concrete hair. When he's cross, his ears redden. Stressed, he has a face like a slammed front door.' Those suits, she wrote, were bought from Charles Tyrwhitt, the mid-range men's clothes shop. Tellingly, she also observed that Starmer has a habit of referring to himself in the third person. First, speaking of their previous encounter, he said to Edwardes, 'You asked me questions that I've never asked myself. That may seem funny, [but] part of being Keir is just ploughing on.' Next, when discussing private healthcare, he explained that he had been forced to give up football for months while waiting for a medical procedure on the NHS. 'So there was a serious issue for Keir Starmer,' he said. Some would take this trait as the surest sign of a swollen ego.

The second head-to-head TV debate, hosted by the BBC in Nottingham, took place on 26 June. On paper, the encounter should have been easy for Starmer. If Sunak said anything positive about Britain, Starmer simply had to reply that Sunak was detached from reality. If Sunak referred to a new policy idea, Starmer could ask why the Tories had waited fourteen years to introduce it. Or he could repeat the mantra that it was time for a change of government. Yet arguably he showed himself to be slower on his feet than Sunak that night, in particular on immigration, as Sunak jabbed and hectored, accusing Starmer of 'not being straight with people' about Labour's plan to 'smash the gangs' to deal with the small boats crisis. Starmer appeared frustrated. Under questioning on this topic he failed to satisfy, though his spontaneous riposte to Sunak's interruptions – 'If you listened to people in the audience and across the country, you may not be so out of touch' – did win approval from the audience. In truth, neither man was felt to have performed brilliantly. When one spectator was invited to share his observations during the debate, he accused Sunak of being 'a pretty mediocre Prime Minister' before turning his fire on Starmer by claiming his 'strings are being pulled' by senior Labour members. He asked, 'Are you two really the best we've got to be the next Prime Minister of our great country?' Sustained applause followed. His question was pertinent. It accentuated the feeling that, as much as the Conservative Party was disliked, there seemed to be little natural enthusiasm for Starmer and the Labour Party.

During one of Starmer's final interviews of the campaign, he told Virgin Radio that if he won power, he would make time for his family, explaining:

> We've had a strategy in place and we'll try to keep to it, which is to carve out really protected time for the kids, so on a Friday – I've been doing this for years – I will not do a work-related thing after six o'clock, pretty well come what may. There are a few exceptions, but that's what we do.

The Tories seized on the admission, using a social media campaign to paint Sunak as better suited to running the country than Starmer and querying the Labour leader's commitment to national security. Starmer, on the cusp of sixty-two, would be 'a part-time Prime Minister'. This was never likely to alter the result of the election, but Starmer's words were considered by some to show a surprisingly relaxed attitude. Were his political instincts going to be found wanting or was he just tired after a long campaign?

One final oddity remained. On 2 July, out of the blue, a barrister called Allison Bailey took to Twitter to warn the world about Starmer. Over 921 words, she wrote of her spell as a pupil at Doughty Street Chambers in 2002. She was highly critical of the Labour leader, believing that he had once 'intimidated' her and that the experience 'may interest those keen to gain insight into the man's character when he thinks no one that matters is looking'. Bailey explained that she had developed a crush on her pupil mistress, Phillippa Kaufmann, who until recently had been Starmer's girlfriend. This, she said, 'was something that was known about' within Doughty Street Chambers. She claimed that everybody she encountered there during her pupillage was helpful to her 'with one standout exception – Keir Starmer'. She went on: 'Keir Starmer never once acknowledged me during all of that time, never said "hello" that I can recall.' Then she relayed the occasion that she said had made her feel uncomfortable. One evening she and Kaufmann, quietly doing some paperwork in an office,

> were joined, entirely by coincidence, first by Paul Brooks, who would become Phillippa's partner and the father of her children, and then [by] Keir Starmer. It was awkward, and it was tense. No one was talking. No one was looking at each other … Keir Starmer seemed to me to be quite furious. We all sat silently: the ex-partner, the new partner to be, and the lesbian with a crush. Sometime later that evening, I walked out of DSC onto Doughty Street. As I did so, I encountered Keir Starmer directly opposite, preparing to ride his bicycle away from chambers. When he saw me, he stopped, faced me, and stood there glaring at me, saying not a word. What do you do when you are a pupil and the leading barrister of his generation, a complete superstar, is apparently trying to intimidate you? I imagine the pupil's handbook would tell me to walk away, now. I stopped, faced him, and glared right back, saying nothing. There we stood, staring each other down from across Doughty Street – Keir Starmer and a lowly pupil, for what felt like minutes. There are some things no amount of education can teach you. I may not have grasped the intricacies of human rights law, but I knew how to stand my ground in the face of what I saw as this man's attempt to intimidate me. Kier [*sic*] Starmer eventually gave up, hopped on his bicycle and cycled away – and only then did I walk away.

Perhaps unsurprisingly, Starmer never commented publicly on Bailey's assertion.

On the night of 4 July, the Starmer family watched the election results roll in not from their own house in Kentish Town but from Lord Alli's penthouse flat in Covent Garden. In Starmer's constituency of Holborn & St Pancras, turnout was low, at 54 per cent, reflecting the national trend. He managed to lose 17.4 per cent of those who had voted for him in 2019. He secured 18,884 votes – more than halving his majority to 11,572. The strongest competition came from Andrew Feinstein, an independent candidate, who from a standing start won 7,312 votes, coming second. 'On the night of the count, Starmer completely ignored me,' remembers Feinstein.

> We were given the results on a piece of paper just before the announcement on stage. I saw his face change colour as he read them. He was puce. He looked very angry. Half his vote vanished. Of course, he hadn't turned out at all in the constituency during the campaign. Labour just used targeted adverts. We'd knocked on about 50,000 doors. My view is he's not popular in the constituency. I think if we'd had six months, we could have seriously embarrassed him.

The national picture was extraordinary in several ways, with Labour's landslide exceeding the expectations of many in the party. Underneath the flurry of results, however, was evidence of how volatile the electorate had become – and of how Labour's performance was not as decisive as it seemed. Labour won 411 seats, up by 209 from the 2019 election. The Conservatives lost 244 seats, returning only 121 MPs to the Commons – the lowest number in the party's history. The Liberal Democrats gained sixty-one seats for a final tally of seventy-two, while the Scottish National Party lost thirty-nine seats, ending up with only nine MPs. Reform UK won five seats and the Green Party won four. In Northern Ireland, Sinn Féin won seven seats while the Democratic Unionist Party's haul was cut from eight to five. Neil Kinnock was jubilant, calling his party's victory 'the greatest comeback since Lazarus'. Yet its shallow nature was plain for all to see. Turnout was 59.8 per cent – 7.5 percentage points lower than in 2019. And once the numbers had been crunched, it transpired that constituencies won by Labour generally had a lower turnout than those won by the Conservatives.

Although Starmer was able to revel in a 174-seat majority, only 9.7 million votes had been required to achieve it – 33.7 per cent of the total cast. The Tories achieved 6.8 million votes. Political scientists were quick to point out that in 2019 Jeremy Corbyn's Labour Party had clocked up 10.2 million votes – and Corbyn had taken Labour to its worst result for almost a century. Gary Gibbon, the political editor of *Channel 4 News*, memorably described Starmer's victory as a 'loveless landslide'. It was a neat phrase, capturing the exaggerations that the first-past-the-post system is capable of delivering. One has only to consider that Reform UK polled 4.1 million votes – 600,000 more than the Liberal Democrats – but secured only five seats to the Lib Dems' seventy-two to see why the debate about Britain's electoral system flickered into life.

Perhaps the most striking statistic to emerge that night was that only one in five registered voters – just 20 per cent of the nation – had voted Labour. The other 80 per cent had supported different parties or not voted at all. The old dictum that oppositions don't win elections, governments lose them had scarcely ever seemed more appropriate.

CHAPTER 16

THE FIRST 100 DAYS

Shortly after midday on Friday 5 July, Sir Keir Starmer arrived at Buckingham Palace for an audience with the King. Having been asked by him to form the next government, the new Prime Minister went to Downing Street to deliver his first speech to the nation. His unease was noticeable. In the seven minutes that he spoke, he glanced down at his notes 158 times, an average of once every two and a half seconds. He began by thanking Rishi Sunak. 'His achievement as the first British Asian Prime Minister of our country – the extra effort that will have required – should not be underestimated by anyone. We pay tribute to that today.' There was a certain irony in Starmer mentioning his predecessor's Indian heritage since Sunak never drew attention to it when he was Prime Minister and actively discouraged his Conservative colleagues from doing so. It says much about Starmer's need to demonstrate his progressive instincts that he did so. The rest of his words that afternoon were aimed squarely at the four-fifths of registered voters who had backed other parties. 'Whether you voted Labour or not – in fact, especially if you did not – I say to you directly: my government will serve you,' Starmer intoned. 'Politics can be a force for good. We will show that. And that is how we will govern: country first, party second.' He spoke of national renewal, of rebuilding the country, of safer streets, of secure borders and of 'a return of politics to public service'. He promised 'wealth created in every community'. Labour, he said, would 'tread more lightly on your lives'. He would have known that the Conservatives and Reform UK combined had secured almost 1.25 million more votes than Labour.

His first task was to appoint his Cabinet. In most cases, those who had been in the shadow Cabinet slotted into their equivalent government posts. There were, however, some surprises. The biggest of these was the elevation to the House of Lords of Starmer's friend Richard Hermer. From there he would fulfil his duties as the Attorney General, the government's chief legal adviser who oversees the Crown Prosecution Service. Hermer was the first person in this post since 1922 not to have served in Parliament beforehand. He and Starmer had known each other for more than thirty years, having run human rights practices at Doughty Street Chambers at the same time in the 1990s. Hermer had given £5,000 towards Starmer's leadership campaign in 2020. He had a long track record of representing controversial clients, ranging from the Irish Republican politician Gerry Adams to Shamima Begum, the Briton who, aged fifteen, joined the jihadist group Islamic State. He is passionately pro-EU, has said that there is a 'moral argument' for Britain to pay reparations for slavery and has a strong interest in international law. The upshot of his unanticipated entry into national politics was that Emily Thornberry, who had been Starmer's shadow Attorney General for the previous two and a half years, was condemned to the back benches. The demotion clearly distressed her. She gave several interviews to make the point that she had served in the shadow Cabinet for 'eight and a half unbroken years ... a longer record of service than anyone else'. If this was her way of saying that Starmer's Cabinet was inexperienced, it was not without validity. Most of its members had never been in government before. Only Ed Miliband, the Energy Secretary, was considered to know his way around Whitehall sufficiently well to make an impact. Indeed, precious few of Starmer's ministers had had any exposure to life outside the public sector and Westminster. More than that, there was a feeling that Labour's key players – including Starmer – had spent so long trying to defenestrate the Tories that they were simply not ready for what came next. As has been observed elsewhere, and in the simplest terms, there was no plan.

After chairing his first Cabinet meeting on 6 July, Starmer held a press conference in Downing Street during which he told reporters that 'self-interest is yesterday's politics' and promised that the 'mindset' in government had already changed. He declared the Rwanda deportation scheme 'dead and buried', insisting it had 'never been a deterrent' and was a 'gimmick'. He also gave notice that it would be 'impossible' to stop the early release of prisoners because of overcrowding. 'We've got too many prisoners, not enough prisons,' he said. 'That's a monumental failure of the last government on any basic view of government.' Sounding something like a 1990s management consultant, he said he would chair 'mission delivery boards' to concentrate on areas of priority to his government. When asked if he would raise taxes, he was unequivocal. 'We're going to have to take the tough decisions and take them early, and we will. We will do that with a raw honesty. But that is not a sort of prelude to saying there's some tax decision that we didn't speak about before.' The next day he made a whistle-stop tour of Scotland, Northern Ireland and Wales before returning to England, seeking to demonstrate that he would govern in the interests of all parts of the United Kingdom.

As Starmer rates himself Britain's most liberal-minded Prime Minister, it was perhaps inevitable that he chose to open his first Commons outing as premier on 9 July with remarks praising the differences between the hundreds of MPs who were assembled there. 'Mr Speaker-Elect,' he said.

> You preside over a new parliament that is the most diverse

> by race and gender that this country has ever seen, and I am proud of the part that my party, and every party, has played in that; and this intake includes the largest cohort of LGBT+ MPs of any parliament in the world.

His next sentence did raise some eyebrows, however.

> Given all that diversity, Mr Speaker-Elect, I hope that you will not begrudge me a slight departure from convention to pay tribute to the new Mother of the House, my right hon. Friend the Member for Hackney North & Stoke Newington [Diane Abbott], who has done so much in her career, over so many years, to fight for a parliament that truly represents modern Britain. We welcome her back to her place.

Just six weeks earlier, Starmer had hoped that Abbott's parliamentary career was finished. His words offended some on the left. One of them, Jeremy Corbyn, was also back in the Commons, this time as an independent MP. To Starmer's profound irritation, Corbyn's personal following in Islington North had easily seen off Labour's candidate, Praful Nargund.

Hours after addressing the Commons, Starmer and his wife, Victoria, flew to Washington for the seventy-fifth anniversary NATO summit. En route, he told reporters of his 'cast-iron commitment' to spending 2.5 per cent of national income on defence. Yet he would not be drawn on a specific date by which the target would be reached, rendering this claim hollow. He used the summit to hold bilateral talks with the German Chancellor, Olaf Scholz, during which they agreed to co-operate on defence. Starmer said he was 'determined to renew Britain's place on the world stage'. He outlined his belief that 'there was a sense after Brexit that the UK had become too inward-looking' and vowed to 'reset' Britain's relationship with the EU. He also used the occasion to assure President Volodymyr Zelenskyy of Britain's continuing £3 billion-a-year support package for Ukraine and to stage a bilateral meeting with President Biden, to whom he gave an Arsenal shirt as a present. By now, questions about Biden's cognitive abilities were being asked openly, leading to talk that he might not stand for re-election. George Clooney, the actor and Democratic Party donor, was among those urging him to retire. Starmer told the BBC that Biden had been 'on really good form' when they met. Bearing in mind Biden opted out of the presidential race eleven days later, it was perhaps unfortunate that Starmer's biographer, Tom Baldwin, had observed of their meeting, 'Sitting next to Biden in the White House, he [Starmer] doesn't look like an unequal.' In an entirely different context, another embattled leader, Vaughan Gething, the Labour First Minister of Wales, also quit his post that month. He had accepted a £200,000 donation from a businessman, David Neal, who had twice been convicted of environmental offences. Starmer had backed Gething before he stood down, a show of support that had counted for little.

Nevertheless, during those opening days in July, in which Starmer also visited Berlin to watch England play in the UEFA Euro final, he was perceived to have begun his political honeymoon. An Ipsos poll carried out within a week of his arrival at No. 10 indicated that his popularity had received a boost, with 40 per cent of voters having a favourable view of him, up six points from the final week of the campaign. Goodwill was not hard to come by. When he began the slow process of moving his family into the flat above 11 Downing Street, its previous occupants, Jeremy Hunt and his family, left a card and some chocolates for the new arrivals, a fact that Starmer revealed to journalists. 'It became quite a big story and [Starmer] sent me a text saying, 'I'm so sorry, I wasn't expecting it to get such big pick-up and I hope the children are OK about it,' remembers Hunt. 'I thought that was very kind. He was thinking about the children.' As for the Starmers' new abode, Hunt has mixed feelings. 'It's a very odd place to live,' he explains. 'It's like being in the middle of Fort Knox. You're surrounded by police officers with machine guns. You're on top of a rabbit warren of offices and it's quite a large and unhomely flat. It's much bigger than most terraced houses in London – it has very high ceilings and it's not particularly cosy. But it's a great adventure for a family to live there.'

More than forty pieces of legislation outlined in the King's Speech on 17 July, including railway renationalisation plans and a National Wealth Fund to attract private investment, helped to underscore the idea that Starmer and his government had begun the term with purpose. Starmerism was still considered an elusive political concept beyond a general notion of social democracy, but it was now coming into sharper focus. With a vast parliamentary majority to speak of, and the economy rated as the fastest-growing in the G7, he crowned his second week in the job by hosting at Blenheim Palace the European Political Community meeting, attended by about fifty leaders from across Europe. And so began what should have been a highly productive summer.

Yet as more ministerial appointments were finalised over the ensuing days, mutterings were heard. First, another unelected friend of Starmer, the former Labour Home Secretary Jacqui Smith, was given a peerage and made a minister in the Department for Education. In 2009, Smith had been forced to resign from the Cabinet after her husband's purchase of pornographic films appeared on her parliamentary expenses. She had also falsely maintained that her main property was her sister's house in London, allowing her to claim tens of thousands of pounds of taxpayers' money for her family home in Worcestershire. In

2012, she had told the BBC: 'I don't think people who have been disgraced should go to the House of Lords.' Was her volte-face reflective of Starmer's own attitude to such matters?

Noses were also put out of joint when it became clear that at least thirteen loyal Labour MPs who had served in junior posts in opposition were to be overlooked. Instead, a string of new and untested MPs who were well known to Starmer and his inner circle were parachuted into favourable posts, prompting cries of nepotism. They included Starmer's longstanding aide Chris Ward. He became Starmer's parliamentary private secretary – the first step on the ministerial ladder, who is known as the Prime Minister's 'eyes and ears' on the back benches. Liam Conlon, the son of Starmer's chief of staff, Sue Gray, was made a PPS in the Department for Transport. Imogen Walker, the wife of Starmer's director of political strategy, Morgan McSweeney, was made a Treasury PPS. Olivia Bailey, another former aide to Starmer, was made a PPS at the Department for Work and Pensions. And Torsten Bell, a further Starmer ally, was made a PPS in the Cabinet Office. Other young new MPs with longstanding Labour connections were given more senior jobs. Hamish Falconer, the son of Lord Falconer, once Tony Blair's right-hand man, was made a minister in the Foreign Office. Georgia Gould, whose father, Philip Gould, was Tony Blair's chief strategist and whose mother, Lady Rebuck, is a Labour peer, became a Cabinet Office minister. (Gould's husband, Alex Zatman, is also a special adviser to Liz Kendall, the Secretary of State for Work and Pensions.) Kirsty McNeill, a charity executive who had served as a director of Center for Countering Digital Hate, an organisation closely linked to Labour Together and Morgan McSweeney, was despatched as a minister at the Scotland Office. And Sarah Sackman, who had worked closely with Starmer's friend Lord Hermer at Matrix Chambers, became Solicitor-General.

Neither was the supposedly impartial civil service immune from allegations of cronyism. Ian Corfield, a banker who had donated £5,000 to Rachel Reeves in August 2023 and £15,000 to other Labour MPs in previous years, was made a Treasury director. His job was not subject to an open contest and the Treasury did not tell the Civil Service Commission, which vets Whitehall appointments, about Corfield's donation to Reeves.

Within Downing Street, Starmer caused surprise – perhaps even alarm – among some who worked there thanks to his seemingly endless obsession with football. One source explains:

> Keir is so set in his ways. When he first came in, one of his diary people was putting all of the Arsenal games into his diary and a civil servant said, 'I wouldn't bother with that, there won't be time.' And this diary person said, 'No, he insists that they're in his diary.' It was an Outlook diary, blocking out the times when Arsenal matches were on.

This supports the view of some insiders who have spoken of a 'blokey' atmosphere among Starmer and his top team, including Morgan McSweeney, in which many conversations are based around football. Anybody who does not share that interest is unable to participate, as Sue Gray would discover. In some cases, they might even be overlooked.

Another source says of those early months that Starmer's default setting is one of reservation bordering on wariness when it comes to engaging with people, meaning that they in turn find it difficult to get to know him. 'Downing Street civil servants usually warm to the principal. Everybody is usually very keen to accommodate themselves to the boss. It's not about politics, it's just the way the building works. I was surprised by the lack of warmth towards Keir. It was quite striking.'

Starmer wasn't the only person in the building who was not universally popular. Reports surfaced that Morgan McSweeney's desk had been moved twice in two weeks, each time getting a little further away from his boss's office. Sue Gray was the chief suspect. Writing in the *New Statesman* on 25 July, the Labour-supporting journalist Kevin Maguire touched on the simmering 'turf war' between Gray and McSweeney. Maguire quoted an anonymous Labour veteran who said of Gray, 'She knows how government works and that is now nine-tenths of the job, so Gray will win.' This would turn out to be a brave prediction to commit to print.

By the end of July, Starmer had faced his first test of parliamentary authority when seven Labour MPs voted against the government on an SNP amendment to scrap the two-child benefit cap, which prevents most parents from claiming Universal Credit or Child Tax Credit for more than two children. The group – most of whom were close to Jeremy Corbyn – comprised John McDonnell, Richard Burgon, Ian Byrne, Rebecca Long-Bailey, Imran Hussain, Apsana Begum and Zarah Sultana. The amendment failed by 363 votes to 103, giving the government a majority of 260, but the truculent MPs were suspended for six months, having to sit as independents instead. Before the vote, McDonnell needled Starmer, saying, 'I don't like voting for other parties' amendments, but I'm following Keir Starmer's example, as he said put country before party.'

There were, however, other, more unexpected, moves afoot. On 21 July, it was announced by Home Secretary Yvette Cooper that the applications of 120,000 immigrants whom the Tory government had said would not be allowed to settle in Britain would now be processed. The Refugee Council said this could result in 70,000 people being granted asylum. The Conservatives believed the figure could be as high as 90,000 and labelled the plan an effective amnesty – an idea that had not featured in Labour's manifesto. And a few days later, thousands of free speech advocates and academics made public their concerns that Bridget Phillipson, the Education Secretary, had announced in a written statement that she had decided to 'stop further commencement of the Higher Education (Freedom of Speech) Act, in order to consider options, including its repeal'. This legislation had been due to come into force the following week and was intended to protect this crucial civil liberty from the creeping erosion to which it had been subjected in the past decade, empowering academics. Suspending it had not been in Labour's manifesto either.

The following week, Rachel Reeves made a Commons statement titled 'Public Spending: Inheritance' in which she said that a review of the public finances had unearthed a £22 billion 'hole'. The previous government was to blame, Reeves alleged. It was guilty of a 'cover-up'. From what she said, it was clear that this overspend would be used to justify tax rises in the next budget, which would take place on 30 October. She then explained that public sector pay would increase across the board. Most workers would receive an above-inflation salary hike of about 5.5 per cent. The wages of junior doctors would rise by 22 per cent over two years. Incredibly, there were no conditions attached. The Treasury calculated that these wage rises would cost the public purse an extra £9.4 billion. Such largesse had not been planned for in Labour's manifesto and this figure accounted for more than 40 per cent of the £22 billion hole that Reeves claimed she had discovered.

Reeves used her statement to discuss billions of pounds of savings that had to be made. They included ending the Rwanda scheme, scrapping transport projects and reviewing the new hospital programme. There would also be an immediate cut to winter fuel payments, worth between £200 and £300 per year per household, for all but the poorest pensioners. This would affect

10 million older people, some of whom were the most vulnerable in society. This unforeseen announcement, made just before recess, gave limited opportunity for parliamentary scrutiny, but MPs from every party plus charities, trade unions and welfare groups were furious when they heard of it, not least because the measure would save only £1.4 billion annually. Targeting pensioners was another course of action that had not been in Labour's manifesto. Indeed, it is noteworthy how few people seemed to be aware that this cut was on the cards, even at the centre of power. One source reports:

> I think people in Downing Street expected Keir to come in and know how he wanted to run things, but he didn't. He is quite suspicious of everybody – including civil servants. They were shut out of meetings. Keir keeps things very tight. Ed Miliband got very cross because he didn't know about the winter fuel cut. He started berating civil servants, but it turned out they didn't know either.

Responding for the Tories, Jeremy Hunt disputed the £22 billion figure, reminding everybody that Reeves had given a revealing interview to the *Financial Times* the previous month. The newspaper had noted that 'unlike previous incoming chancellors she would be unable to arrive at the Treasury and claim she had looked inside the books and realised things were even worse than they looked from the outside, giving a flimsy excuse for immediate tax rises or spending cuts'. Reeves had accepted the *FT*'s analysis, saying, 'We've got the OBR [fiscal watchdog] now. We know things are in a pretty bad state. You don't need to win an election to find that out.' Hunt also reminded her of the Treasury's £14 billion reserve for unexpected revenue costs and its £4 billion for unexpected capital costs, while pointing out its ability to manage down in-year pressures on the reserve. Sure enough, at the end of October 2024, when the OBR had completed a review, it found that £9.5 billion of additional spending pressures were anticipated by the Treasury but not made known to the watchdog – less than half the figure Reeves had quoted.

Looking back on Reeves's statement, Hunt says it is likely that Labour will use every opportunity it can to remind voters of the supposed £22 billion shortfall until the next general election, but he doubts that Starmer had much to do with it. 'My impression is he is hands-off. He left it to her,' says Hunt.

> They'd have agreed on the political strategy to land a narrative that they'd inherited a financial mess from the Tories, but she came in and said we'll accept £9.4 billion of pay awards with no questions asked. That was her decision. And she's counting that as part of the £22 billion. We said the year before, any departments that have pencilled in public sector pay awards of 2 per cent above inflation would have to find it themselves. So we found a different way of funding it. For political reasons, she wanted to thank public sector unions for their support in the election campaign. That was a choice. During her statement, Starmer was sitting next to her and I thought he looked extremely uncomfortable. To me, it looked like he knew perfectly well this was a fabrication. That's not the kind of politics he's comfortable with. I think he sees himself as a morally upright person who's come into politics to do the right thing. I think he's instinctively uncomfortable with falsehood.

It wasn't difficult either for voters to see that the winter fuel payment cut would fund a portion of the £9.4 billion being handed to those on taxpayer-funded salaries, some of whom had spent the previous two years striking intermittently. There was no dressing up the unpopularity of the decision, which has been widely criticised in the media ever since. Partly, this was because of the casual manner in which it was announced – there was no coherent communications plan behind it. But, more than that, it was taken as a worrying sign of things to come. Trust in Starmer and his government was diminished that day. The question for Labour MPs was whether the voters' faith could be recaptured.

• • •

Just a few hours before Reeves made her Commons statement, there was a mass stabbing in the northern town of Southport. Three children were killed and ten other people – eight of whom were children – were injured. Soon afterwards, the attacker was falsely identified online as an Islamist asylum seeker. This was the precursor to a week of riots in twenty-seven British towns and cities. The tragedy and its aftermath were a major test both for the police and for Starmer and his government, a fact that became apparent when, on 30 July, he visited Southport and was heckled by members of the public as he left a bunch of flowers in tribute. Solutions to a complicated set of problems about the state of Britain a quarter of the way through the twenty-first century were needed. The question is whether Starmer acknowledged meaningfully enough the root causes of those problems.

Some of the rioters were opportunists who hijacked the tragedy, using it as a reason to loot shops and damage property, but if any single issue united many of the others who took part in these generally spontaneous violent protests, it was a response to mass immigration. Far-right extremists set upon hotels in which asylum seekers were living, attacked mosques and assaulted police officers. Merseyside Police and government ministers stated that the incident was not being treated as terror-related, but no agency would confirm if the perpetrator was an asylum seeker. It was three days before he was named as Axel Rudakubana, a seventeen-year-old who was born in Cardiff to Rwandan parents.

In the immediate aftermath of the attacks, experienced legal minds criticised the delay in naming Rudakubana. Among them was Jonathan Hall KC, the government's terrorism tsar. In September 2024, Hall told a conference organised by the Counter Extremism Group think tank, 'One of the problems and the consequences of the Southport attack was that there was an information gap, a vacuum, which was filled with false speculation.' He added, 'I personally think that more information could have been put out safely without compromising potential criminal proceedings.'

In many ways the crisis played to Starmer's strengths. His background as the man who had run the CPS when the last major riots had taken place in 2011 came to the fore. It was second nature to him to engage with the police and to assess how the criminal justice system could be used to its best effect. He and his ministers said in interviews that agitators would face the full force of the law immediately. Their words were bolstered by Stephen Parkinson, the Director of Public Prosecutions, and Sir Mark Rowley, the Metropolitan Police Commissioner.

On 2 August, a new National Violent Disorder Programme was announced, allowing police to share intelligence on known violent groups. Facial recognition technology would also be used more widely. On 4 August, Starmer made a statement from Downing Street in which he lambasted the 'far-right thuggery' that had been seen. Yet pleas from some MPs to recall Parliament went unheeded. And on 8 August, when asked by a reporter whether he should engage with underlying unease over immigration, Starmer did not answer. Some found his refusal to discuss the issue curious. Britain's population had increased by almost 10 million since the late 1990s, with almost 1 million legal immigrants arriving in 2023 alone. Illegal immigration had also risen sharply since 2018. Britain's public services were under significant strain and communities in some areas were badly fractured. It was apparent that some protesters felt bitter resentment towards the political class. Some thoughtful politicians believed that behind the rioters stood millions of quieter, non-violent citizens whose anti-immigration opinions were just as strong. Their views on immigration levels in Britain had simply never been sought or addressed.

Starmer has always been conflicted on this issue. In January 2020, he said:

> We need to make the wider case on immigration. We welcome migrants, we don't scapegoat them. Low wages, poor housing, poor public services are not the fault of people who come here: they're political failure. So we have to make the case for the benefits of migration; for the benefits of free movement.

And yet Labour's latest manifesto had accepted legal immigration was too high and promised to cut it. He would also have known that Tony Blair had recently urged him in a *Sunday Times* article to be tough. 'We need a plan to control immigration. If we don't have rules, we get prejudices,' Blair had written. If this was an opportunity for a wider national debate, it was in danger of being squandered. The Tory MP Sir John Hayes was blunt in his assessment. 'There's been too much immigration in this country for too long and a huge proportion of the population knows that,' he told the *Daily Mail*. 'So there are underlying tensions, fears and problems. And now that the thuggery and crime seems to have abated, we need to have a measured national conversation about that and I'm amazed that that's not recognised by the government.'

At the time, Starmer was said to be reluctant to discuss what lay behind the unrest for fear of appearing to justify it. Having cancelled a family holiday to demonstrate that he was still in charge of the response, he could never be accused of not having taken the riots seriously. But it is at least arguable that he appeared to duck the broader issue to focus instead on contemporaneous events. Yet this approach also incited an atmosphere of mistrust. Following an emergency meeting on 6 August, Starmer gave a broadcast interview in which he said, 'I'm now expecting substantive sentencing' for those involved in the riots 'before the end of this week'. Who can know what pressure his statement put on the judges who were tasked with hearing those cases? It seems at least possible that they felt as though they had been leant upon by the Prime Minister, who was watching and – in his word – 'expecting'. Equally significantly, the Home Office put out a tweet a few days later to say there had been 'more than 1,000 arrests related to recent public disorder' and stated, 'These criminals will face the full force of the law.' This message was prejudicial seeing as not all of those arrested had faced trial and so were not in fact 'criminals'.

Starmer also came in for criticism over what some perceived to be the double standards of the criminal justice system. Figures released by the National Police Chiefs' Council showed the scale of the disorder and the rapid response to it. By the end of August, 1,280 people had been arrested, 796 of whom had been charged. Separate government figures confirmed that, as of 2 September, 570 people had appeared in court. The culprits were not just rioters, though. They also included those who had not committed violent offences, such as Julie Sweeney, who posted a comment on a Facebook community group. In response to a photograph which showed people clearing up after a riot in Southport, Sweeney, fifty-three, wrote: 'It's absolutely ridiculous. Don't protect the mosques. Blow the mosque up with the adults in it.' Her words were impossible to defend, but many thought the same was true of the fifteen-month prison sentence she received. Lord Hermer, the Attorney General, had given his consent to charge people for stirring up racial hatred online.

Cases such as Sweeney's had motivated Starmer to warn social media companies and those who run them that violent disorder had been whipped up online. 'That is also a crime,' he said. 'It is happening on your premises, and the law must be upheld everywhere.' In fact, this fuelled accusations of so-called 'two-tier' policing, in which the forces of law and order are said to be more sympathetic to supporters of left-wing causes such as Black Lives Matter – which triggered violent demonstrations in London in June 2020 – than they are to right-wing causes. This perception led to Starmer being nicknamed 'Two-Tier Keir'.

One person who used that moniker against him was the American tech tycoon Elon Musk. Over several days he took to his Twitter account – which has more than 200 million followers – to engage in a war of words with Starmer. Musk responded to a video of the riots to say, 'If incompatible cultures are brought together without assimilation, conflict is inevitable.' When Starmer stated on Twitter, 'We will not tolerate attacks on mosques or on Muslim communities,' Musk goaded him. 'Shouldn't you be concerned about attacks on *all* communities?' he asked. Another reposted video appeared to show police officers arresting a man for making offensive comments on Facebook. 'Arrested for making comments on Facebook!' Musk exclaimed. 'Is this Britain or the Soviet Union?' And he posted another video showing crowds of masked people in a British street, some waving the Palestinian flag. 'Why aren't all communities protected in Britain?' he demanded.

There were consequences to this rather strange spat in which Starmer was portrayed as a leader with authoritarian instincts. To the dismay of many Britons who operate in the business arena, in October 2024 Musk – reputedly the richest man in the world – was the most notable absentee from the British government's International Investment Summit. The BBC reported that he had not been invited because of his provocative exchanges with Starmer, among other controversial posts he had published. Until then, there had been talk of Musk opening a gigafactory in Britain. This plan had supposedly been jettisoned by Musk as a result of the snub. Musk, who allies say is driven by a desire to protect freedom of speech, responded, 'I don't think anyone should go to the UK when they're releasing convicted paedophiles in order to imprison people for social media posts.'

Starmer did touch upon immigration in his Labour conference speech in September 2024, and he spoke of the riots. 'I have always accepted concerns about immigration are legitimate,' he said.

> But whatever anyone thinks about immigration, I will never accept the argument made not just by the usual suspects, but by people who should have known better, who said that millions of people concerned about immigration are one and the same thing as the people who smashed up businesses. Who targeted mosques. Attempted to burn refugees. Scrawled racist graffiti over walls. Nazi salutes at the cenotaph. Attacked NHS nurses. And told people with different coloured skin, people who contribute here, people who grew up here, that they should 'go home'. No – people concerned about immigration were not doing that because they understand that this country, this democratic country, is built on the rule of law.

To some, though, Starmer's view was just too narrow. The argument being advanced by figures including Sir John Hayes was that the riots were a manifestation of deeper frustrations, even if most people who felt antagonised by immigration did not act upon their feelings. Having just arrived in Downing Street, and having once been the DPP, there was an idea that Starmer was ideally placed to order an investigation into the causes of the civil unrest. In 1981, Lord Scarman had chaired a public inquiry into the Brixton riots. His report was influential, ushering in measures that improved relations between ethnic minorities and the police. That Starmer chose not to commission a similar type of review – perhaps on a cross-party basis – risked distancing him from the very communities whose interests he said he wanted to represent.

Shortly after the riots subsided, Starmer found himself in another predicament, this time one that was more damaging to him personally. On 25 August, the *Sunday Times* revealed that Lord Alli, Labour's chief fundraiser, had been given a pass allowing him unrestricted access to 10 Downing Street. As Alli had no official position in public life, this arrangement was highly irregular. It was also reported that he had helped to organise a post-election party in the Downing Street garden. Well-placed sources insisted that the pass had been temporary, but they refused to elaborate. Pat McFadden, the Cabinet minister who invariably speaks for the government in times of trouble, told Times Radio, 'He's not doing a job in Downing Street. I think he had a pass briefly. He's not involved in any government or policy decisions.' These words failed to kill the problem. For one thing, there was no explanation of who had sanctioned the pass or why. For another, the media had already launched its own inquest into Alli's financial relationship with Labour. It was known that Starmer had received thousands of pounds' worth of clothing and glasses from Alli, but it soon turned out that the Prime Minister's wife and several Cabinet ministers were very much in the peer's debt as well. Here was a story – initially dubbed 'passes for glasses' – that not only bore the hallmarks of a conflict of interests but was laced with what many politicians and voters took to be sheer greed on the Starmers' part. Furthermore, it left Keir Starmer open to charges of hypocrisy, for he had spent the previous few years denouncing the Conservatives for corruption and promising to clean up politics. This marked the start of a tense chapter, as sleaze claims stubbornly refused to disappear. Showing a worrying incoherence of approach, Starmer would take weeks to work out how to defuse the situation.

Forty-eight hours after the *Sunday Times* exclusive, Starmer delivered his first set-piece speech. The venue was the Downing Street garden, chosen to remind voters that under the Tories it had been used for lockdown parties several years previously. 'Remember the pictures just over there?' Starmer asked his audience. 'With the wine and the food? Well, this garden and this building are now back in your service.' Ironically, of course, the garden was by then also known as the venue of Labour's recent victory party, as organised by Starmer's fundraiser cum fashion adviser Lord Alli, in an affair that was growing murkier by the day. That fact seemed not to have occurred to whoever had the idea to use the garden as a stage.

The subject of his speech was 'fixing the foundations of our country'. He spoke of a 'deep rot at the heart' of Britain. The riots proved there was not just an economic black hole but 'a societal black hole too'. The UK was a 'deeply unhealthy society'. Having gained power, Labour had discovered that 'things are worse than we ever imagined' and 'will get worse before they get better'. He also cautioned, 'There's a budget coming in October and it's going to be painful.'

Was it necessary – or responsible – to be so pessimistic, some wondered? Hadn't Labour been elected promising hope and change? When asked about Alli and the lengthening shadow of cronyism, Starmer batted away any suggestion of wrongdoing.

> These allegations and these accusations are coming from the very people that dragged our country down in the first place, so you'll forgive me if I take that approach to it ... I'm not really going to take lectures on this from the people who dragged our country so far down in the last few years.

He said Alli was a long-term donor who had done some 'transition work' but who no longer had a pass. This defensive stance only ensured the story would run for longer.

Having delivered the speech, Starmer flew to Berlin for two days of meetings with Olaf Scholz. Foreign policy and economic matters were on the agenda, as they hoped to agree a new treaty as part of Starmer's efforts to strengthen post-Brexit ties with EU states. From Germany, Starmer went on to Paris for forty-eight hours to watch the opening ceremony of the Olympic Games and to hold talks with President Macron. However constructive these trips might have seemed to the PM, they were soon obscured by Tom Baldwin, his biographer, revealing at a Glasgow literary festival that Starmer had removed from his Downing Street study a portrait of the woman he had praised in print just a few months before, Margaret Thatcher. The portrait, painted by Richard Stone, had been commissioned by the former Labour premier Gordon Brown in 2007 and depicts Thatcher just after the Falklands War in 1982. When it was put to Starmer by the BBC that this was a petty decision, he explained somewhat bizarrely that he had got rid of it only because he doesn't like 'pictures of people staring down at me'. It is said to have been hung elsewhere in Downing Street.

If Baldwin's gossipy tale was supposed to distract journalists from the Lord Alli row, it did not succeed. It had been established that the businessman had given about £700,000 to Labour since becoming a peer in 1998. Much of that money had been donated since 2020 – including, as previously described, £100,000 that went to Starmer's leadership campaign. He had also donated £10,000 to Starmer in October 2023 and £6,000 in February 2024 – though initially it was not clear what this money was for – plus, in April 2024, £16,200 of 'work clothing' and 'multiple pairs of glasses' worth £2,485. Starmer had also accepted unspecified 'accommodation' from Alli between 29 May and 13 July, a benefit valued at £20,437.28. Alli had therefore given Starmer more than £155,000 in the space of four years. Separately, he had lent his £2 million New York flat to Angela Rayner for five nights in December 2023 and contributed to her office almost £20,000 of undefined 'support'. At this point it was also known that five-figure sums had been advanced by Alli to the Education Secretary, Bridget Phillipson and to the Foreign Secretary, David Lammy. The new Labour MP Liam Conlon, son of Sue Gray, had received £10,000. Over the next four weeks, journalists mined this deepening pit, unearthing new facts about these and other donations.

One Downing Street veteran explains that the value of privileged access to Alli was potentially enormous. 'If you've got a Downing Street pass, you can wander around the building and you will hear a huge amount,' says this person.

> The reason Cabinet ministers don't have a Downing Street pass is that the PM and his team want to know when Cabinet

> ministers are entering the building so that everyone knows to shut up and not talk about the fact, let's say, that there's a chance this or that Cabinet minister's favourite project is going to be axed. When you're there, people will say, 'X is coming in at this time, be aware,' because you don't want people being loose-lipped. When you wander around the building, you hear so much. The level of information you can pick up by dint of being present is huge. That's why the Alli story was so big.

On 5 September, Bloomberg made the running by revealing that Alli had been working with senior officials for months on a secret project called Operation Integrity, drawing up a list of candidates to fill Cabinet posts and to chair the boards and non-executive directorships of government departments. By then, Starmer was back on the road, this time flying to Dublin for talks with the Taoiseach, Simon Harris. He then watched England versus Ireland in a UEFA Nations League football match. A day later, he gave his first major interview since becoming Prime Minister. The BBC programme *Sunday with Laura Kuenssberg* was furnished with this exclusive. Most conveniently for Starmer, Alli's name was not even mentioned. Instead, the conversation stayed fixed on the riots, the far right, the Grenfell disaster, Ukraine and the difficulties of his political inheritance. He said he was prepared to accept the cost of power, adding, 'We're going to have to be unpopular. Tough decisions are tough decisions.' But some of those who listened to what he said felt his message simply echoed the doom-and-gloom forecasts of the previous two months, with the upshot being a diminishing confidence among businesses. 'Sir Keir claims to want to turbocharge growth, but why would anyone choose to invest in a country described by its own leader as essentially a basket case?' asked the *Daily Mail* the next day. Jenni Russell, the *Times* columnist who describes herself as a

'Labour-inclined voter', complained that the 'miserabilist message' was not what people had voted for. Labour's plan was, seemingly, to blame the Tories for as long as possible.

Another pressing topic that was absent from Kuenssberg's 25-minute interview came to the fore forty-eight hours later when around 1,750 prisoners in England and Wales were released early. This emergency scheme, allowing certain categories of criminals to be freed up to seventy days before the end of their sentence in order to create space on the prison estate, had been in place under the Conservatives. Yet Starmer had been critical of it as recently as May, lambasting Rishi Sunak for endangering the public by not being able to say what type of prisoners were being released. Its continuation under Labour was yet another decision that took voters by surprise, for it had not featured in the party's manifesto, which had promised a 'safe, secure, law-abiding society' in which 'criminals will be punished'. Moreover, the release terms were relaxed further under Labour, with offenders serving less than five years being freed after completing just 40 per cent of their sentence, rather than the usual 50 per cent. Lowering the bar to this level during the premiership of a former DPP ensured Starmer came in for a series of stinging attacks. Worse, for him, was the behaviour of the released prisoners themselves. Some opened bottles of champagne in celebration. Others drove away in expensive sports cars. One, a drug dealer called Djaber Benallaoua, who was forgiven the last six months of his sentence at HMP Isis, a Category C young offenders institution in Thamesmead, announced, 'I'm a lifelong Labour voter now.' With more than 10,000 foreign prisoners in England and Wales – 12 per cent of the prison population – critics suggested that the Justice Secretary, Shabana Mahmood, should deport some of them instead of releasing British convicts.

That day, it wasn't only Starmer's opponents who made their

feelings known about one of his policies. The Tories had secured a parliamentary vote to try to reverse the cut to the winter fuel allowance. It failed by 348 to 228. This was an unsurprisingly comfortable win for the government, but what concerned Downing Street was that one Labour MP, Jon Trickett, voted with the Tories and fifty-two others abstained. Some of them were absent with permission, but coming so soon after a landslide victory, common opinion settled on the notion that rolling out this policy to save £1.4 billion per year had been an error.

While the Lord Alli matter continued to generate questions, the finances of the Labour Party itself came under scrutiny. Official figures showed that it had raised £26 million in the run-up to the general election, over 50 per cent more than the Tories. Trade unions had come up with £5.6 million, but those with an interest in green affairs had donated even more generously. Some £2 million came via the firm Ecotricity, founded by the environmental campaigner Dale Vince. He had formerly bankrolled Just Stop Oil, the protest group notorious for using civil disobedience to promote its aims. Another donor was Quadrature Capital, a Cayman Islands-based hedge fund dedicated to addressing climate change. The party had accepted £4 million from this source on 28 May. It was the biggest single donation in Labour's history and on that basis alone it would have attracted media attention – had anybody known about it. In fact, thanks to the peculiar rules of the Election Commission, it was possible for it to remain secret until after every vote had been cast and counted on 4 July.

The reason for this was that only gifts and loans of more than £11,180 that were received by parties from 30 May – the day on which Parliament was dissolved – had to be declared on a weekly basis during the campaign. By accepting Quadrature's donation forty-eight hours earlier than the cut-off date, Labour avoided having to field questions about its generous new sponsor. After the gift was publicly disclosed, there was scepticism about its origin and the timing of Labour's declaration. Having gone through Quadrature's latest available accounts, which showed that during 2022/23 it paid tax of £5.3 million on profits of £231 million, ITV's political editor Robert Peston noted, 'There will be Labour members and supporters who will be surprised and disappointed that the party is funded by a business that pays considerably less in tax than the official rate.' Would Labour have faced tough questions if it had admitted during the campaign that it had banked Quadrature's money? And whose idea was it to conceal Quadrature's donation from the electorate during the campaign? Those with longer memories recalled that, as mentioned in Chapter 12, Starmer had shown a similar lack of candour during his 2020 leadership campaign when he had refused to reveal his donations contemporaneously, as his rival candidates Lisa Nandy and Rebecca Long-Bailey did. Instead, he had only revealed his backers – who included Lord Alli – via the MPs' register of financial interests after voting had taken place. Quadrature Capital itself explained its £4 million was a 'values-based donation, not a political donation'. This was language – some might call it doublespeak – that was well understood by Labour's eco-fundamentalist Energy Secretary Ed Miliband. His plans to spend tens of billions of public money on carbon capture machines, wind turbines and solar panels were endorsed by his close friend Keir Starmer.

After a brief trip to Washington on 13 September to discuss the wars in Gaza and Ukraine, Starmer returned to Britain and with his wife, Victoria, went to Doncaster racecourse to watch the St Leger Stakes. As they walked through the parade ring, some of the crowd swore and shouted abuse at them, including complaints about the winter fuel allowance cut. The couple appeared to laugh it off, but hours later the *Sunday Times* broke fresh ground on the Lord Alli story by revealing that in June 2024 Victoria had accepted £6,134 of gifts from him. The funds had supplied her with a personal shopper, clothes and alterations. This had not been revealed to the parliamentary authorities within twenty-eight days, as it should have been. The next day, David Lammy, the Foreign Secretary, told the BBC that Starmer had accepted Alli's donations because he and his wife wanted to 'look their best' on behalf of the British public. Lammy claimed – wrongly – that in America the First Lady receives a clothing allowance and implied that one should be available in Britain. More interesting was that, despite growing public anger at what had now come to be known as Freebiegate, another guest on the programme, Piers Morgan, revealed he had been in touch with Starmer the night before. Based on what Morgan said, it seemed that Starmer was not overly preoccupied by what was being written about him. He was more interested in the Tottenham versus Arsenal football match that was to be played that afternoon. 'I can tell you the Prime Minister has a vested interest [in the match],' Morgan boasted. 'He asked me last night – he texted me to say "Are you going to the big game?"'

The next day Starmer was in Italy for a meeting with Giorgia Meloni to discuss Ukraine and people-smuggling gangs, but in a sure sign that Downing Street's PR machine had broken down, Victoria Starmer appeared at an event that morning to mark London Fashion Week. She wore more 'gifted' clothing in the form of a £1,200 dress she had borrowed from the designer Edeline Lee. Under the circumstances, this was seen as tin-eared, possibly even aggravating the situation. Sky News calculated that Starmer had accepted £107,000 of gifts, benefits and hospitality since 2019 – two and a half times more than the next MP, Labour's Lucy Powell. As well as attending Wimbledon and accepting a £4,500 holiday in Wales courtesy of businessman Rod Lloyd, he had taken £40,000 of football tickets alone. The Premier League had given him £12,588 of gifts to various events, including the Taylor Swift concert he had attended in June. This was relevant because Premier League bosses were at that time lobbying against having a football regulator foisted upon them by the government. ITV News also reported that he had been allowed the use of a corporate box all to himself by Arsenal, worth £8,750 per game. Starmer told the BBC that he had to use the box for security reasons. Rachel Reeves was then dragged into the row after the *Financial Times* reported that she had received £7,500 for clothing from Juliet Rosenfeld, a Labour donor.

On 18 September, it transpired that Victoria Starmer – who had accompanied her husband to the Taylor Swift concert at Wembley stadium in June – had returned there to watch another of the American singer's concerts free of charge, this time without the Prime Minister, on 15 August. Other Labour MPs in attendance that night included Health Secretary Wes Streeting, Education Secretary Bridget Phillipson and Culture Secretary Lisa Nandy. They had not had to pay either. Phillipson justified the tickets on the grounds that they were 'hard to turn down' and one of her children was 'keen to go along' to see the pop star perform.

The narrative then changed direction after the BBC reported that Sue Gray was being paid £170,000 per year – £3,000 more than Starmer himself. One source dripped poison by whispering, 'It was suggested that she might want to go for a few thousand pounds less than the Prime Minister to avoid this very story. She declined.' That this information was passed to the state broadcaster surprised Whitehall veterans, who took it as proof of the noxious atmosphere at the heart of Starmer's government after less than three months in power. 'The bitchiness was incredible,' says one.

> Whoever leaked it was intent on damaging Starmer because Sue Gray was his pick. You wouldn't have expected it to happen so quickly. Labour loyalists hated her because she arrived late in the project when Labour were 3–0 up, tapped in a fourth goal and was running round like she was the player of the match. The age difference didn't help. Her rivals were younger and have a different demeanour.

Yet the fact that Starmer had cleared Gray's salary surely showed a lack of political nous on his part. He certainly felt sensitivity about the matter. In a highly unusual move, the Prime Minister secretly recruited Simon Case, the Cabinet Secretary, to try to strangle the story before it became public. Starmer asked Case to contact the BBC to lobby them against broadcasting it. Chris Mason, the corporation's political editor, and Tim Davie, its director general, were both approached. Of course, the fact that a journalist was in effect being asked to censor a report about a publicly funded salary only made it more likely that the information would be aired. When Mason's story duly appeared, Starmer looked twice as foolish: first because the public now knew that Gray was paid more than him; and secondly because those operating in media circles now knew him as a Prime Minister linked to a clumsy scheme of suppression. When the story about Case contacting the BBC became public in February 2025, Starmer's reputation as a meddler was cemented.

By the autumn of 2024, Gray had been causing other problems for Starmer. The *Mail on Sunday* reported that she was preventing him from receiving crucial security briefings, insisting that she be told instead of him. And *The Times* reported that she had been 'subverting' Cabinet ministers by 'personally dominating' talks to try to push the government to fund a £310 million development of the Casement Park stadium in Belfast. When asked about this at a press conference in the city, Starmer snapped that it was 'nonsense'. Few believed him. Gray's connections to Ulster are strong: having been a civil servant since the 1970s, she rose to become the permanent secretary at the Department of Finance in Northern Ireland. And in the 1980s she took a career break to run the Cove Bar, a pub outside Newry, close to the border with the Republic of Ireland. This unorthodox aspect of her CV provoked talk that she had been a spy, a charge she has publicly denied.

Another reason for the animus towards Gray was the intensifying fury in Labour circles that Freebiegate had been allowed to take on a life of its own. Most of the handouts in question had been declared within parliamentary rules, but no thought had been given to public perception. Starmer's friends have said that he was lulled into a false sense of security having recorded the gifts with the Commons authorities and did not anticipate the higher level of testing he would face in government compared with opposition. If true, it shows that he was very poorly advised. For a sitting Labour Prime Minister and his wife to have accepted thousands of pounds' worth of presents shortly before the government cut pensioners' winter fuel allowance was impossible to reconcile. Many believed that Gray should have instructed Starmer not to accept any of Alli's charity. That he had done so, and that she had failed to see off the story, was considered unforgivable. Some in Labour – not least Morgan McSweeney – thought she should be fired. What had begun as a whispering campaign against her in July had turned into something closer to open warfare by September.

But it would surely be wrong to single out Gray for criticism. During this fraught time, many people asked why Starmer – a well-off lawyer with no significant overheads and with his own special pension scheme – should have wanted Alli to buy his and his wife's clothes. Indeed, over the summer Starmer paid off the mortgage on his £2 million London house, giving him even more financial freedom compared with most people, and began renting it out for something in the region of £5,000 per month. Others remembered the righteous indignation he had shown over the so-called Wallpapergate episode, involving the £112,000 refurbishment of Boris Johnson's Downing Street flat. On that occasion, it became apparent that, initially, a Conservative Party donor, Lord Brownlow, had secretly covered the cost of the work before Johnson repaid the funds out of his own pocket. That had been enough for Starmer to demand a formal inquiry into whether Johnson should face criminal proceedings.

One former Downing Street aide says:

> During the first 100 days, Starmer was nowhere near as well briefed in meetings as other PMs are and you can see a lack of focus as well by the mess he got into over Freebiegate. The usual thing to do would be to get all the bad news out at once. But the story kept moving. More and more came to light. For someone who was so pious towards Boris, it's incredible that he didn't realise Alli's donations were going to be a problem. And it's amazing how many veteran Labour figures are still baffled by it. Even people who are quite friendly with Lord Alli still don't understand why Starmer and his wife took so much stuff.

While Gray captured headlines, Freebiegate questions persisted. ITV Scotland cleverly spliced the issue with the winter fuel cut, asking Starmer, 'You earn £167,000 a year. If you need help buying your wardrobe, why shouldn't pensioners on £13,000 get help with their heating?' He offered no convincing answer.

Jonathan Reynolds, the Business Secretary, told Times Radio he had 'no objection' to Starmer receiving free gifts, insisting he deserved 'a little bit of relaxation'. But the former Labour MP Harriet Harman was incredulous, telling Sky News, 'I think doubling down and trying to justify it is making things worse.' Voters seemed to agree. A Survation poll for the *Daily Mail* on the eve of the Labour conference found that Starmer's personal approval rating had dropped from +13 after the election to −13 – a fall of twenty-six points. And 52 per cent of respondents said Labour had not met their expectations.

As delegates gathered in Liverpool on 22 September, Starmer posed for photographs with Prince, a rare breed Siberian kitten worth £1,500 that he gave to his children. The family already had another cat and so did Downing Street in the form of Larry, chief mouser to the Cabinet Office, who has lived in No. 10 since being adopted from Battersea Dogs & Cats Home in 2011. One source claims that Prince is not allowed out of the Starmers' Downing Street flat 'or else Larry, who can be aggressive, would eat him'. Neither has it always been possible for the Starmers to leave their cats in Downing Street alone when they go away, for example to stay at the Prime Minister's country retreat, Chequers. Another source reports that they have been transported there with the family at taxpayers' expense in a chauffeur-driven special protection vehicle, surely making them the best guarded animals in Britain.

The *Mail on Sunday*, like every other media outlet, was unaware of this. That day its interest lay in Lord Alli's £14,000 contribution towards two events to mark the fortieth birthday of the Education Secretary, Bridget Phillipson, in late 2023. Receipt of the funds had been recorded in the MPs' register of interests, but Phillipson had merely said that they covered 'a number of events, including on behalf of the shadow education team'. This story guaranteed that Freebiegate would be a feature of the event that was supposed to mark the first autumn for fifteen years that Labour was in government, dampening celebrations. Sue Gray, pointedly, did not attend, though Lord Alli did.

In his conference speech, Starmer made no mention of Alli or of the controversy. Indeed, even if he had done so, it is debatable whether most people would have been paying attention. Few were able to get past the point early on in his address when he demanded the 'return of the sausages' being held by Hamas. He had meant to say 'return of the hostages'. He was embarrassed again on 25 September when a non-binding conference vote tabled by the trade union Unite calling on ministers to reverse the winter fuel payment cut was passed. Cheers rang out in the conference hall. Unite's general secretary, Sharon Graham, laid into Starmer, saying, 'I do not understand how our new Labour government can cut the winter fuel allowance for pensioners and leave the super-rich untouched. This is not what people voted for. It is the wrong decision and needs to be reversed.' Above and beyond Freebiegate, disquiet about Starmer's leadership was evident. Who in his Cabinet was a true figure of the left, they wondered, as they contemplated the narrow centre of power that existed under him.

Starmer had left Liverpool before the conference ended formally, bound for New York, where he would attend the seventy-ninth United Nations General Assembly and address the United Nations Security Council. Before his plane took off, he gave an interview to Nick Ferrari of LBC in which he refused to apologise for Freebiegate, saying that no rules had been broken. Smiling throughout, he seemed almost amused by the questions Ferrari asked him. 'People come forward and say "I can help" and [they] make a donation,' he explained.

In this particular case it was a Labour peer so he's got nothing

> to gain. He just wanted us to win the election. That's why he did it … That was in opposition, we're now in government and therefore you won't be seeing any declarations from me in relation to clothing now we're in government. We've turned a page.

In New York, he and David Lammy had dinner with the Republican presidential candidate Donald Trump, who was preparing to contest the US election six weeks later. It was the first time they had ever met. Trump's friend Nigel Farage says the event was somewhat flat. 'I heard they didn't exactly hit it off,' reports Farage with a wink. 'There was no enmity in the room, but they have absolutely nothing in common. Trump will know that Starmer is, or has been, anti-monarchy and profoundly atheist. I think these things may matter to Trump more than Starmer realises.'

The Freebiegate row wasn't over and, according to Beth Rigby, the political editor of Sky News, it had rattled Starmer by now. When she interviewed him in New York, she suggested that his fondness for free gifts was evidence of his being 'continuity [Boris] Johnson'. Reflecting later on the way he reacted to this proposition, Rigby alluded to the flash of quiet anger for which Starmer has become well known. 'He was absolutely furious with me,' she reported. 'It was really uncomfortable.'

When the BBC pushed him to divulge more about the £20,000 of accommodation that he had accepted from Lord Alli between 29 May and 13 July, he revealed it had been necessary to move out of the family home in north London so that his son could revise for his GCSE exams 'without being disturbed' by journalists. 'Somebody then offered me accommodation where we could do that. I took that up and it was the right thing to do,' he argued. This did not go down well. Some journalists doubted the veracity of the story, pointing out that in England the first GCSE exam was on 9 May and the final one on 19 June. In other words, the exams had begun three weeks before the Starmers relocated to Alli's flat and finished more than three weeks before they vacated it. Others branded Starmer a hypocrite for using a handout to enhance his son's educational progress while preparing to impose VAT on private school fees. A further group of observers suggested he had used his son, over whom he is fiercely protective, to try to shut down the row and thought it would have been less elaborate to say that his family had needed some privacy. Joan Smith, an author and Labour voter who had met Starmer in the past, wrote disobligingly about him in the *Daily Mail*:

> Each day, it becomes clearer that the country is in the hands of a man without a shred of emotional intelligence. He keeps telling us the economy is in a dire state. It's doom and gloom for most of us, but not for Starmer and his family. Clothes and glasses for himself, clothes for his wife, a box at his favourite football club, the use of a luxury flat in central London – it's been one freebie after another.

This was a theme that Rosie Duffield, the Labour MP for Canterbury, seized upon. On 28 September, she quit the party to sit as an independent in what is thought to have been the speediest resignation following an election in the modern era. In her letter, published in the *Sunday Times*, Duffield condemned Starmer's 'cruel and unnecessary' policies and said Freebiegate proved that among his Cabinet 'sleaze, nepotism and apparent avarice are off the scale'. She wrote that she was 'so ashamed of what you and your inner circle have done to tarnish and humiliate our once proud party'. She went on:

> As Prime Minister, your managerial style and technocratic approach, and lack of basic politics and political instincts,

> have come crashing down on us as a party after we worked so hard, promised so much, and waited a long fourteen years to be mandated by the British public to return to power. Since the change of government in July, the revelations of hypocrisy have been staggering and increasingly outrageous. I cannot put into words how angry I and my colleagues are at your total lack of understanding about how you have made us all appear.

Remarkably, there was still some life left in the Freebiegate saga. At the very end of the month, *The Guardian*, which had already chastised Starmer for the affair, calling it an 'avoidable and self-inflicted wound', broke another story in the same vein. The £16,000 that Alli had donated to Starmer in two tranches in October 2023 and February 2024 had come in the form of clothes yet had been registered using the opaque language that it was an unspecified gift 'for the private office of the leader of the opposition'. In other words, Starmer had not wanted anybody to know what the money was used for when he registered it. Now it was undeniable that the total amount of free clothing that Alli had given Starmer came to £32,200, based on the parliamentary register. Starmer has never revealed what clothes Alli's money bought, nor where they came from. It has been suggested that a number of suits were purchased, yet even a high-end London tailor would be unlikely to charge much more than £5,000 per suit. Was Starmer really the proud possessor of six of Savile Row's finest examples? It didn't look like it. And, puzzlingly, Charlotte Edwardes, the *Guardian* interviewer who had trailed him during the general election campaign, had been told that his suits came from the midmarket retailer Charles Tyrwhitt, where they cost about £500 each.

What was wrong with Starmer's own wardrobe anyway? Those searching for an answer may recall a conversation on Times Radio in March 2024 about the importance of politicians' appearances. One participant was Peter Mandelson, Labour's former spin doctor and a good friend of Lord Alli. He had said that clothes were 'not unimportant' for politicians and observed that 'Starmer needs to shed a few pounds and that would be an improvement'. This barb apparently persuaded Starmer to brush up his image, a project that Lord Alli was only too happy to oversee.

On 2 October, the increasingly beleaguered Prime Minister visited Brussels to meet the European Commission President Ursula von der Leyen. The purpose of this trip – his tenth foreign visit in ninety days – was to establish a 'more pragmatic and mature relationship' with the EU following Brexit. While there, he conceded that he had decided to pay back £6,000 of the gifts that he and his wife had accepted, covering six Taylor Swift tickets, four tickets to the races and a clothing rental agreement with Edeline Lee. He said new principles for donations would be introduced. 'I took the decision that until those principles were in place it was right to repay these particular payments,' he said. This caused bewilderment. Why didn't he repay every penny that he had accepted – or nothing at all? Didn't this partial repayment breathe new life into a story that had almost expired? And shouldn't his Cabinet colleagues who had accepted gifts also repay money? In his *Daily Mail* column, Boris Johnson asked, 'What is the logic of this £6,000 refund? Where is it supposed to leave the rest of the freeboholic Labour front bench?'

There was one further significant bump in the road as Starmer approached his 100th day in office. On 6 October, a week before that milestone was reached, Sue Gray resigned as his chief of staff, saying she 'risked becoming a distraction' to the government. Accepting her resignation was a gamble for Starmer. Her departure was an acknowledgement that she had lost the 'turf war' with Morgan McSweeney, who replaced her. As Gray was one of

Starmer's key confidantes, and because he had been among the last members of his top team to conclude that she had to go, his own authority was obviously diminished by her decision. Now he was open to accusations of governing with the permission of his remaining younger advisers, such as McSweeney. Yet he had no time to lose. A relaunch was initiated in which four staff were hired or given new roles. James Lyons would oversee strategic communications; Vidhya Alakeson and Jill Cuthbertson became deputy chiefs of staff; and Nin Pandit stepped in as a new principal private secretary.

Having spoken to sources with knowledge of how Downing Street operated during this period, it is clear that behind the scenes there was not only tension but also dysfunction. 'Civil servants said that both Starmer and Gray being in their sixties was a problem,' explains one source.

> The physical pace of the job meant they both struggled. Sometimes they didn't eat properly. They were too tired. If one of them had been in their forties, it might have been easier because they could have handled the pace better. Physically, being PM is a very demanding job, even if you're fairly fit.

There were other concerns. This source goes on:

> It was an odd set-up because Starmer and Sue Gray often travelled on a Friday, and Morgan McSweeney goes to Scotland on Fridays because his wife's constituency is there, so No. 10 was like a ghost town on Fridays. Civil servants would say the atmosphere was much more what they'd expect at the end of a government than the beginning in terms of how many people were there. It wasn't a good sign.

Inevitably, several polls to mark the first 100 days were conducted. One carried out by the consultancy More in Common showed the Tories and Labour level pegging on 27 per cent. For the first time in 934 days, Labour had lost its lead. Separate canvassing by YouGov found that 27 per cent of voters had a favourable view of Starmer, while 63 per cent had an unfavourable opinion of him, giving him a net favourability score of –36. Such dire numbers would have been unimaginable to Starmer on the morning of 5 July, when he addressed the country from Downing Street.

On 6 July, a day after that victory speech, John Crace, *The Guardian*'s sketchwriter, had boldly stated, 'The grownups are back in Westminster. The Tory psychodramas inside No 10 have been replaced by a serious Labour government focused on delivery.' The idea of Labour's 'grownups' being in charge was widely quoted for a few weeks afterwards. Yet cronyism, Freebiegate, the winter fuel payment cut and the swift implementation of surprise policies that were not in the manifesto, plus bitter internal rows in Downing Street, had resulted in Starmer having to dispense with the services of a close ally. His authority had been punctured within just three months of reaching No. 10. Nobody who wanted to be taken seriously could any longer be as positive about Starmer's performance as Crace had been three months previously. Moreover, every time voters saw Starmer, they were free to speculate whether he had paid for the clothes and glasses he was wearing or whether Lord Alli had.

If Starmer regarded as trivial any of the issues that had pursued him since July, he had underestimated the reality of life in No. 10. It has always been dangerous for a new Prime Minister to enter government without being able to inform the electorate of a series of positive, detailed policies and then plot a clear course – in the era of digital news, all the more so. Would Starmer's next 100 days in power be any better?

CHAPTER 17

FAILURE TO RELAUNCH

In mid-October 2024, the Labour Party's head of operations, Sofia Patel, posted a message on the networking site LinkedIn that she thought was helpful and measured. In reality, it provoked a diplomatic row, jeopardising Keir Starmer's relationship with Donald Trump just three weeks before the US presidential election and earning the Prime Minister condemnation in America. 'I have nearly 100 Labour party staff, current and former, going to the US in the next few weeks, heading to North Carolina, Nevada, Pennsylvania and Virginia,' Patel wrote in her pro-Kamala Harris message. 'I have 10 spots available for anyone available to head to the battleground state of [North] Carolina – we will sort your housing.' This was the follow-up to an email Patel had sent in August asking Labour colleagues if they were willing to 'help our friends across the pond elect their first female president' and 'show those Yanks how to win elections!' Denunciation was immediate. Marjorie Taylor Greene, a Republican congresswoman, claimed Labour was guilty of breaking Federal Election Commission law. 'Foreign nationals are not allowed to be involved in any way in U.S. elections,' Greene fumed on Twitter. 'Please go back to the UK and fix your own mass immigration problems that are ruining your country.' Elon Musk, a close ally of Trump, was equally furious. 'This is illegal,' he claimed.

Trump's campaign team asked the Federal Electoral Commission to investigate 'apparent illegal foreign national contributions made by the Labour Party of the UK' which had been 'accepted' by Harris's campaign. In fact, there was no evidence of donations to the Democratic Party. As long as these Labour activists were not paid, no law had been broken. Though in fact there is a long history of Labour and Conservative, Democrat and Republican staffers crossing the Atlantic for a stint with their sister parties, the timing of the appeal was explosive and the story had taken off. Patel's LinkedIn post vanished hours after it was first noticed, but the damage was done. When asked about the row soon after, Starmer played it down, insisting he had 'established a good relationship' with Trump. Opponents were unconvinced. This was chalked up as yet another misstep by Labour and, by extension, the Prime Minister. It was compounded when it emerged days later that the British campaign group the Center for Countering Digital Hate, which had been founded by Morgan McSweeney in 2018, had once declared its intention to 'kill Musk's Twitter'. When Musk learned of this via a leaked internal report, he tweeted, 'This is war.' He was not bluffing, as events over the next few months would confirm.

After Trump won the US election decisively in November 2024, there was further embarrassment, as the catalogue of insults directed at him by Starmer and his Cabinet were dusted off and re-examined. For example, in 2019 Starmer had tweeted, 'An endorsement from Donald Trump tells you everything you need to know about what is wrong with Boris Johnson's politics and why he isn't fit to be Prime Minister.' In 2017, David Lammy had written that Trump was 'racist' and a 'Nazi sympathiser'. And Wes Streeting, by now the Health Secretary, had written in the same year, 'Trump is such an odious, sad little man.' In 2020, Deputy Prime Minister Angela Rayner had called Trump 'an absolute buffoon' who 'has no place in The White House', adding, 'He's an embarrassment … he's an absolute disgrace, he's an idiot.' And it was also revealed that, before taking office, Lord Hermer, the Attorney General, had labelled the President an 'orange tyrant'.

Nigel Farage observes that none of this is likely to matter much in the longer term. 'Trump is a much more forgiving person than people realise,' Farage says. 'He doesn't forget, but he does forgive. And since the assassination attempt [in July 2024] you see a much softer side to him.' Even so, because the relationship between Britain and America will be one of the defining aspects of Starmer's tenure in Downing Street, the fact that these senior Labour MPs and some of their colleagues thought it appropriate to publicise their opinions about an American President was taken as more evidence that Starmer's Cabinet is riddled with political naivety.

These hiccups were less significant than some of the foreign policy decisions Starmer's government had made up to that point, however. Within three weeks of taking office in July 2024, Hermer visited Israel to inform officials there that, unlike the Sunak administration, Starmer's government would not object to the International Criminal Court (ICC) application for an arrest warrant against Benjamin Netanyahu for alleged crimes against humanity and alleged war crimes in Gaza. This immediately placed Britain at odds with America, which has never signed up to the ICC. Even the liberal-minded President Biden called the ICC's arrest warrant against Netanyahu 'outrageous'. During Trump's first term in the White House, he told the UN General Assembly that the ICC had 'no jurisdiction, no legitimacy, and no authority'. His view had not changed since. By contrast, Starmer was, seemingly, happy to call Israel an ally while at the same time accepting that its Prime Minister could be treated like a potential war criminal.

Then, in early September, Lammy announced the suspension of thirty out of 350 UK arms export licences to Israel, for items used by Israeli forces in Gaza. Officially, the ban followed a government review of Israel's compliance with international humanitarian law, but it was roundly criticised. Phil Rosenberg, the president of the Board of Deputies of British Jews, said it sent a 'terrible message' in Israel's 'hour of need'. Washington warned British government officials that the move could affect attempts at a ceasefire deal. *The Times* called it 'cynical and performative', reducing the status of an ally to that of 'a pariah state deserving of sanctions normally reserved for brutish tyrannies such as Iran and Russia'. The *Daily Mail* thought it knew what lay behind the ban. 'This shameful decision has been made principally to pacify pro-Palestinian zealots within [the Labour Party],' the newspaper fulminated. As for Trump, who was eight weeks away from winning the election, he had been clear that he did not believe in using international humanitarian law to suspend arms exports. His support for Israel dismembering Hamas and Hezbollah, and so weakening Iran, therefore once again put Britain at odds with his view of how the crisis in the Middle East should be handled.

Lammy had also attracted international attention in early October with his surprise announcement that the British government wanted to cede sovereignty of the Chagos Archipelago, in the British Indian Ocean Territory, to Mauritius. Although negotiations had begun under the previous Conservative government, Labour seemed to be more open to the idea. Britain had controlled this region since 1814, but in recent years China has sought to strengthen ties with Mauritius, fuelling theories that Beijing would benefit from what many British MPs regarded as a dangerous surrender.

The justification was an advisory opinion – not a binding one – advanced in 2019 by the International Court of Justice (ICJ) that Britain's separation of the Chagos Islands from Mauritius – from where Britain had originally administered the islands – in 1965 was unlawful. This opinion was based on a UN General Assembly resolution. Such resolutions are not legally binding. Added to this, Britain has a legal opt-out from any ICJ ruling involving a country that is or was a member of the Commonwealth. This includes Mauritius. Still, under the planned new arrangements, Britain would be granted a 99-year lease over Diego Garcia, the largest island, which is home to a strategically vital UK–US military airbase. This tentative pact had been brokered by Jonathan Powell, once Tony Blair's chief of staff, whom Starmer formally appointed as his national security adviser in November 2024.

In Westminster, MPs were angry that this news had been slipped out during parliamentary recess without any debate. For one thing, what would it cost taxpayers? The government refused to say, though a figure of £90 million a year, rising with inflation, was rumoured. With the world closer to war than it had been for decades, and military leaders emphasising the geographical significance to western nations of the Chagos Archipelago in the face of China's global ambitions, other MPs were concerned about the security implications of the scheme. Nigel Farage, who knows many of Trump's closest political allies, told the BBC the incoming US administration was 'horrified'. Giving a vital asset to a country with links to the Chinese government – and then paying a vast price to lease it back – was apparently seen by some in the US as an own goal of epic proportions.

The common factor in these three controversial decisions was Starmer's close friend Lord Hermer. In mid-October 2024, he used the Bingham Lecture to emphasise the Starmer government's 'deep commitment to international law', singling out the Chagos agreement and 'our arms licensing criteria' as proof of international humanitarian law obligations having been met. He also spoke of 'applying law not politics', adding, 'We have made plain our commitment to our cornerstone international institutions, not least the International Court of Justice and the ICC.' He promised that 'the UK will once again be a champion for international courts and institutions, taking positive steps to promote their importance and to rebuild the respect for them that the populists have sought to destroy'.

It is not necessary to look back very far to understand where Hermer's sympathies lie when it comes to Israel. Although from a Jewish background himself, in May 2023 he was among the signatories of a Lawyers for Palestinian Human Rights letter urging the British government to participate in an International Court of Justice advisory opinion on the legal consequences of Israeli actions in the occupied West Bank, East Jerusalem and Gaza. That letter described the Israeli government as being led by 'a coalition of far-right parties'. More distantly, he wrote a chapter for a 2011 book called *Corporate Complicity in Israel's Occupation* edited by Asa Winstanley and Frank Barat. The title of Hermer's contribution was 'Redress for Palestinian Victims of Human Rights Abuses in the Courts of England and Wales'.

As for why the Chagos pact was seen as such a pressing matter for Starmer's government to settle in its early days, it was noted that another of Starmer's friends, Philippe Sands KC, had acted as Mauritius's chief legal adviser since 2010 in relation to the Chagos Archipelago. Sands had therefore been involved in the process that led to the ICJ's advisory opinion that Britain's separation of the islands had been unlawful. (In fact, the Judicial Power Project, run by the Policy Exchange think tank, concluded in 2022 that the ICJ's decision was legally questionable.) Sands was a co-founder of Matrix Chambers, where Hermer was based until his appointment as Attorney General.

Once the result of the US election was known, there were strong suggestions that Starmer's government wanted the Chagos deal to be completed before Trump entered the White House in

2025. To complicate matters, the original agreement struck in October 2024 by the Prime Minister of Mauritius, Pravind Jugnauth, was rejected by his successor, Navin Ramgoolam, for financial reasons. He wanted Britain to pay a steeper price. Before long, a figure of £18 billion over ninety-nine years was bandied around. One week before Trump's 20 January inauguration, it became clear that the plan to sign away the islands before that event had been abandoned. Members of Trump's top team effectively put a stop to it – at least temporarily. But they did wonder how on earth Britain had got itself into such a position of self-harm. One, Robert Wilkie, called the Chagos giveaway 'haphazard' and told the BBC the situation was 'calamitous'.

Previous holders of the office of Attorney General have tended to focus mainly on domestic law. Not so Hermer. Indeed, the foreign policy priorities of Starmer's government during its first six months in power arguably demonstrated how important Hermer is to Starmer. 'Keir wanted a friend in the role of Attorney General,' says one ally of Starmer bluntly when explaining why Hermer got the job. Theirs is more than a mere friendship, however. They share a political ideology that is crucial to the Starmer project. It is central to both men's thinking that Britain is viewed on the world stage as a country that respects international law. Hermer wasted no time in promoting this aim. Other notable aspects of his Bingham Lecture included his and Starmer's desire to reform the UN Security Council by giving permanent representation to Brazil, India, Japan, Germany and some African countries. 'The rule of law cannot be imposed on developing countries by former colonial rulers but must be grown organically from within by working closely with local communities and institutions,' Hermer announced. He also promised to be 'unwavering in our commitment to tackling climate change, where we know that many of the worst effects are felt by those who have made the smallest contributions to this existential threat'. And he vowed to 'unequivocally support the European Convention on Human Rights, including by complying with requests from the Court for interim measures'. This last point was intended to send a clear message to those on the right who had railed against ECHR judges blocking deportation flights. During Hermer's tenure, such decisions would be accepted without argument. In January 2025, during a visit to Brussels, he bolstered this stance by saying, 'I'd like to be very clear: the new UK government will never withdraw from the European Convention on Human Rights or refuse to comply with judgments of the court or requests for interim measures given in respect of the United Kingdom.'

Hermer's interest in domestic law is just as keen. Having taken office, he issued new guidance to the government's 2,000 lawyers 'to raise the standards for calibrating legality' across government so that they could 'give their full and frank advice to me and others in government and to stand up for the rule of law'. This was interpreted to mean that the government's lawyers would play an ever greater part in the work of elected politicians, potentially fortifying the former and weakening the latter.

• • •

By the time Rachel Reeves took to the despatch box at midday on 30 October to deliver her first budget, its assumed contents had been considered in the media for weeks thanks to well-sourced leaks. This conjecture forced many businesses to take fright and delay decision-making. There was good reason for this nervousness. Hours before she entered the Commons chamber, a photo of Reeves working at her desk had been circulated to the press. Hanging on a wall behind her could be seen a picture of the 1940s Labour MP Ellen Wilkinson. This was not a coincidence. A few weeks previously, Reeves had decreed that on her watch every piece of art in 11 Downing Street would be by a female artist or would feature female subjects. To that end, a picture of the Tory Chancellor Nigel Lawson had been removed to make way for Wilkinson's image. Wilkinson's legacy as a radical socialist and Communist Party member was taken as a statement of Reeves's intent, for the 45-year-old Chancellor was about to stage the biggest tax-raising event in modern times.

One of the key questions to emerge from the pre-budget speculation was the same one Starmer had struggled to answer during the election campaign: how to define the term 'working people'. It had featured twenty times in Labour's manifesto, especially in relation to its central aim, economic growth. 'Labour will not increase taxes on working people, which is why we will not increase National Insurance, the basic, higher, or additional rates of Income Tax, or VAT,' the document promised. The party's plans were 'fully costed, fully funded – built on a rock of fiscal responsibility'. But there was confusion when, five days before the budget, Starmer was asked whether those who have a job and who also receive extra income from shares or property could be classed as 'working people'. He disagreed and said that a working person was someone who 'goes out and earns their living, usually paid in a sort of monthly cheque' and who can't 'write a cheque to get out of difficulties'.

Reeves's budget statement lasted seventy-seven minutes, the longest heard in the Commons chamber for decades. Having once again invoked the disputed £22 billion Tory 'black hole', she said that VAT would be imposed on school fees from January 2025, capital gains tax would rise, stamp duty would rise, inheritance tax would be frozen at current rates until 2030 and the tax regime for non-doms would be scrapped. Tax rises were also imposed on oil and gas companies, sparking fears for the future prospects of industries operating in the North Sea. Alongside these expected tax hikes, several guarantees made over the previous eighteen months were shredded. Chief among them was the manifesto commitment not to raise National Insurance. From April 2025, employer National Insurance contributions would jump from 13.8 per cent to 15 per cent and the earnings threshold at which staff incur this tax was cut from £9,100 to £5,000. Reeves hoped that this step alone would generate £25 billion. Labour had also previously denied it intended to scrap agricultural property relief, which allows farmland to be passed between generations without attracting inheritance tax. Yet Reeves confirmed that this exemption, together with business property relief, would be abandoned so that from April 2026 assets worth more than £1 million could be taxed at 20 per cent.

Another pledge that was junked related to Labour's self-imposed fiscal rules. In 2023, Reeves had said she was 'not going to fiddle the figures or make something to get different results', but in her budget speech the debt target was indeed tweaked, releasing another £70 billion of borrowing to be invested in infrastructure projects as a way of boosting growth. This public spending increase was the largest in real terms for a quarter of a century.

In his final act as Tory leader, Rishi Sunak responded. His energetic performance impressed many as he lashed out at the budget's 'broken promise after broken promise' and lambasted Starmer and Reeves for not having been 'straight with the British people'. He reminded those watching that the Tories had cautioned that Labour would tax, borrow and spend above and beyond what had been set out during the election and took issue with Reeves's £22 billion black hole claim, pointing out that it did not appear in the Office for Budget Responsibility report that was published that day. Far from Labour having inherited a dire economy, he said, inflation was at 2 per cent, unemployment was low and economic growth was stable when the election was called in May. It was somehow appropriate that this former Chancellor turned Prime Minister, who had helped to restore Britain's economy in the wake of Liz Truss's unfortunate spell in Downing Street, had the last word for his party. Three days later, Sunak was replaced as Leader of the Opposition by Kemi Badenoch, who had beaten Robert Jenrick in the final round of voting among party members. She was the fourth Tory leader Starmer had faced since 2020.

Thanks to the remarkable £40 billion of extra taxes that was forecast, a broad consensus was quickly reached that Reeves had produced an anti-growth budget. During the election, voters were assured that public services would be improved from the higher revenues that come from economic growth, yet it was clear that higher tax rates were in fact her preferred method of payment. The OBR predicted that the new measures would result in lower wages for workers and higher prices for consumers. Richard Hughes, its chairman, said: 'This budget delivers one of the largest increases in spending, tax, and borrowing of any single fiscal event in history.'

Both small and large business executives boiled about the National Insurance rise, inevitably dubbed a 'jobs tax'. When taken in conjunction with the new national living wage that Reeves had agreed – up 6.7 per cent to £12.21 an hour – their worries intensified. Deutsche Bank predicted it could lead to 100,000 job losses. Labour's new Employment Rights Bill caused yet more alarm. It had begun its journey into law three weeks earlier and included initiatives such as protecting staff from unfair dismissal from their first day in a job and extending paternity and statutory sick pay eligibility. It was expected to cost businesses an extra £5 billion annually.

Analysts concluded that the inherent contradiction of Reeves's budget was that Labour had been elected on a growth strategy yet wanted to saddle private enterprise – the engine room of growth – with charges and bureaucracy that would have the opposite effect. This fiscal ineptitude fuelled the idea that Starmer's administration was not only deceitful but also ignorant, not understanding how growth is achieved. Again, the lack of commercial experience among Cabinet ministers was considered responsible. Of course, it wasn't just businesses that would be hit. Charities, GPs' surgeries, the police and hospices would be among organisations that would also bear the brunt.

In the weeks after the budget, the counterblast was sustained. Seventy-nine members of the British Retail Consortium, including the boss of Tesco, told Reeves that their collective expenditure was going to rise by £7 billion in the following year alone thanks to her plans. 'The sheer scale of new costs and the speed with which they occur create a cumulative burden that will make job losses inevitable and higher prices a certainty,' they said. That was only the beginning of it. Job vacancies fell, online and high street retail sales declined, scores of non-doms left Britain, companies drew up plans to relocate thousands of jobs to India, investors pulled billions from the stock market and fears of a recession grew.

In late November, thousands of farmers descended on London to protest against the new levies they faced, believing small family farms would have to be broken up and sold in order to pay inheritance tax bills. When Elon Musk read an opinion piece in *The Observer* that sought to defend this policy, he showed sympathy for the farmers' plight, tweeting to his 205 million followers: 'Britain is going full Stalin.' This was an inflammatory reference to Joseph Stalin's policy of forcing private farms into state ownership between 1928 and 1940, no doubt exaggerated for effect. Coming so soon after the winter fuel allowance raid, however, it did emphasise that Reeves was pursuing another section of society whose existence is far more fragile than politicians appreciate. Business journalist Liam Halligan was felt to speak for many when he wrote in the *Sunday Telegraph* that the new rules affecting farmers contained 'a strong whiff of class prejudice, as an overwhelmingly urban party takes aim at thousands of farming families perceived to be wealthy but actually seriously cash-strapped'. There is even a theory that imposing inheritance tax changes on farmland served the dual purpose of helping to achieve Energy Secretary Ed Miliband's astonishingly expensive dream of rolling out solar power on a scale never seen before to make Britain a 'clean energy superpower'. This is because another levy outlined in Reeves's budget was a new fertiliser tax from 2027, something that would dent farmers' profits further still.

By the end of November, growth had slowed to a halt and inflation and borrowing had risen, eliciting fears of higher interest rates. At a Confederation of British Industry summit, Reeves was forced onto the defensive, telling attendees, 'We're never going to have to do a budget like that again.' Forty-eight hours later, Downing Street toned down Reeves's claim by saying that no tax rises on the same scale would be needed – a very different prediction.

At the same time, there were growing questions about Reeves's credentials. She had stated publicly that she was an economist at Halifax Bank of Scotland (HBOS) before entering politics. It transpired, however, that details on her LinkedIn account were changed to reflect that she had in fact worked in retail banking at HBOS. She had previously been found to have listed incorrect dates on her CV, artificially inflating her time at the Bank of England by nine months. In reality, she had spent five and a half years at the bank – including nearly a year studying for a master's degree – which did not prevent her from claiming she had 'spent a decade working as an economist at the Bank of England'. For embellishing her CV, she was nicknamed 'Rachel From Accounts'. It stuck. She also left herself open to accusations of being out of her depth. All the while, those who would be affected by the budget were able to reflect on the fact that Reeves and her civil servant husband, Nicholas Joicey, were among the most well-catered-for people in public life. Their taxpayer-funded salaries combined reached £350,000. Each has a gold-plated pension. Like Keir Starmer, who rents out his north London house, they also have additional income streams. The two London properties they own generate additional income of £75,000 per year while they live rent-free between two grace-and-favour homes: the Downing Street flat and Dorneywood, a 21-room mansion in Buckinghamshire. Joicey left Whitehall for a secondment to the Blavatnik School of Government at the University of Oxford early in 2025.

The former Tory Chancellor Jeremy Hunt believes Reeves's budget was 'unimaginative and conventional'. He comments:

> Compare it to Gordon Brown when he made the Bank of England independent and made the really big call to stick to Conservative spending plans, which cemented his reputation as a Labour Chancellor who would not fall back on tax and spend. With Reeves, there wasn't really anything substantive when it came to growth. The reason why her budget wasn't well received in the markets was that she told the markets she was just going to increase borrowing to fund more capital. In fact she increased it by £29 billion per year and the majority of that is for revenue spending. That's why the markets were quite disappointed with the budget.

Where was Starmer, officially the First Lord of the Treasury, as the budget was being prepared? On 19 October, Peter Mandelson told the *Sunday Times* the new Prime Minister seemed to be spending a lot of time in other countries. 'His diary has been very dominated by foreign affairs and international visits, somewhat inevitably, given all that's going on,' Mandelson observed. 'He knows, though, that at the next election the verdict of the electorate will only partly be on foreign policy and security matters – it's the economy and the state of the NHS which will matter most to people.' He was not wrong. Starmer had notched up ten overseas trips between 9 July and 2 October, costing the public £700,000 in flights alone. One Downing Street veteran thinks his inexperience in economic affairs explains his absences. 'You could tell he was so lacking in confidence on the economy and people who were in No. 10 during his first six months all pointed out that he's doing a huge amount on foreign affairs – way more than you'd expect a newly elected leader to do – and not doing the economic stuff,' says this person. 'It's not that he's not a former chancellor like Rishi Sunak or Gordon Brown. It's that any Prime Minister has to have a focus on the economy. He seems to be steering away from the economy. That will become more difficult as time goes on.' Another says, 'By this point he'd done almost no domestic visits. Cameron, Boris and Sunak were all out in the country two days a week. Starmer had very rarely done stuff like that.'

He was back in the air on 18 October, when he visited Berlin for a meeting with President Biden, Chancellor Scholz and President Macron to discuss the war in Ukraine and the situation in the Middle East. A week later, he was in Samoa attending the Commonwealth Heads of Government Meeting. On 7 November, after the budget had been delivered, he visited Budapest for a European Political Community summit. Four days later, he accepted an invitation from President Macron to attend the Armistice commemoration at the Arc de Triomphe in Paris, the first

Prime Minister to do so since Winston Churchill in 1944. Lord Ricketts, who was ambassador to Paris until 2016, thought this worthy of comment. 'Macron has gone out of his way to signal the importance of the France–UK relationship on this Remembrance Day,' he wrote. 'The drive up the Champs Élysée in a command jeep is very unusual.'

But was it so surprising, in light of Starmer's pro-EU stance? By then the Cabinet Office had quietly begun to assemble a 100-strong team of civil servants dedicated to working on the UK's 'reset' with the EU on matters including food checks, fishing rights and immigration. When this leaked, the government would not set out its plans in detail, convincing many that Brexit was in peril. Negotiations were scheduled to last for months.

Lord Hermer's approval was guaranteed. His belief in the EU project is so strong that in 2020 he had fantasised publicly about introducing a law titled 'The European Union (Please Can We Come Back?) Act 2020'. Donald Trump's senior economic adviser, Stephen Moore, had a different view. He told *The Times* that America would be 'less interested' in a trade deal with Britain if it decided to follow the 'socialist model' of the EU. Moore also said that Reeves's budget suggested Britain was not moving 'towards freedom'. Starmer has made it clear that he thinks it is wrong to suggest that Britain must pick an ally, using the speech he gave at the Lord Mayor's Banquet to make clear that 'the national interest demands that we work with both'.

Nigel Farage agrees with the principle of this position, but as a result of the way Brexit was handled, he is pessimistic when it comes to Britain's trading prospects during Trump's second term. 'The more we reset with the EU, the more impossible it'll be to move towards a free trade agreement with America,' says Farage.

That's a huge mistake. In 2008, the size of the American

> economy was the same as the Eurozone's. Now, it's twice as big. Trump is bewildered by everything that's happened since 2019. He's amazed we haven't made more of Brexit. He doesn't understand what's gone wrong with the Conservative Party. And all Starmer is doing is continuing their programme. The reason he is able to 'reset' with the EU is that the Conservatives didn't take us out of the bloc fully. Kemi Badenoch [as Business Secretary] scrapped the legislation that would have allowed us to get rid of 4,000 directives. We didn't take advantage of Trump's presidency during his first term and it looks unlikely that we will do in the second. I don't think Starmer is going to capitalise on having an Anglophile President in the White House.

Starmer's next stop, on 12 November, was Baku in Azerbaijan for the 2024 UN Climate Change Conference, where he announced Britain's aspiration to cut greenhouse gas emissions by 81 per cent by 2035. The leaders of the thirteen biggest emitters of carbon – including America, China and India – snubbed this conference. That Starmer plus 448 officials did fly there and back left him open to scorn. Was it really necessary for him to have gone? Was it a good use of public money? Didn't it make a mockery of Britain's claim to be ahead of the pack in environmental matters given the large carbon footprint generated by the 5,000-mile return trip?

Yet these questions were soon eclipsed by greater ones. He rounded off his November travels by going to Rio de Janeiro for the G20 summit. There, he held a special meeting with President Xi Jinping. This marked the first time a British Prime Minister had met the Chinese President in person since 2018. Scepticism in Britain was high. Why was a former human rights lawyer – who as recently as 2021 had lambasted China's human rights record – cosying up to the leader of a brutal regime which counts Russia, North Korea and Iran as allies? Starmer had once called for China's treatment of the Uyghur Muslims to be branded 'genocide' and argued that bilateral trade deals should be blocked. Now, he wanted a 'new and pragmatic relationship' with Beijing, bolstering economic and trade ties. Following the talks, Xi praised Starmer and Reeves for their approach to the economy. 'The new UK Government is working to fix the foundations of the economy and rebuild Britain and has set the vision of Britain reconnected,' he said in a written statement that sounded as though it had been copied directly from a Labour Party press release. Hours later, there was more awkwardness for Starmer when a group of pro-democracy Hong Kong lawyers, journalists and activists labelled the 'Hong Kong 47' were imprisoned for subversion. When he was asked at a press conference by George Parker of the *Financial Times* about their incarceration, he summoned up a woolly answer that did not include a word of criticism of the Chinese government. A reminder of the potential perils of doing business with China soon materialised when court documents in London named an alleged Chinese spy, Yang Tengbo, as having accessed the highest levels of the British establishment over a twenty-year period including befriending Prince Andrew and being photographed with former Prime Ministers David Cameron and Theresa May.

• • •

There were palpitations in Westminster on 28 November when it was revealed by Sky News that Louise Haigh, the Transport Secretary, had a fraud conviction dating from 2014, a year before she became an MP. Haigh's version of events was that she had been mugged one night in 2013. She reported this to the police at the time and provided a list of items she believed had been stolen, including a mobile phone given to her by her then employer, Aviva.

She was given a new work phone but later found that the phone she had said was stolen in fact remained in her possession. When she switched it on, the police were alerted. She was questioned by officers and the matter was referred to the Crown Prosecution Service. The case was sent to a magistrates' court, where her solicitor apparently advised her to plead guilty. She was given a conditional discharge.

Haigh resigned within hours of this news becoming public, but that was not the end of the matter. Not only was she the first minister to leave Starmer's Cabinet, it was immediately apparent that much about the story was odd. It remains shrouded in mystery. And it is Starmer, not Haigh, who is responsible for having created this uncertainty. In her resignation letter, Haigh stated that Starmer knew of her fraud conviction when he appointed her to his Cabinet. This prompted questions about Starmer's judgement. Downing Street's explanation was that 'new information' had come to light which resulted in her resignation. Yet when asked about this new information, Starmer said, 'I'm not going to disclose private conversations.' (He had stonewalled in just this fashion over Angela Rayner's inexplicably complicated property arrangements six months previously.) The plot thickened when it was reported that associates of Morgan McSweeney had tipped off the Conservatives about Haigh's conviction during the election campaign. Farcically, the Tories were apparently given the wrong court details and were unable to confirm the story. Still, it was clear that Haigh was neither liked nor trusted by Starmer's inner circle.

When Haigh was installed as Transport Secretary in July 2024, her enemies were minded to go for her a second time. She soon provided the excuse they needed. Just weeks after taking office, the committed trade unionist agreed a 15 per cent pay rise for train drivers, meaning some would receive an £80,000 salary for a four-day week. Following Reeves's announcement that she was ending the winter fuel allowance, Haigh's pay offer created fury among the public. It was not even clear whether Starmer knew of the deal before it was announced, causing maximum embarrassment for the government. And in October 2024, she humiliated Starmer again when she described P&O Ferries as a 'rogue operator' for its past treatment of staff and said the firm should be boycotted. Its parent company, the Dubai-owned DP World, had been preparing a £1 billion investment in a new Thames freeport. When Haigh's remarks surfaced, the firm walked away from the agreement. Only some urgent repair work by diplomats rescued it.

While there is little doubt that these incidents provided the motive for Labour insiders to spread word of Haigh's conviction, more important is why – according to Haigh – Starmer saw fit to appoint a convicted fraudster to his Cabinet in the first place. And if he didn't know the full details of Haigh's criminal conviction, what accounted for his ignorance? Whether he likes it or not, cases such as Haigh's show once again why he has developed a reputation as a man who can be surprisingly badly informed.

Starmer was lucky in one sense, though. The timing of Haigh's departure coincided with the first of several Commons votes on the complicated question of assisted dying. The vote passed by 330 to 275, providing useful cover as the issue dominated the news agenda. Years earlier, Starmer had drafted the third-party intervention for the Voluntary Euthanasia Society in the case of Diane Pretty, whose efforts to change the law following her diagnosis with motor neurone disease made her the focus of a national debate on euthanasia until her death in 2002. Few were surprised when Starmer voted in favour of legalising the right to die. As the voting was underway, sharp-eyed observers witnessed something more unexpected – Starmer crossing the floor of an almost empty Commons chamber to speak to Nigel Farage. 'He'd made a joke at my expense a week before at PMQs and he came to say he hoped I didn't mind,' explains Farage.

> We had a laugh. I then made a couple of serious points to him. I'd emailed a couple of weeks before asking for a meeting, which hadn't materialised. I said to him, 'It's not just Trump. Half his Cabinet are friends of mine and I could be really useful to you, acting as a bridge.' I meant it sincerely. In terms of defence and trade our relationship is much more important than our relationship with the failing EU. He said, 'Just leave that with me.' So it wasn't much of an answer.

More interesting than what the two men discussed, though, was what the encounter represented. Arguably, Starmer's decision to approach Farage in that context, rather than the other way round, was emblematic of what some saw as a power shift taking place in British politics, with Reform UK gaining momentum as the Labour government seemed to be sliding backwards. Within a few weeks, polling showed that Starmer was less popular than Farage, with 25 per cent of voters having a favourable opinion of the Prime Minister versus 28 per cent approving of the Reform UK leader. It wouldn't be long before Reform UK topped several mainstream opinion polls, ahead of Labour and the Conservatives.

During the first week of December, Sir Chris Wormald was appointed as Cabinet Secretary and head of the civil service, one of the most powerful jobs in British public life. Although Wormald is a Whitehall veteran, he was not considered by the panel that drew up the shortlist to be the best suited to this post. However, Starmer is said to have insisted on hiring him. For some, this reflected his own instincts as a technocrat rather than a reform-minded politician who was serious about implementing radical change. A couple of days later, Starmer put himself under the spotlight by going to Pinewood Studios in Buckinghamshire to make what was known as the 'Plan for Change' speech. Although his aides strongly denied it, this was taken by almost everybody who was aware of it to be a relaunch of his administration after a dismal opening five months in power. One poll published on the day of the speech found that voters believed the government was doing a bad job by a margin of fifty-three to nineteen. Most polls showed Labour having slumped. Starmer's personal approval ratings were also historically low.

In the speech, he unveiled six 'milestones' that were to be reached by the time of the next election. They were: for working people to feel better off; to build 1.5 million homes; to ensure 92 per cent of NHS patients are treated within eighteen weeks; to recruit 13,000 new police officers; to make sure three-quarters of children aged five are 'school-ready'; and for Britain to have 95 per cent clean power by 2030. The response to the speech was muted, at best. Some found the name of the initiative to be ill-conceived, pointing out that Labour's election slogan had been 'Change' and yet five months later came the 'Plan for Change'. Shouldn't the plan for change have been set out before the change could be enacted? Other quibbles related to what was absent from his wish list. There was not a word about defence or immigration, for example, even though both topics were more pressing than they had been for decades. It was also noted that the central election pledge to deliver the fastest growth in the G7 was reduced to a far more realistic aspiration that people might 'feel' better off by 2029. But these six milestones came after Starmer had previously given speeches about Labour's 'five missions'; its 'three foundations'; and its six 'first steps'. His message was confused and confusing and it left him open to ridicule.

In one section of the speech, he was more forceful, as he observed that 'too many people in Whitehall are comfortable in the tepid bath of managed decline'. For several hours, it looked as though he was limbering up to tackle the ballooning civil service. With 515,000 staff, it was bigger than ever. But then Dave Penman, the head of the FDA trade union representing senior civil servants, took to the airwaves to reveal that he found Starmer's words 'really damaging' and advised that he 'must work to immediately rebuild trust' with his officials. A day later, Starmer dutifully constructed what was in effect a letter of apology to all civil servants. 'I know first-hand how fortunate this country is to have a Civil Service that is admired across the world,' he wrote. 'For you it is not just a job. You want to change the country and make Britain a better place.' So much for reforming zeal.

Three days later he was en route to the Middle East for trade talks with Sheikh Mohamed bin Zayed Al Nahyan, the ruler of Abu Dhabi, and, separately, with Saudi Crown Prince Mohammed bin Salman. In 2022, he had criticised Boris Johnson for 'going cap in hand from dictator to dictator' trying to drum up Middle Eastern investment. Now he found himself in the same position. As a former human rights lawyer, some of his own MPs and some charities took a strong line on the need for him to raise with Mohammed bin Salman the many human rights abuses of which western leaders had been made aware. Downing Street insisted that Starmer had discussed his concerns, but this was just one more lesson for the Prime Minister that what is said in opposition can take on a very different quality when in power.

From the Middle East he went to Cyprus for bilateral security talks with Cypriot President Nikos Christodoulides and visited British service personnel at RAF Akrotiri, marking his sixteenth foreign trip in less than six months. He was reckoned to have flown around the world the equivalent of three times in that period, causing some to wonder whether he was in fact scared to confront the mounting pile of domestic problems Britain faced.

Just before Christmas 2024, the government sparked a new row by announcing that the Women Against State Pension Inequality (WASPI) campaign would be denied the estimated £10.5 billion compensation its members had been seeking. The group fights for women born in the 1950s who say they were not given due notice that they would have to work up to six years longer before drawing the state pension. Given the economic climate, the government considered their demand too high. Once again, however, Starmer, along with several members of his Cabinet, was labelled hypocritical for having supported the WASPI cause in opposition by vowing to get the women what they wanted. Backbench Labour MPs were furious, with some likening the ruling to the winter fuel allowance cut. There were even fears it could cost several marginal seats.

Two other announcements followed. The first was Starmer's creation of thirty new Labour peers. Six months previously, the Labour manifesto had made clear its commitment to replacing the House of Lords with a second chamber that is 'more representative of the regions and nations'. Apart from beginning the process that would see the expulsion of the remaining ninety-two hereditary peers, that ambition had been ditched. Bolstering Labour's numbers in the Lords was seen as far more essential. Among those to be elevated was Sue Gray, Starmer's former chief of staff. She would be joined by a handful of close friends of Tony Blair, including his former aide Anji Hunter and his former advisers Deborah Mattinson and Phil Wilson, ensuring that Blair himself could remain well briefed on developments in Starmer's administration.

The second announcement concerned another key Blairite, Peter Mandelson, who accepted Starmer's invitation to be ambassador to Washington. Unusually, this would be a political rather than a diplomatic appointment. Much was made of the fact that, like many of Starmer's Cabinet ministers, Mandelson had insulted Trump publicly in the past – in his case by calling him a 'danger to the world' and 'little short of a white nationalist and racist'. What was all too easily forgotten was that during Mandelson's forty years in and around politics he had been forced to quit the Cabinet twice after becoming entangled in financial scandals, the second of which was subject to an independent inquiry which cleared him of wrongdoing. More recently, he had also been close to Jeffrey Epstein, the financier and convicted paedophile who was found dead in an American prison cell in 2019. Sensitivity around this association showed itself when he was asked about it during an interview with the *Financial Times*. 'I regret ever meeting [Epstein] or being introduced to him by his partner Ghislaine Maxwell,' Mandelson said. 'I regret even more the hurt he caused to many young women ... I'm not going to go into this. It's an *FT* obsession and frankly you can all fuck off. OK?'

Still, with Donald Trump threatening to impose a tariff on British exports, Starmer's thinking was that Mandelson's network of international contacts and second career as a business adviser made him the obvious choice to go in to bat for Britain. Some Labour MPs had concerns, emphasising that Mandelson had already been publicly critical of policies championed by Starmer's government – notably the extension of workers' rights, which he believed could damage business. Of greater relevance to the nation, however, is Mandelson's devotion to the EU project. Having been an EU trade commissioner for four years, he is a cast-iron anti-Brexiteer in the mould of Starmer. As Trump is known to look more kindly on Britain's interests now that it is no longer part of the EU, the implications of Mandelson's EU stance could be vast for British taxpayers. 'Mandelson might be good for helping us avoid a tariff regime, but will he take us on to a free trade deal with America? No,' says Nigel Farage. 'He believes our link to the single market is too important. If you consider intelligence sharing, defence and security, the US relationship is clearly far more important than the EU one. I don't believe Mandelson sees that. He still thinks the EU relationship matters more.' As far as Trump is concerned, there are also doubts about Mandelson's perceived links to China.

Starmer went into Christmas 2024 in need of a break but had to postpone his plans to travel to Madeira for a family holiday after his brother, Nick, succumbed to cancer on Boxing Day at the age of sixty. This tragedy was not the only piece of depressing news with which the Prime Minister had to contend. There was also clear evidence from multiple sources that Britain's economy was sliding backwards. Figures showed there was no growth in the first three months of Starmer's administration and inflation had ticked up, from 2 per cent to 2.6 per cent. Businesses remained anxious about Rachel Reeves's high-tax budget. Many suspended plans to hire new staff, while manufacturing was dented and government borrowing rose, hitting the confidence of investors. Reeves's tax rises had not even kicked in but the outlook was already bleak. Stagflation – the lethal mix of low growth and high inflation – seemed possible; stagnation was probable. When Starmer arrived in Downing Street, Britain was the fastest-growing economy in the G7. Six months later, it was the slowest. Paul Johnson, the head of the Institute for Fiscal Studies think tank, predicted there would have to be further tax rises in 2025 if these trends continued.

While Starmer was on holiday, Elon Musk, the owner of car maker Tesla, popped up again. Ash Regan, the Holyrood leader of the Alba Party, had written to him urging him to open a new Tesla gigafactory in Scotland. Musk was dismissive, commenting on Twitter, 'Very few companies will be willing to invest in the UK with the current administration.' This latest public jibe at Starmer was just another reminder that his vision for growing Britain's economy was very far from the thinking of those with influence in the private sector. It was a dealt a further blow in January 2025 when the cost of long-term government borrowing climbed to 5.42 per cent, its highest level since 1998, reflecting investors' negative feelings about Britain's economy. The value of the pound plunged.

During Starmer's first six months in charge, his personal poll ratings had gone through the floor. *The Times* recorded that since taking office he had become one of the most disliked politicians in Britain and was even more unpopular than Jeremy Corbyn at his nadir, with his personal approval rating collapsing to −41. Perhaps inevitably, there was talk of Labour MPs growing restive at the rate of his decline. Outwardly, he maintained that he would do nothing differently if he could relive the previous six months, claiming that he had deliberately taken a series of difficult decisions early on. Yet there were signs of pressure. He was visibly fatigued. He was also said to be in need of being shored up psychologically because of the relentless nature of the job. None of this was helped by reports over Christmas that the official number of illegal immigrants to have arrived in Britain by boat since 2018 had surpassed the 150,000 barrier. The cost of this to taxpayers ran into multiple billions. The number of crossings had accelerated since July and ended up 25 per cent higher than it had been the previous year. Did Starmer's mantra that he wanted to 'smash the gangs' mean anything?

His New Year message was uninspiring, as he was forced to admit that the 'change' he had promised would take time to materialise. In the opening days of January 2025, Donald Trump deviated from his preparations for re-entering the White House to comment that Britain was making 'a very big mistake' by halting the exploitation of North Sea oil and gas. Trump's own business interests in Scotland, where he owns two golf courses, were doubtless a factor. But it was the American oil and gas firm Apache announcing it was ending its operations there by 2029 because of 'uneconomic' high taxes that gave him a reason to intervene. He said Starmer should 'open up' the North Sea and 'get rid of windmills', a reference to Energy Secretary Ed Miliband blocking new North Sea drilling licences in his quest for Britain to become reliant on wind and solar power by 2030. It was later reported that Trump and his advisers were also angry that the contents of a pre-Christmas phone call between the President-elect and Starmer were leaked to *The Times* in early January. The paper claimed that Trump had been 'fixated on the number of birds dying after flying into wind turbines in the US' and had joked that coyotes eating the birds 'were getting so fat that they would need to be given weight-loss drugs'. It was assumed that Starmer's team were mocking Trump.

Then, Elon Musk launched another torpedo, this time over the grooming gangs that had caused such misery to thousands of girls and young women all over the country. In many cases they had been plied with drink and drugs before men, mainly of Pakistani origin, attacked them. Musk alleged that Starmer played a role in the scandal having been Director of Public Prosecutions between 2008 and 2013, when it first entered the public consciousness. 'Starmer must go and he must face charges for his complicity in the worst mass crime in the history of Britain,' he wrote in one of 200 posts on the subject during the first week of January.

On 6 January, Starmer appeared at a press conference to discuss the NHS. It was seen as an adjunct to the government relaunch he had embarked on four weeks previously. Yet it was overshadowed by Musk's outpourings. When fielding questions, Starmer allowed his anger to get the better of him. By then, both Kemi Badenoch and Nigel Farage had joined calls for a new national inquiry into these crimes, estimated to have affected fifty towns and cities. Starmer thought them opportunistic and criticised anybody he deemed guilty of 'jumping on a bandwagon' and being so 'desperate for attention they're amplifying what the far right is saying'. Labelling as 'far right' those who were angry about young girls being abused was seen as desperately out of touch. He also generated suspicion. Was he trying to evade scrutiny of the Crown Prosecution Service's handling of the matter? Badenoch accused him of 'smear tactics'. Farage said he was 'trying to sweep the past failures of the establishment under the carpet'. Once again, Musk had forced Starmer onto the defensive. And the calls for a specific inquiry into the abuse of young girls by Pakistani men only intensified. Starmer argued that a new national inquiry would take time and that it was more important to implement the recommendations from previous inquiries. He had also performed creditably on the issue when he was DPP, as described in earlier chapters. Even so, there was a feeling that he was on uncomfortable ground.

By then, a YouGov poll found that Labour's approval rating had fallen to −47, well below the murky depth of −42 reached by Boris Johnson when he stood down as Prime Minister in the summer of 2022 following a historic mass revolt of his ministers. It was then reported in *The Times* and elsewhere that Musk had been discussing ways to oust Starmer before the next general election by destabilising the government. This was quite a claim, but there was no hard evidence to support it. The obvious question to ask is what lies behind Musk's interest in Britain and its politics? 'He has very strong opinions on what Starmer's government is doing on free speech,' explains Nigel Farage. 'He also has British links on both sides of his family. His view is that Britain is the mother country of the English-speaking world. That matters to him.'

If Starmer was hoping to get onto the front foot as January progressed, he was to be disappointed. The economy was fluctuating. Bond yields were at their highest since 2008 and government borrowing continued to climb, so much so that Rachel Reeves was forced to consider cutting spending or raising taxes to meet her fiscal rules and make sure the markets didn't lose confidence. For some, this was reminiscent of the aftermath of Liz Truss's mini-budget of autumn 2022. Many Labour MPs were dismayed, fearing a return to austerity, which perhaps explains why Starmer began holding regular lunches in his Commons office each Wednesday after Prime Minister's Questions. With more than 200 new Labour MPs on the back benches, offering groups of six or seven of them a Pret A Manger sandwich and a chat was seen as a way to keep them sweet.

When journalists asked Starmer at a press conference about Reeves's future as Chancellor, however, he took the extraordinary step of saying that she would remain in her post for the duration of the parliament. Some thought this foolish. He had made a similar commitment to David Lammy a few months before. By doing so, he not only created what was labelled a 'two-tier' Cabinet in which these two ministers appeared to be untouchable, he had also taken from himself the power to dismiss them – even if they were not doing a good job. Loyalty aside, no previous Prime Minister would have thought it sensible to surrender their authority in this fashion.

Reeves was not the only Treasury figure whose future was in question. Tulip Siddiq, the City minister, was forced to quit her post on 14 January following weeks of headlines about her links to the corrupt regime of her aunt Sheikh Hasina, the former

Prime Minister of Bangladesh, whose critics frequently found themselves imprisoned, tortured and killed. Hasina and some of her allies had been accused of stealing up to £4 billion of public funds over a fifteen-year period. Bangladesh's Anti-Corruption Commission had begun to investigate whether any of the stolen funds had been used to buy Siddiq's multi-million-pound portfolio of London properties. Starmer and Siddiq are close. Her north London constituency borders his and he had refused to sack her until her position became untenable. Sir Laurie Magnus, the independent adviser on ministerial standards, to whom Siddiq eventually referred herself while denying any wrongdoing, suggested it would be impossible for her to carry on as the anti-corruption minister.

This matter only served to raise yet more questions about Starmer's judgement. Why had he appointed her in the first place when it had long been known that she was a figure of suspicion? And why hadn't he actively dismissed her? His supporters wanted voters to believe that Siddiq's resignation – the third high-profile departure in three months, following Sue Gray and Louise Haigh – was a show of Starmer's supremacy. But were those advisers merely myth-building? Many others concluded that Starmer had acted with diffidence in allowing the matter to drag on.

The Prime Minister barely had time to catch his breath before the next set of questions reared up. While some foreign politicians, notably Italy's Prime Minister, Giorgia Meloni, and the Argentinian President, Javier Milei, were invited to Trump's inauguration, Starmer was not. Downing Street played this down, but the newspapers picked it up, also noting that Trump's aides were considering putting Starmer 'at the back of the queue' when it came to meeting the 47th President and possibly vetoing Peter Mandelson's nomination as ambassador to Washington. Six days after Trump's inauguration, the two men did speak by telephone for forty-five minutes. Trump was candid about the differences between them, telling reporters, 'He's liberal, which is a bit different from me.' But no doubt to the relief of No. 10, he added that Starmer was doing 'a very good job thus far'. Some saw significance in the fact that Trump had found time to ring Saudi Crown Prince Mohammed bin Salman and El Salvador's President Nayib Bukele before speaking to Starmer.

Questions about Lord Hermer's past clients also mounted. As described, when he was a practising barrister he had represented the former president of Sinn Féin, Gerry Adams, receiving £30,000 in fees. After Labour's election, the government repealed The Troubles Act, introduced by the Tories in 2023, paving the way for hundreds of Irish Republicans – including, potentially, Adams – to claim compensation over their detention in prison in the 1970s. This was projected to cost British taxpayers £2.7 billion. Hermer was accused of a conflict of interests for failing to say whether he had advised the government over its decision to repeal this piece of legislation. He was learning that being one of Starmer's closest friends made him the target of legitimate press scrutiny.

That was not all. Poor news about the economy continued to trickle in. In late January, the Office for National Statistics said that employment had fallen by 47,000 in December 2024, the steepest drop since November 2020, while government borrowing the same month hit a four-year high of £17.8 billion – £3.2 billion more than forecast. Starmer wrote a piece for *The Times* comparing his government's ambition to 'cut through thickets of red tape' in order to stimulate economic growth with Margaret Thatcher's strategy of deregulation in the 1980s. Once again, Thatcher – whose politics he had professed to hate – was a very convenient political tool.

Starmer's apparently ambivalent relationship to Thatcherism was soon put in the shade by allegations that he had broken Covid lockdown rules in December 2020 by asking his voice coach, Leonie Mellinger, to visit him at his London office on Christmas Eve as he prepared to respond via a virtual press conference to Boris Johnson's Brexit deal. The Tier 4 restrictions in place at the time insisted that 'everyone must work from home unless they are unable to do so'. Mellinger and Starmer apparently believed that she had key worker status, though government guidance at that time was that a key worker in politics included only those in 'administrative occupations essential to the effective delivery of the Covid-19 response'. The revelation that Starmer had a voice coach heaped mockery onto the Prime Minister. Given he is routinely acknowledged as being among the most uninspiring public speakers in Westminster, commentators wondered whether he ought to ask Mellinger for his money back – if indeed he had paid her from his own funds. It was not clear who had footed the bill. The more serious point was that he had majored on scrutinising Johnson's interpretation of the rules during the pandemic. Was he guilty of hypocrisy? The Metropolitan Police declined to investigate, as more than three years had elapsed since the alleged offence. The story did nothing to enhance his reputation, though.

At this point the nation's woes deepened, as economists said the £9.9 billion in 'fiscal headroom' – spare money shielded from the government's spending plans – had evaporated thanks to low growth, high borrowing costs and higher than predicted interest rates. Although the Bank of England cut interest rates by a quarter-point during the first week of February 2025, it halved its growth forecast for the year from 1.5 per cent – which it had estimated in November 2024 – to 0.75 per cent. Inflation was also expected to remain higher than anticipated, with 3.5 per cent now the accepted level against the target of 2 per cent. Britain moved a step closer to the dreaded 'stagflation' that had been speculated upon at Christmas.

When a junior health minister, Andrew Gwynne, was found to have made some highly questionable remarks on a WhatsApp group, he was forced to quit the government, marking the third ministerial resignation since November. The days when Labour was in opposition, and Starmer was able to spend his time criticising his parliamentary colleagues for their supposed lack of probity and competence, seemed a long way off. The opening months of Starmer's tenure in 10 Downing Street had not been favourable as far as his own political reputation was concerned. Being Prime Minister was the job he had coveted for so long. Would history judge that he was any good at it?

POSTSCRIPT

The local difficulty that was Andrew Gwynne's enforced departure from government was swiftly forgotten when, on 12 February, it was revealed that Donald Trump and Vladimir Putin had spoken by telephone for an hour and a half. During their wide-ranging call they discussed a ceasefire in Ukraine. This news was met by geopolitical analysts with a sense of foreboding that, over the following weeks, seemed entirely justified as the future security of the west underwent a radical reassessment.

Within a week of the phone call, Trump caused consternation by calling Volodymyr Zelenskyy, Ukraine's democratically elected leader, a 'dictator'. Then he signalled that on his watch America's continued involvement in European affairs could not be guaranteed, throwing into doubt the transatlantic alliance that had been forged eighty years previously. His scepticism was based on his long-held view that American taxpayers should not fund NATO so generously while European nations do not pay their fair share. And on 24 February, America aligned itself with Russia, Belarus and North Korea in opposing a UN resolution calling for Putin's immediate withdrawal from Ukraine. Not only had America never sided with Russia at the UN before; this decision also meant the world's biggest military power had voted against the interests of its longstanding democratic friends, including Britain. These events were the unsettling prelude to

Starmer's first meeting with Trump since his return to the White House, on 27 February.

Months of preparation are said to have gone into Starmer's trip to Washington. Even before Trump and Putin had spoken, however, it was never going to be easy thanks to mooted tariffs on steel and other imports that it had been suggested Britain would have to endure along with other European nations. With America no longer prepared to commit so much of its defence spending to Europe, and Trump instead urging NATO allies to devote up to 5 per cent of their GDP to defence, Starmer readied himself for the encounter by announcing to Parliament on 25 February his intention to raise UK defence spending from 2.3 per cent to 2.5 per cent of GDP by 2027 – an increase of £6 billion per year – and then raise it again to hit 3 per cent by 2033. He knew this hawkish move would meet with the President's approval and underscored it by explaining that it would be funded by cutting overseas aid from 0.5 per cent of gross national income to 0.3 per cent by 2027. 'That is not an announcement I am happy to make,' he told the Commons, perhaps mindful that these two policies had featured in the manifesto of Reform UK the previous year. 'I am proud of our pioneering record on overseas development, and we will continue to play a key humanitarian role in Sudan, in Ukraine and in Gaza, tackling climate change, supporting multinational efforts on global health and challenges like vaccination.' He added that 'at times like this the defence and security of the British people must always come first. That is the number one priority of this government.' Some in the Labour Party condemned him as heartless, but he enjoyed qualified praise from the wider majority. On his first day in office he had uttered the words 'country first, party second'. This decision could be held up as proof to all voters that he had meant what he said.

The meeting with Trump was easily the most significant

moment Starmer had faced since becoming Prime Minister. He was visibly nervous on arrival. Trump made a remark about his suit as they greeted each other. (Did he know about the Lord Alli scandal?) Starmer broke the ice by hand delivering at a televised meeting an invitation from the King for a second state visit to the UK. Sounding almost Trumpian in his language, he said, '[A second state visit] has never happened before. It's so incredible. It will be historic.' Clearly tickled at this choreographed piece of diplomacy, Trump heaped praise on the Prime Minister in a manner that some might have considered patronising, referring to his wife, Victoria, who had not accompanied him, as a 'beautiful, great woman' and complimenting Starmer's 'beautiful accent'. (Was this a dig at his recently discovered use of a voice coach?) He acknowledged Starmer's new defence spending commitment. He also opened the door to a possible trade deal. At the time, this was interpreted by Starmer's supporters as potentially sparing Britain from American tariffs. The following month, Starmer was forced to concede that there would be no exemption. To the surprise of many, Trump also appeared to offer his tacit approval of the plans for the Chagos Islands, subject to scrutiny. Yet on the most important subject, the war in Ukraine, Starmer failed to convince. Having voiced his wish to deploy British soldiers to the war-torn country to act as part of a peacekeeping force, he would need US military support in the form of aerial intelligence and air cover. Trump was not prepared to give it.

Nevertheless, Starmer's mood on the flight back to London was buoyant. He even made the thumbs-up sign to journalists at the back of the plane. His core mission – to show deference to Trump and therefore win his favour – had been completed. The obvious political differences between the two men were put to one side. There is no doubt that many Britons baulked at the bizarre display of backslapping, shoulder patting and handshaking that they indulged in. And no sooner had Starmer landed in Britain than the Development Minister, Anneliese Dodds, resigned from the Cabinet in protest at the foreign aid budget cut. But on the strength of his meeting with one of the most unpredictable politicians in the world, it was widely felt that Starmer had shown himself to be competent and pragmatic. With Trump due to occupy the White House for the remainder of Starmer's projected political term, a good personal relationship between them will, of course, be essential come what may.

President Volodymyr Zelenskyy's bilateral meeting with Trump at the Oval Office the following day was, as is well known, altogether different. Trump and his Vice-President, JD Vance, turned on the Ukrainian President as television cameras rolled in what surely ranks as one of the most uncomfortable episodes in recent international politics, shouting at him in a way that was unprecedented among world leaders. Zelenskyy was accused of 'gambling with World War Three' and criticised for not expressing sufficient thanks for the US aid deployed to defend Ukraine against Russia's invasion. Eventually, Trump asked him to leave. The central purpose of their meeting, the US–Ukraine mineral resources agreement, went unsigned. Many believed the episode left the west facing its biggest crisis since 1945, as the concept of the NATO alliance was comprehensively undermined. It also meant Ukraine faced the prospect of what has been described as a 'loser's peace' in which 20 per cent of its territory and millions of its citizens would be subsumed by Russia.

On 1 March, Starmer threw a literal and metaphorical arm around Zelenskyy when he arrived in London, promising him Britain's 'full backing'. The King also granted Zelenskyy an audience at Sandringham. Yet questions were being asked about the wisdom of Starmer believing so wholeheartedly that Trump had spoken to him as sincerely as his thumbs-up sign suggested in their meeting forty-eight hours earlier. Others who were appalled by Trump's behaviour towards Zelenskyy insisted that the unprecedented invitation for a second state visit should be revoked. Starmer sidestepped the issue, saying it would be a decision for the King.

The following day, he hosted a summit at Lancaster House in London attended by Zelenskyy and the leaders of the major European nations, plus Turkey and Canada, to draft a peace plan to take to America. He called them a 'coalition of the willing', the same phrase that had been applied to the multinational force established during the Iraq War in 2003. A four-point plan was produced that would be reliant upon America's support. Despite his lack of experience in matters of international defence or world politics, Starmer was suddenly cast in the role of global statesman leading the effort to support Ukraine while simultaneously keeping Washington onside on behalf of European interests. To that end, he told MPs the next day, 'We must strengthen our relationship with America.' He received the backing of most of the House. Hours later, when Trump suspended US military aid to Ukraine, leaving the traditional western alliance stuck at a crossroads, Starmer pressed ahead with his attempt to keep both parties on board. But with America seemingly intent on pursuing an isolationist position globally, Europe must confront a host of extremely complicated questions about its future.

At the time of writing, Starmer seemed determined to continue playing a central part in tackling those questions. However laudable this may be, sooner or later he will have to ask himself for how long he can devote himself full-time to solving the world's problems. He will also have to balance the moral considerations of putting British 'boots on the ground' with economic ones given the chronic underfunding endured by UK armed forces in recent years. Were he to commit British troops to Ukraine, as he has outlined, it would mark quite a turnaround from the man who in 2020 seemed most preoccupied with telling voters about his unconscious bias training and taking a knee in solidarity with the Black Lives Matter movement.

After such a poor start to his premiership domestically, the events of February and March 2025 provided a much-needed shot in the arm to Starmer's personal standing. Every British Prime Minister has hoped that the world stage might provide them with an opportunity to burnish their reputation. Starmer is no different. Yet he faces a litany of challenges in Britain which demand his attention, from the cost of living and hated tax rises to high immigration and the potentially calamitous economic ramifications of pursuing a net zero agenda. It remains to be seen to what degree his newfound status as an architect of global peace will improve his popularity at the ballot boxes in the constituencies Labour must hold to remain in power.

EPILOGUE

As 2024 drew to a close, Diane Abbott gave an interview to the BBC in which she chose to remind voters that Sir Keir Starmer has not been a member of the Labour Party for very long. Asked why she thought this relevant, the veteran MP answered, 'Because he doesn't have a feel for the Labour Party and politics in general.' Abbott's words echoed those of Jon Cruddas, a Labour MP until July 2024, who wrote of Starmer in his recent book *A Century of Labour*, 'He is clearly an honest, decent man engaged in politics for principled reasons. Yet there are few contributions to help reveal an essential political identity and little in the way of an intellectual paper trail.'

Starmer's supporters would surely argue that these two opinions are not representative of the thousands of people who are actively involved in Labour politics. They would say that he does have sound instincts and ideas. How could a man who converted the Labour Party from a Corbynite sect into an election-winning machine be devoid of any political touch, they would ask. They may have a point. However, there is a perception among voters that he comes across as more of a bureaucrat than a politician – 'a lawyer not a leader' in the words of Boris Johnson, or 'an empty suit' as his erstwhile friend Benjamin Schoendorff described him in Chapter 4. This notion is given credence by his status as a former DPP who is relatively inexperienced in Westminster terms. The most successful postwar Prime Ministers, Margaret Thatcher and Tony Blair, had been in the Commons for twenty years and fourteen years respectively before taking office. As we have seen, Starmer reached the top of the Labour Party just five years after becoming an MP. Four years later, he entered No. 10 with no government experience to his name. Was that enough time for him to develop the characteristics that would make him a Prime Minister of consequence? While it may be too early to form a definitive judgement, one barrister colleague who has known him since the 1990s doubts that he has ever had the ability to be anything other than a follower.

'Keir can't speak with conviction because he has no convictions,' says this person.

> That passion that you hear in politicians who come across as erudite – there are some who can just turn it on like an actor, but most often it really hits the spot when it comes from a position of conviction. The mind works that way. The mind provides you with the language and the emphasis if you are reasonably articulate and you believe what you're saying. The best evidence of Keir's weak personality is the way he would argue cases in court. He'd make concessions that would undermine the main issue and they'd be binding on everybody. If you make a concession in an Appeal Court case and that gets recorded in the judgment, that's the law. He made concessions that were completely wrong just because he thought that was the way the court was thinking and he was trying to play to their existing way of thinking. That's the man through and through. He's the same as an MP as he was as a lawyer. I've always thought the thing he's most scared of is being found out for being a mediocre individual.

Some will find this criticism unduly harsh, but it is important to look at his record during his first months in power before considering whether he is less suited to Downing Street than he himself thought. Allowing Rachel Reeves to announce the cutting of the winter fuel allowance just twenty-four days into his first term remains the best evidence of Starmer's general ineptitude, according to a senior Labour figure. 'My concern is that Keir hasn't been able to set out any narrative,' says this person.

> It's been a series of mistakes. The clunkiness of the winter fuel cut is the obvious one. The way it was announced was bizarre. There was no sequencing, no preparation. It came ahead of everything else. Yes, he inherited an unstable underlying situation, but he did so with great parliamentary strength – yet he's a guy who doesn't know how to handle it. He's very inexperienced in parliamentary and political terms. Look at the way he handled Brexit. He had a detailed focus, but it was a very narrow focus. He's had no political experience outside of that issue. I remember during his first year in Parliament he went with Andy Burnham on little tours around the country, but he doesn't have any history pre-2015 of political campaigning or political management and I think it shows in his record both as Leader of the Opposition and as Prime Minister. His political antennae are very weak.

British politics has undergone an extraordinary shift since 2019. In the space of a single five-year parliamentary term, the country went from electing a Conservative government with an eighty-seat majority to giving a Labour government a majority of 174. Such a violent swing of the pendulum is highly unusual, even accounting for the peculiarities of the first-past-the-post system.

But in fact, as mentioned already, the 2024 result was almost certainly more of a negative vote against the outgoing Conservative government than it was a positive vote for Labour under Starmer. The clamour for change in the run-up to that outcome was so loud that when the result was known it was labelled the 'revenge' election by some commentators. But how many voters who backed Labour knew what to expect from Starmer's supposedly moderate government? And how many already feel duped? They would be forgiven for any confusion they have experienced. In the space of a few months, Labour made enemies of pensioners, farmers, small business owners, big business leaders, free speech advocates, female pensioners and parents who pay school fees, to name just some groups who have been affected by their policies. In an already volatile political environment, will any of them vote Labour next time? An ally of Conservative Party leader Kemi Badenoch says:

> Kemi's view is that the Sue Gray debacle showed Starmer had a plan for the election, but none for government. He genuinely believed the Conservatives were the problem with the country and, with us gone, all would be fixed. His hinterland is the law and lawfare, which he sees as the solution to most things but which is actually the root cause of many of the UK's problems. Things will get worse.

Starmer was elected as Labour leader in April 2020 using a prospectus that paid tribute to Jeremy Corbyn's politics. Under the circumstances, some would say this showed necessary pragmatism on his part. Over the next four years he seemed to renounce Corbynism by tacking towards the centre. As soon as power was secured, however, his administration pursued policies of which Corbyn would be far more likely to approve than would a centrist like Tony Blair. Within the first month, nearly £10 billion was lavished on public sector pay rises on an unconditional basis. Since then there have been a further £40 billion of tax rises; £70 billion of public spending announcements in areas ranging from railway renationalisation to green energy; the imposition of VAT on private school fees; the promotion of workers' rights at an estimated cost to businesses of £5 billion per year; a reversal of changes made by New Labour and later the Tories to the education system; and a foreign policy programme that appears to put international court rulings above British interests. As I have watched this unfold, it has been impossible not to conclude that this government is ideologically extreme. Perhaps it is not so difficult to understand why Starmer was so happy to serve in Corbyn's shadow Cabinet between 2015 and 2019.

Strikingly, Britain turned left shortly before several other major democracies turned right. Since Starmer's victory, Joe Biden in America, Olaf Scholz in Germany and Justin Trudeau in Canada have either resigned or been removed from their posts, leaving him without three fellow progressive leaders on the world stage. Within the EU, Italy, Finland, Slovakia, Hungary, Croatia and the Czech Republic already had right-of-centre parties in government by July 2024. The right has also gained ground in France. If Starmer's government continues on its current trajectory, Britain risks assuming the role of odd man out both economically and in terms of social policy. It is hard to believe that Starmer would be comfortable in that position.

The success of the relationship that Starmer constructs with Donald Trump is likely to define his own premiership to a great extent. As Britain's closest and most important friend, America has begun liberalising its economy in a way that is diametrically opposed to Labour's impulse to tax and spend. That presents Starmer with a conundrum which could set the tone for the future of the so-called 'special relationship', especially if America's economy grows and Britain's stalls. The problem for Starmer is twofold. How will he remain on positive terms with Trump in the face of US tariffs while simultaneously achieving his aim of moving Britain back into the orbit of the EU – Trump's least favourite trading bloc – in areas such as farming and goods standards? Trump has also sworn to tear up the diversity, equality and inclusion philosophy that dominated his country during the first half of this decade, believing it to be a restriction of personal freedom and economic growth. To that end, he signed dozens of executive orders on his first day in office. Will Starmer have the courage to mirror the US President by re-examining whether these concepts have enhanced the productivity of the civil service, universities and businesses in Britain? Another area of concern for Starmer will be his government's cripplingly expensive green agenda. Trump's America has joined China in effectively abandoning climate change targets. If this is the attitude of the two biggest economies on the planet, many British voters will want to know why the UK economy is so heavily geared towards expensive environmental concerns given the country produces less than 1 per cent of the world's CO_2 emissions.

Global events of February and March 2025 show that foreign affairs are likely to dominate the next few years. Even if Starmer's reaction to the future of Ukraine and associated matters turn in his favour, things are far from certain for him domestically, despite Labour's overwhelming parliamentary majority. For Britain faces the fascinating prospect of the traditional two-party system disintegrating. Successive polls show that the rise of Reform UK had, at the time of writing, transformed UK politics into a three-horse race between itself, Labour and the Conservatives. It is all the more complicated for that. Large numbers of voters still believe that the last Tory government damaged the economy, unnecessarily pursued expensive net zero policies and facilitated high immigration long before Labour was in power. In many ways, Labour's stance in these three areas is seen merely as a continuation of the Tory years (though it is worth acknowledging that in March 2025 Starmer announced plans to axe NHS England and tackle the ballooning welfare bill, two policies that might have been expected of a Conservative government). As a new party, Reform UK has the reputation of being a 'clean skin'. With trust in both mainstream parties slipping, it has the potential to shake up the entire system. Internal rows that were aired in public in March 2025 were thought to have done the party some damage. Yet it is undeniable that, when compared with the traditional organisations, Reform UK has the aura of an exciting start-up business and the advantage of a household name, Nigel Farage, running it. He predicts that one issue will soon tower above most others. 'Labour's energy policy is going to be the next Brexit,' says Farage. 'The public will wake up to how much they've been paying on their bills. We have the most expensive electricity in the world. Under Starmer, we're de-industrialising. Wait until people realise the only beneficiary is China.'

Most people who are politically engaged are aware of the potential impact of this mini political revolution on the Conservatives, but Labour is in the firing line just as much – and perhaps more so. In July 2024, Reform UK came second in ninety-eight constituencies – eighty-nine of which are held by Labour. Farage says that Starmer will struggle because, as a member of the metropolitan elite, he does not connect with Labour's base. 'He went into government without any real policies,' he says.

> They were all vague. It's clear that because so many events are beyond a Prime Minister's control, the only way they can get through governing is by having some underlying ideology.

> His is based around a vague world order, and the law, and this is part of his metropolitan outlook. He seems wholly unconcerned with the immigration issue. It was the same with Boris. He's making a mistake. UKIP did far more harm to Labour in the 2015 general election than it did to the Tories. Those who are the most patriotic, the most socially conservative and the most concerned about the effect of mass immigration are traditional Labour voters. Most of our highest-priority areas for the 2025 local elections mirror the old mining communities – Nottinghamshire, South Yorkshire, bits of the north-east, Derbyshire, Kent. We treat the Tories and Labour as the uniparty. There's nothing between them. Should Labour be worried about us? They should be terrified.

The arrival of an insurgent political party in Britain leads to other, more fundamental questions. The French writer Michel Houellebecq, author of the political novel *Submission*, concluded in 2024 that people in his country no longer want to be represented by professional politicians. There may be something in this idea. In the digital age, the leaders of established parties in some countries are being rejected in favour of those who seem less conventional. Arguably, this desire for a new type of political leader began in Italy in the early 2000s with the rise of the former comedian Beppe Grillo, who led the anti-politics Five Star Movement. Donald Trump, whose political philosophy is built around his 'Make America Great Again' brand, and Argentina's Javier Milei, a former economics professor who has used a chainsaw as a political prop, are other obvious examples of unorthodox figures who are prepared to cater to the needs and wants of modern electorates. In Britain, Nigel Farage has built up a significant following by using the media to present himself as a political outsider who is ready to break the existing monopoly. So far, his approach has produced some remarkable results, with Reform UK having a greater number of members than the Conservative Party. Some might say that Elon Musk, though unelected, is the ultimate example of those who fit the 'unconventional' mould. As the owner of Twitter, he has used that channel to further many of his aims – notably, as we have seen, in British politics, by tracking and attacking Keir Starmer and sometimes humiliating him onto the back foot.

By comparison, Starmer runs the risk of looking like a figure from another age. At this point of the twenty-first century, it is clear that personality very much matters in politics – perhaps more than ever. Yet his temperament does not lend itself to flamboyance, humour, exhibitionism, great flights of oratory or much else that is truly memorable. Rather, he is a man who likes to be in control; who doesn't like being thwarted; who can be stubborn. He also has to be scripted, as he struggles to speak off the cuff. This makes it difficult for him to emote. He comes across as rigid. His lack of warmth makes it hard for voters to relate to him. Even if he is essentially decent, his path would be easier if he had a coherent political credo to sell – a set of ideas that could be called Starmerism. If such a thing exists, most Labour parliamentarians have so far found defining it to be a challenge. There is no consensus on what it means beyond woolly talk of the centre-left and social democracy, leading some to reason that he is a somewhat apolitical politician. A friend of Conservative Party leader Kemi Badenoch comments:

> Kemi's view is that he's odd, very partisan, more so than average, yet she doesn't think he likes politics at all. Occasionally you can see him trying not to be like that, but it doesn't last long. It seems he ended up in politics because he wasn't sure what to do after being DPP. Also, he doesn't seem to take

> women seriously – just think of Sue Gray, Angela Rayner, Rosie Duffield, Louise Haigh, Tulip Siddiq, Annaliese Dodds, the list goes on. He sees women as window dressing, then puts them in unsuitable positions from which they eventually have to resign.

It should also be said that he may have used up whatever human capital he has so far relied on as the former DPP. His professed ignorance of two high-profile CPS cases while in post – Savile and Al Fayed – has come back to bite him. His allowing the convicted fraudster Louise Haigh into his Cabinet raises questions about his own judgement. And the grooming gang scandal remains a running sore.

As for his performance in the Commons chamber, friends of the woman who faces him across the despatch box each week at Prime Minister's Questions, Kemi Badenoch, are unimpressed.

> Kemi finds it an amusing experience. He simply does not like answering questions. He feels he is being put on trial, but it comes across as dismissive and self-important. The lawyer in him is absolutely terrified of saying anything that could be prosecuted later. He prefers to be the prosecutor. It's an interesting role reversal. Kemi loved answering questions when she was in government and demonstrating she was on top of her brief. She thinks Starmer is better suited to asking questions.

Attention has already turned to who could succeed him as Labour leader, whether via a coup (though this is far from straightforward under Labour Party rules) or in an orderly fashion. The two names mentioned most often are Labour's deputy leader, Angela Rayner, and the Health Secretary, Wes Streeting. Both are seen as good communicators who have made their way to the top table through talent, perseverance and luck. During the research for this book, one Labour figure told me that Rayner is unpredictable enough to worry Starmer, however. She resented having to fight so hard to be given the use of a grace-and-favour flat. Starmer's team, perhaps mindful of the recent controversy over her housing arrangements in Stockport, was resistant to this idea. At one point they apparently tried to fob her off with a property in Northern Ireland, though it remains hard to see how she would have commuted there at all easily. Eventually, in December 2024, she secured an apartment in Admiralty House. But she is still prone to stirring up trouble. 'Angela has already threatened to quit the Cabinet several times,' says this person.

> Most recently, Tony Blair rang her to talk her down. This tells you how important Blair is to the Starmer project. She'd threatened to quit because she felt she'd been set the impossible target of Labour building 1.5 million new homes by 2030. She is also to the left of Morgan McSweeney and therefore not part of his team and it's said she has a target on her back. But of course she's useful to Starmer. She's necessary, in some respects.

Who can say whether Rayner could move against Starmer one day? For now, the thinking seems to be that from his perspective it is safer to keep her on the front bench rather than the back benches.

Streeting is seen as a more serious figure, although, as one of his friends tells me, his motivations may not be entirely altruistic. 'Wes's one ambition is for him and his boyfriend to be the first gay couple in No. 10,' reports this parliamentarian. Even if this is true, there is more to him than that, as a senior Labour figure explains. The danger that he poses to Starmer's leadership is significant. 'Starmer is in hock to a factional group in Labour which has a different agenda from his own,' says this person.

> So far, Starmer's been happy to use that. He positioned himself as centre-left but I would say he's not very fixed in that at all, whereas Morgan McSweeney and his allies in the party and elsewhere *are* fixed in what they want. Their agenda is different and the candidate they'd like to roll it out is Wes Streeting. He is the guy they want [as leader]. The Blairites were never keen on Keir to start with. They were always suspicious of him. Then, as far as they were concerned, he came good and they were very happy about that and came to love him dearly, but it was always a very transactional and conditional love. It would take a lot to dislodge Keir, but it's not just a question of personal ambition and individuals. It's also about the people like McSweeney who are currently running the Keir show. In the longer term, Wes Streeting is their guy, not Keir.

Another former colleague adds, 'Keir is brittle, literal, process-driven. He's very good at holding a line in public, but he can't do what Wes Streeting can do, which is to expand on a point off the cuff and jump back and forth. Keir can't go off his brief. He's very limited in that sense.'

Assuming that Starmer wishes to lead the Labour Party into the next general election, which must take place by the summer of 2029, two factors are in his favour: he has time and he has a parliamentary majority that should allow him a tremendous amount of latitude. This is a luxurious position for any premier to be in. And yet the feeling that he is an accidental Prime Minister, a leader who is in power because of his opponents' weaknesses rather than as a result of his own strengths, has been ever-present since July 2024. Rachel Reeves's Spring Statement did nothing to bolster his position. Reeves was forced to admit that Britain's growth forecast had halved to 1 per cent and that overall the economy was deteriorating. To compound matters, on 2 April Donald Trump announced tariffs on all goods being imported into America. Britain was saddled with a levy of 10 per cent. Starmer's efforts at negotiating short-term dispensation had failed, certainly at the time this book went to press. The only chink of light was that the levy wasn't higher. The rate imposed on the EU was 20 per cent. The irony that Starmer, who had devoted years of his life to trying to overturn the Brexit vote, should have been the beneficiary of this 'Brexit dividend' was lost on nobody. It is not difficult to imagine confidence in Starmer draining away rapidly should he allow himself to be overtaken by events. However admirable his virtues, he may find that he, too, falls victim to the curse of matters moving beyond his control.

[illegible]

[illegible] having worked closely with Hermer at Matrix Chambers, was made Solicitor General and then Justice Minister.

Kirsty McNeill, ex-director of the Center for Countering Digital [illegible]

THE WEB

Since July 2024, the national Labour Party, the Parliamentary Labour Party and the Labour government have been conspicuous by the number of people working within them who owe their position to nepotism, favouritism or cronyism. In some cases, of course, individuals have achieved their place through merit. Below is a list of prominent men and women whose status has caught my eye while working on this book.

FAST-TRACK ELEVATION

Keir Starmer's aide Chris Ward was parachuted into the Brighton Kemptown seat in May 2024. He won it in July 2024 and became Starmer's PPS.

Olivia Bailey, once an aide to Starmer, won Reading West & Mid Berks in July 2024 and became a PPS at the Department for Work and Pensions.

Richard Hermer – Starmer's longstanding friend who donated £5,000 to his leadership campaign in 2020 – was given a peerage in July 2024 and made Attorney General.

Sarah Sackman, a lawyer who won Finchley & Golders Green in July 2024, having worked closely with Hermer at Matrix Chambers, was made Solicitor General and then Justice Minister.

Kirsty McNeill, ex-director of the Center for Countering Digital Hate, an organisation founded by Morgan McSweeney, won Midlothian in July 2024 and became a minister at the Scotland Office.

Ian Corfield gave Rachel Reeves £5,000 in August 2023 and was made a Treasury director in July 2024. His job was not subject to an open contest and the Treasury did not tell the Civil Service Commission, which vets Whitehall appointments, about Corfield's donation to Reeves.

Jess Sargeant, formerly of Labour Together, was appointed deputy director in the Cabinet Office's Propriety and Constitution Group in July 2024.

Emily Middleton, formerly of Labour Together, was made a director general in the Department for Science and Technology in July 2024.

Jacqui Smith was given a peerage in July 2024 and made a minister in the Department for Education. In 2009, she quit as Home Secretary after her husband's purchase of pornographic films appeared on her parliamentary expenses. She had also falsely maintained that her main property was her sister's house in London, allowing her to claim tens of thousands of pounds of taxpayers' money for her family home in Worcestershire. In 2012, she told the BBC, 'I don't think people who have been disgraced should go to the House of Lords.'

SONS AND DAUGHTERS

Liam Conlon – son of Sue Gray (Starmer's chief of staff until Oct 2024) – won Beckenham & Penge in July 2024 and was appointed a PPS in the Department for Transport.

Hamish Falconer, son of Lord Falconer, once Tony Blair's right-hand man, won Lincoln in July 2024 and was made a minister in the Foreign Office.

Olivia Blake, elected MP for Sheffield Hallam in 2019, is the daughter of Baroness Blake, a Labour whip in the House of Lords.

Georgia Gould, daughter of Philip Gould, Tony Blair's chief strategist, and Lady Rebuck, a Labour peer, won Queen's Park & Maida Vale in July 2024 and was made a Cabinet Office minister.

Baroness Smith of Cluny was made Advocate General for Scotland in August 2024. She is the daughter of Baroness Smith of Gilmorehill and the late Labour leader John Smith.

PARACHUTES

Torsten Bell MP was parachuted into Swansea West in May 2024. He was made a PPS in the Cabinet Office in July 2024 and Parliamentary Under-Secretary of State for Pensions in January 2025.

Luke Akehurst MP, Starmer's 'enforcer', who played a key role in removing dozens of Corbynites as prospective parliamentary candidates over the previous few years, was parachuted into North Durham in May 2024.

Josh Simons MP, the director of the Starmerite think tank Labour Together, was parachuted into Makerfield in May 2024.

James Asser MP, former co-chairman of LGBT+ Labour, was parachuted into West Ham & Beckton in May 2024.

Alex Barros-Curtis MP, Starmer's aide and Labour's executive director of legal affairs, was parachuted into Cardiff West in May 2024.

MARRIAGES AND PARTNERS

Wes Streeting's partner Joe Dancey was appointed Labour's executive director of policy and communications, a £100,000-a-year role, in October 2024 after failing to win Stockton West at election.

Alex Zatman, husband of minister Georgia Gould, was made a special adviser to Liz Kendall, the Secretary of State for Work and Pensions, in July 2024.

Imogen Walker, wife of Morgan McSweeney, won Hamilton & Clyde Valley in July 2024 and was made a PPS in the Treasury.

Baroness Chapman, Starmer's former aide, is married to Labour MP Nick Smith.

Alex Norris MP, a housing minister, is married to Emma Foody MP, who was elected in July 2024.

Pat McFadden MP, Chancellor of the Duchy of Lancaster, is married to Marianna McFadden, formerly Labour's deputy campaign chief and now a special adviser.

Jonathan Ashworth lost his seat in July 2024 and was appointed director of Labour Together. He is a former boyfriend of Ellie Reeves MP and is now dating Stephanie Peacock MP, a minister in the Department for Digital, Culture, Media and Sport.

Stuart Ingham, head of the No. 10 policy unit, is married to Jess Leigh, special adviser to Home Secretary Yvette Cooper.

Jonathan Reynolds MP, Business Secretary since July 2024, is married to Claire Reynolds, director of Labour Women's Network and from October 2024 political director in Downing Street.

Rachel Reeves MP is married to Nicholas Joicey, second permanent secretary at Defra until early 2025, when he left Whitehall for a secondment to the Blavatnik School of Government at the University of Oxford.

Ellie Reeves MP, sister of Rachel, is Labour Party chair and Minister Without Portfolio. She is married to Lord Cryer, a former whip, who left the government in February 2025.

Alexandra Baker MP is married to Jason Keen, who was appointed special adviser to Keir Starmer in January 2025.

FAMILY TIES

Hilary Benn MP, Northern Ireland Secretary, is the brother of Viscount Stansgate, a Labour peer.

Angela Eagle MP, a border security minister, is the twin sister of Maria Eagle MP, a defence minister.

Olaf Bell – the twin brother of Torsten Bell MP – became director of the No. 10 Policy Unit in January 2025.

INDEX